What's on the CD?

The CD-ROM included with the *MCSE: Internet Information Server 3 Study Guide* contains several valuable tools to help you prepare for your MCSE exams. The contents of the folders you'll find on the CD, and the steps for installing the various programs, are described below. Please consult the README file located in the root directory of the CD for further product information.

Custom Files and Software for Creating Dynamic Web Pages

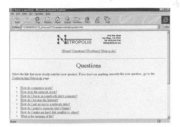

Includes sample Web pages, CGI executables, database files, and ISAPI DLLs. The documents, scripts, and programs located in the SAMPLES folder are used in conjunction with the chapter exercises located throughout the book. Also contains the full Perl5 package for Windows NT and Internet Information Server (both command-line executable and ISAPI DLL interpreters with associated libraries and documentation). With this software package, you can use Perl scripts to create dynamic web pages.

The Edge Tests: *Internet Information Server 3* Exam Preparation Software

This Edge Test demo provides sample test questions similar to those you'll encounter when you take the MCSE Internet Information Server 3.0 exam. Two versions of the test are provided, one for Windows 3.1 & 3.11 systems, and one for Windows 95 and NT systems. To install the Edge Test for Windows 3.1, Windows NT, or Windows 95 run the SETUP.EXE file located in the EdgeTest folder.

Transcender Corporation's *InternetCert™ 3.0* Demo & Certification Sampler

An evaluation copy of Transcender's *InternetCert 3.0* exam prep software, which provides you with a selection of sample test questions similar to those you'll encounter in the Implementing and Supporting Internet Information Server 3.0 exam. To install the Windows demo, run the SETUP.EXE file located in the TRANSCENDER folder. You'll also find a collection of Transcender's other Microsoft exam simulations. Note: The NT 4 version of the Transcender software may not be fully compatible with NT 4 running on NTFS.

Microsoft *Train_Cert Offline* Web site and *Internet Explorer 3.0*

Look to Microsoft's *Train_Cert Offline* Web site, a quarterly snapshot of Microsoft's Education and Certification Web site, for all the information you need to plot your course for MCSE certification. You'll need to run *Internet Explorer 3.0* to access all of the features of the *Train_Cert Offline* Web site, so we've included a free copy on the CD. To install *Internet Explorer 3.0*, run the SETUP.EXE file located in the MICROSOFT\IE3\CD folder. To install the *Train_Cert Offline* Web site to your system, run the SETUP file located in the MICROSFT\OFFLINE folder.

MCSE: Internet Information
Server 3 Study Guide

Microsoft
CERTIFIED PROFESSIONAL
Approved Study Guide

October 9, 1996

Dear SYBEX Inc. Customer:

Microsoft is pleased to inform you SYBEX Inc. is a participant in the Microsoft®
Independent Courseware Vendor (ICV) program. Microsoft ICVs design,
develop, and market self-paced courseware, books, and other products that
support Microsoft software and the Microsoft Certified Professional (MCP)
program.

To be accepted into the Microsoft ICV program, an ICV must meet set criteria. In
addition, Microsoft reviews and approves each ICV training product before
permission is granted to use the Microsoft Certified Professional Approved Study
Guide logo on that product. This logo assures the consumer that the product has
passed the following Microsoft standards:

- The course contains accurate product information.
- The course includes labs and activities during which the student can
  apply knowledge and skills learned from the course.
- The course teaches skills that help prepare the student to take
  corresponding MCP exams.

Microsoft ICVs continually develop and release new MCP Approved Study
Guides. To prepare for a particular Microsoft certification exam, a student may
choose one or more single, self-paced training courses or a series of training
courses.

You will be pleased with the quality and effectiveness of the MCP Approved
Study Guides available from SYBEX Inc.

Sincerely,

Holly Heath

Holly Heath
ICV/OCV Account Manager
Microsoft Channel Programs, Education & Certification

MICROSOFT INDEPENDENT COURSEWARE VENDOR PROGRAM

MCSE: Internet Information Server 3 Study Guide

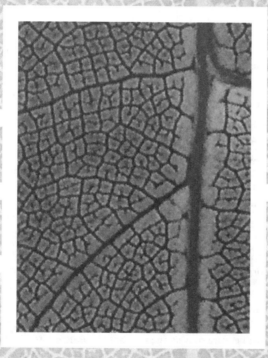

Matthew Strebe
Charles Perkins

NETWORK PRESS®

SYBEX

San Francisco • Paris • Düsseldorf • Soest

Associate Publisher: Guy Hart-Davis
Acquisitions Manager: Kristine Plachy
Acquisitions & Developmental Editor: Neil Edde
Editor: June Waldman
Project Editor: Jeff Chorney
Technical Editor: Jim Polizzi
Book Designer: Patrick Dintino
Graphic Illustrator: Patrick Dintino
Electronic Publishing Specialist: Bob Bihlmayer
Production Coordinator: Alexa Riggs
Proofreaders: Charles Mathews and Theresa Gonzalez
Indexer: Nancy Guenther
Cover Designer: Archer Design
Cover Photograph: FPG International

Library of Congress Card Number: 97-67415
ISBN: 0-7821-2110-1

Manufactured in the United States of America

10 9 8 7 6 5 4 3 2 1

Matthew Strebe: To Christy
Charles Perkins: To Dawna

Acknowledgments

Matthew Strebe: My wonderful wife has been a tremendous supporter of my writing, even though it steals time away from her. Thanks, Neil, for letting us run with this one. Thanks, Jeff, Jim, and June, for your patience and long suffering. Thanks, James, for putting the series together and bringing us aboard in the first place. And thanks to my father, Leroy Strebe, who didn't get to see his name in print.

Charles Perkins: Thanks, Matt; without you the book would have been much smaller! Thanks, Christy, for putting up with us while we wrote late into the night. Thanks, Neil, Jeff, June, and Jim, without whom this book would have been much larger, less focused, and more bizarre in its use of language.

Thanks again, Mike, for getting us into all of this.

Contents at a Glance

Table of Contents

Table of Exercises

Introduction

The Internet exploded onto the computer industry suddenly in 1995, after years of relative obscurity in the academic realm, largely because of the powerful new multimedia hypertext protocol called the World Wide Web. Everything changed. Applications as diverse as spreadsheets and word processors became "Internet enabled," and the mark of dominance among operating systems was Internet support and services. Every current network operating system now supports serving the Internet protocols.

Windows NT is Microsoft's premier operating system. Its modular architecture made adding Internet and Web services easy—so easy, in fact, that Microsoft does not charge extra for these capabilities. Internet Information Server (IIS) is now in its third release and has moved from simply supporting Internet protocols for Windows NT servers to setting the pace for new interactive Internet technologies such as server-side scripting with Active Server Pages, multimedia content delivery with NetShow, and industrial strength searching and indexing with Index Server. IIS is truly one of the very best Internet service packages available.

Whether you are just getting started or are ready to move ahead in the computer industry or the Internet, the knowledge and skills you have are your most valuable assets. Microsoft, recognizing this strength, has developed its Microsoft Certified Professional (MCP) program to certify your ability to work with Microsoft products effectively and professionally. The MCP credential designed for professionals who work with Microsoft networks is the Microsoft Certified Systems Engineer (MCSE) certification. The MCP credential designed for professionals who work with the Internet is the Microsoft Certified Product Specialist: Internet Systems.

This book covers IIS and Index Server for Windows NT. Here you will find the information you need to acquire a solid foundation in the field of Internet service provision, prepare for the IIS and Index Server exam, and take a big step toward MCSE and MCPS: Internet Systems certification.

Is This Book for You?

If you want to learn how the Internet and IIS work, this book is for you. You'll find clear explanations of the fundamental concepts you need.

If you want to become certified as a Microsoft Certified Systems Engineer (MCSE) or Microsoft Certified Product Specialist in Internet Systems, this book is also for you. The MCSE is *the* hot ticket in the field of professional computer networking, and the MCPS:IS will clearly distinguish you from the pack in the fields of Internet service provision, content creation, and systems integration.

What Does This Book Cover?

Think of this book as your guide to IIS. It begins by covering the most basic Internet concepts, for example:

- What is the Internet?

- How do you put together a Web site?

Next you learn how to perform important tasks, including:

- Working with user accounts

- Configuring security for public or private sites

- Creating an interactive Web site

You also learn how to configure the operating system services that relate to the Internet, tune your Internet server's performance, and troubleshoot your system.

How Do You Become a Certified Professional?

Achieving Microsoft Certified Systems Engineer (MCSE) status is a serious endeavor. The exams cover a wide range of topics and require dedicated study and expertise. Many technicians who have earned other computer industry credentials have found the MCSE certification more difficult to achieve, which is why the MCSE certificate is so valuable. If achieving MCSE status were easy, MCSEs would flood the market and the certification would become quite meaningless. Microsoft, keenly aware of this fact, has taken steps to ensure that the certification means its holder is truly knowledgeable and skilled.

To become an MCSE, you must pass four core requirements and two electives. To become an MCPS:IS, you must pass three exams. Most people select the following exam combination for the MCSE core requirements for the 4.0

track (the most current track) because it provides both certifications with the minimum number of exams:

MCSE Client Requirement

70-73: Implementing and Supporting Windows NT Workstation 4.0

MCSE Networking Requirement

70-58: Networking Essentials

MCSE Windows NT Server 4.0/ MCPS:IS Requirement

70-67: Implementing and Supporting Windows NT Server 4.0

Windows NT Server 4.0 in the Enterprise Requirement

70-68: Implementing and Supporting Windows NT Server 4.0 in the Enterprise

MCSE Electives/ MCPS:IS Requirements

70-59: Internetworking Microsoft TCP/IP on Microsoft Windows NT 4.0

70-77: Implementing and Supporting Microsoft Internet Information Server

For a complete description of all the MCSE options, see the Microsoft Train_Cert Offline Web site on the CD that comes with this book.

This book is a part of a series of MCSE study guides, published by Network Press (Sybex), that covers four core requirements and two electives—the entire MCSE track.

Where Do You Take the Exams?

You may take the exams at any of more than 800 Authorized Prometric Testing Centers (APTCs) around the world. For the location of an APTC near you, call (800) 755-EXAM (755-3926). Outside the United States and Canada, contact your local Sylvan Prometric Registration Center.

To register for a Microsoft Certified Professional exam:

1. Determine the number of the exam you want to take.

2. Register with the Sylvan Prometric Registration Center that is nearest to you. At the time of this writing, the fee is $100 for each exam, and you are asked to pay when you register. You must take the exam within one year of payment. You can schedule exams up to six weeks in advance or as late as one working day prior to the date of the exam. You can cancel or reschedule your exam if you contact Sylvan Prometric at least two working days prior to the exam. Some locations offer same-day registration, subject to space availability. Where same-day registration is available, you must register a minimum of two hours before test time.

3. After you receive a registration and payment confirmation letter from Sylvan Prometric, call a nearby Authorized Prometric Testing Center (APTC) to schedule your exam.

When you schedule the exam, you will receive instructions regarding appointment and cancellation procedures and ID requirements, as well as information about the testing center location.

What the Exam Measures

The Internet Information Server 3.0 and Index Server 1.1 exam covers concepts and skills required for the support of Windows NT servers running IIS. It emphasizes the following areas of IIS support:

- Standards and terminology

- Planning

- Implementation

- Troubleshooting

This exam can be quite specific regarding IIS and Windows NT requirements and operational settings, and it can be particular about how administrative tasks are performed in the operating system. It also focuses on fundamental concepts relating to the operation of Internet Information Server. Careful study of this book, along with hands-on experience with Windows NT Server, Internet Information Server, and Index Server will help you prepare for this exam.

Tips for Taking the Exam

Here are some general tips for taking the exam successfully:

- Arrive early at the test center so you can relax and take one last review of your study materials, particularly tables and lists of exam-related information.

- Read the questions carefully. Don't be tempted to jump to an early conclusion. Make sure you know *exactly* what the question is asking.

- Don't leave any unanswered questions. They count against you.

- When answering multiple-choice questions you're not sure about, use a process of elimination to get rid of the obviously incorrect answers first. This approach improves your odds if you need to make an educated guess.

- Because the hard questions will eat up the most time, save them for last. You can move forward and back through the exam.

How to Use This Book

This book provides a solid foundation for the serious effort of preparing for the Internet Information Server 3.0 and Index Server 1.1 exam. We suggest the following study method:

1. Study a chapter carefully, making sure you fully understand the information.

2. Complete all hands-on exercises in the chapter, referring to the chapter so that you understand each step you take.

3. Answer the exercise questions related to that chapter. (You will find the answers to these questions in Appendix A.)

4. Note which questions you did not understand and study those sections of the book again.

5. Study each chapter in the same manner.

If you prefer to use this book in conjunction with classroom or online training, you have many options. Both Microsoft-authorized training and independent training are widely available. Free network training referral services, such as Keeler Education at (800) 800-1638, can help you locate available resources.

To learn all the material covered in this book, you will need to study regularly and with discipline. Try to set aside the same time every day to study in a comfortable and quiet place. If you work hard, you will be surprised at how quickly you learn this material. Good luck.

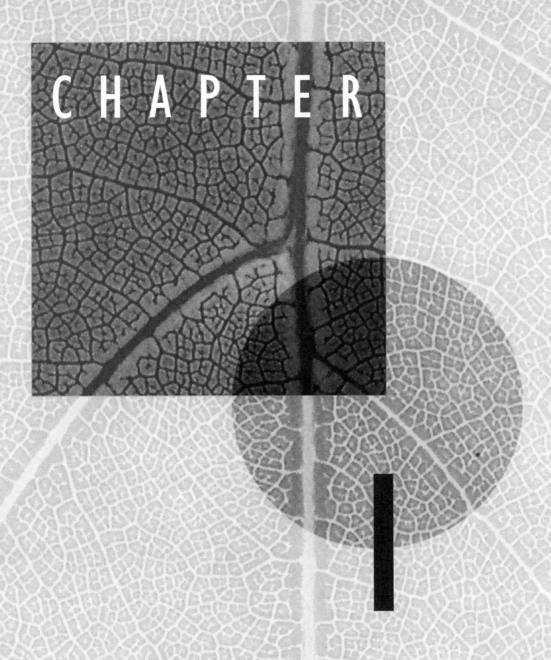

CHAPTER

1

The Internet and the World Wide Web

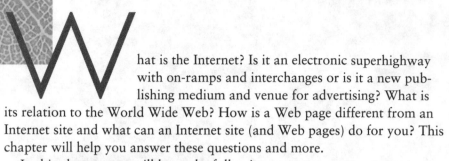

What is the Internet? Is it an electronic superhighway with on-ramps and interchanges or is it a new publishing medium and venue for advertising? What is its relation to the World Wide Web? How is a Web page different from an Internet site and what can an Internet site (and Web pages) do for you? This chapter will help you answer these questions and more.

In this chapter you will learn the following:

- What the Internet is

- What the World Wide Web is

- The origins of the Internet and World Wide Web

- The structure of the Internet and World Wide Web

- What you can do with the Internet and World Wide Web

- The most popular new use of the Internet

- The cause of the recent explosive growth of the Internet into the business world

- The protocols that form the logical structure of the Internet

- The telephone and network links that form the physical structure of the Internet

This chapter takes you on a tour of the Internet. The purpose of the tour is to show you how various companies and organizations are using the Internet to improve their businesses.

What Are the Internet and the World Wide Web?

You see and hear them everywhere: two or three words separated by periods (called "dots") with `http` in front or prefixed by a name and an at (@) sign. These cryptic statements are World Wide Web page locations and Internet e-mail addresses; they appear in newspaper advertisements and on television and radio—even TV sitcoms have Web sites. Almost every business card you get nowadays includes an Internet e-mail address alongside the standard business telephone and fax numbers that you've come to expect.

Some people consider these Internet addresses a sign of being cool or connected and use them as status symbols. As time progresses, however, the Internet connection (like the fax machine of the last decade) is turning into an essential business tool and is no longer optional. As more and more people and businesses connect to the Internet, the more useful the Internet becomes—and the more essential it is for late adopters to get their act together.

Many people speak of these two revolutionary computer constructs (the Internet and the World Wide Web) as if they were the same thing. They are not. Although the World Wide Web is both a new phenomenon and newly created (the first Web pages made their appearance on the Internet just a few years ago), the Internet is older than the authors of this book. (Thus the Internet can measure things in real generations, not just computer generations. A computer generation is about 18 months long because that's about how long it takes for computers to double in power. The Internet actually predates the microprocessor.)

Moore's Law is an observation that the logic density of an integrated circuit doubles every two years. Moore himself isn't too sure what he originally postulated, but an authoritative source states that the law predicts chip-density doubling every two years but effective speed of computers doubling every 18 months due to other factors. This growth rate, combined with advances in computer architecture (how that logic is used), results in a corollary: the effective doubling of computer power every 18 months. This phenomenon explains why you keep buying new computers and why old computers depreciate so rapidly. They are not really any slower than they were when you bought them—but you have come to expect the level of performance of the latest generation of computers.

The Internet

People talk about the Internet as though it is one big thing, perhaps mythical, like Godzilla or Kansas. However, the Internet is not one big thing; it is how a group of things (computers, big and little) are tied together.

> The Internet is a concept, like the economy. You can't touch the economy. However, when you get a job or start a business, you participate in the economy. Similarly, when you connect your computer or your LAN to an Internet service provider, you have "connected to" the Internet.

Companies, organizations, and governments have been linking computers together for a long time. When computers in one location (such as a school or office building) are linked, the result is called a *local area network,* or a LAN. LANs are usually made with special cables just for carrying computer data. When the computers are farther apart (such as across the town, across the state, or across the world), telephone lines, rather than special cables, usually link the computers. A network of this type is called a *wide area network,* or WAN.

In 1969 the Advanced Research Projects Agency of the Department of Defense created a WAN to link researchers and Department of Defense research centers. A great deal of the research was done at universities, and the networking protocols used in the WAN were also the product of a research project. These protocols became the *TCP/IP suite*, which comprise the protocols of the Internet. (You will learn more about TCP/IP in Chapter 5, which covers Internet protocols.)

During the 1970s most of the larger universities in the United States and many research centers throughout the world linked themselves together using the same TCP/IP protocols, extending the original (ARPANET) network beyond its original scope of linking Department of Defense computers. The extended network became known as the *network of networks* (since many schools and organizations already had LANs linking their local computers), or the Internet.

As corporations joined with universities to develop technologies (especially computer technologies) and to turn those technologies into commercial products, these corporations joined their networks to the Internet as well. Alumni and researchers leaving this academic environment often convinced their new employers that they needed Internet access, and so the Internet moved into the business world.

Although ARPA (and its successor, the Defense Advanced Research Projects Agency, or DARPA) created the nucleus of the Internet, these organizations do not control the Internet. For a while ARPA and DARPA guided its evolution, and government subsidy of the Internet backbone (the main high-speed links connecting geographic areas) limited commercial traffic over the Internet. DARPA then decreed the Internet "research program" a success and spun off support of the backbone to private industry (mostly to the long-distance telephone companies). No single organization is "in charge" of the Internet today.

The following sections describe

- How the Internet is structured

- How companies and organizations control various parts of the structure (Internet service providers, Service Access Points, Internet backbones)

- How the controlling organizations cooperate to maintain Internet service

The Internet, as well as being a network of networks, is also a network of cooperating organizations and companies. See Figure 1.1 for a diagram of the Internet.

FIGURE 1.1

The Internet is a web of computers linked by telephone lines.

The Internet is how computers around the world are connected together. It is the realm of protocols and operating systems. Its purpose is to transport data. What that data is and what you use the Internet for is another matter entirely. You can put information on your computer (connected to the Internet) and let other computers elsewhere on the Internet access that data. This is the realm of Web servers and Web clients, respectively.

The Internet connects computers. World Wide Web servers make information available on a computer connected to the Internet, and World Wide Web browsers show you information stored on a Web server over the Internet. The World Wide Web requires the Internet to function.

The purpose of the Internet is to link computers. What you do with the link is a matter of software. One of the earliest software programs written to use the Internet protocols is Telnet. *Telnet* allows you to connect to and use UNIX computers with a command-line interface. Another program that has been around a long time is FTP, which allows you to store and retrieve files on any remote computer that supports the FTP protocol.

The World Wide Web

Most early Internet programs were command-line programs. The World Wide Web has changed all that. Instead of requiring you to know arcane commands, the World Wide Web gives you a graphical view of the Internet. The Web is easy to use; it is also easy to create Web pages and to link them to other Web pages. You don't have to learn esoteric programming languages to create a simple Web site. (But the more complex Web pages do require some programming.)

Although the World Wide Web uses the Internet, the Web is based on another concept entirely. That concept is *hypertext*, and it is referred to in the names of the standards and protocols that the World Wide Web uses: Hyper-Text Markup Language and HyperText Transfer Protocol (HTML and HTTP).

The idea that hypertext explores is that, unlike paper documents, electronic documents don't have to be static. When you run across an interesting word or concept in a printed newspaper article, for instance, you (the reader) must go to a dictionary or encyclopedia or library to look up references yourself. The most the article can do is to cite references in footnotes.

However, if a hypertext article is displayed for you on a computer screen, the computer can bring the references right to you. Instead of merely giving the reference name, the hypertext article contains pointers to a web of interrelated documents, each with links to more articles with similar subjects or examples or "digressionary" (but interesting) subjects. All you would have to do is click the reference.

The World Wide Web delivers what hypertext promises, and more. The Web goes beyond merely interlinking textual documents. Web features such as JavaScript and CGI allow individual Web pages to interact with the user, and Web servers can create Web pages that are based on dynamic information such as the weather or the contents of a database. Some Web pages even display the moment-by-moment state of coffee machines and pop dispensers (so that you can know whether your next drink will be fresh or cold if you happen to be anywhere near these Web-enabled devices). Or if you are technically inclined, you can Web enable a device yourself.

The World Wide Web protocols (HTML and HTTP) allow any Internet site to provide (or host) Web pages. Any Web page can refer to any other Web page, even without the knowledge of the other page. You don't have to ask anyone's permission (outside of your own company or organization) to set up a Web site. This open method of linking documents makes it incredibly easy for people to set up their Web pages and to make information on them available to anyone on the Internet.

How Do the Internet and the World Wide Web Work?

The Internet and the World Wide Web share a similar structure because the World Wide Web uses Internet protocols. When you explore the protocols and structure of the Internet, you are also exploring how the Web works. By learning how the Internet works you can better use the Internet and understand some of its baffling behavior.

The mechanics of the Internet are, of course, secondary to its uses. The common Internet services (Web, Mail, News, and FTP) have turned the original ARPANET from a research tool into a new tool for business, and much more.

Protocols

The Internet uses TCP/IP to link computers. TCP/IP stands for Transmission Control Protocol/Internet Protocol, which are two significant parts of what is now also known as the *Internet Protocol Suite*. The feature that makes TCP/IP different from many other networking protocols is that it was designed to link networks instead of just linking computers in a network. The design of TCP/IP allows each individual network to be managed separately, so different organizations that do not wish to give complete network access to each other (for instance a military research department and an academic computer science department) can still exchange information.

Protocols define how computers (or any group of entities) communicate. Communications protocols define such things as when a computer may transmit or must listen, how to address another computer so that a message will arrive at the correct destination, and what to do if there are errors in the received message. Protocols are explored further in Chapter 5.

The first TCP/IP specifications were circulated as Requests for Comments (RFCs). The original developers and the Internet Engineering Task Force (the current open-membership standards body for TCP/IP and the Internet) maintained the tradition of producing RFCs that describe any new Internet standards or revisions to older standards. All the RFCs for TCP/IP protocols are available for download on the Internet.

The Internet protocols in the TCP/IP suite are arranged in layers. Protocols at each layer are used by the next. The layers are as follows:

- The network interface layer

- The Internet layer

- The transport layer

- The application layer

The diagrams in Figure 1.2 compare the TCP/IP suite of protocols to the OSI stack and some Windows NT operating system components.

F I G U R E 1.2

The TCP/IP protocol suite compared to the OSI stack and some Windows NT operating system components

OSI Model
Application
Presentation
Session
Transport
Network
Data Link
Physical

TCP/IP Model
Application
Transport
Internet
Network Interface
Hardware

TCP/IP Protocols

RSH	TFTP	Rlogin	NFS	SNMP	DNS	Ping	SMTP	Telnet	FTP	HTTP

TCP					UDP		

IP	ICMP	ARP	RARP	Routing

Network Driver and NIC

The Network Interface Layer

The network interface layer handles hardware-dependent functions and presents a standardized interface to the Internet layer of TCP/IP. You can have several network interfaces in your computer, each of which can carry the TCP/IP data traffic over a different type of physical network.

For instance, you may have an Ethernet adapter connecting your computer to an Ethernet network and a token-ring adapter connecting your computer to a token-ring network. In addition, you might have a serial connection through a modem to your Internet service provider (ISP). Each network interface uses different physical and data link protocols, but they all appear the same to the Internet layer of TCP/IP.

Under Windows NT the network device driver implements the network interface layer. If the connection is made via the Remote Access Service (RAS), then the RAS WAN wrapper performs this function, making your modem connection into a network connection.

The Internet Layer

The Internet layer moves information from the source to the destination through a network. The source and destination computers may not be on the same local area network; in fact, the source and destination computers may be in different computers on different continents, and the data being transferred may have to go through many intermediate computers and networks to reach its destination.

- **Internet Protocol (IP)** is the core of the TCP/IP protocol suite. This protocol provides a directionless best-effort data delivery service for data sent within and between networks. Therefore, data that is sent is not guaranteed to arrive at the destination, and data packets are not guaranteed to arrive in the same order in which they were sent.

- **Internet Control Message Protocol (ICMP)** uses IP to control the flow of data over networks and to report error and congestion conditions on the network links.

- **Address Resolution Protocol (ARP)** is used in a local area network to determine a destination computer's physical hardware address when the source computer has the destination computer's Internet address.

- **Reverse Address Resolution Protocol (RARP)** is a mechanism whereby a computer that does not yet have an Internet address can obtain one.

- **Dynamic Host Configuration Protocol (DHCP)** is a newer protocol for obtaining an IP address as well as other TCP/IP information on an IP network. DHCP is more flexible than RARP and automates many tasks that must be done manually with RARP.

Microsoft uses DHCP, not RARP, in its TCP/IP implementation.

The Transport Layer

The transport layer provides end-to-end data delivery services for the TCP/IP application layer above it.

TCP/IP provides two types of transport layer services. Which service upper layers use depends on the nature of the network communication that the upper layer service needs. The two transport layer protocols provided by TCP/IP are

- **User Datagram Protocol (UDP)** adds very little to the underlying IP transmission service. *Datagrams* are small, fixed-sized packages of data sent over a network. Like IP, UDP neither guarantees that the data (transmitted as datagrams) will arrive in order or even that the data will arrive at its destination.

  UDP is useful in applications under these conditions:

  - Sending many small units of data

  - Speed is more important than guaranteed delivery

  - The application will make sure that data is received

- **Transmission Control Protocol (TCP)** is a connection-oriented transport layer protocol that ensures that the data arrives and that it arrives in the correct order. TCP sets up a connection between the sender and the receiver; it uses the services of IP to send and receive data. TCP reorders information that is received out of order and will request that information that was not received be sent again.

The Application Layer

The application layer in a typical TCP/IP implementation contains the following network applications (which are included in Windows NT unless otherwise noted):

- **Ping** is a utility that tests connectivity between computers on the Internet. It uses Internet Control Message Protocol echo request and echo reply packets to time how long it takes for information to get to the other computer and back.

- **Telnet** is a utility that gives you a character mode interactive session with another computer. You'll take a closer look at Telnet in the section on Internet Services.

- **Rlogin** is like Telnet in that it gives you a command-line interface to another computer, but it also does more for UNIX computers to make the connection transparent to UNIX programs. Rlogin is not part of the Windows NT TCP/IP package.

- **Rsh** allows you to type commands on your local system that will be executed on the remote system with the results returned to you on the local system.

- **File Transfer Protocol (FTP)** is a utility that transfers files to and from remote computers over TCP/IP. The remote computer must have an FTP server. Windows NT provides both an FTP utility and an FTP server. You'll take a closer look at FTP in the section on Internet Services.

- **Trivial File Transfer Protocol (TFTP)** is a file transfer protocol usually used to download operating system code for UNIX networked client machines.

- **Simple Mail Transfer Protocol (SMTP)** sends and receives Internet mail. Windows NT does not include an SMTP mail client, but many mail packages do, and Microsoft Exchange Server will route your LAN mail on and off the Internet. You'll take a closer look at Mail in the section on Internet Services.

- **HyperText Transport Protocol (HTTP)** transfers World Wide Web documents from a Web host to a Web browser such as Netscape or Internet

Explorer. You will explore the Web further in the section on Internet Services and throughout the rest of this book.

- **Domain Name Service (DNS)** translates human-friendly Internet addresses such as `electriciti.com` to numerical Internet addresses such as `198.5.212.8`, which the computer needs to find the receiving computer. Windows NT workstations use the DNS protocol to look up names stored on DNS servers elsewhere on the network, such as on a Windows NT server.

- **Simple Network Management Protocol (SNMP)** has become the most widely used protocol for monitoring network devices such as hubs, routers, workstations, and computers. Windows NT supports SNMP.

- **Network News Transport Protocol (NNTP)** is the mechanism whereby Usenet News is exchanged over the Internet. Windows NT Server does not support NNTP, but many software packages for Windows NT do.

Structure

The previous section explained how each protocol works with the next to create an Internet connection. This section shows you how each computer works with the next to create the Internet. As an example of this process, look at the links required for a typical home user in Chicago to access a Web server run by a company in Washington. Refer to Figure 1.2 while you trace the connection.

1. The user connects to an Internet service provider and sends a request.

2. The Internet service provider forwards the request to the nearest Service Access Point.

3. The request is routed to the Service Access Point nearest the destination.

4. The Service Access Point sends the request to the destination's Internet service provider.

5. The destination's Internet service provider sends the request to the router on the LAN that contains the destination computer.

6. The destination computer receives the request and sends the requested document back along the same path.

The actual connections required to get the request from the user's computer to the remote Web site are much more complicated and elaborate than the route just described. The following section explores this example in greater detail.

Don't be baffled by new terms such as ISDN, T1, leased lines, and routers. Later chapters in this book explain all of these services and devices for Internet connectivity. Just follow along and refer to this example again to put these terms in context.

The user at home first has to connect to the Internet. Most Internet connections from home are made over the telephone lines using regular modems. Some lucky users can connect via cable modems or Integrated Services Digital Network (ISDN) connections. Users may someday connect via Asymmetric Digital Subscriber Line (ADSL) high-speed data phone lines, or via radio or satellite or...who knows? Assume that the user in Chicago connects via the telephone line and a modem and that the user requests a Web page from the Web document in Washington.

What does the user connect to? Remember that there is no such tangible thing as *the Internet* to connect to. You have to connect to a part of the Internet. Most users will connect to an Internet service provider. For most people an Internet service provider is just a local phone call away. Most larger cities are served by several Internet service providers. The function of an Internet service provider is to provide many low-speed connections and a few high-speed connections to end users. These end users may be individuals at home connecting just one computer via a modem or they may be businesses connecting entire networks to the Internet via a T1 leased line or an even faster connection. The Internet service provider is then connected via a high-speed link (usually a T3 leased line) to a Service Access Point. In our example, the Internet service provider in Chicago forwards the Web page request via a T3 line to the Service Access Point nearest the Internet service provider.

Service Access Points throughout the United States are connected by Internet backbones (the high-speed data links that connect geographically distant locations), which are maintained by the long-distance phone companies. Data can cross over from one backbone to another at these Service Access Points. The user's Web page request may travel along backbones provided by Sprint and AT&T before it reaches the Service Access Point nearest the destination Web server in Washington.

The Service Access Point forwards the request to the Internet service provider that the business in Washington uses. The business is probably connected by a higher-speed link rather than a regular modem line so that it can serve many users at once. The Internet service provider forwards the request down the leased line to the business. Most businesses connect a router on their LAN, instead of a regular computer, to their Internet service provider because the router allows all the computers on the LAN to communicate over the Internet, instead of just the one that is connected. The request is then sent over the LAN at that business to the computer that is hosting the Web site. The Web host sends the requested Web page over the same links, and the entire process occurs again in reverse order.

As you can see, a simple Internet message (such as a Web page request or an Internet mail message) must take many steps to get from the sender to the recipient. The basic mechanism is the same, though, whether the user sends a message from one computer to another in Chicago or from a computer in Chicago to one in Tokyo. The only difference is that a message from Chicago to Tokyo travels through more intermediate devices (routers and computers) than a message from one side of town to another.

Clients and Servers

The Internet comprises *server computers* and *client computers*. As an internetworking professional, you should be familiar with the types of computers that are servers and clients on the Internet.

One assumption in the preceding description of how the Internet works is the presence of Internet clients (such as the user in Chicago) and servers (such as the Web site in Washington). With the advent of the Web browser and the proliferation of Internet service providers making the Internet available to just about everyone, you will find that most Internet clients are personal computers running Windows or the Macintosh operating system. UNIX workstations, which are the original home of the Internet and the World Wide Web, are still natural network clients but there are many more personal computers out there than there are UNIX workstations.

Don't assume, though, that all your clients will be using Mac and Windows Web browsers. You can already buy World Wide Web peripherals for your television, and many more devices will start showing up with the ability to connect to the Internet. One hot new feature of handheld computers is Web connectivity. You can browse the World Wide Web right now from an Apple Newton, for example. The key when creating Web pages is to make them flexible enough to be viewed from any device. You don't want to limit your audience to just Windows users, do you?

Unlike Internet clients, you will find that Internet servers are mostly UNIX, Macintosh, and Windows NT computers. Almost any computer can be a Web server, though. (You can even find Novell Netware file servers hosting World Wide Web data.) Each operating system has its strengths for serving Internet data. One of the virtues of Windows NT is that it comes with all the software you need to be an Internet host. This book will show you how to use Windows NT Server and the Internet Information Server software package to create a complete Internet server.

Internet Services

Internet hosts commonly provide four Internet services:

- **Internet mail** is one of the oldest and still one of the most useful Internet services. Hundreds of thousands of messages are exchanged daily within and between companies worldwide via Internet mail.

- The **World Wide Web** is the most visible Internet tool today. It presents information textually and graphically and turns the Internet into an information resource and marketing tool unlike any other.

- **FTP** is a command-line interface to archives on the Internet (but you can also use your Web browser to access FTP sites).

- **Internet news** gives individuals with common interests (from cooking to large system database administration) a new way to exchange information on almost any subject.

Internet Mail

You can use Internet mail to send e-mail messages to other individuals anywhere in the world. If you have a dedicated Internet connection and your LAN e-mail package is set up to route e-mail to the Internet, you do not have to do anything special to send Internet mail. In fact, you may not even need to have TCP/IP installed on your computer if some other computer on your network does the e-mail conversion.

If you are using Microsoft's desktop e-mail package (Microsoft Messaging [or whatever it is called today], formerly known as Exchange) as your e-mail package, you can either use Microsoft Exchange Server to route your e-mail to the Internet or, if you checked the Internet option when you installed the desktop e-mail product, send mail directly to the Internet from your computer. Many Internet e-mail packages are available for most client operating systems. Here are some of the popular e-mail features:

- Address books

- Inboxes and outboxes

- Mailboxes for specific correspondence

- Delayed message sending and offline mail reading

- Multiple e-mail account checking

- Automatic mail forwarding and mail checking

- Mail filters and automated mail processing

- File attachment and flexible mail formats

See Figure 1.3 for an example of a package that can send Internet mail.

FIGURE 1.3

Microsoft's e-mail software can send messages over the Internet.

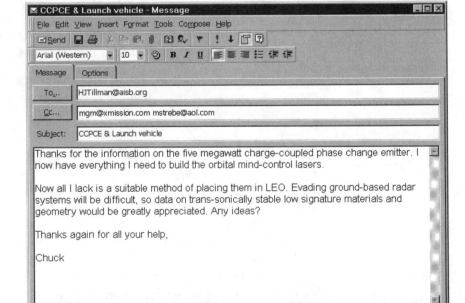

In Exercise 1.1 you will send an e-mail message over the Internet using Microsoft's desktop e-mail software in Windows 95 or Windows NT.

EXERCISE 1.1

Sending an Internet E-mail Message Using Microsoft Exchange

1. Start the Microsoft e-mail package. (Double-click the Inbox icon on the desktop.)

   - If the e-mail package is not configured, you may have to configure it. The Installation Wizard will guide you through the process. If you have difficulty installing the software, consult the documentation that came with the software.

2. Select New Message from the Compose menu.

3. Type the address **mcseiissg@aol.com** in the To: box.

4. Type **Exercise 1.1** in the Subject: box.

5. Type the following sentence in the text area of the window: **Exercise 1.1 completed. I will be a Microsoft Certified Systems Engineer soon.**

6. Select Send from the File menu.

7. *If you are working offline* (check your configuration and refer to step 1): Select Tools ➤ Deliver Now Using ➤ Internet Mail option in the Inbox - Microsoft Exchange window.

8. Select File ➤ Exit and log off.

World Wide Web

The World Wide Web has given businesses the most compelling reason since e-mail to connect to the Internet. Before the World Wide Web, the widely used Internet programs were character based. The World Wide Web allows graphical as well as textual information to be displayed, and innovations in World Wide Web technology support not only continuous sound and video transmission but also dynamic displays based on executable code.

You can use the World Wide Web to search for product information, download changes to software and firmware, keep abreast of information published in electronic newsletters, research any subject from auto mechanics to zoology, and much more.

You can also publish your own information on the World Wide Web. (That's what this book is about!) If you have a constant connection to the Internet, the information can be stored on your workstation or on your LAN server. If you have a dial-up connection, your Internet service provider usually will provide space on its server for your World Wide Web information.

Several World Wide Web browsers are in wide use today. Netscape is a very popular and feature-filled Web browser. Microsoft includes a Web browser with Windows NT and Windows 95 called the Windows Internet Explorer. Web browsers may support some or all of these features:

- Bookmarks for favorite Web sites

- Multiple browsing windows

- Frames or multiple views within a window

- Multiple outstanding requests to Web servers

- User settings for colors and other aspects of screen appearance

- Web interface to FTP and Gopher Internet sites

- Secure data transmission

- User-configurable helper applications for new data types

- Java and other scripting languages support

Figure 1.4 shows Microsoft Explorer, which is a Web browser that Microsoft includes with Windows NT.

You will use Internet Explorer for most of the exercises in this book, and we made most of the screen shots in this book with it. (However, we also used other browsers, especially when another browser exhibits a feature you should be aware of.) Chapter 11 examines other popular Web browsers.

FIGURE 1.4

Internet Explorer is
your graphical interface
to the Internet.

In Exercise 1.2 you will access and search the World Wide Web using Microsoft's Internet Explorer.

EXERCISE 1.2

Access the World Wide Web Using Microsoft Explorer and Search for Windows NT Information

1. Start Internet Explorer. (Double-click the Internet Explorer icon on the desktop.)

   If your Internet Explorer is in its default configuration, you will be viewing the Microsoft Network Web site (www.msn.com).

2. Replace http://www.msn.com in the Address field with **http://www.sybex.com** and then press Enter. Internet Explorer will now show you Sybex's Web site.

3. Select Add To Favorites from the Favorites menu. In the Add To Favorites window, click the Add button. The Sybex Web site will now appear in the Favorites menu.

4. Replace http://www.sybex.com in the Address field with **http://www.yahoo.com** and then press Enter. You will be taken to the Yahoo! home page that contains a list of categories.

5. Click once on the underlined <u>Computers and Internet</u> category. This *link* will take you to the Computers and Internet subcategory.

6. Select the Search Only in Computers and Internet search option.

7. Type **"Windows NT"** (including the quotation marks) in the text box before the Search button and then click the Search button. Yahoo! will display a list of Web pages that refer to Windows NT.

8. Select the Sybex entry from the Favorites menu. You will be returned to the Sybex home page.

9. Close the Internet Explorer by selecting File ➤ Exit.

FTP

FTP is a protocol for transferring files over the Internet, and many FTP utilities are available for Windows NT and Windows 95. Microsoft ships an FTP utility with the Windows NT and Windows 95 operating systems; it is installed when you install the operating system.

The FTP utility is a *command-line utility*; that is, you type commands from within the utility to perform the file transfer operations. You can set up an icon that will start the FTP utility, or you can invoke it from the command line.

Many additional graphical FTP utilities are available. (And many of them are free for download on the Internet.) These utilities provide a graphical interface and translate the actions you perform on graphical objects (such as selecting a file from a file list on a remote computer and then clicking Get) into the textual commands that the FTP protocol expects (e.g., get *filename*). See Figure 1.5 for an example of Microsoft's client FTP software being used.

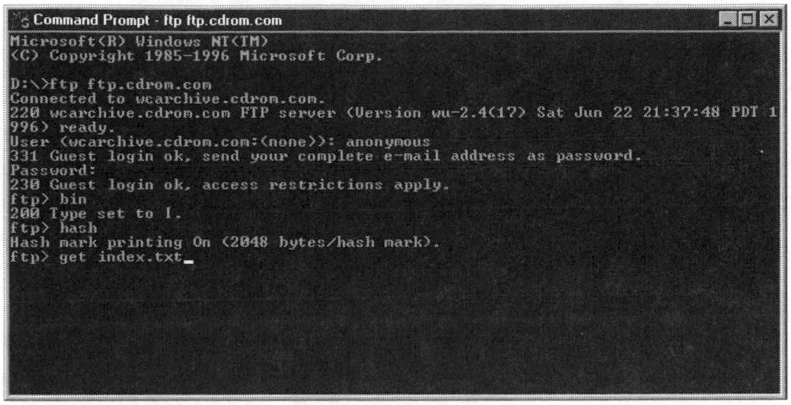

FIGURE 1.5

FTP retrieves files
over the Internet.

```
Command Prompt - ftp ftp.cdrom.com
Microsoft(R) Windows NT(TM)
(C) Copyright 1985-1996 Microsoft Corp.

D:\>ftp ftp.cdrom.com
Connected to wcarchive.cdrom.com.
220 wcarchive.cdrom.com FTP server (Version wu-2.4(17) Sat Jun 22 21:37:48 PDT 1
996) ready.
User (wcarchive.cdrom.com:(none)): anonymous
331 Guest login ok, send your complete e-mail address as password.
Password:
230 Guest login ok, access restrictions apply.
ftp> bin
200 Type set to I.
ftp> hash
Hash mark printing On (2048 bytes/hash mark).
ftp> get index.txt_
```

Telnet

Telnet is a utility that gives you a text terminal interface to another computer over a TCP/IP network. Telnet is usually used to connect to a remote UNIX computer.

If your Internet service provider provides you with a UNIX shell account, Telnet is most likely how you will access that shell account. If you have a dial-up connection, your mail will probably be delivered to this account. Although accessing this e-mail account is easier if you use a TCP/IP e-mail package as described above, you can use Telnet and the UNIX shell account command-line programs to send and receive e-mail. You may also have to use the UNIX command line in order to manage World Wide Web files in this UNIX account if you are using the Internet service provider to publish your Web pages to the Internet.

Windows NT comes with a Telnet utility that is installed when you install the operating system. See Figure 1.6 for an example of Telnet being used.

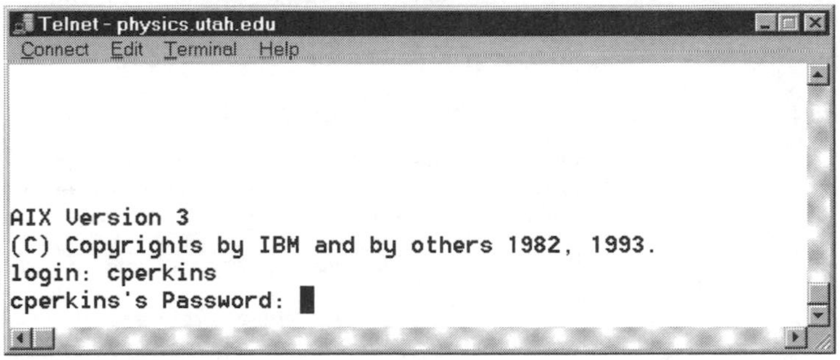

FIGURE 1.6

Telnet enables you
to access command-
line accounts on
other computers.

```
Telnet - physics.utah.edu
Connect   Edit   Terminal   Help




AIX Version 3
(C) Copyrights by IBM and by others 1982, 1993.
login: cperkins
cperkins's Password: ▊
```

UseNet News

UseNet News is a worldwide replicated bulletin board network with tens of thousands of topics that individuals around the world discuss constantly. You will find that it is an unparalleled resource for solving technical problems, especially computer and computer networking problems. For any problem you face, you can be assured that someone has probably already faced that problem—and found a solution to it. Many progressive companies also provide technical support in newsgroups.

Internet newsgroups are not limited to technical subjects. You will find newsgroups on topics ranging from boat building to politics. The subjects of newsgroups are only as limited as the imaginations of the individuals on the Internet.

In order to access Internet News, you will need to install a newsreader program and have access to a UseNet server supplied on your network or by your Internet provider (most UseNet servers are limited to subscriber access). Many newsreaders are available for most operating systems, and you may find other Internet tools that include a newsreader. Both Internet Explorer and Netscape contain a newsreader and an Internet e-mail package. See Figure 1.7 for an example of Internet News being used.

FIGURE 1.7

With Internet News you can communicate with other people interested in a topic.

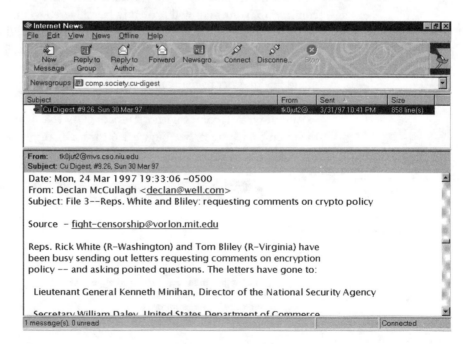

Why Do You Need the Internet and the World Wide Web?

You now know what the Internet is, where it came from, and how it works. You may also have some idea of what the Internet can do for you. This section considers the question, Why should you (or your organization) be connected to the Internet?

The Internet connects you to your customers so that they can learn what you do, receive information and technical support, and even buy your products over the Internet. In addition, the Internet connects you to employees who either work from remote sites (e.g., telecommuters who work from their home offices) or roam (e.g., outside sales people or customer support technicians). Finally, on the Internet you will find a wealth of information on almost any subject.

In short, the reason to "get wired" is that when you are online, you are not just connected to the Internet. You are also connected to everyone and everything that is connected to the Internet.

This section surveys what the Internet can do for you in each of the following categories:

- Online commerce
- Customer service
- Organizational support
- Information

The best way to show you what the Internet can do for you is to describe what the Internet has done for other companies. The following examples were all valid at the time of this writing; however, the Internet is a fluid place, and some of the Internet sites mentioned in the text may no longer be in existence or may have changed significantly. Nevertheless, you should be able to find hundreds of companies using the Internet in a manner similar to the examples shown here.

Online Commerce

Everyone seems to be putting up a Web site these days. Of course, computer companies (such as Microsoft at `http://www.microsoft.com`) have Web sites. But you can also find bookstores (try `http://www.amazon.com`) and book publishers (`http://www.sybex.com`). You can find florists (`http://www.ftd.com`), sandwich shops (`http://www.subway.com`), automobile tire shops (`http://www.bigo.com`), greeting card companies (`http://www.hallmark.com`), manufacturers of chocolates (`http://www.hersheys.com`), and motion pictures (`http://www.paramount.com`), and the list just keeps going (`http://www.energizer.com`).

Most big companies have Internet sites (the preceding companies are all international, national, or regional companies), and many small companies and local organizations are also exploiting the power of the Internet. At the time of this writing you can rent boats in San Diego (`http://www.millenianet.com/seaforth`) and check this weekend's performances at the Utah Symphony Orchestra (`http://www.aros.net/~utsymph/`). You can get a haircut in Pennsylvania (`http://www.phillyzone.com/enjolie/`) or a bicycle in Idaho (`http://www.skilookout.com/index.html`). The Internet, like streets and freeways (which are often compared to the Internet for some reason), yields its benefits to the smallest local shops as well as to the largest multinational conglomerates.

Whatever your business, the Internet can help you do it.

As you browse through the Web pages mentioned here (and whatever else attracts your interest), you will notice that the Internet is helping these companies sell their products and services. Most Web sites provide online customers with one or more of the following:

- Company information
- Catalog of products and services
- Custom product specification
- Product brochures
- Online product ordering
- Online product delivery

In the next section you will see examples of static Web pages and dynamic Web pages. A *static Web page* is not created automatically when the user requests the page; it remains the same from one access to another. A *dynamic Web page* is automatically created or has portions that are automatically created when the page is accessed (e.g., a page that includes product descriptions, images, and pricing pulled from a database) or a page that interacts with the user via CGI scripts, Java, or another programming language.

The next section shows you how companies implement these services on the Internet. You'll just be looking at portions of Web sites for new ideas; you'll learn how to tie together all this information and build your own Web site later in the book.

Company Information

The most basic thing you can do with a World Wide Web site is tell the world about yourself. Sybex describes itself in the Web page `http://www.sybex .com/about.html` (see Figure 1.8). You can give the viewer a little (or more) information about your company, and how you present the information tells the surfer a lot about your company. Sybex shows you one informal (and yet informative!) page. Another example of a company description (for John Deere, `http://www.deere.com/aboutus/index.htm`) spans many pages and covers many aspects of the company's operation, including the company's financial standing (see Figures 1.9 and 1.10)

You might include the following information about your company on your Web page:

- The company name (obviously!)

- The company logo or logos

- The company's address, phone number, and other contact information. (You can even include the location of the Web page because it might be printed out and paper has no reload button.)

- A description of what your company does (an overview of the services it offers, the products it manufactures, etc.)

- A glimpse into the human side of your company (e.g., community involvement, partnerships with charities and foundations, and programs for employees such as educational benefits or flexible working arrangements). If you have a company song, post it! You might even include a sound sample of your employees singing it.

■ Recent information about the company's activities such as press releases and product announcements

FIGURE 1.8

The Sybex About page gives you some information about the company.

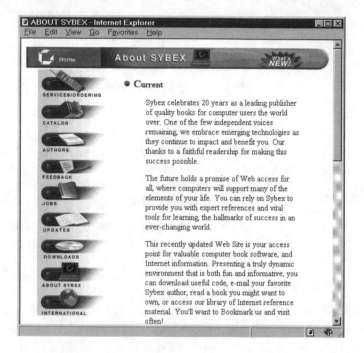

FIGURE 1.9

The John Deere information pages are well organized.

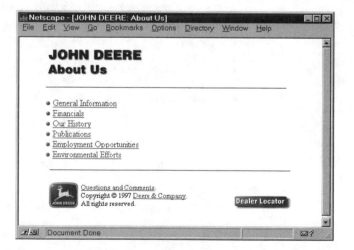

FIGURE 1.10

You can learn about the financial standing of Deere & Company from its Web site.

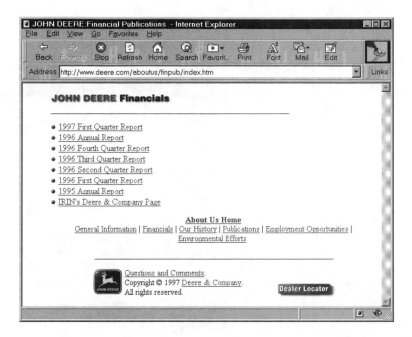

You don't actually have to have an Internet site of your own to put up this kind of Web page. Most Internet service providers will host Web pages and make it look as if you have a site of your own. (You even get your own domain name.) This kind of Web page is also not technically difficult to produce. Your primary concerns will be the content of your ad copy and informational brochures. The content of your Web pages should be well structured and technically accurate, should use proper grammar and punctuation, and should be of a quality and style that reflect well on your organization.

Catalog of Products and Services

If your company exists to provide products or services to the public, listing those products and services is the next obvious thing to do with a Web site. Take a look at what Sybex offers on its catalog page (`http://www.sybex.com/books.html`) and then click the <u>Whole List</u> link (see Figure 1.11).

This kind of Web page can be as simple to produce as the company information Web page, or it can be moderately complex technically to produce, depending on whether or not you create a Web page that is automatically updated from a database. For a simple product line with infrequent changes

FIGURE I.II

The Sybex catalog lists the books that Sybex has in print.

and static prices, you can create a list of products and services the same as you would create any other Web page or printed catalog.

A company that has a wide range of goods and services may need to put forth a great deal of effort to keep its catalog up-to-date if all online changes are made by hand (or by word-processor). However, if you have a database of your products on the computer, you don't have to make the changes by hand. With a little more work, you can create dynamic Web pages that automatically reflect new catalog entries, new prices, and even new pictures and captions for whatever your company sells.

This sort of page requires more technical support than does a simple static Web page. You will need to set up software components to link the Web page with the database. You may use CGI scripts or ODBC Java applets to make the link, and creating a dynamic page in this manner requires more than just writing or graphical arts skills.

Some Internet service providers will host Web pages that support dynamically created pages like this, but you may find that you can better manage these pages and serve the data if you have your own Internet server.

Custom Product Specification

Your catalog can be a simple listing of each product and service that you sell (like Sybex's) with a phone number to call to order. You can also create catalog pages that allow users to choose options and customize their purchase and see the results of their choices over the Web. You can see an example of this approach at Dell's Web site (`http://www.dell.com/products/dim/xpspro/index.htm` and then click the Configure/Price/Buy box; see Figure 1.12).

FIGURE 1.12

This Dell Computer Web page helps you custom configure a computer.

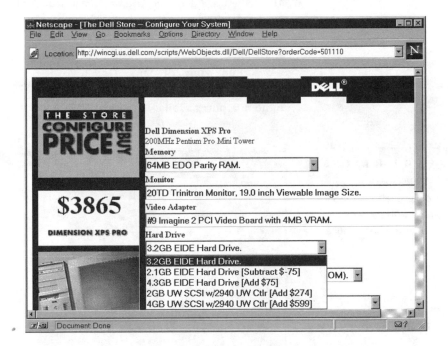

This kind of Web page is one of the most complicated to make because it requires programming. The program may be written in Java or Javascript, or it may be an ActiveX control or a Perl script. But it is a program, and as such it requires programming skill to get right.

Product Brochures

With the explosive growth of the Internet and the new ways consumers can access it, many more customers are turning to the Internet for information with which to make informed purchasing decisions. (Capitalism and free markets, as you may recall from school, depend on a reasonably informed consumer. Or so the theory goes.) You can give your company's products an edge in the marketplace by making information about them easily available.

If your company produces technical products, this sort of Web page is especially important (and even expected if it is an electronic or computer product). You can see an example of a product brochure for a high-tech product at the 3com Web site `http://www.3com.com/0files/products/dsheets/400211a.html` (see Figure 1.13), and you can see a product brochure for another exotic product at the Folbot Web site `http://www.folbot.com/grnland.htm` (see Figure 1.14).

Electronic brochures don't need to be any more complicated than the Web pages describing your company. Your focus here will be on information and presentation rather than the Internet and Web technology that it takes to make the brochures available.

FIGURE 1.13

This 3com Web page brochure tells you about 3com networking products for the home office.

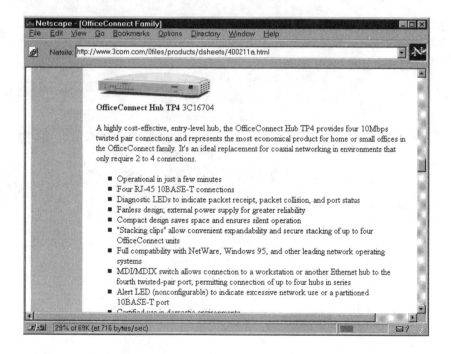

FIGURE 1.14

You can get the details about FolBot folding kayaks from its Web page.

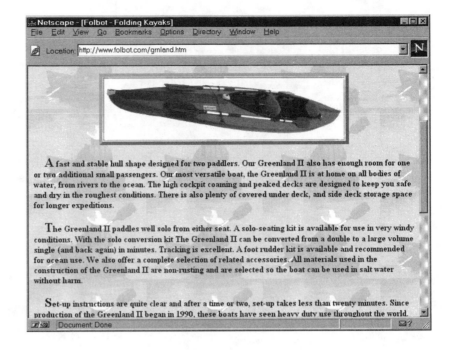

FIGURE 1.14

You can get the details about FolBot folding kayaks from its Web page.

Online Product Ordering and Payment

A natural extension of your online catalog is online ordering and payment. A well-crafted Web page encourages customers to browse, select, customize, order products, and even pay for them using their credit cards.

Amazon.com (`http://www.amazon.com`) is a bookstore on the Internet that allows you to browse through its selections and order over the Internet. See Figure 1.15 for an example of a Web page that allows you to order a product.

Different browsers have different methods of telling you a link is encrypted. (Chapter 11 explores the differences between browsers.) The whole key symbol on the bottom of the window is Netscape's way of telling you that the connection is encrypted.

This kind of Web page is a little more difficult to construct than a simple company information page or a static catalog. You can create a basic order

FIGURE 1.15

You can order books over the Internet from Amazon.com's Internet site.

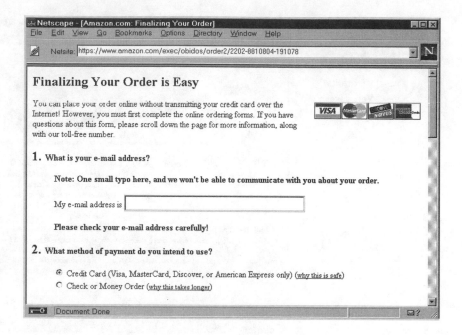

page using standard HTML forms, or you can create sophisticated "shopping cart" pages that automatically add up your purchases, apply sales tax, and inform you of the total.

You should be careful when you set up your site for online ordering, because the Internet was not originally designed to provide secure connections. If you accept credit card numbers over the Internet, for example, you should provide for and require secure, encrypted connections for the credit card number transfer. Chapter 8 goes into more detail on securing your Web site.

Online Product Delivery

If your product is information (or computer software, if you must make a distinction), then you can even deliver it over the Internet! You must craft this kind of Web site with care, however, in order to make the site secure.

Creating an online product delivery Web site can be simple if your product can only be unlocked if the customer phones you to get a password. If you want customers to be able to purchase the product as well as download it over the Internet, you must establish a secure connection as you do for online product ordering and payment.

Customer Service

You can also use a Web site to support your customers once they have purchased your product or service. You can view one company's excellent customer support Web site at `http://www.hp.com/cposupport/eschome.html` (see Figure 1.16). Some things you can include in a customer support Web site are

- Product technical references

- Troubleshooting guides

- Tips, tricks, and application notes

- Order and shipment tracking

FIGURE 1.16

HP provides an excellent customer support site on the Internet.

Only the last kind of support page (order and shipment tracking) requires sophisticated Web-page creation skills. The other pages are simply documents that you can make available on the Internet.

Creating an order and shipment tracking Web page requires more technical skills than the others because you will have to link the Web page to some kind of order-tracking database. You may have to do some programming to create this kind of a Web site.

Organizational Support

You can also create a Web site that supports people inside your organization, rather than customers outside it. You don't even have to connect this kind of Web site to the Internet. An internal Web site is often called an *intranet*. Some things you might include in an intranet are:

- Contact information, job descriptions, and so on for employees of your company

- A company newsletter, complete with back issues

- Memos and organizational correspondence, including an online forum for group communication

- Organizational information such as the company handbook or policy and procedures manual

- Databases for organizational use, such as customer contact lists and inventory tracking

Information

Another use for a Web site is to collect information on a subject or discipline. An electronic engineering firm may collect a lot of data on devices and circuits, and it may make that data available to the engineering community. Software firms may collect and distribute publicly available software tools. A CAD company with a loyal following may create a Web site containing CAD automation files that users have created and placed in the public domain.

Exercise 1.3 takes you on a tour of the Internet to see how some companies present themselves via World Wide Web pages.

EXERCISE 1.3

Viewing Company Web Sites

1. Start Internet Explorer. (Double-click the Internet Explorer icon on the desktop.)

If your Internet Explorer is in its default configuration, you will be viewing the Microsoft Network Web site (www.msn.com).

EXERCISE 1.3 (CONTINUED FROM PREVIOUS PAGE)

2. Replace `http://www.msn.com` in the Address field with **`http://www.sybex.com`** and then press Enter. Internet Explorer will display Sybex's Web page.

3. Replace `http://www.sybex.com` in the Address field with **`http://www.deere.com/aboutus/index.htm`** and then press Enter. Internet Explorer will take you to the John Deere About page that contains a list of categories.

4. Click once on the word <u>Financials</u>. This link will take you to the company's financial information Web page.

5. Replace the address in the Address field with **`http://www.sybex.com/books.html`** and then press Enter to go to the Sybex Books page. (You can also reach this page from the Sybex home page.)

6. Replace the address in the Address field with **`http://www.folbot.com/grnland.htm`** and then press Enter to go to the Folbot page that describes the Greenland II folding kayak.

7. Replace the address in the Address field with **`http://www.hp.com/cposupport/eschome.html`** and then press Enter to go to an HP customer support page.

8. Close the Internet Explorer by selecting Close from the File menu.

Summary

Your company needs to be connected to the Internet. Why? Because the Internet (as the fax machine before it) is quickly becoming an essential business tool.

The Internet comprises computers and networks that are connected to each other. No one individual or organization is in charge of the Internet; instead, the Internet is managed by the cooperation of its constituents. The Internet uses the TCP/IP protocol to move information from one computer to another, and Internet applications such as Telnet, FTP, Internet mail, UseNet News, and the Web require the TCP/IP protocol to operate.

You can use Telnet to run programs on remote UNIX computers and FTP to store and retrieve files. Internet Mail allows you to exchange messages with anyone else on the Internet. UseNet News contains discussion forums on almost any topic, and the World Wide Web gives the Internet a graphical interface and an easy way to navigate through data stored on the Internet.

Your Web site can be as simple as a page describing your company or as complicated as an online catalog that allows you to configure and download software and pay for it over the Internet. The simpler Web pages require little technical skill (a good command of the English language and a good perception of style will suffice to create good Web pages of this nature) but the more complicated pages that interact with the user require a familiarity with Internet tools and perhaps even programming skill.

Review Questions

1. You need a computer (and operating system) to serve as a World Wide Web server for your company's Web site. Which of the following can you use to host the Web site? (Choose all that apply.)

   A. UNIX

   B. MacOS

   C. Windows NT Server

   D. Novell NetWare

2. You have created a simple company Web site that contains information about your company and brochures about your company's products. You would like to put this Web site on the Internet with the minimum of fuss and cost, but you want a large number of people to be able to access it simultaneously. You want customers to connect to the Web site using the address www.yourcompany.com. What is your best option?

   A. Lease a T1 line and purchase a UNIX workstation. Set up the workstation to host the Web site and connect it to the Internet with the T1.

   B. Put a 33.6Kbps modem into a PC running Windows NT Workstation. Dial in to your local Internet service provider and leave the PC constantly connected. Serve your Web site using Peer Web Services.

C. Contract with your Internet service provider to host your Web site. Place the Web pages on the Internet service provider's Web server.

D. Get a personal account on an online information service such as AOL. Place the Web pages under your personal account.

3. Your company sells garden tools. You would like customers to be able to browse your Web site, select tools and supplies, have the selections itemized and totaled, and then order and pay for the items over the Internet using a credit card. You have a database containing tools and prices and customer information. You don't want anyone outside of your company to be able to access those credit card numbers. What is your best option for fast and secure hosting of this kind of Web site?

A. Lease a T1 line and install Windows NT on a computer. Set up the computer with Internet Information Server to host the Web site and connect it to the Internet with the T1.

B. Put a 33.6Kbps modem into a PC running Windows NT Workstation. Dial in to your local Internet service provider and leave the PC constantly connected. Serve your Web site using Peer Web Services.

C. Contract with your Internet service provider to host your Web site. Place the Web pages on the Internet service provider's Web server.

D. Get a personal account on an online information service such as AOL. Place the Web pages under your personal account.

4. Which of the following Internet services would you use to get files off the Internet? (Choose two.)

A. FTP

B. Telnet

C. Usenet News

D. World Wide Web

CHAPTER

2

Planning Your Site

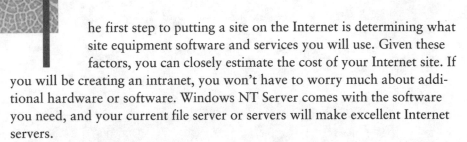

The first step to putting a site on the Internet is determining what site equipment software and services you will use. Given these factors, you can closely estimate the cost of your Internet site. If you will be creating an intranet, you won't have to worry much about additional hardware or software. Windows NT Server comes with the software you need, and your current file server or servers will make excellent Internet servers.

If you are creating a site that will be attached to the Internet, however, you should take a good hard look at the hardware and services you will need before you decide to plunge in. This chapter covers the hardware and services you need to have in place before bringing an Internet host online. The information in this chapter and your cost analysis may cause you to change any plans you've already made for building an Internet site.

In this book we use the term *Internet server* for a server that serves Internet protocol higher-level services such as World Wide Web, file transfer protocol, Gopher (served by IIS), network news transfer protocol, and simple mail transfer protocol (served by Exchange Server). The term does not denote whether the server is attached to the global Internet or a private intranet— the same term refers to both. We have avoided using the term *Web server,* as hypertext services are only one of the many Internet protocol services that these servers typically provide.

To Serve or Not to Serve

Is providing Web services an effective way to draw more business or a money pit that will never really return your investment? Assuming you could adequately determine what you might save with a Web site, it's still nearly impossible to predict exactly how much an Internet presence will increase your sales. No measurement can tell you what the financial impact of a corporate Internet presence will be. Often, you do not have any hard evidence to justify the purchase cost of a new server or software and (especially) the recurring cost of Internet and leased-line services for a Web server.

Serving a Web site requires dedicated hardware, high-bandwidth leased telephony lines from a telephone company, service from an Internet service provider (ISP), and operating system and Internet server software. In return, you get to invite strangers into your networked computers. Considering the expense and potential security problems, one might wonder if it's worth the bother.

On the other hand, the promise of providing information and support to your customers automatically without tying up expensive human resources or incurring per minute long-distance telephone line charges is compelling. Internet sites function as both billboards for casual browsers and informative brochures for interested customers. Certain industries and types of companies will be able to operate completely on the Internet, reducing their overall operating costs dramatically. And when workers can work from home and still accomplish everything they accomplish at the office, the company reduces costs, the employee saves both time and money, and the environment is spared a daily commute.

The answer to the vexing question of whether you should host your own Web site lies in the amount of interactivity that you want from your Web site. If you are merely posting information or providing a site where Web surfers can find your company contact information or get information on your products and services, serving a Web site with your own equipment probably doesn't make much sense. Corporate-presence Web sites exist more as billboards than as storefronts. They tell people about your organization, but they aren't interactive and they don't change much over time.

Your ISP more effectively serves this corporate-presence style of Web site. Nearly all ISPs provide the service of hosting Web sites, charged on a per hit, per megabyte stored, or per bandwidth used basis. Most ISPs also put their Web servers on their high-speed backbones, making access to your site far faster than it would be through the lower-bandwidth commercial leased-line service your organization can afford. Typically, ISPs charge about $100 per month to host your Web site; users have to contact you via a posted telephone number or e-mail address to avail themselves of your services.

Per hit refers to metering a service based on the number of distinct IP addresses that attach to the service in a given time frame, usually one day. *Per megabyte stored* refers to metering the cost of a service based upon how much disk space is required to store the service. *Per bandwidth used* refers to metering a service based upon the load it generates for the ISP. These different styles of metering indicate the emphasis of the provider: providing value, conserving resources, or passing through direct costs.

Paying for Web hosting services has the following advantages:

- No investment in equipment or software
- Very low recurring monthly rate for corporate presence Web sites
- No security risk to your network
- Usually less expensive for smaller organizations
- High-bandwidth connection

On the other hand, if you want to create a major presence, host an Internet-based business, store and provide vast amounts of information, or host an Intranet site for the internal use of your organization, you should host your own Web site. Few ISPs will allow you to make your Web site truly interactive with Common Gateway Interface (CGI) scripts and Internet Server Application Programming Interface (ISAPI) applications. Many charge per megabyte stored, which makes providing library services like shareware-download sites prohibitively expensive. And if you have an extremely popular Web site, your ISP may not be willing to use its servers at its normal rates to host your site. And, of course, the purpose of an intranet is to keep data private, so having your ISP serve it doesn't make much sense.

Hosting a Web site has the following advantages:

- No metered costs—less expensive for large or popular sites
- Allows the use of interactive CGI or ISAPI applications
- Keeps intranets private and secure
- Cost-effective if you already have or need a leased line to the Internet

If you don't know which method will be more cost-effective for you, you should start by paying for a hosting service. Paying a third-party to host your Web site is far less expensive when your site is newer, less popular, and smaller. You can determine both the size and popularity of your site rather quickly once your site is available on the Internet. When you decide to host the site yourself, you can easily buy the server, get the leased-line circuits installed, make arrangements with your ISP, move your site onto your own server, and update your domain name to reflect the new IP address of your server. The change will be transparent to your customers.

The reverse strategy—that is, paying for telephony and Internet services and a server up front—is far more difficult to opt out of if you determine that your site is not worth the expense. You typically must agree to lease your digital telephone trunk line and Internet service for at least a year, which you must continue to pay whether or not the leased line and ISP service are of use to you. You'll also be left with a server, router, and software that are no longer of any use to you.

This book shows you how to set up and run your own Web site using Internet Information Server, Windows NT, and Index Server. Even if you start out with a hosted Internet site, you should understand the issues involved with Internet technology as well as the costs and benefits of providing your own site services. Then, when you are ready, you'll be properly prepared to serve your own site. Of course, none of the security or bandwidth issues apply if hosting an intranet site is your primary interest.

Site Requirements

When you finally decide to put your site on the Internet, you'll need the following hardware, software, and services:

- **Site content**—The content is the HTML pages you've created to provide the function of your site and the files you'll be making available for download.

- **HTTP server software**—For Windows NT, the server software is usually Internet Information Server. If you intend to serve protocols other than HTTP, FTP, and Gopher, you'll need additional server software, such as Microsoft Exchange Server that serves SMTP and NNTP for mail and news services.

- **Network operating system**—Your operating system could be Windows NT Server, UNIX, MacOS, OS/2, or even Windows 95. Internet Information Server runs only on Windows NT. Other operating systems have different Internet server packages.

- **Host computer**—Your host computer should have enough storage space for the operating system, Internet service software, and your site. Internet servers usually do not need to be very fast, since connections to them are usually slow compared to the speed of a LAN.

- **Data link adapter or router/firewall**—If your host computer will also function as your network router, it will need two network interface adapters. Consider using a firewall if you are attached to the public Internet to keep your site secure.

- **High-bandwidth physical data link to your ISP**—In most cases this link is a 56K frame relay leased line for light use or niche Web sites and T1 for sites that handle moderate traffic. If your site has more than moderate traffic, you should consider having it hosted on at least a T3 (45Mb/s leased line) backbone.

- **Internet service providing a permanent TCP/IP address**—Your ISP can help you with many of the details of setting up your site. Most ISPs will lease the CSU/DSU (the channel service unit/digital service unit is a device used to attach leased lines to a router) and router necessary for a small additional fee, which means that all you have to provide is the Web server. Most ISPs will now also provide a packet-filtering function that can make your site more secure.

- **Domain name registration**—Domain names provide an easily remembered name for your site, such as www.microsoft.com. You register domain names with InterNIC, an organization created to provide a unified domain name registration service. Registration will cost about $50 dollars, and a yearly fee of $50 is required to keep your domain name registered. This fee exists simply to keep frivolous registrations to a minimum and to make sure names are registered only for as long as they are needed. You can contact InterNIC at www.internic.com.

Figure 2.1 shows an Internet host in a typical network. The next few sections detail the software services and hardware required to bring your Internet site online. The discussion in this chapter is a broad survey of the entire process and relatively generic in nature; it applies to any operating system environment.

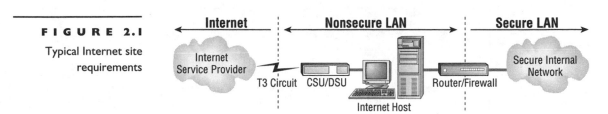

FIGURE 2.1

Typical Internet site
requirements

Services

An *Internet host* (a computer attached to the Internet that hosts an Internet site) usually requires more than just hypertext or FTP service software. Especially if your Internet host is the primary link to the Internet for other computers in your organization, you will probably want to run more Internet-related services than just Internet Information Server.

Name Services are services that resolve computer names to IP addresses. You may also want to run the Distributed file system Service to allow other computers to store files made available to the Internet from your Internet host. Dfs allows one computer to operate as an Internet host with IIS software installed but to serve FTP and hypertext files stored on other computers.

Name Services

To reach your Web site, client computers will have to know the name of the Internet host that stores the files that make up your site. They will also need access to a database that translates that name into an IP address. Servers that perform the name lookup and IP address resolution are called *name servers,* and the process is called *name resolution.*

The two types of name servers are

- Windows Internet Name Service (WINS) servers

- Internet Domain Name Service (DNS) servers

WINS servers translate NetBIOS names (e.g., \\boomerang) that have traditionally been used in IBM/Microsoft networks into IP addresses to support browsing across broadcast domains. DNS servers translate Internet domain names like www.microsoft.com into the IP address of the Internet host that contains the Microsoft Web site.

Terminology

The terms *network, subnetwork,* and *internetwork* are used differently in different contexts. To reduce confusion, we will use the following definitions throughout this book:

- A *subnetwork* is a network of computers directly connected through hubs or on the same coaxial cable segment. The term *Ethernet segment* is synonymous with subnetwork.

- A *network* is a group of subnetworks connected by data link layer equipment such as bridges or switches (but not routers) and characterized by the fact that broadcast packets are forwarded across these bridges so that any two computers can communicate over the data link directly. *Network* is synonymous with local area network.

- An *internetwork* is a group of networks connected by network layer equipment such as routers or multihomed servers and characterized by the fact that broadcasts are not forwarded through routers so that computers on different networks can communicate only by using network layer protocols such as IPX or TCP/IP. This condition remains true even though IPX forwards broadcasts (because the data link technology does not).

Windows Internet Name Service

Computers on a Windows Network simply browse through a list of computers and share names when they need access to a shared resource. This list is maintained by browsers that operate by broadcasting requests for names to all the computers on the same network. Each computer responds with its name and address information. Client computers then cache the list of computer names and IP addresses provided by the network browsers on the network. One Windows network may have up to three browsers no matter how big the network gets.

Because Windows name resolution relies on broadcast packets, browse requests are not forwarded through routers to computers on other networks. This situation is very problematic: Computers on other networks will not show up in the Network Neighborhood of client computers, making access to their shared resources difficult even though a path to the computer exists. Essentially, you would simply have to know the IP address of the computer and the share if you wanted to access a shared resource—there's no way to discover it.

So why doesn't TCP/IP simply forward broadcast packets the way IPX does? Broadcast packets work well only in small to medium-size networks. When the number of clients in a network reaches the tens of thousands, broadcasts from all those clients take up most of the available network bandwidth. Large internetworks (and especially the Internet) would be impossible to implement unless broadcasts are kept local to small domains.

The Windows Internet Name Service (WINS) service solves this problem by acting very much like an Internet DNS server for NetBIOS names. When you run a WINS server, it communicates with all the master browsers on each attached network and compiles a master list of network names and IP addresses for all the resources on the network. When a client computer needs to resolve a NetBIOS name, it first checks with the master browser on the same network. If that browser cannot resolve the name, it checks the WINS server that keeps the master list of all available network names on the network.

Windows NT Server 4 includes WINS so you can automatically resolve NetBIOS names across networks in your organization.

Domain Name Service

Domain Name Service (DNS) is a client/server Internet protocol that responds to requests for the name resolution of Internet domain names. A client passes a domain name such as www.microsoft.com to the DNS server, and the DNS server returns the IP address of the server that name refers to.

As you might have suspected, name resolution is actually a little more complex than that. Since the Internet relies on a master list of all Internet hosts, the entire Internet theoretically requires only one DNS server. In reality, no single computer could possibly respond to the volume of name requests that occur on the Internet, and routing that traffic to a single point on the Internet would not be possible, so a caching localization scheme is used.

Most networks attached to the Internet have a DNS server that maintains a list of all the recently resolved DNS names and addresses. When a client on that network requests name resolution, that DNS server checks its list and responds in one of the following ways:

- If the name appears in the list, the server returns the address.

- If the name does not appear in the list, the DNS server checks its DNS server.

- If that server can't resolve the name, that server checks its DNS server.

This process repeats until a DNS server without a DNS parent server is reached. This server returns an error message indicating that the DNS name cannot be resolved. The final server in the chain is normally the master domain name server of the Internet (maintained by the InterNIC organization, also called a *root server*) in networks connected to the Internet, or simply the master DNS server in private IP networks not connected to the Internet.

Windows NT Server 4 includes the DNS service that allows your network to maintain its own DNS server. Having a DNS server local to your network speeds DNS name resolution considerably for domain names that have already been accessed once. After the first access, the names appear in the DNS cache on your local network and therefore do not require a trip through your connection to the Internet. Name resolutions that fail will always take a long time because the name servers have to search all the way to the master DNS server (or a high-level server that caches the entire InterNIC database) before a fail is returned.

Distributed File System

Windows NT 4 (and Windows NT 3.51 Service Pack 5) supports a new service called the Distributed file system (Dfs). Dfs allows you to create directory trees wherein the shared resources of other servers and workstations in your network appear as subdirectories to a monolithic directory structure on the Dfs server. Dfs also supports multiple trees, so you can create different hierarchical views of your network for different purposes.

If your Internet service root directories (`wwwroot`, `ftproot`, `gopherroot`) are implemented as Dfs trees, you can attach shared directories on other servers inside these directories, effectively making documents on those servers available to browsers attached to that Internet server. This method allows you to spread the files in your site around to minimize the load and to change the physical location of files without modifying your hypertext links.

Routing and Subnets

Routing seems to be one of the least understood concepts in TCP/IP networks, but it's really quite simple once you grasp the underlying idea. *Routers* connect different networks, thus allowing data to be forwarded to other data links of any type. For example, let's say you open your browser and attach to a Web site across the country. Here's an example of the routing that can occur:

1. Your computer sends Ethernet frames containing the request in an IP packet to your router.

2. Your router receives the Ethernet frame and removes the IP packet contained within it. The router checks the IP packet's address against the routing table stored in the router and determines that the host is located on the Internet, so it transmits the IP packet through a frame relay frame on your company's T1 link to your company's ISP.

3. Your ISP's router receives the frame relay frame from your company's router and removes the IP packet contained within. The router checks the IP packet's address against the routing table stored in the router and determines that the host is most closely located on a link to a different ISP attached through a different router in the room, so the current router sends the IP packet over the local FDDI ring to the appropriate router.

4. That router receives the IP packet inside the FDDI frame and examines it, determining that the packet should be forwarded to the Commercial Internet Exchange. It transmits the packet over the T3 link to CIX.

5. The router at CIX assigned to that ISP receives the packet, examines the IP address, and determines which major ISP's router the packet should be forwarded to. It then transmits the packet over the 2.2Gb/s SONET network to the router that attaches to the ISP hosting the destination Web site.

6. The next router receives the IP packet from the SONET network and forwards it onto the T3 link to the destination ISP.

7. The destination ISP receives the packet over its T3 link to CIX and forwards it to the ATM-155 network attaching all their Internet servers. The ATM cells are switched to the appropriate Internet server, which assembles the base IP packet from that traffic. The server then decodes the IP address, determines that the packet is local to the machine, removes the data contained in the packet, and passes it to the higher-level service (the Web service software) that will respond to the traffic.

This process occurs for each IP packet traveling in each direction. To make a rough analogy, consider a cargo container designed for cargo ships. Large trucks tow flatbed trailers that carry cargo containers. The truck sits at the factory warehouse until its container is full of widgets. It then travels to the docks, where a crane lifts the cargo container from the flatbed trailer and sets it down on a ship. The ship then leaves port and steams to the destination port. At the destination port, a crane lifts the cargo container off the ship and loads the container onto another truck. That truck travels to the customer's warehouse where the container is unloaded. Figure 2.2 shows this analogy graphically.

F I G U R E 2.2

A routing analogy

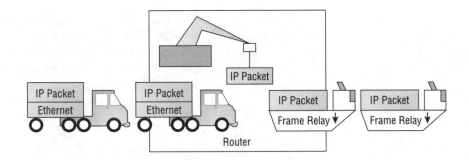

In this example the truck is one type of data link technology (say, Ethernet) and the ship is another type (say, frame relay). The port facility and crane perform as the router, and the cargo container is the IP packet. Just as the cargo container travels the complete route over different transport mechanisms, IP packets travel their complete routes over different data links. Routers are the port facilities that move packets between the different data links.

The important aspect of routing is that it is entirely transparent to the data in the IP packets and to the user. You don't have to care about the number or types of networks that your data flows through, just as when you send a package through the mail, you don't care how many mail trucks carry out the delivery. Your only concern is that the package gets to the destination intact and as quickly as possible.

Stand-Alone Server

With a single Internet server, you probably don't have to worry about routing. The destination for all your Internet traffic should be local (on the same network) to all your computers. If you have more than one network, your networks should all be directly connected to a single multihomed Internet server. If your server is multihomed, you will need WINS if any of your clients need to access shared resources on clients attached to other networks.

A *multihomed* server is a server attached to more than one network through multiple network adapters. This server normally serves as a router among the various networks in addition to any other file or Internet services it may perform.

Single Domain

A single Internet domain is defined by the fact that routing need not occur between any two computers within it. If you are using a single domain, you won't have to worry about routing TCP/IP or providing WINS or DNS service.

Don't confuse the concepts of a Windows NT Security domain with an Internet domain—they are entirely different. A *Windows NT Security domain* is merely a connected group of servers (the connection method doesn't matter) that use the same security accounts database. An *Internet domain* is a single network in which two computers can communicate without routing.

Multiple Domain

If you have multiple TCP/IP domains in your network, you will have to provide at least WINS, and perhaps both WINS and DNS services, to allow the computers on your networks to communicate across routers. Windows NT relies upon the services of WINS and DNS to browse the resources of computers located across routers. If these services are not available, the only way for Windows NT to know about nonlocal computers is to simply refer to the servers by their IP address. Chapter 5 covers the different IP protocols, including WINS and DNS in complete detail.

Security Planning

If one could say that the growth rate of the Internet is currently limited by any factor, that limiting factor would be security. Initially, the Internet was set up without regard for security because it was far more important to simply begin sharing data. Everyone involved thought there would be time for security planning later. The Internet pioneers simply didn't put material they didn't want to make available to the public on Internet hosts. Since the original purpose of the World Wide Web was to publish scientific documents in an easily retrievable format, security simply wasn't a major issue. In fact, the reason for the phenomenal growth of the Internet to date is this very lack of security—nothing keeps people out.

However, the absence of security that once fostered growth is now a limiting factor. An environment without security is an environment where commerce cannot occur on a large scale. Commerce was not a factor when the Internet was planned. Its original purpose was simply the publication of timely scientific and academic information—no commercial interests existed before 1994. If the Internet is to become anything more than an interesting toy, commercial enterprises must be able to use it either to make money directly or to reduce costs indirectly. Because Internet security is not widely understood and because the threat of stolen secret information for many organizations is more important than information dissemination over the Internet, many organizations are keeping the Internet at a distance by attaching only temporarily through dial-up connections.

Intranets

Keeping data on an intranet private is just as easy as keeping any other set of files private. Since intranets run on your file server, you can simply use file system permissions to keep different Web pages or FTP files private. Users who attempt to access Web pages for which they don't have permission will receive an access-denied message.

WARNING   You should disable anonymous logon to your Web site if it is used strictly for intranet access. Since all your users will be logged on anyway simply to access the server, allowing anonymous logon serves no purpose.

Internet Hosts

Many methods are available to implement security mechanisms for an Internet server. The most common methods follow:

- Firewalls

- Filtered packet services

- Internet service restrictions

- File and directory permissions

- Encryption

- Secure Socket Layer

None of these methods precludes the use of any others. In fact, you can (and probably should) implement all of them or as many as you can reasonably justify for the level of protection required by your data.

Firewalls

If you attach your local area network directly to the Internet through a router, you risk intrusion into your network from the Internet. Many routers now function as devices called *firewalls,* which allow you to restrict the information flowing through the firewall by type (for instance, only HTTP or FTP information), IP address of the computers, and many other factors. Firewalls are the best way to protect your network from intrusion via the Internet, but they come without a guarantee.

Filtered Packet Services

Some ISPs provide a firewall service. They will automatically filter traffic to and from your network by type; if you desire, they will also restrict access to your network to certain IP addresses or subnets. These measures are generally less expensive than purchasing your own firewall, but they are also a little less secure.

Internet Service Restrictions

Most Internet service software, including Internet Information Server, includes security mechanisms to prevent functions like listing the files in a Web site or uploading files to an FTP site. The Internet service software implements these security mechanisms, and they operate independently of all other security mechanisms. You should implement security mechanisms that will enhance security without restricting the behavior you desire, regardless of the other levels of security you've enabled. You will find a complete discussion of the WWW service security restrictions available in Internet Information Server in Chapter 8.

Some Internet service software contains bugs that allow security loopholes. Internet Information Server 1.0 had a very serious security loophole that could be exploited to take control of a Web server. Poorly written CGI scripts and ISAPI applications are also a major source of security problems. Test every piece of software you use on your Internet server very thoroughly and stay up-to-date on software revisions from the manufacturer.

File and Directory Security

Keeping the data you publish on the Internet private seems somewhat easier, but again, there are perils. If you put up your own Web server, you can require users to log on to the server. This method allows you to use regular Windows NT file-level security to keep documents secure. The problem is that your data will still pass over the Internet in an unencrypted form. Anyone running a promiscuous mode packet sniffer (like the Network Monitor that comes with SMS Server, for instance) attached to a network between the source and destination will be able to see your traffic and even piece together the packets flowing between computers. HTML pages are relatively easy to reconstruct from this sort of data. Even the passwords used to log on are passed in these packets and may not be encrypted unless you've set up your site correctly.

Encryption

You can further secure your server against these sorts of intrusions by using MS-CHAP encryption and the Point-to-Point Tunneling Protocol (PPTP). These two services encrypt the data that flows over the Internet so that even if it were intercepted between two computers, it would be very nearly impossible to decode.

Secure Socket Layer

Another advance in Internet security is the Secure Socket Layer (SSL) protocol supported by most browsers and Internet servers. The Secure Socket Layer establishes an encrypted link between the Internet server and browser in a manner similar to that provided by the PPTP except that SSL is user independent. You don't have to log in or provide credentials for SSL to work. SSL is useful for keeping transactional data from being compromised while you work on the Web, but it doesn't keep the public from using your Internet site the way a firewall would.

Hardware

Internet servers do not have to be particularly buff machines. Last year's file server will do fine, as will a client computer with perhaps an additional network adapter to perform the routing function if necessary. So long as the machine conforms to a reasonable minimum for the operating system, it will make an adequate Internet server if your Internet link is slower than a T3 leased line (the vast majority are).

Your Web server must be powerful enough to run any ISAPI applications or CGI scripts required of it, and if the same computer is used to host a database server, it must be capable of running the database server software. The basic rule is this: Your computer must be able to run all the software required by your site without the IIS software in order to run the IIS software.

Now that you are overloaded with information, let's review what you will need to run Windows NT Server 4 and Internet Information Server properly. (These guidelines are not Microsoft's official minimum configurations; they are commonsense minimums. The official minimums are detailed in the companion book *MCSE: NT Server 4 Study Guide*.)

- Pentium 100MHz or greater for simple IIS services. Running other services, such as a multiprotocol router, DNS, WINS, or other Internet services, such as Internet Relay Chat or an ISAPI application, will require more power.

- 24MB RAM (32MB RAM for RISC-based machines), but a minimum of 32MB is preferable.

- 250MB disk space minimum *plus* the size of your content files *and* room for return data from CGI scripts or ISAPI applications. Disk space will depend on the size of your content files.

- Network adapter(s), including hardware to connect to your ISP's site.

- Tape backup hardware.

If the computer you expect to use for an Internet or intranet host does not conform to these minimums, consider upgrading it. Computer hardware is now so inexpensive that using less-than-adequate equipment doesn't make sense.

Internet Service Providers

Internet Service Providers (ISPs) are companies that connect you to the Internet. These companies either form the backbone of the Internet or are connected to companies that do.

If you are constantly connected to the Internet to provide an Internet service, you will most likely attach to your ISP's wide area network via a telephony leased line. If you simply need a temporary connection to the Internet to browse the Web or download a file, you will probably attach to your ISP's wide area network using a dial-up modem.

The top-tier ISPs connect at one or all of four commercial Internet exchange (CIX) network access points (NAPs) in San Francisco, Chicago, Los Angeles, and near Washington, D.C., in Virginia. At these exchanges the top-tier ISPs have routers attached to the same high-speed network. These routers exchange data among their large networks and handle nearly all Internet traffic (although some traffic is routed by optimized routing links).

ISPs all do the same thing: route data off your computer or network and onto the Internet. So what is the difference between ISPs? Functionally, there is none. ISPs differ only in the following categories:

- **Price**—Like anything, low cost providers sell a lower quality of service. The top-tier ISPs all have similar charges—about the same as your leased-line monthly charge. Second- or third-tier providers (i.e., connected to the Internet through one or two other ISPs) are usually cheaper.

- **Percentage of capacity sold**—Many smaller ISPs oversell their capacity by an order of magnitude. This means that all customer connections will be slow and that connections may begin failing during busy times on the network. For instance, a small ISP may have only a single T1 connection to the Internet, but sell four or five T1 connections to other businesses and 200 or 300 dial-up connections. During peak access hours, all subscribers will have very poor service.

- **Customer service**—Some ISPs do nearly everything for you, from registering your domain name with InterNIC to arranging for your leased line to be installed. Others don't have the ability to help you at all; they merely wholesale Internet connections.

- **Services**—All ISPs offer variations of their basic Internet connection services. Some ISPs will put a firewall on their end of your connection so you won't have to buy one yourself. Some service options will allow you to operate as an ISP; others won't. Some will provide you with a permanent IP address for a dial-up connection so you can host a Web site from your own machine; others will not. Many other service variations exist.

You can't get a feel for the differences between providers just by comparing their ad brochures, and sales representatives rarely know enough about what their company does to answer tough questions—but they should be able to put you in touch with someone who can.

Don't assume that large providers are always better than small ones; small providers are often far better at customer support and offer very customized services. They may even come to your site and set up the connectivity hardware for you.

You should ask each ISP you interview the following questions to discover that provider's basic capabilities:

- **Who is your ISP?** Unless the ISP is a top-tier ISP, it will be connected to one. An ISP's quality of service depends directly on its provider's quality of service. Don't accept silly answers like "We're directly connected to the Internet" or even "We don't have one" because they most likely do. A top-tier ISP will answer with something like "We're a top-tier provider connected directly to the Internet backbone" or "We have routers at the CIX NAPs."

- **What is your bandwidth to your ISP?** This response will tell you how much capacity the ISP can handle. Answers like "multiple T1" don't mean much. Ask how many T1 lines the ISP has. Insist on a provider that has at least one T grade higher than you are leasing. For instance, if you are leasing a T1 service, don't go with a provider that has "multiple T1s"; you should find a provider with a T3 link. (T2 is not widely available.)

- **Can you help me subnet my network?** Questions like this, even if you don't need the help, test the ISPs customer support knowledge and capability. Don't worry if the sales rep can't help you—that's typical. But if he or she can't put you in touch with someone that knows how this technology works, you shouldn't go with that provider.

- **How many leased-line customers do you have in the area?** Try to get a feel for how much of the ISP's capacity is already sold. Many ISPs oversell their actual capacity by a factor of five or ten. Good providers always have more capacity than customers.

There's no good way for a single customer to "shop" for Internet service provision because you generally have to sign a lengthy service lease. So familiarize yourself as much as you can with an ISP before you get stuck with its service. Try to find comparisons among providers in trade magazines or on the Internet itself.

Networks and Communications

No server is a computer unto itself. The ability to communicate with other computers is fundamental to the purpose of an Internet server. Internet servers attached to the public Internet must somehow be attached to an Internet service provider. Internet servers that will be serving private intranets are attached to the network the same way that other servers are attached. Typically, they will be located on the primary backbone of your organization. Since Internet protocols operate well over low-bandwidth connections and use fewer network resources than file services use, optimizing for network bandwidth is usually not necessary.

You will be dealing with two types of network data link technologies: wide area networks and local area networks. Quite obviously, the difference is the distance limitations imposed by the connection methods. However, that simple difference also leads to differences in speed and cost.

Large networks are created using local area technologies in areas of high computer density and connecting these smaller areas by routing to wide area data links. Because the Internet is the largest wide area network in the world, you should understand the underlying data link technology.

Wide area data links can transmit digital data over great distances. These protocols are invariably *point to point,* meaning that they connect two and only two communication devices. Originally, wide area networks were always slower than local area networks. Optical fiber has changed this situation. Wide area transports now exist that are many times faster than the fastest local area transports. A new data link technology called ATM promises eventually to merge the data link technologies of the wide area and local area into one seamless whole. Whether or not ATM succeeds (or is even really necessary) will depend entirely on how cost-effective the technology becomes.

Leased Lines

Constantly connected digital circuits (called *leased lines*) leased from the local telephone company are by far the most popular way to link distant network sites. Leased-line grades of service are indicated by a T (in the United States and Canada) or an E (in Europe, South America, and Mexico) and then a number that codifies the bandwidth of the connection. Table 2.1 shows the bandwidth, aggregations, and typical cost of different leased-line services in the United States and Canada, and Table 2.2 shows the bandwidth and aggregation for European, South American, and Mexican telephone systems.

TABLE 2.1

North American Digital Circuits

Carrier	Bandwidth	Aggregation	Initial	Cost/Month
T0	56Kb/s	1 voice circuit	$700	$400
T1	1.544Mb/s	24 T0	$2,500	$1,500
T2	6.312Mb/s	4 T1		
T3	44.736	28 T1	$5,000	$25,000
T4	274.176	168 T1		

TABLE 2.2 European Digital Circuits	Carrier	Bandwidth	Aggregation
	E0	64Kb/s	1 voice circuit
	E1	2.048Mb/s	32 E0
	E3	34Mb/s	16 E1

T0/E0 is the digital equivalent of a single-voice channel. T0 operates at 56Kbp/s, and E0 operates at 64Kbp/s. The difference in bit rate occurs because the North American systems use an older signaling protocol that guarantees the creation of an alternating current using the eighth bit that magnetic inductance transformers will not block, whereas the European standard uses the eighth bit to convey information. T0 and E0 channels form the basis of higher-rate digital services because all telephone trunk lines can carry digitized voice conversations. All telephone company digital lines are optimized for voice services. Figure 2.3 shows the number of channels that are aggregated to form higher-rate carrier services.

FIGURE 2.3

Leased-line multiplexed data rates

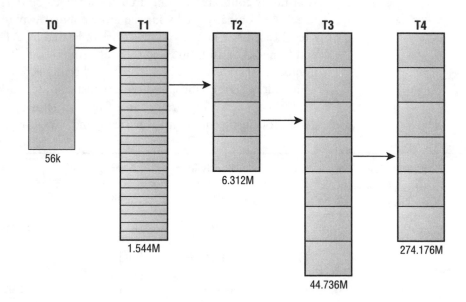

In addition to the straight E/T grades of service, many carriers offer fractional services that allow you to purchase any number of T0 channels in a T1 line, or any number of T1 channels on a T3 line. For instance, if you determine that you need 336Kb/s of bandwidth to support your site (or, more likely, that's all your budget will support), you can purchase six channels of T0 service that operate over a T1 line. Your CSU/DSU must be able to support fractional channels. Your telephone company will then charge you a fraction of the T1 line charges for the fraction of the bandwidth you use.

To implement a network between two sites with clear channel leased lines, you must lease the telephone circuit segments between the two sites. Your telephone company then connects the segments you lease. Current leased-line rates run between $10 and $20 per mile per month for 56Kb/s lines. As you can see, leasing a circuit between the east and west coasts can be prohibitively expensive for most companies. Because of the popularity of frame relay and X.25, most telephone companies no longer lease individual long-distance circuits.

Leased lines are attached to the serial ports of computers or routers through a CSU/DSU. The CSU/DSU is the interface from the telephone company's data lines and protocols to the format required by the serial port of your computer. The CSU/DSU is a digital converter; it is not a modem.

Frame Relay and X.25

You may have heard the term *frame relay* or *X.25* used to describe leased-line services. X.25 is the original protocol for routable data transmission over leased lines.

- X.25 uses address and error correction information in a manner similar to most local area networks.

- X.25 allows digital frames to be routed over a wide area by the telephone company.

Frame relay provides a cost-effective alternative to X.25 by implementing permanent virtual circuits rather than packet-by-packet routing. The telephone company programs its switches to always route frames from one specific location to another—thus creating a "virtual" circuit between two points. This technology eliminates the addressing and error-correction overhead of X.25 and allows the telephone company to more accurately predict the network load.

With both X.25 and frame relay, you pay only for a circuit between you and the closest telephone company central office, and for the use of the other circuits. Using frame relay is generally less expensive than leasing a clear channel circuit between two points, especially over long distances. Most leased-line services sold today are frame relay.

ADSL

Analog Digital Subscriber Line (ADSL) is a new variant of standard digital leased telephone lines that operates over normal voice telephone wiring. ADSL implements a low–data rate up-link and a high–data rate down-link similar to the service provided by cable modems but provided by the telephone company. ADSL was developed to provide an alternative television service from telephone companies, but it promises much more as a high–data rate, low-cost link to the Internet for consumers.

ADSL works by providing a very high power transmission from the telephone company. Since copper cables attenuate (or lose power) very quickly, they are not very suitable for high-bandwidth communications. ADSL overcomes this limitation simply by cranking up the power at the transmitting end, thus allowing a much higher bandwidth than would normally be available. The up-link channel cannot be powered the same way from your house, so the return channel operates at a much lower data rate that is similar to ISDN.

ADSL data rates operate from 1 to 6 Mb/s on the down-link channel (depending upon how far your site is from the local telephone company central office) and between 16Kb/s on the low end to 640Kb/s on the high end for the up-link channel. Typically, the up-link channel will probably operate at 64Kb/s when the service is available in your area.

ISDN

Integrated Services Digital Network (ISDN) is a dial-up digital circuit. Unlike leased lines, which are permanently connected to the terminal equipment on each end, ISDN allows you to make and break connections at will between any two ISDN adapters. Unlike leased-line services, ISDN is available in residential areas for high–bit rate connections to the home because ISDN operates over the same physical wire technology as normal voice telephony. Therefore, your local telephone company can easily convert analog telephone lines into ISDN lines by changing the terminal equipment at the central office.

ISDN is divided into the following kinds of channels:

- Data (B) channels that operate at 64Kb/s

- Control (D) channels that operate at 16Kb/s (basic rate) or 64Kb/s (primary rate)

User data travels over the B channels, and signaling data travels over the D channel. No matter how many B channels are part of an ISDN connection, there is only 1 D channel.

In-band signaling refers to dialing and control data that occurs in the primary data channel. For instance, when you dial with a touch tone telephone, you hear the dialing tones because they occur inside the voice channel. *Out-of-band* signaling refers to dialing and control data that occurs in another channel so that it does not consume bandwidth in the data channel(s).

ISDN is traditionally available in two basic rates: the residential basic rate and the commercial primary rate. Some telephony providers do not have the correct wiring and terminal equipment to provide basic rate service, so they provide variants of the basic rate that operate at 64Kb/s or 56Kb/s. These variations operate as only a single B channel.

ISDN adapters provide a function similar to the CSU/DSU terminal equipment used in digital leased lines. However, unlike the constant CSU/DSU connection, ISDN adapters are able to dial out and answer digital ISDN connections. ISDN adapters are sometimes referred to as "ISDN modems" (even by the marketing departments of ISDN adapter manufacturers) because they perform a similar function to the modems used over analog lines. However, ISDN adapters *are not* modems; they perform neither a modulation/demodulation function nor an analog-to-digital conversion.

ISDN pricing is similar to normal telephone service pricing: you pay a basic low monthly charge for the service and then a charge per minute for local access and a higher rate for long distance service. The vast majority of ISDN connections are now used to dial into an ISP in the local area.

Because ISDN is not a constantly connected service, the Internet address assigned by your ISP will change each time you dial in unless you find an ISP that will guarantee you a reserved IP address (most will not). For this reason, ISDN is not appropriate for hosting an Internet site unless you've negotiated a reserved IP address with your ISP. Most ISPs will not support efforts to host a Web site from a dial-up connection, and you will not be able to register for a domain name from InterNIC without a permanent IP address.

InterNIC is the organization that maintains the master database of permanently assigned IP addresses. InterNIC assigns all *new* IP addresses, but your ISP might assign your IP address because it is subnetted from the ISP's address.

Basic Rate

Basic rate ISDN operates with two 64Kb/s B channels and a 16Kb/s D channel over normal telephone wire providing a bandwidth of 128Kb/s. Basic rate is available in most areas in the United States and Europe at a rate somewhat near the cost of normal telephone service.

Primary Rate

Primary rate ISDN operates with twenty-three 64Kb/s B channels and a 64Kb/s D channel over T1 line circuits providing a bandwidth of 1472Kb/s. Primary rate can handle the high–data rate dial-up connectivity that large organizations may require.

ATM

Asynchronous transfer mode (ATM) is a new type of data link technology being implemented in the major telephone trunk lines run between cities by the major telephone companies. ATM allows the phone company to charge different rates for different levels of data service on a per packet basis. For instance, if you require real-time guaranteed packet delivery (for telephone or two-way video), you pay the highest rate; in return, the phone company guarantees that all the data you transmit will be available within microseconds at the receiving end. Table 2.3 shows the various classes of ATM service.

TABLE 2.3 ATM levels of service	Class	Service	Representative Use
	A	Real-time, guaranteed delivery	Two-way audio; video
	B	Real-time, non-guaranteed delivery	One-way audio; video
	C	Non–real-time, guaranteed delivery	Data services that do not use a higher-level protocol (e.g., a long-distance network bridging service)
	D	Non-guaranteed, non–real-time delivery	Data services that have a higher-level protocol or in which data does not need to get through (e.g., the Internet)

Another major benefit of ATM is that it operates independently of the physical media. ATM is divided into channels that contain cells all operating at a constant bit rate. When data is switched between circuits of different sizes, the switch multiplexes data onto larger and smaller circuits as necessary. Common ATM circuit sizes are shown in Table 2.4.

TABLE 2.4 ATM Transmission Rates	Designator	Bit rate	Comments
	ATM-T1	1.5Mb/s	ATM over T1 circuit
	ATM-25	25Mb/s	1/2 STS-1 rate Designed for LANs using UTP cable
	OC-1	51Mb/s	One ATM channel over optical fiber (rarely used)
	ATM-T3	45Mb/s	ATM over T3 circuit
	OC-3	155Mb/s	3 ATM channels Referred to ATM-155 in LAN environments if over unshielded twisted pair
	OC-12	622Mb/s	12 ATM channels Used in smaller telephony trunks and as campus area backbones

TABLE 2.4	Designator	Bit rate	Comments
ATM Transmission Rates (continued)	OC-48	2.4Gb/s	48 ATM channels Long-distance intercity telephony trunks, metropolitan area networks, large campus backbones
	OC-192	9.6Gb/s	192 ATM channels Sometimes implemented as four OC-48 links using wave-division multiplexing (WDM)

Analog Telephone Lines

Modems that operate over normal telephone lines have progressed from an absolute maximum bit rate of 2.4Kb/s to 33.6Kb/s in less than ten years. New modems that connect to the Internet at 56Kb/s already operate at the maximum theoretical bit rate for an analog telephone line. No faster bit rates will be available unless the telephone companies change the equipment at the central office (which is what they did to support the higher bit rates of ISDN).

Although the data rates that analog modems support might be sufficient to host a light-use Internet site, most ISPs will not provide a permanent IP address to dial-up connections.

Non-Telephony Options

You may not have to lease service from a telephone company to connect to the Internet at a high data rate or create a private wide area network. Many different non-telephony data services exist. These services differ from telephony in that they are not universally available. Since these companies are trying to compete with telephone companies, they operate only in those areas that provide the highest return on their investment. Major metropolitan areas provide more customers for smaller networks.

Local Fiber Optic Loop Providers

Many data service companies in metropolitan areas have created their own fiber optic networks. Unlike telephone networks, these networks are created entirely with high-bandwidth, single-mode optical fiber, even up to the point of demarcation at the end user's site. When connected through a router to local area networks, these networks can transfer network data faster than the networks at your sites can consume it. If you need to connect many sites in the same metropolitan area, these data service providers will probably be less expensive and provide a faster service than telephone companies.

Many of these companies have expanded their services by providing an Internet connection to their networks. Typically, the fiber optic metropolitan area network connects through a T3 or better service to a higher-level service provider. This configuration shares the bandwidth of that T3 connection among all the subscribers on the fiber optic metropolitan area network. In other words, even though the local loop may operate at 2.2Gb/s, the connection to the Internet is still only as fast as the digital line connecting to the Internet, which in this example is only 45Mb/s.

The Internet then becomes a wide area transport between any two dissimilar metropolitan area networks so long as they are both connected to the Internet. You should use encryption software to keep your data private if you use the public Internet as a wide area transport in this manner. Encrypting private data over the Internet is called *IP tunneling* because it creates a virtual clear and secure channel over the public Internet.

Because these services vary widely from location to location, you should research the data networking companies available in your area. These services are generally not available to residential, suburban, or rural areas.

Cable Modems

Cable modems are now becoming available in many areas with cable service. Cable modems are broadband modems that operate at very high data rates. These services are usually not symmetrical in that they provide many times more download bandwidth than upload bandwidth. In some cases the cable infrastructure does not support sending data back through the cable system, so a regular dial-up modem is used for the upload channel. A typical true cable modem provides a download channel of 10Mb/s and an upload channel of 768Kb/s. Generally, they are interfaced to your computer through an Ethernet adapter because serial connections are too slow to handle the high-download data rate. Many services will allow you to connect an entire small network to a single cable modem and will provide a unique IP address for each computer on the network.

True cable modems (those that provide both channels over the cable) can provide upload channels of up to 768Kb/s—half the speed of a T1 connection. Cable modems are constantly connected, unlike telephone modems, so if you can negotiate a permanent IP address with your cable service provider (not likely, but possible) you may be able to create a compelling medium-speed

Web site from a residential, suburban, or rural area. Cable companies do not typically market to businesses, so you may not be able to take advantage of this technology from a commercial site.

A Web server that uses a temporary dial-up connection and simply never hangs up is called a *Web toaster*. Your service agreement may specifically prohibit this type of use. Some service companies may also hang up after a certain (long) time to keep you from maintaining a certain IP address.

Summary

As with all network operations, planning is the first step to creating a practical and effective Web site. After studying your options, you may determine that the most cost-effective strategy—at least initially—is to have a hosting service host your Internet site. This option allows you to determine how much response your Web site generates and allows you to accurately justify the costs involved.

When you decide to serve your own Internet site, you'll need some computer hardware and specialized software. More important, you'll need to lease a high-bandwidth circuit to your Internet service provider. If your Internet host also functions as a router, you should consider using the WINS and DNS services to resolve Internet names for computers on your local network.

With access to the Internet comes access from the Internet. Hackers can exploit the many security loopholes in the Internet protocols to gain access to private local area networks. Firewalls, packet filtering services, and good security planning can prevent loss or disclosure of private information from the Internet.

Leasing an Internet circuit is likely to be the most expensive recurring cost of an Internet Web site, but many options are available. Upgrading circuits may not be easy, so you should try to accurately gauge what your required bandwidth is and what your budget will support before leasing a telephony circuit. Study the non-telephony network providers in your area to find out what other high-speed Internet connectivity options exist.

Review Questions

1. After having your Web site hosted for six months, your Internet service provider tells you that your site on average consumes 400Kb/s during business hours. You've decided to move the Web site onto your own server to support running some CGI scripts to take customer orders. You estimate this switch may double or triple the bandwidth required for your site. Which data link technology should you use?

   A. 56K frame relay service from the local telephone company (cost: $500/mo).

   B. T1 frame relay service from the local telephone company (cost: $2,000/mo).

   C. T3 frame relay service from the local telephone company (cost: $15,000/mo).

   D. Access to an FDDI metropolitan area network provided by an alternate carrier (cost: $5,000/mo).

2. After running a public access Web site about treatment options for athlete's foot for a few months, you notice some files are missing in the wwwroot directory. You suspect someone may have gained access through the Internet and somehow deleted the files. How can you prevent this kind of intrusion in the future without inhibiting normal access?

   A. Require a logon to the server and use NTFS file permissions to restrict the files to read only.

   B. Disconnect the Web server from the Internet and make it an intranet.

   C. Implement PPTP or Secure Socket Layer to encrypt the data.

   D. Put in a firewall.

3. You are considering using your Pentium-150 desktop computer as an Internet server. It has 16 megabytes of RAM and a 420 MB hard disk drive. You load Windows NT Server 4 and Internet Information Server and configure all the services. You also will be using the server to route

traffic to the T1 circuit from your Ethernet LAN and to resolve Internet and NetBIOS names. This computer:

A. Won't work.

B. Will work, but will be very slow because the hard disk is small.

C. Will work, but will be slow because it doesn't have enough RAM.

D. Will work very well.

4. You've just installed a leased 56K circuit and an Ethernet router to allow Internet access for all the clients on your 30-computer LAN. Your network is segmented into four networks each attached to the server through a network adapter. After adding TCP/IP services to each client computer, you remove the NWLink service from the server to increase efficiency. Users now complain that they can't see some network printers and computers in their Network Neighborhood windows. You verify that you can PING the computers and printers from computers on different subnets, so the server must be routing properly. No one is having problems accessing the server or the Internet. What is wrong?

A. You need to implement the WINS service.

B. You haven't properly configured the default gateway setting.

C. You haven't configured the server to forward TCP/IP broadcasts.

D. You need to implement the DNS service.

CHAPTER

3

All about Web Servers

hat is a Web server, and why would you choose one Web server over another? This chapter gives you a brief overview of some Web servers (there are far too many for an exhaustive review) and a look at the operating systems they run on.

The survey starts with the operating systems that are most commonly used to host Web sites:

- UNIX

- Windows NT Server

- NetWare

- MacOS

- Windows 95

Then it describes several packages (two from Microsoft, one from Netscape, one from Sun, and a few from those crazy people on the Internet who write software and give it away for free) that provide Web services:

- Internet Information Server

- Peer Web Services

- Netscape Enterprise Server

- MacHTTP

- NCSA HTTPd

- Fnord! Web Server

- Novell Web Server

Although the material in this chapter does not directly bear on the MCSE Internet Information Server exam questions, it does give you context for the exam and essential knowledge for your career as an Internet expert. If you do not understand the merits of your own system relative to others, then you do not fully understand your own system whether it is operating system software or Web server software.

Operating Systems

You can run your Web site on virtually any operating system. In fact, every operating system in use today has probably hosted a Web site at one time or another. (Don't be surprised if you find an Apple II out there somewhere hosting its own Web pages.)

UNIX computers, of course, can host Web data because the World Wide Web was born on UNIX. Windows NT is a natural environment for Web services, and Microsoft has worked hard to make hosting Web sites with NT incredibly easy. In addition, NetWare Loadable Modules allow NetWare servers to host Web sites, and the graphical nature of the Web has made the MacOS a popular operating system platform choice. Finally, even Windows 95 can host a Web site if you aren't too concerned about security or high performance.

UNIX

UNIX makes a natural World Wide Web and Internet server because UNIX is the birthplace of both the World Wide Web and of the Internet. All UNIX computers support TCP/IP as their networking protocol, and the UNIX operating system structure efficiently supports services that are simultaneously accessed by many users over the network. This section starts with a discussion of the advantages and disadvantages of UNIX in general and then examines today's most popular versions of UNIX.

Advantages of UNIX

UNIX is an extremely powerful and flexible operating system. It supports multiple simultaneous users, and UNIX security mechanisms (when properly configured) protect the users from each other and the computer from network intrusion.

UNIX workstations are usually much faster than PC-compatible computers. They typically have faster microprocessors, more memory, larger hard drives, and faster internal buses. Therefore, UNIX workstations can typically handle more simultaneous users than regular PC computers can handle. If you anticipate a heavy load on your Web server or if you will also use your Web server computer as a gateway or firewall, you should at least consider using a UNIX workstation for the job.

Disadvantages of UNIX

Unlike Windows NT, Windows 95, OS/2, or the Macintosh, UNIX does not come from just one vendor. Consequently, programs for one brand of UNIX may not run on another brand. Sometimes the programs will run on several brands of UNIX but you must compile the program for the brand of UNIX that you are using.

UNIX is typically either very expensive to purchase—and very well supported by the manufacturer—or it is free to download off the Internet and use but arguably less well supported than the commercial versions of UNIX.

UNIX can be more difficult to set up and administer than other operating systems (such as Windows NT or MacOS) if you are not familiar with the UNIX environment. The commercial versions of UNIX reduce the difficulty of administration, but they do not eliminate the need to understand how UNIX works.

Sun (Solaris)

Sun produces the most popular line of UNIX workstations, and it produces a workstation (the Netra i) specifically designed and configured for hosting Internet Web and FTP sites (check out `http://www.sun.com`). The Netra i uses the SPARC RISC microprocessor; it operates in a networked environment and can handle a lot of data and many network connections efficiently. Solaris on the Netra i workstation supports more simultaneous Web and FTP accesses than regular PC-compatible computers can.

Sun also makes a version of Solaris for Intel-based computers. Solaris Internet software combined with the relatively inexpensive Intel-based hardware platform is a powerful solution if you are comfortable and familiar with the UNIX environment.

Santa Cruz Operation

One of the original implementers of UNIX on Intel-based computers is the Santa Cruz Operation. The SCO UnixWare and SCO Open Server implementations of UNIX run on standard PC-compatible computers.

One of the strengths of the SCO versions of UNIX is their support for other Intel program environments, especially DOS and Windows. SCO Merge and SCO Wabi are software packages that allow you to run many DOS and Windows programs within the SCO UNIX environment.

Silicon Graphics (IRIX)

The primary uses for Silicon Graphics workstations are computer graphics and visualization, engineering, and computer-aided design. The powerful computing hardware and the extensive support for professional graphics make Silicon Graphics workstations natural hosts for the graphical content of Internet Web sites.

Silicon Graphics workstations use the IRIX variant of the UNIX operating system and use the powerful MIPS RISC family of microprocessors. Silicon Graphics workstations emphasize graphical and computing performance, and they can be expensive. The Silicon Graphics acquisition of the Cray supercomputer company illustrates Silicon Graphics's commitment to high performance.

Linux/NetBSD

You can get versions of UNIX that are less expensive than even Windows 95 or Windows NT. Linux and NetBSD are versions of the UNIX operating system that were developed on the Internet and may be used for free. These operating systems support all of the functionality of UNIX, and Internet Web servers are also available free of charge.

Both Linux and NetBSD are available (still free of charge) for computing platforms other than Intel. You can download Linux and NetBSD for the Digital Alpha and the PowerPC, for example. You can even get Linux for the Sun SPARC workstations—but why would you want to replace a fine operating system that comes with the computer and is supported by the company?

One disadvantage of both Linux and NetBSD is that they require more knowledge of the operating system, applications, and networking environment than do the other versions of UNIX if you want to use them to set up and run an Internet site. Another disadvantage to freeware is that you can't really hold anyone responsible if it doesn't work as advertised. On the other hand, if you actually pay for an operating system, you can hold the operating system vendor to some standard of product usability and support (theoretically, anyway).

Digital Equipment

Digital Equipment Corporation supports a number of operating systems for its Digital Alpha line of workstations and servers. In addition to Windows NT (which is described below) and VMS, Digital has its own brand of UNIX called Digital UNIX.

One of the strengths of Digital UNIX is the support for programs that manage extremely large data sets, huge files, and very precise numbers. The Alpha microprocessor is a true 64-bit microprocessor, which means that it can process very large numbers quickly and access terabytes of virtual memory space. Most other microprocessors used in PCs and workstations today are only 32-bit microprocessors, which means that they manipulate 64-bit numbers in chunks and are limited to 4GB of addressing space. Digital UNIX was written to exploit the large addressing space and the large numbers of the Alpha microprocessor.

Hewlett-Packard

The HP-UX operating system on Hewlett-Packard's line of PA-RISC–based workstations is another high-performance operating system on powerful but expensive hardware. HP workstations and servers are most often used in engineering environments and in data-processing centers of large corporations.

The most common use of a Hewlett-Packard server as an Internet server is to provide a Web interface to organizational data stored in databases or transaction-processing systems.

Other Major Vendors

Every major computer manufacturer has written a version of UNIX. IBM (AIX), Apple (A/UX), and many others have created versions of UNIX that are customized for their hardware platforms and usually provide some sort of compatibility features with other operating systems the vendor supports. These versions of UNIX are less widely implemented because typically the manufacturer supports them only to round out its operating system offerings and to appease customers who demand a UNIX environment.

Windows NT

Windows NT Server is an excellent platform for providing Internet services such as the World Wide Web, FTP, and Gopher. Windows NT uses the same graphical user interface as Windows 95, which makes most operations easy to figure out for users who are familiar with Windows 95. Internally, however, the operating system is robust and modular, and it easily supports Internet services.

Windows NT Server does more than just support Internet services. Internet services software (in the form of Microsoft Internet Information Server) is included on the Windows NT installation CD, and the OS installation process asks you if you want to install Internet services with the rest of the operating system.

Windows NT Server makes an excellent choice for an Internet site host if you are also using NT to provide network file and print services for a LAN. Using the same operating system for all your network services (LAN and Internet) reduces the complexity of your network and makes network administration easier.

You can also use Windows NT Workstation to provide Web services. However, Windows NT Workstation supports fewer incoming connections than Windows NT Server supports. The Internet server package for Windows NT Workstation is less complex than the server package for Windows NT Server. (For example, the NT Workstation version doesn't include Web site indexing.) The package for Windows NT Workstation is called Peer Web Services.

Windows NT runs on Intel-based computers, which have the price advantage of mass market production, and also on computers with the RISC microprocessors, which usually have a performance advantage but cost more.

NetWare

Just as the natural platform for Internet services in a Windows 95 and NT network is a Windows NT server, the natural platform for Internet services in a NetWare network is a NetWare file server. Many software packages allow a NetWare server to host Web, FTP, and Gopher files.

The primary reason to choose NetWare to host your Web site is that you are already using NetWare for the file servers on your network.

You should be careful, however, in selecting the Internet hosting software for your file server because NetWare does not provide the same level of interprocess protection that UNIX and Windows NT provide. This situation is not an oversight or a bug in NetWare software—Novell chose not to pay the performance cost that the extra protection would require. You are simply trusted to run software that will not crash the server.

Because NetWare file servers are more difficult to administer than many other operating systems and because the operating system does not provide many of the security and stability features now standard in network operating systems, you should consider using another server for your Internet/ intranet services. As long as your clients have the TCP/IP protocols installed, your Web servers do not have to run the same operating system as your file, print, and application servers.

MacOS Web Servers

The Macintosh, like Silicon Graphics workstations, is a natural environment for graphics. The number of Macintoshes in use is much greater than the number of Silicon Graphics machines, and Macintoshes are also often used for desktop publishing and document layout and production. Much Web page content (especially Web pages that contain professionally produced graphics) is produced on Macintosh computers.

It is a small step from creating the Web pages on the Macintosh to hosting them on the Macintosh, and taking that step in a Macintosh LAN environment makes sense. This approach means that you have only one type of operating system to administer, and if you are familiar with MacOS, you don't have to learn how to use a foreign operating system just to host your Web site.

Windows 95

You can even host a Web site using a personal computer running Windows 95. However, you will not be able to support as many simultaneous network connections as you can on other servers. You may not be able to support many of the features (e.g., CGI, database connectivity, and Web site indexes), but you will be able to set up a Web site inexpensively on the desktop operating system that you are probably using anyway.

Windows 95 is most often used for temporary or personal Web sites. You would probably not use Windows 95 to host information for your organization, but you might use it to host a Web site containing Web pages of personal interest.

Operating System Comparison

Table 3.1 compares operating systems in terms of performance, ease of use, price, and fault tolerance.

TABLE 3.1 Operating System Comparison				

Operating System–Hardware	Performance	Ease of Use	Price	Fault Tolerance
Solaris–SPARC	High	Medium	High	Medium
Solaris–Intel	Medium	Medium	Medium	Medium*
SCO–Intel	Medium	Medium	Medium	Medium*
IRIX–MIPS	High	Medium	High	Medium*
Linux/BSD–Intel	Medium	Low	Very low	Low
Linux/BSD–Digital Alpha	High	Low	Medium	Low
Digital UNIX–Digital Alpha	High	Medium	High	Medium*
HPUX–HP-PA	High	Medium	High	Medium*
Microsoft Windows NT–Intel	Medium	High	Medium	High
Microsoft Windows NT–Digital Alpha	High	High	High	High
NetWare–Intel	Medium	Low	Medium	Medium*
MacOS–PowerPC	Medium	High	Medium	Low
Windows 95–Intel	Low	High	Low	Low
Mainframe/Mini	High	Low	Very high	High

*additional packages for RAID, etc.

The questions in Exercise 3.1 will help you understand the workings of the operating systems you have just read about.

EXERCISE 3.1

Selecting an Operating System

1. You have a peer-to-peer network of Macintosh computers using EtherTalk to communicate with each other and using TCP/IP to communicate over the dedicated link to the Internet. You would like to set up a simple Web site that displays information about your organization.

■ Which platform will best serve your needs?

2. You administer a large network containing several file servers and hundreds of client computers.

■ Which network and organizational characteristics would lead you to choose NetWare as the Web server host?

3. You have a small peer network of eight Windows 95 computers for your mail-order firm. You would like to expand your business on to the Internet. You need your Web server operating system to be able to handle a large amount of traffic, and you will be buying a new computer to host the Web site. You and your coworkers are most familiar with the Windows 95 operating system and interface, and you want to minimize the learning curve of another system.

■ Which operating system best suits your needs for your new Web server computer?

Web Service Software

The first part of this chapter described operating systems that you can use to host Web service software. For this book, however, the purpose of the operating system is to allow your Web service software to run. Therefore, this part of the chapter reviews some (but not all!) Web servers that are available for Windows NT and for other platforms. This comparison will help you understand the features of Internet Information Server (IIS) and its advantages and disadvantages relative to other Web server software.

This cursory survey includes the following software packages:

- Internet Information Server

- Peer Web Services

- Netscape Enterprise Server

- MacHTTP

- NCSA HTTPd

- Fnord! Web Server

- Novell Web Server

This section examines the performance of each Web server package in respect to the following issues:

- **HTTP communications**—How many simultaneous connections the server can handle and whether the server is single threaded or multithreaded

- **Administration**—How you set up and administer the site

- **Security**—Access restrictions, how users are authenticated, and how (or whether) secure communications are handled

- **Scripts, includes, and automation support**—How Web pages are created dynamically

- **Database integration**—How the Web server links Web pages to database information

- **Web site indexing**—Features for searching the Web site for information

- **Virtual Web site support**—How the software can make one Web site look like many independent Web sites

Many concepts introduced in this quick survey (CGI and ODBC, for example) are explained in detail later in the book as we explore the capabilities of IIS.

A quick survey cannot possibly do justice to the complex software that makes up these Web servers. In many cases a feature that is not directly supported is indirectly supported through other mechanisms that this review does not cover. Also, software changes quickly—some features are updated, other features are dropped, entire product lines appear and disappear. When you choose software for your organization, you must gather your own information and try the packages to see if they meet your needs.

Internet Information Server (IIS)

Microsoft now includes IIS on the Windows NT Server installation disk, which means that you do not have to purchase it as an additional software package. You can also download the software—as well as updates—from Microsoft's Web site. See Figure 3.1 for a view of IIS.

FIGURE 3.1

Internet Information
Server

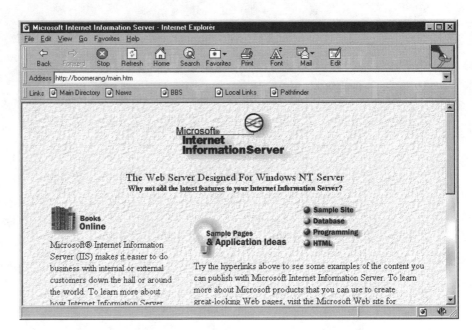

Although you can use other Web server software with Windows NT, you should strongly consider IIS for use on a Windows NT Server computer. Not only is it free with the operating system, but Microsoft has produced an Internet server package that integrates extremely well with the Windows NT operating system. This integration results in a software package that is secure, easy to manage, and fast. You can expect Microsoft to bring the operating system and IIS even closer together in the future. In fact, in the future you may not be able to tell the difference between Internet Explorer and IIS on one hand and Desktop Explorer and the Server network service on the other.

In addition to Web services, IIS also supports FTP and Gopher access.

This chapter summarizes the various aspects of IIS so that you can compare it to the other Web servers. Later sections of this book expand on many of these topics.

HTTP Communications

IIS runs as a service in the operating system, which means that a user account does not have to be open on the computer in order to run the service. (In contrast, a Web server that is implemented as an application requires that a user account be logged on in order for the application to run.)

Its multithreaded architecture enables IIS to handle many simultaneous Internet connections. IIS can also act as a proxy Web server (with Microsoft Proxy Server software). *Proxy servers* are Web gateway servers that load Web pages on behalf of a pool of client computers and then cache them for rapid access in the future. Proxy servers also provide a modicum of security by hiding clients from the Internet.

IIS supports the HTTP/1.0 standard. It does not support some of the features of HTTP/1.1 (such as the new specification for PUT).

One useful feature of IIS is that it can restrict the bandwidth used to service Web requests. This feature enables you to keep Web requests from swamping your connection to the Internet and to reduce what you may have to pay for your network connection if you must pay for bandwidth use as well as for the connection itself.

Administration

Microsoft has provided two ways to administer IIS—from the Internet Services Manager program and from the Internet Services Manager Web pages. The program and the Web pages both give you a graphical interface for managing the Internet services.

Because much of the security in IIS is tied into Windows NT users and groups, you will also use the User Manager or User Manager for Domains to create a Web site that uses more than the default security of IIS.

Security

IIS and Windows NT Server together provide the tools to create a secure and flexible Web site. IIS uses Windows NT users and groups to implement security on the Web pages as well as on files and directories. (Because Web pages are files and FTP directories are directories on the hard drive, Microsoft merely had to make NT security mechanisms available to IIS, rather than implement new security measures.)

In addition to file and Web page security, IIS also can log transactions to a log file, establish secure connections between the client and IIS via the Secure Socket Layer (SSL), require a password for access to the Web page, and disallow access from certain computers or from certain Internet subnets.

Scripts, Includes, and Automation

IIS supports server-side includes (including forced includes that may be inserted in a document whether or not the document specifies it), CGI scripts (with access to CGI state variables supplied by the Web server software), and supports built-in image-map handling and ISAPI components.

Database Integration

IIS supports database integration. IIS Web sites can be closely linked to databases via the ODBC (database) connector, and IIS will redirect data queries through the database connector to be satisfied by an ODBC data source such as Microsoft SQL Server that can actually be running on the same server. Few other operating systems can support this level of application integration.

Database integration is very important. Nearly every commercial use of the Internet requires some sort of database integration capability. Catalogs, purchase orders, and customer lists are most easily handled with database software, so the ability to tightly integrate database applications like SQL Server or Microsoft Access is perhaps the most important feature of Web service software.

Web Site Indexing

Microsoft Index Server is a companion product of IIS. Index Server is a search engine for IIS, and its features include virtual Web site support (only returning information contained on the virtual Web site accessed by the user) and security integration with IIS and Windows NT users and groups.

You've probably already used Web site indexing software. AltaVista, Digital Equipment's amazing Web search page, uses the AltaVista search engine and indexing software similar to Microsoft Index Server to index Web sites and respond to search queries.

Virtual Web Site Support

This Internet server package allows you to create virtual Internet sites. If your computer is registered with and responds to multiple IP addresses, the IIS software can appear to be many different Web sites. This feature is especially useful if you are providing a Web hosting service for other companies or organizations.

Most Internet service providers use this type of software to host many different customer Web sites on the same large server. For instance, if Bobco, Fredco, and Janeco are customers of Webco, Webco could host their Web sites (www.bobco.com, www.fredco.com, and www.janeco.com) with one server and enable each customer to have its own home page. Simply pointing each domain name to the server would otherwise show only Webco's default home page (www.webco.com).

Peer Web Services

IIS runs on Windows NT Server. Windows NT Workstation comes with a different Web server package—Peer Web Services. Peer Web Services is a version of IIS for individual use, rather than for organizational or corporate information.

The idea is that you will use Peer Web Services to host personal information on a LAN or on the Internet. See Figure 3.2 for a view of Peer Web Services.

FIGURE 3.2

Peer Web Services

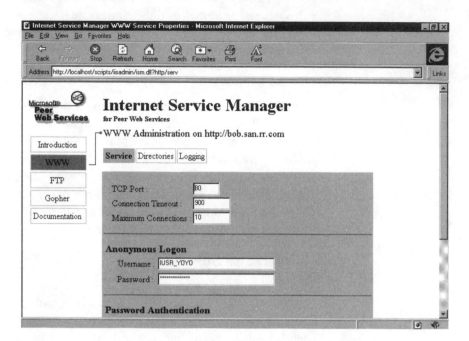

 Peer Web Services, like Internet Information Services, hosts FTP and Gopher data as well as World Wide Web data.

HTTP Communications

The primary difference between IIS and Peer Web Services in the area of communications is that Peer Web Services on Windows NT Workstation is limited to ten simultaneous Internet connections. Therefore, you would not use Peer Web Services to host a popular Internet site or an organizational site that would be accessed often.

A related communications limitation of Peer Web Services is that it (unlike IIS) cannot ration its network use. Since Windows NT Workstation can only support ten simultaneous network connections, the outgoing bandwidth is effectively limited anyway; therefore, that factor should not affect your choice of a Web server for an NT Workstation computer.

Administration

Administration for Peer Web Services is the same as it is for IIS—you can manage the services through either the Internet Service Manager or through the Internet Services Web pages that are installed when you install Peer Web Services. Both provide a graphical interface for administration.

Security

Security is the same for Peer Web Services as it is for IIS because Peer Web Services uses the same Windows NT security model (users, groups, and permissions) that IIS does.

Unlike IIS, however, Peer Web Services does not allow you to restrict access to the Web site based on the IP address of the client computer.

Scripts, Includes, and Automation

Peer Web Services supports server-side includes, CGI scripts, and ISAPI applications in the same manner as IIS does.

Database Integration

Peer Web Services allows Web pages to access database content through ODBC components in the same manner as IIS.

Web Site Indexing

Peer Web Services does not include Microsoft Index Server, but Index Server can be used to index Peer Web Services pages. You can download Index Server from the Microsoft Web site or install it from this book's companion CD-ROM.

Virtual Web Site Support

Peer Web Services does not support virtual Web sites provided by the same computer.

Netscape Server Software

Despite what you may infer from Microsoft publications, Microsoft did not invent the World Wide Web. Microsoft is actually a newcomer to the Internet and World Wide Web scene. Many people who have been there from the beginning (of the Web, at least) work for Netscape. Netscape and Internet Explorer are the primary competitors in the Web browser market, and it is not surprising that Netscape makes the Web server software that (in functionality and market penetration) Microsoft contends with. Currently, Netscape owns more than 75 percent of the Web browser market (if you can call a niche where software is given away for free a market). See Figure 3.3 for a view of a Netscape page for managing the server.

FIGURE 3.3

Netscape

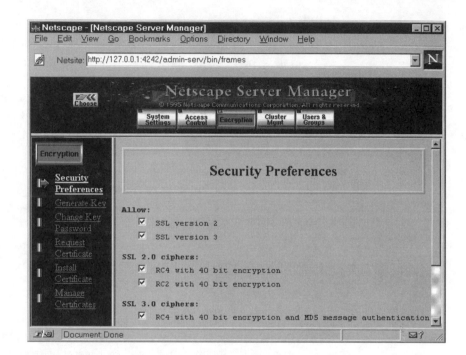

Netscape runs on Windows NT Workstation and Windows NT Server, as well as on many versions of UNIX. Netscape Web server software comes in several versions, ranging in complexity (and expense) from the basic Netscape Commerce Server to the powerful and capable Netscape Enterprise Server, which is Netscape's top-of-the-line server product.

Netscape does not provide FTP and Gopher access. (On the UNIX platform, the operating systems usually provide at least FTP.) The following survey describes the features of Netscape's Enterprise Server.

HTTP Communications

The Netscape server for Windows NT runs as a service, as do IIS and Peer Web Services. (Netscape for UNIX runs as a separate process as most UNIX network services do.) Like IIS, The Netscape server is multithreaded; it can easily handle many simultaneous accesses.

Unlike IIS and Peer Web Services, Netscape servers support features of HTTP V1.1 such as PUT, byte ranges, and persistent connections, and will likely be the first to support new HTTP protocols like v2 and v3 when they become standardized. Netscape servers do not support Active Server Pages.

Administration

Netscape servers are administrated via Web pages. Netscape goes beyond the simple administration of the server's operation to include Web page construction and management via Web pages.

Security

Netscape servers support a complete suite of user access security features, but they are not based on Windows NT users and groups. Instead, Netscape servers use the Lightweight Directory Access Protocol, or LDAP, which keeps track of user and group security for the Web site and allows several Web sites to use the same security information.

Netscape servers are often used in sites that require secure information exchange between the Web browser and the Web server (such as an order and purchasing Web page). Netscape supports the Secure Socket Layer versions 2 and 3 to make the secure link.

Scripts, Includes, and Automation

Netscape servers provide a full range of mechanisms to make dynamically created pages such as server-side includes, forced includes, CGI scripts, and image map handling. Netscape server does not support ISAPI or Active Server Pages, but does have proprietary application services of its own.

Database Integration

Netscape servers also can provide direct connections to databases using ODBC. However, Netscape does not publish any database server software, so you must find and integrate a database server (usually from Oracle or Informix) yourself. Because the software components come from multiple vendors, integration may be a bit difficult.

Web Site Indexing

Netscape servers include a flexible search engine that cooperates with LDAP and the virtual Web sites to provide appropriate and secure search pages.

Virtual Web Site Support

Netscape servers easily support the creation of virtual Web sites, where the server responds to the browser client with a different set of pages depending on which of the server's IP addresses the client is connecting to. Most Internet service providers use the Netscape server to provide service for hundreds of virtual Web sites.

MacHTTP

All of these NT and UNIX Web servers are fine, but what if you have a wholly Macintosh network and you don't want to complicate things with a foreign operating system?

A number of Web servers are available for the Macintosh operating system. ExpressO and WebStar Mac are two of the many commercial Macintosh Web servers. However, you do not have to pay for a commercial software package to host a simple Web site on the Macintosh or any other platform. Many high-quality free and shareware Web server packages are available for download off the Internet. These packages may not support all the features of commercial software, but they are often just as reliable (or even more reliable!) and can easily provide all the features required by most small organizations or individuals.

MacHTTP is an excellent shareware Web server for the Macintosh. (It is the most widely used shareware Web server for the Mac.) Although MacHTTP does not provide FTP and Gopher services, it is an excellent choice for a Web server when you just want to host some files from your computer.

HTTP Communications

MacHTTP depends on the underlying communications subsystem of the MacOS. The communications subsystem is interrupt driven and responsive, but the applications are cooperatively multitasked; therefore, heavy use of the MacHTTP service may cause uneven response in other applications (and vice versa). You should consider dedicating your Macintosh server to Web services and limit its use for other purposes.

MacHTTP does not support many of the new features of the HTTP V1.1 standard, such as PUT, byte ranges, and persistent connections.

Administration

MacHTTP includes a graphical administration program that runs on the Macintosh and allows you to configure and run your Web site. Unlike most other Web server programs, you cannot manage your Web site via Web pages.

Security

MacHTTP does not support the elaborate security mechanisms that other Web servers do. Although it supports simple user authentication (i.e., user and password), you must set up more elaborate mechanisms with CGI scripts.

MacHTTP can prohibit access from domain names and IP addresses.

Scripts, Includes, and Automation

Most of the customization of a MacHTTP Web site is done through CGI scripts. MacHTTP does not support ISAPI applications or complex server-side includes, so a programming knowledge of Perl or C is required to generate complex pages.

Database Integration

MacHTTP does not directly support access to database information. Database access must be constructed through CGI scripts. This sort of integration is very difficult to perform properly, so you should consider using a different package if database integration is a requirement on your site.

Web Site Indexing

You can use AppleSearch with MacHTTP to create a search engine for your Macintosh Web site.

Virtual Web Site Support

MacHTTP does not directly support the creation of virtual Web sites.

NCSA HTTPd

The great granddaddy of all Web servers comes from the National Center for Supercomputer Applications. NCSA's free HTTPd runs on UNIX computers.

Its many years of use around the world in many different network environments makes HTTPd one of the most tested and debugged Web servers you can get. The NCSA HTTPd server has evolved as the World Wide Web has evolved and incorporates features you expect in a Web server such as server-side includes, CGI scripts, user authentication, access determination based on source IP addresses, and so on.

NCSA HTTPd, like Netscape server and most other server software, does not provide FTP and Gopher services. On UNIX computers (the vast majority of NCSA HTTPd installations are on UNIX computers), the operating system or other software traditionally provides these services. A large fraction of World Wide Web servers on the Internet are hosted by UNIX computers running NCSA HTTPd.

HTTP Communications

NCSA HTTPd runs under UNIX as an application, like most other UNIX services. HTTPd can be continuously active, or it can be activated automatically when Web browsers request information. This second option releases RAM for use with other programs when HTTPd is not being accessed, but it also increases the time for the Web server to respond to some requests.

HTTPd supports the HTTP v1.0 standard. It does not support v1.1 features such as PUT, byte ranges, and persistent connections.

Administration

Administration is done from the UNIX command line. You can remotely administer an HTTPd server using the Telnet program. HTTPd does not provide administrative Web pages for graphical or remote management.

Security

HTTPd uses UNIX security mechanisms much as IIS uses Windows NT security mechanisms. HTTPd also supports Kerberos and MD5 security systems.

HTTPd can require a username and password for access to Web pages and can prohibit access to the server by the incoming user's Internet domain name and by the incoming user's IP address.

Scripts, Includes, and Automation

HTTPd supports server-side includes, image maps, and CGI scripts.

Database Integration

HTTPd does not directly provide database connectivity. You must use CGI scripts instead, which require a programming knowledge of Perl or C. Therefore, if your site requires database connectivity, you should consider using IIS or Netscape Enterprise server instead.

Web Site Indexing

HTTPd includes an internal search engine and also connects to external Wide Area Information System (WAIS) databases. WAIS is an Internet database connectivity protocol that supports searching for data across multiple databases over the entire Internet. Hosts must respond to the WAIS protocol the same way they must respond to any other Internet protocol.

Virtual Web Site Support

HTTPd serves different virtual roots for different server IP addresses (i.e., it supports virtual Web sites).

Fnord! Web Server

Even though Windows 3.11 and Windows 95 computers can host Web sites, a number of free and commercial Web servers are available for these platforms (more of them for Windows 95 than for Windows 3.11). One such Web server is the Fnord! Web server, which is free to use. See Figure 3.4 for a view of Fnord!

FIGURE 3.4

Fnord! Web server

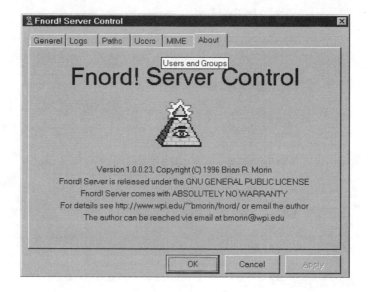

Fnord! provides Web service only. It does not provide FTP and Gopher services.

HTTP Communications

Since Windows 3.11 and Windows 95 cannot handle a large number of simultaneous network accesses, you would not use the Fnord! Web server to host a high-use Web site. Fnord! Web server on either of these platforms is perfectly adequate to host a personal Web site, however.

Fnord! Web server does not support HTTP V1.1 features such as PUT, byte ranges, and persistent connections.

Administration

Fnord! Web server is graphically set up and maintained using the FNORDctl program. You cannot manage the Web server remotely, however.

Security

Fnord! Web Server does not provide much security beyond the simple user authentication (username and password, and user groups) and does not allow you to exclude access based on Internet domain names. However, it does allow you to exclude access based on IP addresses.

Scripts, Includes, and Automation

Fnord! supports CGI scripts, but does not support the Windows variant of CGI scripts. It does not directly support image maps.

Database Integration

Fnord! does not directly provide database connectivity. Database access with a Fnord! Web server must be made using CGI scripts.

Web Site Indexing

Fnord! does not include a search engine for automatic Web site indexing.

Virtual Web Site Support

Fnord! does not support virtual Web sites.

IntranetWare

If you use NetWare servers to provide file and print service on your network, you may not want to install another computer and operating system just to host a Web site. Now you don't have to because Novell has created a Web server that runs in the unique environment provided by a NetWare file server. IntranetWare includes the Novell Web Server HTTP NLM.

HTTP Communications

Novell Web Server is optimized for speedy communications. Novell Web Server can support numerous simultaneous HTTP requests.

Novell Web Server supports the HTTP/1.0 standard. It does not support some of the new features of HTTP/1.1 (such as the new specification for PUT, byte ranges, and persistent connections).

Administration

Novell Web Server, like IIS and Netscape, allows you to manage the Web site via Web pages. You can also manage the Web pages remotely via this interface.

Security

Novell Web Server (like IIS and NCSA HTTPd) uses the mechanisms of the underlying operating system to implement account security (in this case, the NetWare Directory Services [NDS]).

Novell Web Servers (like most commercial servers) can deny access to computers by domain name or IP address.

Scripts, Includes, and Automation

Novell Web Server supports server-side includes, CGI scripts (Perl, BASIC, and Java are built in), and server-based image maps.

Database Integration

Novell Web Server does not, however, provide a direct connection to databases. Database access must be through the CGI mechanism.

Web Site Indexing

Novell Web Server also does not incorporate indexing software. You must use external search engines instead.

Virtual Web Site Support

Novell Web Server also does not provide different directory roots for different IP addresses, which limits its support for virtual Web sites.

Exercise 3.2 tests your understanding of the features and requirements of the Web servers discussed in this chapter.

EXERCISE 3.2

Choosing a Web Server

1. You have a peer network of Windows NT Workstation computers. You want to make your Web pages available to individuals on your local network.

   ▪ Which software package best meets your needs?

2. You want to provide members of your Windows NT domain access to certain parts of your Web site but deny access to those pages to everyone else. You want the Web server to automatically use NT domain information—you don't want to enter user account changes in two places.

   ▪ Which software package automatically integrates with Windows NT security?

3. You will be hosting Web servers for other organizations. Your server will be assigned IP addresses for these other organizations, and you want to be able to create virtual Web servers by providing different directory roots for each IP address.

   ▪ Which Web servers support this feature?

4. You manage a large corporate internetwork with UNIX and Windows NT servers. You want to standardize on a single Web server for your whole organization.

   ▪ Which Web server package can you use?

Summary

You can use many operating systems and Web server software packages to host your Web site. Each operating system and Web package has advantages and disadvantages, and each has a niche where it is the best available solution. In some cases cost is the overriding consideration. (Actually, cost is the main consideration in most installations.) In other cases the best approach is to use the platform that is being used for everything else on the network. Familiarity is sometimes the deciding factor because the cost associated with learning a new environment and software package may be more than the cost of buying a more expensive or more automated package for a familiar operating system.

Windows NT is an excellent choice for an organizational Web server because of its stability, excellent network support, and ease of use. If you already have an NT-based network or if you are familiar with the Windows 95 interface, the learning curve of a Windows NT–based Web server is short.

IIS is an excellent choice for a Web server on Windows NT for the following reasons:

- It comes free with the operating system.

- It provides a comprehensive security system for Web sites with private and public areas.

- It supports many kinds of dynamic page mechanisms, including server-side includes, CGI, ISAPI, image maps, and ODBC support.

- It is closely integrated with the NT operating system and will be even more closely integrated in the future.

Review Questions

1. You need a Web server for your Windows NT Server computer that will allow you to establish virtual Web sites. Select the most correct observation.

    A. Windows NT will run any Web server software, and all Web server software packages support virtual servers.

    B. Only Microsoft IIS both runs on Windows NT Server and allows you to create virtual servers.

    C. Both IIS and Netscape Enterprise Server run on Windows NT Server and support virtual Web servers.

    D. Both IIS and Novell Web Server run on Windows NT Server and support virtual directories.

2. If the Web server you select does not support direct database access via ODBC, which Web server mechanism can you use to provide database access?

    A. You can use LDAP to access database information.

    B. You cannot access database information if you do not have direct support for ODBC in your Web server.

    C. You can use server-side includes to access database information.

    D. You can use CGI scripts to access database information.

3. You need to support the FTP and Gopher Internet services as well as the World Wide Web. Which of the following observations are true?

    A. IIS, Peer Web Services, Netscape Enterprise Server, and NCSA HTTPd all support all three Internet services.

    B. You can use IIS and Peer Web Services to provide all three Internet services.

    C. Only IIS provides all three Internet services.

    D. FTP and Gopher services are always provided by separate software packages.

4. You need a Windows NT Server Web Server package with search capability. Which of the following fits your needs? (Choose all that apply.)

    A. Peer Web Services

    B. NCSA HTTPd

    C. IIS with Index Server

    D. Netscape Enterprise Server

CHAPTER

4

Installing IIS and Index Server

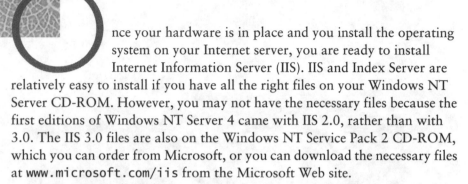

nce your hardware is in place and you install the operating system on your Internet server, you are ready to install Internet Information Server (IIS). IIS and Index Server are relatively easy to install if you have all the right files on your Windows NT Server CD-ROM. However, you may not have the necessary files because the first editions of Windows NT Server 4 came with IIS 2.0, rather than with 3.0. The IIS 3.0 files are also on the Windows NT Service Pack 2 CD-ROM, which you can order from Microsoft, or you can download the necessary files at www.microsoft.com/iis from the Microsoft Web site.

HTTP, FTP, and Gopher are protocols, not services. IIS is a package of services used to serve these protocols. Table 4.1 shows the relationship between the services and protocols of IIS. You can view the services yourself in the Services control panel program.

T A B L E 4.1 Protocols and Services	Protocol	Service
	FTP	FTP Publishing Service
	Gopher	Gopher Publishing Service
	HTTP	World Wide Web Publishing Service

IIS at Home and Abroad

You can install IIS in two environments: the Internet and private intranets. The installation of the tools, services, and protocols is generally the same for both environments. The differences between the two environments fall into three general categories, none of which has much to do with the IIS software:

- Hardware
- Security
- Content

Hardware for Internet servers is more esoteric than the hardware for intranet servers. For example, any old file server is probably fine for use as an intranet server without modification. Internet servers, on the other hand, are generally attached to leased-line adapters or routers, in front of security firewalls, and set up to serve other Internet protocols not served by IIS such as SMTP and NNTP. In general, you must use a more powerful and more expensive machine for Internet service than for intranet service.

Intranet servers should usually be configured to the same specifications as a file server with plenty of hard disk space but light on processing power, whereas Internet servers should be configured to the same specifications as an application server with plenty of processing power and RAM but lighter on hard disk space.

Security is also quite different in the two environments. Internet servers use firewalls to keep hackers at bay but tend to publish information to anyone who requests it using anonymous logons. Intranet servers, on the other hand, generally require a logon, aren't concerned with intrusion, and use NTFS file security to protect different files based on your logon permissions.

Finally, content can also be quite different in the two environments. Internet server content must be concerned with the slow download speeds of a typical analog modem—flashy graphical splash screens and multimedia content must be kept subdued and minimal in order to deliver timely information. Since intranets are usually connected to the network at a minimum of 10Mb/s, download speed is of no concern. Intranet sites can get very flashy without ever being concerned about download speed. Table 4.2 summarizes the differences between Internet and intranet servers.

T A B L E 4.2 Service Differences between the Internet and an Intranet	**Factor**	**Internet**	**Intranet**
	Security	Must be well secured against attacks from hackers. Use SSL for sensitive transmissions and NTFS to keep stored data secure. Disallow storing files on the server.	Server is probably behind a firewall and requires only the same security as other file/application servers inside your organization.
	Content	Must be optimized for slow download speed—smaller graphics, lots of text. Use Java and ActiveX sparingly.	Go crazy. You have lots of bandwidth and no serious security problems, so you can use custom content any way you want.
	Network Hardware	You'll probably need a T1, ISDN, or at least a 56K leased line to the Internet. You'll need a router or leased-line adapter and a CSU/DSU.	Same as your other machines. Consider putting your intranet servers on your high-speed backbone for fair access to all.
	Server	Lots of RAM and processing power to handle hundreds of simultaneous connections, especially if you're using ISAPI, CGI, or ActiveX applications. Public sites are usually not all that large, so you should not need that much disk space.	Few connections won't require much in the way of RAM or processing power, even if you do a lot with ISAPI apps or CGI scripts. A lot of organizational data will probably wind up on the intranet server though, so be prepared with plenty of disk space.

But again, these factors do not really affect the installation of IIS—the process is the same for both environments. Before you install IIS, you need to have a few things in place:

- An operational server with enough disk space and RAM to run Windows NT, IIS, and to hold your content files.

- Windows NT Server 4 installed and running. Your specific version of IIS may require a specific service pack installation—check the `readme.txt` file for details.

- A TCP/IP connection to an intranet or the Internet. Make sure your TCP/IP connection works correctly before installing IIS by pinging other computers on the network.

Pinging another computer means using the ping.exe utility that comes with most operating systems that support TCP/IP to see if an IP packet can be sent to a specific computer's IP address and returned. If you can Ping another computer, you've verified that the network is operational and that TCP/IP is working correctly.

Given these prerequisites, you are ready to install IIS.

Installing Internet Information Server

Installing IIS is a little complicated because the technology has changed so rapidly. If your Windows NT 4 server came with IIS 2.0, you must install that version (as shown in Exercise 4.1), the current Windows NT Server 4 Service pack (Exercise 4.2), and then the current version of IIS (Exercise 4.3).

EXERCISE 4.1

Installing Internet Information Server

1. Insert the Windows NT Server 4 CD-ROM into your CD-ROM drive.

2. Double-click My Computer.

3. Right-click your CD-ROM drive and select Open.

4. Double-click the I386 folder or the folder corresponding to your RISC microprocessor.

5. Double-click the Inetsrv folder.

6. Double-click Inetstp.exe.

7. Read the first sentence of the dialog window. If it reads "Welcome to the Microsoft Internet Information Server 2.0 Installation Program," you have an obsolete version of IIS. However, you must install this version in order to install version 3.0. Click OK.

---

8. Check the Internet Service Manager (HTML) selection so that all components are selected for installation.

9. Click OK to accept the default installation directory.

10. Click OK to accept the default service root directories.

11. Click OK if you get an error stating that you don't have an Internet domain name declared in the networking control panel.

12. Click OK to clear the ODBC drivers message if it appears.

13. Click OK to finish the installation.

If you need to install IIS 3.0, you will have to install Windows NT Service Pack (also included on the Service Pack CD-ROM) if you haven't already done so. When you boot your Windows NT Server, the initial boot screen should state that Windows NT Server 4.0 Build 1381 (Service Pack 2 or higher) is loading. If it does not show a service pack or shows Service Pack 1, use Exercise 4.2 to install the current service pack.

EXERCISE 4.2

Installing the Current Service Pack

This exercise may change slightly depending upon the current service pack release. Follow the instructions that come with the service pack if they vary at all from the exercise shown here.

1. Insert the Windows NT Service Pack CD-ROM that you can order from Microsoft. Alternatively, you can download the required files from the www.microsoft.com Web site.

2. Double-click My Computer.

3. Right-click your CD-ROM drive and select Open.

4. Double-click the folder corresponding to your microprocessor, usually i386.

EXERCISE 4.2 (CONTINUED FROM PREVIOUS PAGE)

5. Double-click the Update icon.

6. Click Next.

7. Click Next.

8. Select whether or not you wish to create an Uninstall directory in case you decide to remove the service pack later.

9. Click Next.

10. Click Finish. The service pack files will now install on your computer.

11. Click OK to restart your computer.

After you've completed Exercise 4.1 and determined that you need to install the current version of IIS, use Exercise 4.3 to walk through the steps.

EXERCISE 4.3

Upgrading to the Current Version of Internet Information Server

This exercise may change slightly depending upon the current service pack release. Follow the instructions that come with the service pack if they vary at all from the exercise shown here.

1. Insert the Windows NT Service Pack 2 CD-ROM that you can order from Microsoft. Alternatively, you can download the required files from the www.microsoft.com Web site.

2. Double-click My Computer.

3. Right click your CD-ROM drive and select Open.

4. Double-click the iis30 folder.

5. Double-click the asp folder.

6. Double-click the folder corresponding to your microprocessor. Usually this is the I386 folder.

7. Double-click the Asp.exe file to start the installation process.

8. Return to step 1 of Exercise 4.1 to install IIS 2.0 if you get an error message stating that you must have IIS 2.0 installed to install this version of the IIS.

9. Click the license statement: I agree to accept the terms of the Microsoft software license.

10. Click Next to continue the installation process.

11. Click OK to stop the Internet services *if* you get a message stating that Internet services are running and must be stopped before proceeding.

12. Check all available options for installation.

13. Click Next.

14. Click Next to accept the default installation directory.

15. Click OK to acknowledge that the installation has completed.

16. Click OK to acknowledge the start menu shortcuts.

17. Click OK to start the Internet services.

Configuring Internet Protocols

Now that your server is configured to serve Internet protocols, you are ready to begin customizing IIS to meet your specific needs. This section briefly explains how to manage the three protocols served by IIS using the Internet Service Manager. Figure 4.1 shows the Internet Service Manager.

FIGURE 4.1

The Internet Service Manager

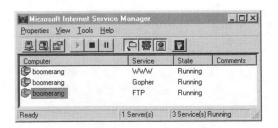

HTTP Settings

You control HTTP service settings through the WWW Service Properties window of the Internet Service Manager. Exercise 4.4 shows you how to access this window. Refer to this exercise as you read the following discussions of the features of the WWW Service Properties window. Figure 4.2 shows the WWW Service Properties panel of the Internet Service Manager.

FIGURE 4.2

The WWW Service
Properties window

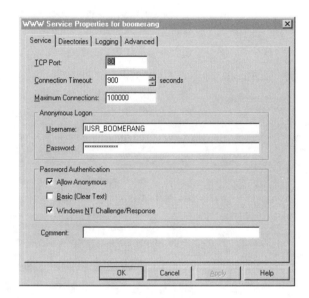

Controlling User Connections When a user requests a page from your Web server using an HTTP (see Chapter 5) connection, that user must provide logon credentials. Normally for Internet services, this credential is an anonymous user without a password. When IIS receives anonymous logon credentials, it logs that user on using the account specified in the Internet Service Manager—by default this account is the IUSR_*servername* account created when you installed Internet Service Manager.

The anonymous logon connection exists so that you can control permissions assigned to inbound HTTP connected users who do not provide logon credentials. By assigning NTFS file permissions to this user, you can control which HTML pages anonymous users can connect to. You can change the Internet anonymous user account to an existing user account that fits your security structure better. However, it's generally easier to simply assign permissions to the default account.

EXERCISE 4.4

Tour of the WWW Service Manager

1. Select Start ➤ Programs ➤ Microsoft Internet Server ➤ Internet Service Manager.

2. Double-click your server name in the WWW service row.

3. Notice the options available in the Service panel. From this panel, you can control the following:

   ■ TCP/IP port number of the HTTP service
   ■ Connection time-out and the maximum number of connections
   ■ Anonymous user account
   ■ Logon options

4. Click the Directories panel. From this panel you control the following:

   ■ Which directories users have access to
   ■ Default document options
   ■ Whether or not directory browsing is allowed

5. Click the Logging tab. From this panel, you control logging options that allow you to profile how your server is being used and by whom.

6. Click Advanced. From this panel you control which specific computers or subnets will be denied or granted access. In addition, you can specify how much network load you will allow Internet services to demand from your server.

7. Click OK to close the WWW Service Properties window.

8. Close the Internet Service Manager.

Logon Requirements   Using the Internet Service Manager you can also specify how users must log on to your site. When your Web browser initially contacts a Web server, it provides credentials without a password. If the Web server does not accept anonymous credentials, it will send back a message rejecting the logon. At that point your Web browser will pop up with a dialog box asking for your username and password (basic) or your username, password, and possibly your domain (Windows NT Challenge/Response). If you see a logon box, you must enter logon credentials in order to gain access to the page. Once you've provided credentials for one page for that server, the same credentials will be provided any time that server rejects an attempt to load a page on that site for that browsing session.

Three logon options are available with IIS:

- **Allow Anonymous Logon** allows users providing anonymous credentials to log on to your server as the anonymous account. Use this setting for most servers attached to the public Internet.

- **Basic (Clear Text)** is generally used with Secure Socket Layer (SSL) to provide encrypted authentication. Web browsers that don't support Secure Socket Layer may log on using clear text passwords that are unencrypted and could be intercepted in route. This setting transmits a valid Windows NT account for your Web server without encryption; you should disable this setting for servers attached to the Internet unless you know exactly why you want it enabled.

- **Windows NT Challenge/Response** allows users that provided encrypted credentials to log on to your server with their Windows NT account permissions. This setting is generally used in intranets and Internet servers that provide special access for specific users. This type of access currently works only between Windows NT Servers and Internet Explorer 3.0 Web browsers. If you don't also allow Anonymous or Basic, users of other types of browsers, including Netscape 3.0, won't be able to attach to your Web site. Use this setting for most intranets if you are using a browser that supports it.

If you must use basic authentication over the Internet, create a Windows NT global group for all the accounts that log on from the Internet. Allow those accounts access only to your HTML files, not to the rest of the objects on your server—and don't allow the groups Domain Users or Everyone access to anything. Create another group for all users who log on internally if they need access to everything. This method prevents hackers who have found an unencrypted password from gaining access to anything else on your network.

Some browsers (e.g., Internet Explorer) automatically provide Windows NT Challenge/Response encrypted credentials if you are already logged on to a Windows NT domain, thus obviating the need for a logon box to ask for them. No browser will automatically transmit basic logon authentication without your knowledge, however, because the password is not encrypted and could be intercepted by hackers.

If you are serving for an intranet, you will generally use only the Windows NT Challenge/Response logon requirement. This setting assures the same level of security that your Windows NT server normally requires to gain access to any files. If you are serving for the Internet, you will usually use the Allow Anonymous Logon requirement unless you will also be providing additional services to account holders.

CGI scripts enable you to create logon authentication independent of the operating system, but these systems are complex and prone to security holes. You are much better off using the security features built into Windows NT and IIS to perform security checking for you.

Port Settings You can use the Internet Service Manager to change the TCP/IP port setting that IIS responds to. The normal convention for HTTP is port 80. All public Internet Web servers must be set to this setting for usual access, and most firewalls are configured to pass this port number. You would change the port setting only if you are creating a private intranet or passing private HTTP data over the Internet. Every client that attaches to your site must be configured to transmit to the specific port you specify here—if you change from the default, users will have to know which port to attach to in order to request HTML documents from your server.

Using an atypical HTTP port number over the public Internet does not guarantee security. Any hacker with a packet sniffer will be able to tell immediately what port number your HTTP server is responding to and set a Web browser to use that port. If you are truly concerned about security, use encryption and NTFS file permissions rather than nonstandard port settings.

The Connection time-out duration field is the maximum amount of time a connection that is not responding to the server will be left open. If a client does not respond within this duration, the server will close that connection. This mechanism keeps inactive connections or connections that are too slow to usefully connect from consuming network resources.

The Maximum connections field specifies how many clients you will allow to connect to your Web server simultaneously. The default value is set to 100,000 (ridiculously high) simply to simulate no limit. If your site is extremely popular, you may actually want to limit the number of simultaneous connections so that users will be able to get something done, since they must all share the bandwidth of your network trunk. About 100 Internet users can usefully share a single T1 line. Allowing more than 100 can bog down your server access to the point where it's not very productive for anyone. Use Table 4.3 to determine how many useful connections your server can support through specific types of network interfaces. If your server has more than one network interface, add up the totals for each type.

Table 4.3 was created by dividing the real available bandwidth by 14.4Kb/s (1.8KB/s)—the speed of a slower analog modem and rounding to the nearest meaningful number in faster connections. Nondeterministic shared data links like Ethernet are assumed to be loaded at 33 percent utilization. Note that Table 4.3 also presumes the data link is not used by any other data services. If it is, make an estimate of what percentage of the data link will be available for use by Internet services and multiply the number of users by that percentage.

TABLE 4.3

Useful Connections by Data Link

Data Link	Users
28.8Kb/s analog modem	2
56Kb/s leased line	4
128Kb/s ISDN line	9
768K cable modem	50
T1 leased line	100
Ethernet	300
T3	3,100
Fast Ethernet	2,300
FDDI	7,000
ATM-155	8,600
OC-12	34,400
OC-48	140,000
OC-192	550,000

Because HTTP connections are by nature not constant, you can multiply these useful maximums by a factor of up to ten if your Web server does not make use of large or complex graphics, Java applets, or otherwise serve large files, and if you don't mind providing sporadic service. These connections should be strictly observed for FTP sites, however, since file transfers are not transitory and consume bandwidth steadily throughout the duration of the transfer.

Virtual Directories   Virtual directories allow you to provide access to files and directories located in areas other than your www root and on other machines on your local area network. When you add a directory to the WWW Service Manager, you specify whether that directory is a home directory (meaning a root WWW directory) or a virtual directory that will appear as a subdirectory to a home directory.

This functionality, somewhat similar to the functionality provided by the Distributed File System for Windows NT, allows you to make other directories appear as subdirectories of the WWW home directory even if they exist on other machines. The computer storing the page can run any operating system or platform as long as your Windows NT Server can log on to the other computer to retrieve the Web page. Virtual directories are referred to by their alias in the directory structure. (Virtual directories are covered in detail in Chapter 6.)

Virtual Servers   Virtual servers allow you to make a single Web server look like two or more—for instance, the same actual Web server can host both www.yourorg.com and www.myorg.org. Each virtual server has its own home (default) page, so when you connect to the different Web sites, nothing indicates that they are running on the same machine.

Virtual servers are fundamentally different from virtual directories—don't confuse the two concepts. *Virtual servers* allow one server to host more than one Web site. *Virtual directories* allow more than one server to store files for one Web site. (Virtual servers are covered in detail in Chapter 6.)

The IP address of each virtual server must be bound to the network adapter attached to the Internet. If you have assigned more than one IP address to your network adapters, you must specify which IP addresses have access to which directory. If no IP addresses are specified, that directory will be visible to all virtual servers.

Default Pages   When users attach to your Web server, they usually don't specify a specific Web document. If your server receives an attachment request without a specific document, it will send the document specified in the Directories tab of the HTTP Service Manager (`default.htm`). You can disable sending a specific document by unchecking the Enable default document option, or you can specify a different default document in the default document input box.

FTP Configuration

You control the FTP configuration through the FTP Service Properties window of the Internet Service Manager. Exercise 4.5 gives you a brief overview of the FTP options, and the rest of this section details what the FTP service options control. Figure 4.3 shows the FTP Service Properties window of the Internet Service Manager.

FIGURE 4.3

The FTP Services
Properties window

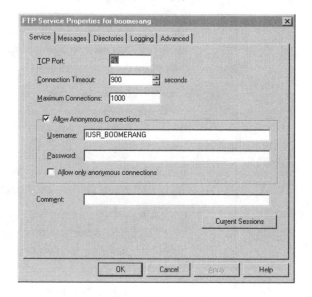

Controlling User Connections   When a user opens a connection to your FTP server, that user must provide logon credentials. Normally for Internet services, this credential is an anonymous user without a password. When IIS receives an anonymous logon credential, it logs that user on using the account specified in the Internet Service Manager—by default this is the IUSR_*servername* account created when you installed Internet Service Manager.

EXERCISE 4.5

Tour of the FTP Service Manager

1. Select Start ➤ Programs ➤ Microsoft Internet Server ➤ Internet Service Manager.

2. Double-click your server name in the FTP service row.

3. Notice the options available in the Service panel. From this panel you can control the following:

   - TCP/IP port number of the FTP Service
   - Connection time-out and the maximum number of connections
   - Anonymous user account
   - Logon options

4. Click the Messages panel. In this panel you can enter a Welcome message that appears automatically whenever an FTP connection is opened to your server, an exit message shown when it is closed, and a message to users who will not be allowed in because too many connections are already in use.

5. Click the Directories panel. From this panel you control which directories users have access to and what the directory list style will be. The default is UNIX style because most FTP servers run on UNIX hosts.

6. Click the Logging tab. From this panel you control logging options that allow you to profile how your server is being used and by whom. This panel is the same as the Logging panel in HTTP options.

7. Click Advanced. From this panel you control which specific computers or subnets will be denied or granted access. You can also specify how much network load you will allow Internet services to demand from your server.

8. Click OK to close the FTP Service Properties window.

9. Close the Internet Service Manager

If a user account password has been specified for the account set at the anonymous connection account, users will not be able to log on to your FTP site unless they know that password. For most purposes, the anonymous user account password should be empty if you want to allow public access to the site. If you want to have some protected directories, uncheck the Allow only anonymous connections and then create a new account for those directories.

The anonymous logon connection exists so that you can control permissions assigned to FTP-connected users. By assigning NTFS file permissions to this user, you can control which FTP directories and files anonymous users can open. You can change the Internet anonymous user account to an existing user account if one exists that fits your security structure better. However, it's generally easier to simply assign permissions to the default account.

Logon Requirements   If you are providing service on the Internet, you should allow anonymous FTP connections. You do not need FTP services on an intranet, though, since file servers perform the same function and are much easier to use.

If you don't need to protect certain files on your site from public access, you should also check the Allow only anonymous connections setting. This setting prevents account names and passwords that are valid for your network from being transmitted without encryption over the Internet.

Welcome and Exit Messages   You can set the Welcome, Exit, and Maximum connection messages for your FTP site in the Messages panel. Typically, you would put information about your organization, the data contained in the site, copyright and legal notices, and greetings in the Welcome message. The Exit message is usually just a cheerful note or thank you, and the Maximum Connections message is generally a notice that the server is not accepting connections and that the user should try again later. Simply type your message to have it appear when the user connects to your FTP sites.

Port Settings   Like HTTP (and all other Internet protocols), FTP has a default port number. Port numbers provide a way to create more than one data stream over a single IP connection. The default TCP/IP port for FTP is 21, which you should use unless you have a compelling reason to override it. FTP clients must be configured to use ports other than port 21, so don't change this number unless you want to deny access to most users by default.

The connection time-out setting and the maximum connection setting are the same as the HTTP settings described earlier. You'll notice, however, that the default is only 1,000—1/100 of the default allowed for HTTP connections. This default setting reflects the fact that FTP connections typically consume far more bandwidth than HTTP connections consume. FTP connections are designed for large file transfers, rather than for the sporadic transfers typical of HTTP connections.

Directories   The Directories panel allows you to specify which directories on your server will be made available to FTP connections. All subdirectories of the directories shown are automatically made available as well.

Directory listing styles lets you choose between MS-DOS–style directory listings or UNIX-style directory listings. Because most FTP hosts are UNIX computers, you should choose UNIX style unless you have a reason not to. Some software depends on receiving UNIX-style directory listings. The difference between the two styles is minor, as shown in Figures 4.4 and 4.5.

You must stop and restart the FTP service for a change in directory style to take effect.

FIGURE 4.4

MS-DOS–style directory listings

```
331 Anonymous access allowed, send identity (e-mail name) as password.
Password:
230-Welcome to the private site.
| blah blah blah.
230 Anonymous user logged in.
ftp> dir
200 PORT command successful.
150 Opening ASCII mode data connection for /bin/ls.
07-31-96  05:54PM               300762 F0201.tif
07-31-96  05:54PM                60602 F0202.tif
07-31-96  05:54PM               111802 F0203.tif
07-31-96  05:54PM               152762 F0204.tif
07-31-96  05:54PM               227002 F0205.tif
07-31-96  05:54PM               271802 F0206.tif
07-31-96  05:54PM               306522 F0207.tif
07-31-96  05:54PM               250042 F0208.tif
07-31-96  05:54PM               268602 F0209.tif
07-31-96  05:54PM               243642 F0210.tif
07-31-96  05:54PM               124806 F0211.tif
07-31-96  05:54PM               163270 F0212.tif
07-31-96  05:54PM               208602 F0213.tif
07-31-96  05:54PM               271802 F0214.tif
226 Transfer complete.
700 bytes received in 0.00 seconds (700000.00 Kbytes/sec)
ftp>
```

FIGURE 4.5

UNIX-style directory listings

```
F0212.tif
F0213.tif
F0214.tif
226 Transfer complete.
154 bytes received in 0.01 seconds (10.27 Kbytes/sec)
ftp> dir
200 PORT command successful.
150 Opening ASCII mode data connection for /bin/ls.
            1 owner    group           300762 Jul 31  1996 F0201.tif
            1 owner    group            60602 Jul 31  1996 F0202.tif
            1 owner    group           111802 Jul 31  1996 F0203.tif
            1 owner    group           152762 Jul 31  1996 F0204.tif
            1 owner    group           227002 Jul 31  1996 F0205.tif
            1 owner    group           271802 Jul 31  1996 F0206.tif
            1 owner    group           306522 Jul 31  1996 F0207.tif
            1 owner    group           250042 Jul 31  1996 F0208.tif
            1 owner    group           268602 Jul 31  1996 F0209.tif
            1 owner    group           243642 Jul 31  1996 F0210.tif
            1 owner    group           124806 Jul 31  1996 F0211.tif
            1 owner    group           163270 Jul 31  1996 F0212.tif
            1 owner    group           208602 Jul 31  1996 F0213.tif
            1 owner    group           271802 Jul 31  1996 F0214.tif
226 Transfer complete.
980 bytes received in 0.03 seconds (31.61 Kbytes/sec)
ftp>
```

Virtual Directories   Virtual directories allow you to provide access to files and directories located in areas other than your FTP root and on other machines on your local area network. When you add a directory to the FTP Service Manager, you specify whether that directory is a home directory (meaning a root FTP directory) or a virtual directory that will appear as a subdirectory to a home directory.

This functionality is somewhat similar to the functionality provided by the Distributed File System for Windows NT. Virtual directories allow you to make other directories appear as subdirectories of the FTP home directory even if they exist on other machines. Virtual directories are referred to by their alias in the directory structure.

Virtual directories will not appear in FTP directory listings. You must tell users the exact URL to the virtual directory for them to connect to it.

Virtual directories don't have to be located on the Internet server; they can be located on network drives. If you specify a network directory, you have to include an account and password that has access to that network drive (see Chapter 6).

Virtual directories located on network drives must be in the same Windows NT Authentication domain.

Gopher

By now you've probably noticed quite a bit of similarity between HTTP service options and FTP service options. Gopher settings are similar to both of these— every service option available for Gopher settings has already been covered either under the HTTP section or the FTP section. Take a few moments to browse around the Gopher service panel using Exercise 4.6. The Gopher Service Properties window is shown in Figure 4.6. Because the options are the same as the HTTP and FTP services already presented and because the Gopher service is obsolete, we will not describe them in detail here.

Gopher services are largely obsolete—the services of HTTP can provide all the functionality of Gopher and more. Gopher services are included with IIS for two reasons: They were easy to add, and they enable sites already having a Gopher site to use Windows NT and IIS. If you are creating a new Internet site, you should base it on HTTP rather than on Gopher protocols.

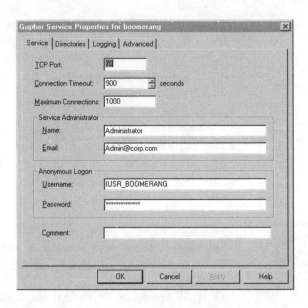

EXERCISE 4.6

Tour of the Gopher Service Manager

1. Select Start ➤ Programs ➤ Microsoft Internet Server ➤ Internet Service Manager.

2. Double-click your server name in the Gopher service row.

3. Notice the options available in the Service panel. From this panel you can control the following:

   ■ TCP/IP port number of the Gopher service
   ■ Connection time-out and the maximum number of connections
   ■ Anonymous user account

4. Click the Directories panel. From this panel you control which directories Gopher users have access to. The virtual directories work the same way as described for HTTP and FTP.

5. Click the Logging tab. From this panel, you control logging options that allow you to profile how your server is being used and by whom. This panel is the same as the logging panel in HTTP options.

6. Click Advanced. From this panel you control which specific computers or subnets will be denied or granted access. You can also specify how much network load you will allow Internet services to demand from your server.

7. Click OK to close the FTP Service Properties window.

8. Close the Internet Service Manager.

Installing Index Server

Index Server enhances IIS by providing a method to search for documents like Web pages, Word documents, or any other document type with an installed *content filter* on a server by keyword rather than by name. Index Server creates a database of words contained in documents that are stored on the server. You can then simply enter a plain language search phrase, and Index Server will return a list of documents that satisfy the search phrase. Search phrases are called *queries* in database and indexing parlance.

Index Server is administered and queried through HTML pages. The pages you include in your Web site to allow users to query Index Server are called *Query HTML pages*. Index Server can index any type of document that you've installed a content filter for. Content filters are plug-ins that Index Server uses to read a specific type of file. Index Server comes with content filters for HTML and for the Microsoft Office applications. Index Server cannot index documents for which there is no installed content filter.

Index Server works by creating a dictionary of all the words in all the documents on your site. Each dictionary entry lists the documents that contain that word. Queries return only those documents that are listed in all the dictionary entries for each of the search words. For example, if you queried Index Server with the phrase *Internet Information Server,* then Index Server would return all the documents on your server that contained those words as links in a new Web page that it creates.

The dictionary is called a *catalog,* and technically, the catalog doesn't search your entire site. It searches only the virtual roots you specify, which by default is your entire site. This feature allows you to remove virtual roots that you don't want indexed.

You may need to have more than one catalog if you have more than one virtual server. Each virtual server should have its own catalog to prevent documents contained on one site from showing up on queries in another. Queries cannot span more than one catalog.

By default, Index Server catalogs are automatically connected to the wwwroot of the server upon which Index Server is installed. If you need to index other virtual servers, you will have to create a catalog for each server and connect that catalog to that server. (Creating additional catalogs and connecting virtual servers to them is covered in Chapter 6.)

After installing the correct service pack and version of IIS, installing Index Server is easy. Follow the steps in Exercise 4.7 to install Index Server.

EXERCISE 4.7

Installing Index Server

1. Insert the Windows NT Service Pack 2 CD-ROM that you can order from Microsoft. Alternatively, you can download the required files from the www.microsoft.com Web site.

2. Double-click My Computer.

3. Right-click your CD-ROM drive and select Open.

4. Double-click the iis30 directory.

5. Double-click the index11 directory.

6. Double-click the directory that corresponds to your microprocessor.

7. Double-click the is11enu icon.

8. Click Yes to install Index Server 1.1.

9. Click Yes to agree to the license after reading it. Click Continue.

10. Type the path to the IIS scripts directory. If you accepted the default installation location, this path is c:\inetpub\scripts.

11. Click OK to accept the default path to the wwwroot directory.

12. Type **C:\Inetpub** when prompted to provide a location for the index files.

EXERCISE 4.7 (CONTINUED FROM PREVIOUS PAGE)

13. Note the location of the sample search page.

14. Click Exit to Windows.

Index Server starts automatically when the first query is issued from a query HTML page; Index Server stops when IIS stops.

You cannot start or stop Index Server manually.

Configuring Index Server

Index Server requires minimal administration. All Index Server administration is performed using HTML pages. After installing Index Server, a new entry is created in the programs group in the Start menu containing links to the administration pages for Index Server. Exercise 4.8 shows how to launch the Index Server administration page. Figure 4.7 shows the Index Server administrator running inside Internet Explorer 3.0.

A *virtual root* is the same thing as a virtual directory.

EXERCISE 4.8

Administering Index Server

1. Select Start ➤ Programs ➤ Microsoft Index Server ➤ Index Server Administration.

2. Enter your Windows NT logon name and password to gain entry. If the Web page rejects your name and password when they are correct, Enable Clear Text passwords in the WWW Service Properties window of the IIS, stop and restart Web services, and try again.

Remember that this step does pose a security risk, so you should update to a browser that can handle Windows NT Challenge/Response encrypted logon or downgrade to anonymous logon if possible.

EXERCISE 4.8 (CONTINUED FROM PREVIOUS PAGE)

3. Click View/Update Indexing of Virtual Roots. Note the virtual roots indexed by Index Server.

4. Click Back.

5. Click Index Statistics.

6. Scroll down and look at the indexing statistics.

7. Close the Web browser.

FIGURE 4.7

Index Server
Administration page

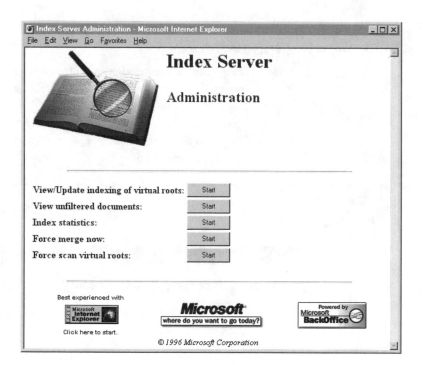

The Index Server Administration Page has the following options:

- **View/Update indexing of virtual roots** shows you which virtual roots are currently indexed and allows you to select which virtual roots you want to have indexed.

- **View unfiltered documents** shows the documents that could not be indexed due to file corruption or a problem with the dynamic link library that filters that type of file.

- **Index statistics** shows cache and index statistics such as the size of the index and the number of files indexed.

- **Force merge now** merges all the master indexes for virtual roots into a single master index. This feature speeds query time, but the merge itself is processor and time intensive for larger sites.

- **Force scan virtual roots** causes the virtual roots to be rescanned for files that may have been added since the last full scan. Scanning is automatic and normally does not need to be performed.

Some types of shares that may be set up as virtual roots, such as Windows 95 computers and Novell servers, do not support the automatic change notification required for a typical incremental scan, so Index Server performs a periodic full scan of these directories. You may want to force a scan if you don't want to wait for the periodic scan (after adding a large number files, for instance). You will also need to force a scan after installing a content filter to index a certain type of file (such as a database). Content filters are implemented as dynamic link libraries (DLLs) and are called *filter DLLs*.

Index servers can open an interesting security loophole. Since the index process runs as a system process, it has higher security access to documents on the server than many logged on users have. Therefore, a query issued to an index server could return fragments of files that the user does not have permission to access—thus alerting the user to the presence of the document and possibly revealing sensitive information.

MS Index Server 1.1 prevents this situation by automatically cataloging the security access control list (ACL) for each file it indexes. When a user issues a query, each document that satisfies the query (called a *query hit*) is checked against the user's permissions. If the user would not normally have permission to view the document, the query is removed from the results list and no indication of the documents existence is revealed.

Summary

Internet Information Server (IIS) provides the functionality of an HTTP server, FTP server, and Gopher server in one easy-to-use package. Index Server enhances this service by providing the ability to search for documents using natural language queries.

IIS is administered using the Internet Service Manager. From the Internet Service Manager, you can stop and start each of the Internet protocol services that IIS 3.0 supports, and you can manage connection and security settings for each service.

IIS will serve files stored on other machines and in directories not attached to the service root directories. These directories are called virtual directories, and they can be assigned and administered for each of the three supported Internet protocols using the Internet Service Manager. For HTML, IIS can also create virtual servers that create the illusion of multiple physical servers on a single machine. Virtual servers allow the HTTP service to respond to different IP addresses with a different set of default pages and with different Index Server query catalogs. Therefore, you can use the same physical server to host more than one Internet site.

The small amount of administration Index Server requires is performed through a set of HTML documents. Index Server is largely self-administering—you typically need to administer Index Server only if you wish to exclude certain virtual directories from queries or if you have set up virtual servers.

Review Questions

1. One of your users is having trouble attaching to your Web site. From your Internet Explorer browser, you have no problem attaching with your test user account. You try attaching at the server and also have no difficulty. But when you try attaching from that user's computer running Netscape 3.0 with your account, you get an Access Denied message. You check the Advanced options in the Internet Service Manager and determine that all computers are by default allowed access and no specific exclusions are listed. What is wrong?

   A. The HTML page is protected with NTFS security restrictions for that user.

   B. The computer does not have the TCP/IP protocol stack installed.

C. The user is using the wrong password.

D. The HTTP service is only using Windows NT Challenge/Response security.

2. You want to provide FTP file access to some documents stored on an older NetWare server at your site. Your Web server doesn't have enough storage space for them, you have no budget for upgrades, and the users that own them don't want you to move the files from their current location. What should you do?

A. Create a virtual server that is configured to access the NetWare server.

B. Create a virtual directory that specifies the network drive attached to the NetWare server.

C. Create a virtual root and index it using Index Server. This step will create a local catalog that can be browsed on the Web server.

D. Convert the NetWare server to Windows NT Server 4, install IIS, and specify the file location as the wwwroot directory.

E. You cannot provide this type of file access because of the restrictions in the system.

3. Your company purchases a small competitor and wants to retain that company's brands, logos, trademarks, and other image-related properties. The acquisition's Internet site is closed, and its employees move to your facility. You copy the Web site files onto your server but want that site to appear as it always has on the Internet. What should you do?

A. Put a link on your company's home page to the default.htm file of the newly acquired company.

B. Inform InterNIC that the company's IP address has changed to your company's IP address. This action will forward requests to www.them.com to your server.

C. Create a virtual server, update the IP address for the company's domain name to reflect a new unique IP address in your subnet, and install the original site files in the virtual server root.

D. Create a virtual directory, update the IP address for the company's domain name to reflect a new unique IP address in your subnet, and install the original site files in the virtual server root.

4. You install a new content filter in Index Server designed to display Post-Script files. When you run a query using words that you know appear in Display PostScript Documents in your wwwroot directory, no Display PostScript files appear in the query. What should you do?

A. Force a scan to activate the new content filter.

B. Add the wwwroot directory to the Index Server list of scanned directories—it's not included by default.

C. Force a Master Merge to include the catalog created for PostScript files.

D. Create a new catalog for displaying PostScript files.

CHAPTER

5

The Internet Protocols

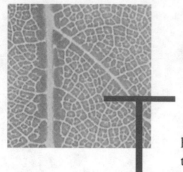

This chapter concisely describes the various lower-level protocols that form the basis of the Internet. The text defines many terms and explains several 12important concepts—probably more than you'll be able to grasp in one sitting if the concepts are new to you.

You should reread this chapter when you complete the rest of the book to brush up on the terminology and review the concepts after you've seen how they work in the Internet and in Windows NT.

Internet protocols enable computers on different networks to communicate. Internet protocols provide the logical connection between your computer and the *Internet host* server that serves the Web site (or other information); they are the foundation of all Internet services. The Internet Protocol (IP) works by routing *packets* (or small pieces, also called *datagrams*) of a continuous stream of data over all the networks between two computers.

The term *Internet Protocol* (IP) refers to the specific protocol that forwards packets on the Internet. The term *Internet protocols* (plural) refers to the entire body of protocols that use the services of the Internet Protocol and are used on the Internet.

You can use Internet protocols on a stand-alone network, but they would be less efficient than protocols designed specifically for single networks. However, using the TCP/IP suite will allow you to use the higher-level Internet protocols like HTTP to form an *intranet,* or a private network architecture based on the principles and software of the global Internet.

Networks and Routing

A *network* is a physical group of computers wired together so that they can communicate directly with each other using the same data link protocol and do not require routers to connect them. For instance, any computer on an office Ethernet network can address any other computer on the network directly—there's no need to forward information between two different shared media networks (for instance, between an Ethernet and a token-ring network).

Computers may be connected with hubs, switches, or bridges, but remain a single network because data can be transmitted between any two computers over the same data link protocol. In some cases, switches perform minor changes in the data link protocol (for instance, bridging fast Ethernet and Ethernet) because these technologies use the same data link protocols but operate at different speeds.

The terms *transport protocol* and *network protocol* are somewhat synonymous. *Transport protocol* is the more generic of the two and includes protocols such as NetBEUI that cannot be used to forward data between networks. *Network protocol* is specific to protocols such as TCP/IP or IPX/SPX that can forward data between networks. Specifically, *network protocols* provide packet forwarding between networks (the IP portion of TCP/IP), and *transport protocols* provide flow control, error correction, and connection services (the TCP portion of TCP/IP). Most actual software services perform both with the same software. Microsoft uses the term *transport protocol* to refer to any suite that provides all these services.

An *internetwork* is a group of networks connected by *routers* that are configured to forward (or *route*) data between the networks based on a set of forwarding rules. The different networks do not need to be of the same data link type, because the router (sometimes called a *gateway* in UNIX circles) can connect to any type of data link. The router examines every packet's destination address and determines which of its ports is closest to the destination computer. One of the following events happens:

- The router can match the packet directly to an entry in the routing table and transmit the packet directly to the host or router.

- If the router doesn't have enough information to determine where a packet should go, it simply sends the packet to another router (its default gateway) that it trusts will know how to deal with the packet.

- If a router does not know how to forward the packet and does not have a default gateway, the destination is *unreachable* because the two networks are not connected properly.

Figure 5.1 shows a hypothetical communication between two computers on different networks. The solid lines in Figure 5.1 show the physical data links, and a dashed line shows the route taken by data. Each dashed line indicates the path between two routers. Notice that a multihomed server (a server with more than one network connection) performs the routing function in two places on the internetwork.

FIGURE 5.1

Routing data between computers on different networks

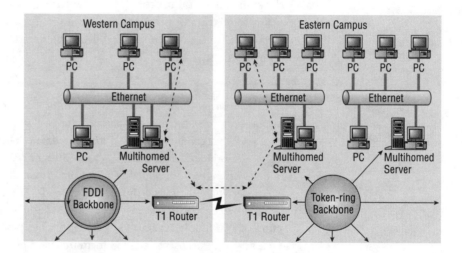

Any computer with routing software can function as a router, but networks that use nondedicated routers experience more time delays (*latency*) and hardware bottlenecks than networks that use dedicated routers experience.

Dedicated routers are simply computers that are optimized for the routing function and do not perform other general-purpose functions. They do not require video displays or keyboards, usually do not have hard disk drives, and may use esoteric RISC microprocessors; otherwise, dedicated routers are similar to general-purpose computers in hardware and most run a small variant of the UNIX operating system. They are rather expensive—generally twice the price of a multihomed server capable of performing the same routing function. You may find you can live with the lower overall throughput of a multihomed server acting as a router in your networks.

The *Internet* is a single large internetwork based on the TCP/IP protocol suite. Nearly every large corporation and university in the world, as well as many small businesses and individuals, are connected to the Internet. *Intranets* are private networks that may or may not be attached to the Internet; intranets are also based on the Internet protocols. *TCP/IP* is a suite of protocols that the government and universities have developed over the last two decades that enable very large networks to be connected. The rest of this chapter discusses the various protocols embodied by the TCP/IP suite that are most important to the creation and connection of networks.

The TCP/IP suite embodies many other protocols, but they either are not nearly as important or are not implemented in many versions of the suite. The entire suite is referred to collectively by the two most common and most important protocols, TCP/IP (Transmission Control Protocol/Internet Protocol), or as the Internet protocols.

Internet Protocol

The Internet Protocol (IP) is the basis upon which all other Internet protocols operate. IP provides the basic mechanism for the forwarding of data between two computers on separate networks. IP can also fragment packets if they are too large for some older networks to forward, but this feature is largely obsolete because all routers built in the past decade are able to pass large IP packets.

IP packets are simply handed from computer to computer until they reach their destination. The computer sending the packet and the computer receiving the packet are called *end systems* because they are at the ends of the communication session. The computers between the end systems are called *intermediate systems*. Intermediate system is a generic and more theoretical term for computers more commonly called *routers, gateways,* or *multihomed hosts*.

- **Router** usually refers to specially designed computers optimized for routing packets.

- **Gateway** refers to general-purpose computers that are simply used as routers and perform no other function.

- **Multihomed host** refers to general-purpose computers that perform some other function in addition to routing packets such as file service or Internet site hosting.

The term *hosts* is commonly used in the UNIX and Internet communities to mean any computer (client, server, or peer) that is directly attached to the Internet.

Services of IP

IP provides the functions of addressing and fragmentation only to support packet forwarding; it does not presume or implement any other functionality.

- IP cannot guarantee that a packet will reach its destination.

- IP has no ability to perform flow control.

- IP performs no error correction.

- IP performs no error detection for the data payload.

- IP does not guarantee that packets will arrive in order and does not order them sequentially.

IP relies on the data link to transmit data in an error-free condition and does not attempt to provide any guarantees of service. Other protocols, which are transported within IP packets, add information such as packet serial numbers and error-correction codes. The destination system can check to see if all the packets have arrived, arrange them in the correct order, and request that any missing packets be sent again based on this additional information. TCP performs all these functions, as explained in the next section.

IP treats each packet as an independent entity, unrelated to any other packet being transmitted. IP does not have logical or virtual connections, circuits, sockets, or any other mechanism to provide associations between packets. These functions are all provided by higher (or occasionally lower) level protocols.

IP does not perform error correction. IP does, however, implement limited error checking to verify that the header information is correct; damaged header information could result in the packet being forwarded to the wrong address. If, at any time, a router on the path between the sending computer and the receiving computer detects that an IP packet's address header has become damaged (by comparing the header with the header's checksum), the router will simply discard the packet without notification of any kind. Again, higher-level protocols will determine what data is missing and generate a request for retransmission. This header checksum does not detect errors that may have crept into the data portion of the packet; that function also is the responsibility of higher-level protocols.

IP does include information about how long a packet should remain "alive" in a system. Every IP packet contains a *time-to-live indicator* and decreases this counter by one each time a router forwards the packet or whenever one second of real time elapses. The time-to-live counter usually starts at 255, the maximum possible value. When a packet's time-to-live counter reaches zero, the packet is discarded.

This event can occur in three (rare) cases:

- When the network is too busy to forward packets in a timely manner

- When a circular route exists and packets are simply being passed around it

- When the route between two computers is simply too long to be useful

In all three cases, the route is not usable so communications should not continue.

Internet Addresses

All computers attached to an IP network (such as the Internet) are uniquely identified by a 32-bit number, usually expressed in decimal notation and with each byte (or octet) separated by a period. Because each portion of the address specifies two bits, the decimal range is between 0 and 255 for each of the four bytes. For example:

10.191.31.10

If you ever see an IP address expressed in decimal notation with a number higher than 255, the address is not a valid IP address.

This address must be unique to the specific computer to which it is assigned—no other computer can have this address if it is attached to the same internetwork (i.e., the Internet). If two computers ever do have the same address, unpredictable routing errors will result. IP addresses are analogous to house addresses in that no two are ever the same and each element (in the case of house addresses, elements would be states, cities, streets, and numbers) is increasingly specific.

Subnets

IP addresses are not simply assigned at random. All computers on the same data link network are within the same *subnet,* or range of IP addresses. For instance, if you have an office Ethernet of 25 computers, all 25 computers would have IP addresses within the same short range.

The following example explains how IP addresses are assigned and how networks are *subnetted*, or divided into IP networks. Let's say that BT&T, a telephone company and Internet service provider (ISP), has been assigned the 10 address range. Within that range, BT&T is able to split up and sell ranges of IP addresses.

Now let's say that American Internet, a regional ISP that serves the east coast, purchases from BT&T high-capacity network connections and the right to act as a second-tier Internet service provider. BT&T assigns the 191 range of its 10 address range to American Internet, which is now free to assign any addresses more specific than 10.191.

Digital Widgets, a small company that makes a digital version of the ubiquitous widget and has 200 computers, leases a T1 service and the ability to assign its own IP addresses within the company from American Internet. American Internet gives Digital Widgets the 64 address range so that Digital Widgets is free to assign any IP address more specific than 10.191.64 to their own computers.

Sara, the forward-thinking network administrator of Digital Widgets, assigns the IP address 10.191.64.1 to the router attached to the T1 line. She assigns the address 10.191.64.2 to the corporate server and sets up DHCP on the server to automatically assign the remaining addresses to client computers as they attach to the network.

DHCP is a protocol that dynamically assigns IP addresses to clients as they request them. DHCP is explained in the last section of this chapter.

When Sara boots her networked client computer, it automatically receives the IP address 10.191.64.3 because it was the first computer to request a DHCP lease.

Sara could have assigned an individual IP address to each computer, but that process is a great deal of work. In addition, assigning IP addresses manually wastes IP addresses because computers that aren't attached to the network at that time still use up an IP address.

Classes

Internet addresses were originally segmented on byte boundaries. Large networks on which the first byte specifies the network number and the last three bytes are the local addresses are called *Class A domains*. Medium-size networks on which the first two bytes specify the network number and the last two bytes specify the local addresses are called *Class B domains*. Smaller networks on which the first three bytes specify the network number and the last byte specifies the local addresses are called *Class C domains*. In the preceding example, BT&T has a Class A domain, American Internet has a Class B domain, and Digital Widgets has a Class C domain.

Classless Addressing

It is also possible to subnet at any point within the 32 bits of the IP address, not just on byte boundaries. This method of dividing network numbers from local addresses is known as *classless addressing*.

Originally, most Internet addresses were segmented on byte boundaries simply because it was easy, but as IP addresses became scarce, the more conservative practice of segmenting based on the actual estimated size of a network became more common.

To explain this system, let's say Digital Widgets has 1,000 computers rather than just 200. Since you can't fit 1,000 IP addresses into the 254 allowed addresses of the last two bits of an IP address, American Internet has to provide a larger subnet to its customers.

If you thought eight bits could provide 256 addresses (because 2 to the 8th power is 256), you'd be right. But in this case two addresses in every subnet are reserved. The "all zeros" address specifies the entire subnet. `10.191.61.0` specifies Digital Widget's entire network; `10.191.0.0` specifies American Internet's network; and `10.0.0.0` specifies BT&T's network. The "all ones" address specifies an IP broadcast, so sending an IP packet to `10.191.61.255` means that all computers should receive it. Therefore, to calculate the number of available addresses in a subnet, you raise 2 to the number of bits in the subnet portion of the address and then subtract 2.

Each additional bit of address space doubles the number of hosts allowed on a network, but divides the number of possible networks in half. So by adding 1 bit to an 8-bit subnet, we can address 510 computers ($2^9 = 512 - 2 = 510$). Adding another bit doubles that to 1,022 ($2^{10} = 1,024 - 2 = 1,022$), which is large enough to cover the required number of computers. Sara realizes that 1,022 possible client addresses leaves very little room for growth. She adds another bit as a safety margin, resulting in an 11-bit subnet that can accommodate 2,046 computers and requests an 11-bit subnet from American Internet. This solution also leaves room for Sara to create her own subnets within Digital Widget's network.

Subnet Masks

Every IP address has two portions:

- The network number
- The local host address

Because both numbers are contained in the same 32 bits and because the size of the network varies greatly from organization to organization, some method is required to determine which part of the IP address is the network number and which is the host's unique identifier.

The subnet mask determines which portion of the IP address is the network number and which portion is the local host address. The subnet mask is a 32-bit number consisting of all ones to the left and all zeros to the right that specifies how large the network number is. The switch between ones and zeros occurs at the bit size of the network. In the preceding example Sara determined that she would need 11 bits of address space to address all the current and future hosts in Digital Widget's network. The following subnet mask supports this division:

```
11111111.11111111.11111000.00000000 = 255.255.248.0
```

The ones mean that the network number is 21 bits long, and the zeros mean that an 11-bit range is available for host addresses.

The subnet mask determines whether the destination computer and the source computer reside on the same local network or whether the transmission will require routing. When a computer creates an IP packet, it masks off the host address of the destination computer, leaving only the network number. It compares this network number to its own network number, and if the two are equal, the computer transmits the packet directly to the destination computer because the two computers are on the same local data link. If the two numbers are not equal, the computer transmits the packet to its default gateway. The default gateway performs a similar comparison. This process continues until the packet eventually reaches the data link to which it is local and is received by the destination computer.

Routers, Gateways, and Multihomed Servers

Routers, gateways, and multihomed servers perform the *routing function*. They forward datagrams received on one network to another network that is closer to the destination. Consequently, these devices must be attached to both networks and have an Internet address that is local to each network. (Obviously, the devices need more than one IP address.)

IP addresses are assigned to each network interface, not to each computer. If a server has two network interfaces, each attached to a different network, it is a multihomed server. Since most clients have only one network interface, clients have only one IP address and can be referred to by that IP address. Multihomed servers, routers, and gateways all require more than one address; they are generally referred to by the IP address of the adapter through which the default gateway for that multihomed host is reached.

Figure 5.2 shows a small portion of a very large Internet. Each interrupted ellipse represents a network. The network number portion of that network appears in bold face, and the host number portion appears next to each host. The complete IP address(es) for a host is formed by appending the host number to the network number—for instance, host number 1.3 on network number 10.191 has an IP address of 10.191.1.3. The computers that sit between two networks are multihomed hosts acting as routers—they have more than one IP address. As you can see in the figure:

- Multihomed computers have an IP address for each network to which they are attached.

- Multihomed hosts connect the networks by forwarding data between them.

- Bottom tier networks have larger network numbers, usually three bytes long. Hosts on these networks are only one byte long.

- Medium tier networks have two-byte network numbers and two-byte host identifiers.

- Top tier networks have one-byte network numbers and three-byte host identifiers.

- Multihomed hosts are usually attached to networks with somewhat similar network numbers, but this convention is not a requirement.

- More than one path can exist between any two end systems.

A trace route using the `tracert.exe` utility from host 10.191.61.4 to host 14.3.1.7 would produce the following IP address list:

1. 10.191.61.4

2. 10.191.1.2

3. 10.1.1.2

4. 1.1.1.1

5. 14.2.1.1

6. 14.3.1.1

7. 14.3.1.7

This trace shows that seven routers are involved between the two end systems—an average size for any typical Internet connection. Routers are shown by the port that the packet travels from, not the port that the packet travels into.

F I G U R E 5.2

An IP network

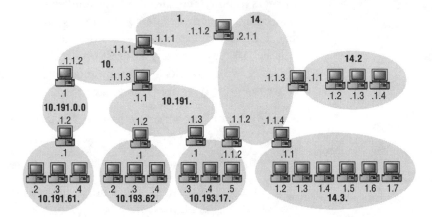

The Default Route

Without more specific routing information, the default route specifies which router to send packets to. A router may have any number of network interfaces, and for each interface the router will maintain lists of routes called *routing tables* about the network to which that interface is attached and the networks that are reachable from that network. The router forwards the packet to the network port (and therefore, network) that is closest to that packet's destination.

If a router's routing tables don't tell the router specifically where a packet should go, the router sends the packet to its default gateway. This route is called the *default route* because packets with no matching entry in the routing table are forwarded there. The default route can be followed until the packet reaches a high-level router that has no default route because it is at the top of the routing hierarchy. The final router either knows where to route the packet or the packet is dropped and the route is unreachable.

Thanks to an obscure bug, Windows NT allows you to specify a default route for every adapter installed in a multihomed server but uses only the default route established for the first bound network adapter. If the first bound adapter is not the network interface on the same data link as the router that connects to the Internet, your server will not route packets to the Internet.

 Never specify more than one default route for a multihomed computer! Enter a default gateway only for the adapter on the same data link as the router that routes to the Internet.

Routing Information Protocol

Routing Information Protocol (RIP) is an Internet protocol that routers, gateways, and multihomed hosts use to trade routing information. For instance, if a higher-level router notices that a lower-level router is actually attached to a network that can reach the destination address in fewer hops, that higher-level router will send a RIP datagram to the router informing it of the closer route. That router will make an entry in its routing table, and all future datagrams going to the same address will be able to take the shorter route.

RIP is built into Windows NT 4.0 and can be added to Windows NT 3.51 by installing the Multi-Protocol Router package on the Windows NT 3.51 service pack CD-ROM. With RIP for IP installed and more than one network adapter, your Windows NT Server can act as a fully functional multihomed host by automatically updating its routing tables based on information received from other routers.

Transmission Control Protocol

Transmission Control Protocol (TCP) provides the services that IP is missing:

- **Reliable delivery**—TCP will request lost packets until the transmission is complete or return a valid and useful error message. TCP guarantees that as long as a data path exists between two end systems, a reliable stream of data can be transmitted.

- **Sequencing**—TCP will put out-of-order packets back in order so a sequential stream of data is maintained.

- **Constant connection**—TCP makes data streams act somewhat like files that can be opened, read from, and closed. It abstracts the packet-based protocol away from the user's application.

- **Error detection and correction**—TCP adds a checksum to the data payload. If the checksum shows that a packet is damaged, it is discarded and retransmitted automatically.

- **Flow control and handshaking**—TCP implements mechanisms to adapt to the reliability of lower-level systems and improve throughput based on current data link conditions.

- **Multiplexing**—TCP uses the concept of sockets and ports to create many simultaneous streams of data between the end systems.

TCP does not need any guarantees of service from lower-level protocols. It can use (technically anyway) any packet-switched or connection-oriented network protocol as long as two-way communication actually exists between the two end systems. The ability to provide a reliable stream of communication between two systems from an unreliable packet-based transport makes TCP the perfect foundation for higher-level services that require error-free communications.

The TCP specification also provides a modicum of security, but these security mechanisms are obsolete (because they don't really work), so they are not discussed here. Encryption services that work above the TCP layer provide true security by reimplementing the socket services with encryption. These services are collectively referred to as *tunnels,* and at the TCP layer they make up the Secure Socket Layer (SSL).

Ports and Sockets

As mentioned earlier, TCP provides a multiplexing mechanism to allow multiple data streams to be transmitted between end systems. This multiplexing feature is implemented through ports, sockets, and connections.

A *port* is a TCP connection number. TCP has 16 bits for port numbers, so two end systems may establish up to 65,535 simultaneous separate communications streams. A *socket* is a port, and the IP (or other protocol) address of the end system necessary to form a complete path to data; it is usually specified in the form 10.191.61.2:80, where the first four bytes are the IP address and the number after the colon (:) is the port. A matched pair of sockets between a client and a host forms a connection.

Once a connection is established, data can be transmitted between systems bidirectionally until the connection is closed. TCP connections are full duplex, or bidirectional.

Well-Known Ports

When you attach your Web browser to an Internet host, the Web browser knows which port to use because the developers of the HTTP service agreed to use the same port number for HTTP servers and clients. This condition is known as the convention of *well-known ports*.

The well-known ports convention specifies that Internet servers of a certain type should "listen" on a certain TCP port for connection requests from client software. The various server software components (such as the Internet Information Server component services) simply open up their socket (local IP address + well-known port for that service) and wait for connection attempts from remote clients. Table 5.1 lists some common (and some silly) services and the well-known port that service uses.

TABLE 5.1 Some Well-Known Ports	Port	Service	Function
	17	Quote	Quote of the Day
	21	FTP	File Transfer Protocol
	23	Telnet	Telnet
	25	SMTP	Mail transfer
	37	Time	Time
	53	DNS	Domain Name Server
	67	BootP	BootP Server
	70	Gopher	Gopher
	80	HTTP	World Wide Web
	110	POP3	Post Office Protocol 3

Many more well-known ports are in use, but the vast majority of them are of no consequence except in special systems. Those listed in Table 5.1 are more general in nature and used by most Internet hosting systems.

The Internet Assigned Numbers Authority of the Internet Engineering Task Force assigns all well-known port numbers below 1024. Port numbers above 1024 are available for public use in any manner. Some nonofficial protocols like Internet Relay Chat (IRC) have simply chosen their own port numbers (in this case, :8000). By convention, everyone knows to use port 8000 for IRC, so it has become a de facto standard. This usage is, after all, how the well-known port numbering system came to be.

Installing TCP/IP

Now that you know more about TCP/IP than you ever cared to know, it's time to actually install TCP/IP in Windows NT. Before performing this installation, gather the information you will need:

- The IP address for the computer

- The subnet mask

- The IP address of the default gateway

Ask your network administrator for these numbers for your computer. Or you can use the numbers suggested in Exercise 5.1 if you don't really intend to use the numbers permanently. Exercise 5.1 shows you how to configure TCP/IP for Windows NT manually.

This exercise suggests using an IP address of 10.1.1.1—if you don't have another IP address—because the entire 10 Class A network is reserved for private use. Internet routers will not forward data to or from IP addresses beginning with 10, so you should use this number for any IP network not actually connected to the Internet. This practice prevents conflicts if you ever do attach the network to the Internet.

This exercise shows you the manual way to configure a TCP/IP address even though we recommend you use DHCP. If you plan to use DCHP to assign IP addresses for this computer, go back to the TCP/IP configuration panel and select Obtain IP Address from DHCP Server.

You must manually configure the IP address of a DHCP server.

EXERCISE 5.1

Installing TCP/IP

If you already have TCP/IP installed, you can skip Exercise 5.1.

1. Select Start ➤ Programs ➤ Control Panel.

2. Double-click the Network Control Panel.

3. Click the Protocols Tab.

4. Click Add.

5. Double-click TCP/IP Protocol in the Network Protocols pick box.

6. Click No when asked if you have a DHCP server (for the purposes of this exercise). You can change this later if you have a DHCP server on your network.

7. Insert your Windows NT CD-ROM into your CD-ROM reader and click the Continue button. If you need to correct the path, do so.

8. Click OK.

9. Click Yes if a message appears asking if you want to configure TCP/IP to work with RAS. Then click Network, check TCP/IP, click OK, and click continue.

10. Click Close.

11. Select your first network interface. If your computer has only one network interface, it will already be selected.

12. Enter the computer's IP address. If you don't have an IP address for your computer, enter 10.1.1.2.

13. Enter the subnet mask. If you don't know what the subnet mask should be for your computer, enter 255.255.255.0.

14. Enter the IP address of your default gateway. If you don't have a default gateway, leave this address blank.

15. Click OK.

16. Click Yes to restart your computer.

Domain Name Service (DNS)

Domain Name Service (DNS) enables Internet clients and hosts to refer to one another using human-readable names like www.microsoft.com or www.sybex.com, rather than IP addresses like 207.68.156.61 or 206.100 .29.83, which are harder to remember and convey no information about the site.

DNS works by accepting a name as a parameter for establishing a connection. The TCP/IP client protocol suite then connects to a name server known to it (either because the name server is assigned with the IP address or its address was provided by a DHCP server) and provides that name server with the name to be looked up, or resolved. If the name server finds that name in its database, the name server will return the IP address to the requesting client. Otherwise, the name server will check its own name server for the name; this process continues until a name server that does not have a DNS server above it is reached. This top-level server resolves the address if the name is registered or returns an error message.

In either case the response is propagated back down through the hierarchy of DNS servers until it reaches the client. The response is also added to the database of all the servers down the hierarchy so that queries for that name can return a response faster in the future (this process is known as *caching*). In an intranet that is not connected to the Internet, the top-level name server is maintained by the owning company. On the Internet the top-level name server is maintained by the InterNIC organization, which was formed specifically for registering and maintaining a unique Internet name database.

The local caching of Internet names is required to keep the domain name system from becoming bogged down with name requests. Imagine if the single top-level name server at InterNIC had to respond to every name request generated by every Web browser on the planet. Quite obviously that system would quickly break down. The caching nature of name servers means that after the initial request, lower-hierarchy name servers can resolve a particular name themselves. This structure of cached database information is referred to as a *distributed database,* because the data is distributed to many servers to improve overall performance.

Name servers also propagate domain name updates and changes to name servers they serve. Because of the distributed nature of the DNS system and the number of name servers involved, an address change update can actually take days to propagate through the system during which name servers could provide an address that is no longer valid. This potential source of confusion is the trade-off for a system of this size that actually functions at all and typifies the DNS philosophy that access to information is more critical than instantaneous updates or guarantees of consistency.

Each name entry maintains with it a period of validity, after which the name server must again check with its name server for a data update. This system guarantees that name database information maintains some "freshness." InterNIC also now requires a small annual fee to keep domain names registered, so old names are not simply perpetuated in the DNS system unless the owner is willing to pay for their presence.

Most Internet clients (including Windows NT) maintain a HOSTS text file that implements a small and simple DNS table for quick resolution without going out to a DNS server. In Windows NT this file is maintained in the `c:\winnt\system32\drivers\etc\hosts` text file. (Replace the `c:\winnt` portion with your system directory.) Note that changes to the HOSTS file are not made, so you must manually update any names that become invalid if you chose to use this file.

WARNING Avoid using the HOSTS file to assign domain names. Your HOSTS file will not be updated when an IP address for a domain name changes, so all computers that rely on that HOSTS file will no longer be able to attach to that resource. You should use the HOSTS file only when a DNS server is not available.

Anatomy of a Domain Name

The domain name system exists as a tree structure of names, as shown in Figure 5.3. The root of this tree is the InterNIC primary database. Domain names are broken down into nodes, or sections separated by periods, that describe the path to the root of the DNS tree. For instance, the domain name `www.microsoft.com` contains three nodes, `www`, `microsoft`, and `com`. Each node can be up to 64 characters long (but few approach that length—after all, the point of the DNS system is convenience), but the total length of a domain name is limited to 255 characters no matter how many nodes it contains. Node names are currently case insensitive (i.e., `www` is equal to `WWW`) but that may change in the future.

Each branch of the DNS tree is a name server that is responsible for resolving names within its domain. For example, the `com` name server is the top-level name server for all domain names ending in `.com`, like `microsoft.com` or `hp.com`. The name server at `microsoft.com` is responsible for resolving names with the `microsoft.com` domain such as `www.microsoft.com`. This level of indirection can continue; for instance, `web1.www.microsoft.com` is a host known to the name server `www.microsoft.com`.

The above example is an oversimplification of the actual system. Once a domain name (such as `microsoft.com`) is registered with the `com` name server at InterNIC, the owner is free to create or delete subdomains underneath the registered domain name. For example, `www.microsoft.com` and `ftp.microsoft.com` can be created under the `microsoft.com` domain without registering that name with the higher-level name server as long as the domain name (`microsoft.com`) points to a host that is a name server and can resolve those subordinate domain names. That name server then resolves references below the `microsoft.com` domain and propagates the response back to the original requester.

If that host (`microsoft.com`) is not a name server, every host below it must also be registered with InterNIC (in this case, `www.microsoft.com` and `ftp.microsoft.com`) to be resolved. DNS does not provide any clear indication of the level at which a name is being resolved, but because of the distributed nature of the DNS tree, the level doesn't really matter. In fact, one of the policies of DNS is that the structure be as general and nonrestrictive as possible.

FIGURE 5.3

The tree structure of the domain name system

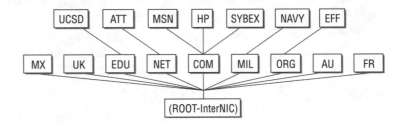

Do You Need This Service?

If you own a domain name and you want to create and delete subdomains without registering them with InterNIC, then you should install and provide the DNS service. Otherwise, you probably don't need to provide domain name service. You don't really need to maintain your own DNS server if your Internet Service Provider provides one. You can simply use the ISP's name servers. If you are using a Microsoft network, you are better off providing WINS service for the internal resolution of NetBIOS names, rather than using Internet domain names internally, unless your network is extremely large in which case you should be creating subdomains.

The one situation in which you would want to maintain this service (when you aren't going to create your own subdomains) is to use services on an Internet host that perform a reverse DNS lookup to verify the identity of each computer that is attached. Some services (especially ftp sites) will attempt to perform a reverse lookup on the IP address you provide to verify that your computer is a valid Internet host, not a hacker using a spoofed (forged) IP address.

A *reverse lookup* is a DNS resolve where an IP address is provided and a domain name is returned. For instance, if you attach to `ftp.microsoft.com` and you get the message that the connection was refused because you do not have a host name (or words to that effect), then no name server responded with a domain name for your IP address. If you were running a DNS server, that server would have confirmed your IP address by returning `clientname.yournetwork.com` as the domain name.

However, before you install a DNS server to avoid this problem, know that many ISPs will provide automatically generated domain names for any reverse lookup requested within their domain, precisely to keep this security measure from affecting their customers. Therefore, you may still not need to provide a DNS server to avoid this problem.

Your best bet is not to install a DNS server unless you know that a service you must use requires a reverse DNS lookup.

Multiple Server Names

Nothing prevents multiple server names from being registered for the same IP address—in fact this situation is quite common. If you have only one computer but you want to use service-related domain names like `ftp.you.org`, `www.you.org`, and `gopher.you.org` to point to that one machine, you can simply register all three names using the same IP address.

Installing DNS

Installing DNS is easy—configuring it is somewhat more difficult. After you've installed DNS server (see Exercise 5.2), you configure it using the DNS manager as shown in Exercise 5.3. Exercise 5.3 shows only a sample DNS configuration, as all installations are unique.

> **EXERCISE 5.2**
>
> ### Installing DNS
>
> 1. Select Start ➤ Settings ➤ Control Panel.
>
> 2. Double-click Network.
>
> 3. Click the Services tab.
>
> 4. Click Add.
>
> 5. Double-click Microsoft DNS Server.
>
> 6. Insert your Windows NT Server CD-ROM, verify the path to your installation files, and click Continue.
>
> 7. Click Close.
>
> 8. Click Yes to restart your computer.

Configuring to Serve DNS

Once you have installed the DNS manager, it will start automatically; however, before it can do anything useful, you have to install some DNS zones. In particular, you should create two primary DNS zones—one to hold host records for your domain and one to hold reverse mappings for those hosts. (A reverse mapping allows a computer to ask which Internet name goes with an IP address.) Exercise 5.3 shows you how to create these zones. Figure 5.4 shows the DNS manager.

FIGURE 5.4

The DNS manager

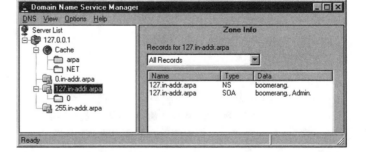

Exercise 5.3 is intended to introduce you to the DNS manager. It will not completely configure the DNS server for actual use on the Internet. You will need to confer with your ISP to determine exactly how your DNS server should be installed.

EXERCISE 5.3

Creating a Primary and a Reverse DNS Zone with the DNS Manager

1. Select Start ➤ Programs ➤ Administrative Tools ➤ DNS Manager.

2. Select New Server from the DNS menu.

3. Enter the host name for the computer that will be the DNS server.

4. Select the server that you have just created (click it).

5. Select New Zone Item from the DNS menu.

6. Select Primary and click Next.

7. Enter the name for your zone (the name for your domain, such as oeadm.org) and click Next.

8. Click Finish.

9. Select your server again.

10. Select New Zone Item from the DNS menu (again).

11. Select Primary and click Next.

12. Enter the in-addr.arpa name for your zone. For example, if your zone (Class C) network address is 192.5.212(.0), then you would type **212.5.192.in-addr.arpa**. Click Next.

13. Click Finish.

Once you have created zones, you can start adding host records. These are the records that map Internet names to IP addresses (such as bob.oeadm.org to 10.5.212.32). You should start with the computer that is hosting the DNS service. Exercise 5.4 shows you how.

EXERCISE 5.4

Adding a Host Record

1. Select Start ➤ Programs ➤ Administrative Tools ➤ DNS Manager.

2. Select New Host from the DNS menu.

3. Enter the host name (but not the network name). For example, if you have a computer with the Internet name of bob.oeadm.org on the zone oeadm.org, you would enter bob as the host name.

4. Enter the IP address of the host.

5. Select the Create Associated PTR Record check box. (You must have created the reverse mapping in the previous exercise.)

6. Click Add Host.

7. Click Done.

The preceding exercises presented a cursory overview of how to set up and configure DNS on a Windows NT Server. In addition to creating zones and host records, you can do many more things with DNS. For example, you can (and should) set up mail records so that Internet mail will be routed to the right computer. You can also set up subnets and other DNS servers that will resolve addresses for portions of your network. DNS is a complex and powerful service. Exercises 5.2, 5.3, and 5.4 should get you started.

You can find more information on DNS configuration and installation in the companion titles *MCSE: Windows NT Server 4 in the Enterprise Study Guide* and *MCSE: TCP/IP Study Guide*.

Windows Internet Name Service (WINS)

You've read about DNS and its ability to resolve Internet domain names, but what happens if you want to resolve the NetBIOS names of computers that are not on the same network? For instance, let's say you have a multihomed server with four network adapters in it. Two of the adapters serve Ethernet networks, and two serve Fast Ethernet networks. You've configured the server to route IP packets between the networks, but you notice that you cannot connect to shared resources from one network to another. This problem occurs because TCP/IP cannot route NetBIOS browser information; TCP/IP does not forward Ethernet broadcasts. WINS solves this problem by creating a distributed NetBIOS name database the same way DNS creates a distributed database of Internet domain names.

Once you install WINS on a server and point all your clients to it either manually or with a DHCP record, they will be able to resolve all the NetBIOS names on your internetwork.

Installing WINS

As with DNS, installing WINS is easy; but unlike DNS, configuring WINS is also easy. In fact, configuring WINS is completely automatic. Exercise 5.5 shows you how to install WINS. The only thing you need to know about the WINS manager is that it exists only to report certain statistics. If you want to experiment with the WINS manager, you can find it in the Administrative Tools menu.

EXERCISE 5.5

Installing and Configuring WINS

1. Select Start ➤ Settings ➤ Control Panel.

2. Double-click Network.

3. Click the Services tab.

4. Click Add.

5. Double-click Windows Internet Name Server.

6. Insert your Windows NT Server CD-ROM, verify the path to your installation files, and click Continue.

7. Click Close.

8. Click Yes to restart your computer.

Dynamic Host Configuration Protocol (DHCP)

The Dynamic Host Configuration Protocol (DHCP) makes implementing a TCP/IP network considerably easier. At the dawn of time, it was necessary to manually install a unique TCP/IP address, subnet mask, and default gateway (at least) for every computer on a network. It was easy to unintentionally reuse IP addresses (causing no end of confusion), mess up a subnet mask, or specify the wrong default router—all problems that can wreak havoc on your network installation and make you the butt of jokes at network integrator parties (had there ever been any).

Manual configuration also made reconfiguring an existing large network virtually impossible. If the idea of manually reconfiguring the IP addresses on every computer in your network between closing on Friday and opening on Monday doesn't stop you, the fact that you simply won't be finished in time will get you fired.

Oddly enough, it wasn't the pain of manual configuration that provided the impetus for automatic IP configuration. The originators of the Internet protocols were real integrators who had no fear of manual configuration, and they knew that if the network didn't work on Monday, they wouldn't get fired because no one else would be able to figure out how their network worked. But the challenge of the diskless workstation intrigued them. Without a hard disk to boot from, a computer could not be permanently configured with an IP address. Booting from a floppy disk was too easily implemented to appease them, so they wrote a protocol that broadcasts a plea for an IP address and a service that provided the address. They burned their protocol into the boot EPROMs of the network adapter cards; thus was born the automatic Boot Protocol (BootP) and the era of the network administrator who could be fired.

The original BootP protocol was somewhat limited in that it provided only an IP address, subnet mask, and default gateway. More complex networks require additional information, such as the address of a WINS server, or additional gateways. DHCP evolved from BootP to provide these (and any other) automatic configuration protocol addresses. DHCP can be forwarded by routers that forward BootP requests, thus removing the requirement that a DHCP server exist on each local network.

DHCP is a client/server protocol in that the booting client requests network information and a server that provides that information. The DHCP server is responsible for allocating network numbers so that no two clients get the same IP addresses. If you have multiple DHCP servers, you must configure them so that no two servers can provide the same address to different clients.

DCHP supports three models of IP allocation:

■ **Automatic allocation** assigns a permanent IP address to a host. Whenever a client boots, it will get the same automatically generated but
permanently assigned IP address.

■ **Dynamic allocation** assigns IP addresses for a limited period of time
(lease duration) or until the client relinquishes the address. This model
does not guarantee that the same address will be provided to that client
in the future.

■ **Manual allocation** assigns a specific IP address to a specific host permanently. This model assigns IP addresses for resources whose IP addresses
must be known because they provide some service to the network, such
as a file or name server.

All three allocation methods can be used on the same network as needs
dictate. Dynamic allocation is often the most useful because IP addresses can
be conserved. With dynamic allocation, IP address assignment is based on the
number of clients actually attached, rather than on the number of clients that
exist. In other words, dynamic allocation can reserve IP addresses for those
clients that are actually using the network at any one time without reserving
them for clients that are not in use.

DHCP will automatically avoid manually assigned addresses already in use
on the network. If you have a router with an assigned IP address, DHCP will
not assign that IP address. Proper implementations of DHCP provide service
to BootP clients (but the Windows NT implementation of DHCP currently
does not; Microsoft has committed to fixing this problem).

IP addresses are assigned in ranges called *scopes*. A scope is simply a range
of IP addresses that the DHCP server is allowed to assign, along with the
DHCP options that go along with that range. DHCP options are IP parame-
ters that would normally be assigned manually, such as the default gateway,
WINS server, and DNS server. These parameters can also be set as global
DHCP options if the same parameters apply to each of your DHCP scopes.
That way, you have to set up the parameter information only one time.

You can also specifically exclude IP addresses or ranges when you set up a
DHCP scope. An exclusion prevents DHCP from assigning IP addresses in the
excluded range. This technique is useful for situations in which more than one
DHCP server may assign the IP address or when you want to reserve a range
for future expansion.

Installing DHCP

Installing DHCP is just as easy as installing DNS and WINS. The installation procedure is shown in Exercise 5.6.

EXERCISE 5.6

Installing DHCP

1. Select Start ➤ Settings ➤ Control Panel.

2. Double-click Network.

3. Click the Services tab.

4. Click Add.

5. Double-click Microsoft DHCP Service.

6. Insert your Windows NT Server CD-ROM, verify the path to your installation files, and click Continue.

7. Click Close.

8. Click Yes to restart your computer.

Configuring to Serve DHCP

DHCP, being a complex service, can be difficult to configure, especially when you are using a multihomed server because each adapter will require its own DHCP scope. The basic rules are easy:

- Every subnet you define will require a unique scope.

- Each domain should have one set of global options to assign DNS and WINS addresses (assuming they are the same for every client).

- Every scope should contain a range of IP addresses that can be dynamically assigned.

- Every scope must provide a valid subnet mask.

- Every scope should provide a default router that points to the gateway to other networks.

- If you have a WINS server, provide its address with DHCP as a global option.

- Provide the address of your (or your ISP's) DNS server as a global option.

These rules cover most of the work. If you don't send a default router field with the DHCP message, your clients will not be able to route off their local network. Exercise 5.7 shows these basic steps in a DHCP configuration. Figure 5.5 shows the DHCP configuration manager.

FIGURE 5.5

The DHCP configuration manager

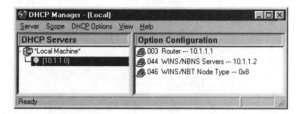

EXERCISE 5.7

Configuring DHCP

1. Select Start ➤ Programs ➤ Administrative Tools ➤ DHCP Manager.

2. Select Scope ➤ Create.

3. Enter the lowest IP address you wish to dynamically assign in Start Address. If you are using the 10 Class A domain for a private TCP/IP network, type **10.1.1.10**. This address provides nine numbers for static assignment to servers, routers, and print servers that may not work with DHCP services.

4. Enter the highest IP address in the subnet in End Address. For a Class C domain within the 10 Class A domain, this number is 10.1.1.254.

5. Enter the subnet mask for this scope in Subnet Mask. If you are creating a single scope for a Class C domain, this number should be 255.255.255.0.

EXERCISE 5.7 (CONTINUED FROM PREVIOUS PAGE)

6. Click OK.

7. Answer Yes to activate the scope now.

8. Double-click Local Machine to reveal local defined scopes.

9. Select the scope you just defined. If you are using the values in this example, this is scope 10.1.1.0. (Remember that .0 refers to the network.)

10. Select DHCP Options ➤ Scope.

11. Select option 003 Router in the Unused Options pick box.

12. Click Add->.

13. Click Value>>>.

14. Click Edit Array.

15. Enter the IP address of your router in the New IP Address input box. If you are using our sample values, type 10.1.1.1.

16. Click OK.

17. Close the DHCP Manager. Your server will now provide enough information for DHCP clients to operate on your network.

Summary

This whirlwind tour of the Internet protocols was brought to you by the letters I and P and by the number 10. The Internet protocols form the basis of all Internet services by providing a method for any two computers on connected networks to establish communications sessions.

Internet Protocol implements a simple packet-forwarding service with no guarantees of reliability or service. IP exists simply to get packets of data from one location to another across an internetwork.

Transmission Control Protocol adds the ability to provide reliable streams of information on top of an unreliable protocol like IP. TCP guarantees that all the data transmitted will arrive at the destination computer in order and free of errors. TCP also implements mechanisms to allow multiple simultaneous communication sessions to occur through the same network connection.

Domain Name Service provides a method for resolving human-readable computer names to Internet Protocol numbers in a manner that is scalable from a single organization to the entire global Internet.

Windows Internet Name Service provides a function similar to DNS for networks based on NetBIOS such as the Microsoft and IBM families of network products. WINS resolves NetBIOS computer names to IP addresses in NetBIOS over TCP/IP (NetBT) networks.

Dynamic Host Configuration Protocol allows you to automatically configure IP client computers from a centrally configured server. DHCP clients can request a range of information such as their IP address, subnet mask, and default gateway, as well as many other product-specific optional parameters.

The global Internet is based upon these fundamental Internet protocols. These protocols have proven their worth and their ability to operate well in packet-based networks of any size with the expansion and success of the Internet. Installing and configuring these protocols is a major step on the path to a fully functional Internet server.

Review Questions

1. You have a multihomed server with two network interfaces installed. All client computers can communicate with the server correctly, but you can attach only to resources shared by peers on the same physical data link; in addition, your browser does not show computers on the other network. What service should you install to correct the problem?

   A. DCHP

   B. DNS

   C. WINS

   D. TCP/IP

2. You've set up a single Fast Ethernet network based on TCP/IP. Your file server and primary domain controller also acts as a DHCP server. Everything works fine until you attach a router that connects to a T1 line attached to your new Internet Service Provider. You find that none of your clients seem to be able to attach to servers on the Internet. When you try to Ping an address you know exists on the Internet, you get an error message stating that the destination is unreachable. What is wrong?

   A. The WINS service is not correctly configured.

   B. You need to enable IP forwarding on the server.

   C. Your ISP is not providing DNS.

   D. The DHCP server did not assign a default gateway.

3. You are responsible for a network of 358 clients and 16 servers. You expect to add about 50 computers over the next two years to keep up with normal company growth. You are about to start the process of attaching your network to the Internet. How many bits of local address space should you request when you request your domain?

   A. 7

   B. 8

   C. 9

   D. 10

4. You are responsible for a TCP/IP domain of 3,488 computers. Assuming that you have not subnetted your original 12 bit local address space, what should your subnet mask be?

   A. 255.255.240.0

   B. 255.255.248.0

   C. 255.255.254.0

   D. 255.255.255.0

5. You have a multihomed server that serves three Ethernets. For some reason, only clients on the same data link as your Ethernet-to-T1 router can attach to the Internet. You check your server and verify that IP forwarding is set up, no conflicting IP addresses exist, and that every network adapter in the server shows the address of the router as the default route. What is wrong?

A. You must install DNS to resolve names across the network.

B. You need to install WINS for clients on other data links to see the router.

C. The DHCP server did not assign a default gateway.

D. You've specified more than one default route, but only one exists.

6. You have a 50-computer network, and you want to use a single server with three network adapters to attach to three different Ethernet network hubs so you can maximize your network bandwidth. One Ethernet network has 12 computers, one has 22 computers, and one has 16 computers. What is the smallest subnet mask that will work with your network?

A. 255.255.255.248

B. 255.255.255.240

C. 255.255.255.224

D. 255.255.255.192

CHAPTER

6

Managing Internet Services

So far in this book, you have learned what the Internet is and seen what a Web server can do for you (Chapter 1), investigated the requirements for hosting a Web site (Chapter 2), explored the features of operating systems and Web servers (Chapter 3), installed Internet Information Server (IIS) and Index Server (Chapter 4), and configured the TCP/IP protocols (Chapter 5). This chapter explores the features of IIS and Index Server and explains how to use the Microsoft Internet Service Manager (and Web pages) to control Internet services.

For IIS you will discover:

- How to set up a Web site, including virtual Web sites

- How to share files via FTP

- How to set up a Gopher tree

- How to work with keys and certificates

- How to configure MIME types, Internet Server Application Programming Interface (ISAPI) applications, and Common Gateway Interface (CGI) scripts

For Index Server you will learn:

- How Index Server works

- How to configure Index Server

- How to administer Index Server

Internet Information Server

IIS is easy to administer. Most of the time you spend administering a Web site will most likely be with other aspects of site maintenance, such as creating HTML content or managing the server computer and the network connection.

You do, however, have to set up your Web site in the first place, and Microsoft gives you two tools: Microsoft Internet Service Manager and Internet Service Manager HTML pages. You can perform most functions from both the Manager program and the HTML pages, but some functions require the Manager program.

Microsoft Internet Service Manager

When you installed IIS, you also installed the Microsoft Internet Service Manager program. You can start this program by clicking Start ➤ Programs ➤ Microsoft Internet Server (Common) ➤ Internet Service Manager. (See Figure 6.1 for a view of Microsoft Internet Service Manager.)

FIGURE 6.1

You administer your IIS from the Microsoft Internet Service Manager program.

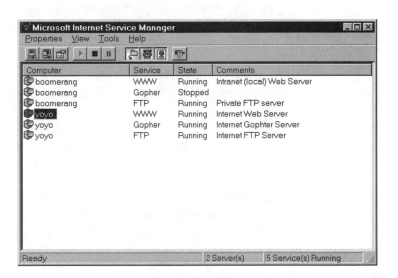

At first glance, Microsoft Internet Service Manager doesn't seem to ask very much of you. When you start the program, you will see a list of Internet services. You don't have to run the program from the same computer that is hosting the Web site, but if you do, you will see the three IIS WWW services: WWW, Gopher, and FTP.

Microsoft Internet Service Manager can manage Internet services on more than one computer. The Properties menu allows you to connect to specific other IIS servers in your network or to find all the servers in the Windows NT domain. Once you are viewing more than the three services for one IIS server, it makes sense to view that list in different ways. Specifically, the View menu allows you to view the servers and their services in the following ways:

- **By Server**—The Internet services are arranged in a tree structure with the server computer name at the base of each tree.

- **By Service**—This view places the type of service (FTP, Gopher, and WWW) at the roots of the trees, with the names of the servers below.

- **By Report**—This view of the services lists the Internet services individually. When you select this option, the Sort view options become available and you can sort the report by server, service, comment, or state.

The Tool menu contains just one menu item—Key Manager. Selecting this option starts the Key Manager program that allows you to create keys and install certificates in your Web server. You learn how to use this important program in the Key Manager section later in this chapter.

You will use the main Internet Service Manager program window mostly to start and stop services. An important feature of the Internet Service Manager is that you can start and stop each service individually. Many of the administrative changes you will make to the services (such as installing a key certificate) won't take effect until you stop and restart the service. You can stop and start a service either by selecting that service and then clicking the Stop button and the Play button on the button bar or by selecting the Stop Service and Start Service menu options in the Properties menu.

You can administer each service listed in the Microsoft Internet Service Manager window separately, and you configure each service by clicking the service and selecting Service Properties from the Properties menu. You also can configure these settings from the Internet Service Manager HTML pages.

Internet Service Manager HTML Pages

The Internet Service Manager HTML pages allow you to do almost everything that the Microsoft Internet Service Manager program allows you to do. Three exceptions are

- You cannot stop and start the services (WWW, Gopher, or FTP) from the HTML pages.

- You cannot configure keys or certificates. To configure keys and certificates, you need to launch the Key Manager program from the Service Manager.

- You cannot browse your domain from Internet servers.

When you use the Internet Service Manager HTML pages, you are configuring the services for a particular server. You will be able to configure the
WWW, FTP, and Gopher settings for that server. If you wish to administer a
different server using the HTML pages, you must connect to that server instead.

You can get to the Internet Service Manager primary HTML page by connecting to the `iisadmin` directory of that IIS server using Microsoft Internet
Explorer. (You must have Windows NT Challenge/Response enabled.) To
connect to the Internet Server on the server computer BOOMERANG, for
example, you would type the URL `http://BOOMERANG/iisadmin` into the
Address field of Internet Explorer. Figure 6.2 shows you the first HTML
administration page.

FIGURE 6.2

You can administer the
Internet Information
Server's WWW, FTP,
and Gopher services via
the Internet Service
Manager HTML pages.

Clicking the WWW, FTP, or Gopher hypertext links on the first HTML
administration page takes you to a sequence of Web pages that mimic the
appearance and behavior of the WWW, FTP, and Gopher Properties windows
in the Microsoft Internet Service Manager program. The next three sections
("WWW Properties," "FTP Properties," and "Gopher Properties") describe
what you can configure for each service.

In most—but not all—cases, administering the services via HTML is exactly the same as administering the services via the Microsoft Internet Service Manager program. For example, you can uncheck the Windows NT Challenge/ Response option from the HTML pages, but you will not be able to recheck it via the HTML pages (because using the HTML pages requires Windows NT Challenge/Response!). The differences between the program windows and the HTML pages are described in the following sections.

WWW Properties

You will find most of the important management features of your Web server in the Properties window of the Web service. (One exception is the Key and Certificates management tool that you access from the Tools menu of the Microsoft Internet Service Manager.) Four tabs cover various aspects of your Web site:

- **Service**—This tab controls basic aspects of how your Web site is presented to the operating system and to the Internet protocols.

- **Directories**—The whole point of a Web site is to allow remote users to access hypertext documents. Those documents reside in directories, which may all be in one place, reside in several places on your server, or even reside on other computers in your network.

- **Logging**—IIS, just like any other service, records its status and any error conditions to the Event log. In addition, IIS can log accesses to the Web site, to a text file, or to an ODBC database.

- **Advanced**—This tab allows you to restrict access to your Web site based on the network location of the client and also limit the amount of bandwidth the Web server will use.

The HTML pages have a similar set of "tabs" (actually, hypertext links) that take you to Web pages that perform the same functions as the tab-separated sections of the Internet Service Manager program. Compare Figures 6.3 and 6.4 to see the similarities between HTML pages and Service Manager program windows.

Service Tab

From this tab (or page), you configure the interface between IIS and the operating system. In order for Web browsers to connect to your site, your Web server needs a TCP port number. IIS allows you to specify an upper limit on

FIGURE 6.3

You can configure basic connectivity options such as the TCP port and the anonymous logon account from HTML pages.

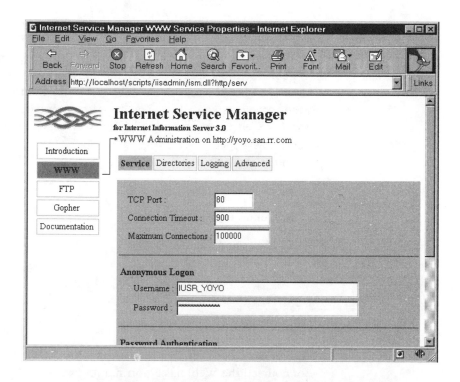

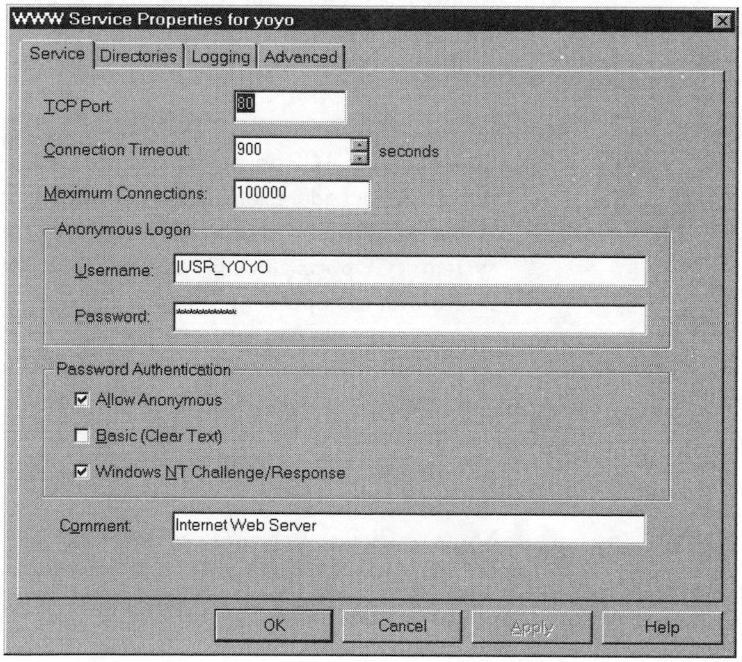

FIGURE 6.4

You can configure the same options from the Microsoft Internet Service Manager program and from the Internet Service Manager HTML pages.

how many browsers may simultaneously connect to your server and a time-out duration for connections that may have "hung."

Because IIS security is based on the security mechanisms of the operating system, you must specify a username for Web users who connect anonymously. When the user doesn't connect anonymously, you can specify what kinds of logons you allow. You can also enter a comment that will show up for this Web server when you list the Web servers in the Microsoft Internet Service Manager.

In the Service tab you can view and change the following service settings:

- TCP Port

- Connection Time-Out

- Maximum Connections

- Anonymous Logon

- Password Authentication

- Comment

TCP Port   Each Internet service that uses TCP/IP (such as FTP, Gopher, and [of course!] the Web) has a port number assigned to it. The port number that is usually reserved for the Web server on a computer is port 80. When you connect to a Web server without specifying a port number, your browser will attempt to connect to port 80 by default.

Don't confuse TCP ports with the port addresses of PC-compatible computers. A port address for a PC-compatible computer allows adapter cards (Ethernet adapters, SCSI adapters, etc.) to communicate with the operating system. TCP ports allow networking protocols (HTTP, FTP, etc.) to communicate with the operating system.

You don't have to connect to port 80, though. A Web server can be configured to respond to any available port number. Many individuals run Web servers on computers to which they don't have administrative permission. On these computers they can't use the regular port, so they set their Web servers to use port 8080.

Some restricted Web sites use nonstandard port numbers to discourage unauthorized users from finding the Web site, and some Web packages (but not IIS) use another port number (in addition to the regular port 80) to administer the

Web site. However, if you don't have a good reason to change this number, you should leave it as it is because using a nonstandard number makes it harder for people to browse your Web.

Connection Time-Out   The time-out value sets how long IIS will allow an HTTP connection to remain inactive before dropping the connection. You may wish to lengthen this setting if the connection to your site is slow or exhibits unusually long delays. The default is 900 seconds.

Maximum Connections   Some Web servers can serve more simultaneous Web requests than others. The default IIS setting is very generous (100,000!), but unless you have a very fast computer and a link to the Internet with tremendous bandwidth available, you should leave the default setting. Because refusing an HTTP connection takes almost as much computation time as satisfying it, you should not reduce this number for a server that is heavily loaded, either. Consider increasing the capacity of your server to handle HTTP requests instead.

Anonymous Logon   IIS uses the Windows NT and NTFS security mechanisms to protect access to HTML pages and other Web components (images, sounds, etc.). When someone browses an IIS Web site anonymously, that user's actions must be associated with a Windows NT user account for the operating system to know whether that user should be allowed to access the Web page (or sound or graphic or script).

When you install IIS, you also specify a username for IIS to use for all of these actions. This field shows that account name and allows you to change it. You should be careful about changing the name, though. If the new account name you specify doesn't exist in the Windows NT security system, then anonymous users won't be able to access the Web site!

The default for this setting is IUSER_<computername>. If your computer's name is WEBSERVER, then the default will be IUSER_WEBSERVER. The password is also generated automatically. If you change it here, you must also change it in the User Manager for Domains program.

Password Authentication   You can enable three authentication options for your IIS, and you can enable more than one option at a time:

- **Allow anonymous** allows access from any Web browser without requiring the user or the Web browser to provide a username and password. You would check this setting if you are hosting Web pages that you want everyone to be able to access.

- **Basic Clear Text** allows Web users with browsers that don't support Windows NT Challenge/Response authentication to give a username and password to access restricted Web pages. If you are implementing an intranet or want to allow members of your organization to access Web data over the Internet from non-Microsoft Web browsers, you would check this option.

- **Windows NT Challenge/Response** allows secure Web access without sending unencrypted passwords over a network that may be subject to eavesdropping. Microsoft's Internet Explorer supports this authentication method. You enable this setting if Microsoft Web browsers will access your Web site (and what site won't be?), and you must enable this setting if you want your site to require Secure Socket Layer protection for certain directories of your Web site. If you will use IIS to engage in commercial transactions over the Web (for example, to accept orders for products and to receive credit card numbers over the Internet), then you certainly should enable this option.

Comment   This field contains the text that shows up next to the Web server entry in the Microsoft Internet Manager window. If you have multiple Web servers on your network, this feature helps you tell them apart. The text you enter should describe the function or location (or both!) of the Web server.

Directories Tab

The structure of the directories in which the HTML pages are stored reflects the structure of the Web site because directories are an excellent way to organize information. Different parts of your Web site may need different security settings. (For example, you may want to allow everyone to access your company information page, employees to access internal memos, and only you to access the administration Web pages.) The easiest way to set up strong security is to store the various Web pages in different directories and to set different permissions on the directories.

You can easily set up a Web site when all the HTML files are stored in directories under the Web site home directory. (If you've installed IIS with its default settings and haven't created any virtual servers, the Web site home directory is the `WWWroot` subdirectory in the `InetPub` directory.)

But what if you don't have all the HTML files in one place? Perhaps you have already filled up one hard drive, or you want to publish HTML files directly from a CD-ROM drive, or you want to allow users on your network to have a Web subdirectory in their home directory. Perhaps different parts of your organization (such as the finance and marketing departments) are responsible for creating their own Web content that they store on their own servers.

Virtual directories allow you to combine directories and subdirectories that are scattered throughout your server and your network into a coherent Web site that Web users can browse from a single home page.

The Directories tab shows you the directories that are a part of the IIS Web site and allows you to configure how IIS uses each directory.

From within the Directories tab you can view and change the following settings:

- Directories

- Default Document

- Directory Browsing

Directories   When you click the Directories tab, you see a list of directories that IIS is publishing. Each entry has four values:

- **Directory**—The UNC path describes the location of the directory on the server or on the network.

- **Alias**—This value is where the directory will appear in the Web structure. It can be a home directory, or it can be a subdirectory elsewhere in the Web structure. It does not have to have the same name or be in the same place relative to the rest of the directories in the site.

- **Address**—This value describes the virtual server for which the directory will be in effect.

- **Error**—When IIS starts up it verifies that it can access each of the directories listed. If it encounters any difficulties, an error condition is reported on the directory list in addition to the more detailed error report that is written to the Event log.

Adding, Removing, and Editing Directories   You manipulate the list of directories through the three buttons at the bottom of the list (Add, Remove, and Edit) or, if you are using the HTML administrative pages, you can click the hypertext links (Remove, Edit) after each entry or the Add link at the end of the list. Figure 6.5 shows the WWW Service directory edit screen.

FIGURE 6.5

You configure WWW Service directory settings such as the location of the directory and which virtual server it will be in effect for in the Directory Properties window.

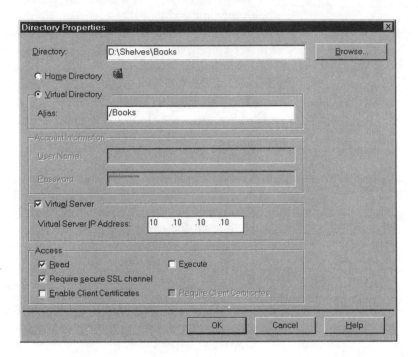

After you make changes to the list, you have the option of canceling those changes (using the Cancel button at the bottom of the window) or confirming them (using the Apply button at the bottom of the window). Clicking the Add button or selecting a directory and clicking Edit both bring up the same window showing the properties of an IIS directory. (If you clicked Add, the fields will be blank.)

The Directory Properties window or page allows you to fill (or edit) the following fields:

■ **Directory**—Here you enter the path to the directory. The directory may be anywhere in the Windows NT domain. If you enter a UNC path to a directory on another computer, the Account Information area will become active so that you can enter the username and password for IIS to use to connect to that network share. If you have installed dfs, you can enter a dfs tree location here. See Chapter 7 for a review of dfs.

- **Home Directory/Virtual Directory and Alias**—A directory may be either a home directory or a virtual directory. By setting a directory to be a home directory and also associating that directory with an IP address, you can create virtual servers. This directory will be the home directory (the directory at the base of the Web tree) for Web browsers that are connecting to the server using that IP address. The Alias describes where the directory will be in the Web structure if it is not the home directory for a virtual Web server. Virtual directories can also be tied to an IP address, making them a part of a virtual server's Web site.

- **Account Information**—When you specify a directory location that resides on another computer on the network, this field becomes active. You should enter the account name and password that IIS will use to access that directory.

- **Virtual Server**—Here you enter the IP address for the virtual server this directory is a part of (if this directory is a part of a virtual server). If you leave this field blank, then this directory will not be a part of a virtual server.

- **Access (Read and Execute)**—You can specify whether network users have read permission and/or execute permission for this directory. These permissions are in addition to (and evaluated independently of) the regular Windows NT security mechanisms. The user's account may have NTFS permission to read the directory and be denied from IIS, or vice versa, and in either case IIS will not supply the Web page to the Web browser. Only users with both permissions can browse pages in the directory. IIS requires Read permission for a user to browse a page in the directory and requires Execute permission to execute a script, ActiveX control, or other extension to IIS that uses the ISAPI DLL interface within the directory.

- **Require Secure Socket Layer**—If you are using IIS to conduct business over the Internet and you need secure and private communications between your customer and your Web server (in order to accept a credit card number, for example), you should require Secure Socket Layer communications on the directories that contain the credit-card-number–taking Web pages. You can require Secure Socket Layer communications only when you install a key and certificate in your server, however, and you must also enable Windows NT Challenge/Response. Web pages in this directory are available only to Web browsers that make the network connection using SSL.

- **Enable/Require Client Certificates**—By enabling client certificates, you allow network users (via their Web browsers) to present authorization certificates to your server. If you require client certificates, you can restrict access to the directory to users who (via their Web browsers) present valid certificates. This security measure is more flexible than username- and password-based security because it allows other trusted entities to create the certificates. You would use this mechanism when you don't really care who the user is, but you do care that someone has authorized him or her to access your site. Client certificates must, of course, be enabled before you can require them.

All Directories   The two other directory settings (applying to all directories, rather than to individual directories) are the default document and the directory browsing behavior.

- **Default document**—When a Web browser connects to the home directory of a Web site, or when a Web browser gives a URL path to a directory rather than to a specific HTML file, this setting names the HTML file (in that directory) that will be sent to the browser.

- **Directory browsing**—This check box allows you to select whether to display a list of the files in the directory when the directory does not contain a default document and the user doesn't specify any particular Web page (just the directory). Directory browsing helps people find resources on your Web site. (But many people are quite capable of making their own way around your Web site if you let them. If you want to make your Web site easy to use, use this setting.) On the other hand, if you don't want people to access certain Web pages without following the links you provide to those Web pages, you can disable Directory browsing. You should note, however, that disabling directory browsing is not a very strong security measure. If the individual has other access to files in the directory, then that user merely has to type your Web page location into a Web browser to access your page, regardless of your links.

In Exercise 6.1 you will configure WWW service directories and create a virtual Web site. Note that this example allows one directory (the Common directory) to appear in both the virtual Web site (when the Web server is responding as the IP address 10.10.10.10) and the regular, default Web site.

EXERCISE 6.1

Configuring the WWW Service Directories and Creating a Virtual Web Site

1. Log on to the Administrator account.

2. Open the My Computer icon on the desktop.

3. Open the C: drive

4. Select File ➤ New ➤ Folder from within the C: drive window and then change the new folder's name to VirtualTest.

5. Select File ➤ New ➤ Folder from within the C: drive window and then change the new folder's name to Common.

6. Start the Microsoft Internet Service Manager program. (Select Start ➤ Programs ➤ Microsoft Internet Server (Common) ➤ Internet Service Manager).

7. Click the WWW service and then select Properties ➤ Service Properties.

8. Click the Directories tab.

9. Click the Add button.

10. Type **C:\VirtualTest** in the Directory field.

11. Select the Home Directory option.

12. Select the Virtual Server option.

13. Type the Virtual Server IP address **10.10.10.10** (or select a free IP address in your subnet).

14. Click the OK button.

15. Click the Add button.

16. Type **C:\Common** in the Directory field.

17. Select the Virtual Directory option.

18. Type **/Common** in the Alias field.

19. Select the Virtual Server option.

20. Type the Virtual Server IP address **10.10.10.10** (or select the same free IP address in your subnet).

21. Click the OK button.

22. Click the Add button.

23. Type **C:\Common** in the Directory field.

24. Select the Virtual Directory option.

25. Type **/Common** in the Alias field.

26. Do not select the Virtual Server option. (Leave it unchecked.)

27. Click the OK button.

28. Click the Apply button.

29. Click the OK button.

30. Click the Stop button to stop the WWW service.

31. Click the Start button to start the WWW service.

32. Exit the Microsoft Internet Service Manager.

Logging Tab

An important feature of every Web server is logging. A Web browser should not only record error conditions to a system log but also be able to record accesses (successful and unsuccessful) to various parts of the Web site. This information helps the Web administrator (you!) know which parts of the Web site are being accessed, and how much. It also helps you troubleshoot problems with the Web site and to fend off attempts at unauthorized access to your Web site.

The logging tab of the Microsoft Internet Service Manager (or page of the Internet Service Manager HTML pages) allows you to configure how IIS logs access attempts (successful and not) to your Web site.

From the Logging tab you can view and change the following WWW Service logging settings:

- Enable Logging

- Log to File/Log to SQL or ODBC Database

- Log Format

- New Log Cycle

- Log File Directory

- ODBC Data Source

Enable/Disable   The first thing you should consider on this tab is whether or not you want to log access attempts to your Web site. This check box allows you to enable or disable the logging of access attempts on your Web server.

You might disable logging if you don't care about security or the diagnostic help logging will give you, if you have very little free disk space, or if you need the minimal performance improvement that disabling logging will give you. Since properly configured logging will take up very little disk space and logging has very little overhead, you should not seriously consider the last two options good reasons for disabling logging.

If you disable logging, the rest of the options on this tab will be grayed out.

Log to File/Database   The next choice you have is whether you will log to a file or to a database. Logging to a file is simpler to configure because it does not require an ODBC data source on your server, but logging to a database allows you to use database tools to interpret, archive, and otherwise make use of the logged information.

Log Format   You can choose between the Standard format (which Microsoft has used in past versions of IIS) and the NCSA format (which some third-party tools can use to generate statistics and analyze the patterns of access to your Web site).

Open New Log   If you enable the Automatically open new log option, you can choose whether a new log is started every day, week, month, or every time the log grows to a certain preset size.

Log File Directory   This setting specifies where the log files will be stored on your server. This directory does not have to be (and, in fact, shouldn't be!) in a directory that your Web site makes accessible to the Internet.

OBDC Data Source   If you are logging access attempts to an ODBC data source rather than to a file, you must give IIS four pieces of information:

- **Name**—Your server can host several ODBC data sources, and each ODBC data source has a name. You must specify the name of the ODBC data source you will use.

- **Table**—Each ODBC data source can contain many tables. You must enter the name of the table that the log data will be written to.

- **Username**—IIS requires a username to access the ODBC source. (ODBC data sources can give different levels of access to different users, and IIS must be given a username that has sufficient access to add data to the ODBC table.)

- **Password**—IIS will use this password with the above username to connect to the ODBC data source. The password must match the actual password for that username.

Chapter 13 covers ODBC data sources in greater detail. Refer to that chapter for examples of how to connect to ODBC data sources. Refer to Chapter 8 on security and Chapter 15 on performance tuning and optimizing for discussions on what to look for in the logged data to keep your IIS server secure and running smoothly.

Advanced Tab

You use this tab (or HTML page) to restrict access to your Web site based on the Web browser's source. You can also limit how much network bandwidth your Web server will use.

In the Advanced tab you can view and change the following WWW Service settings:

- Default Access

- Exceptions

- Maximum Network Use

Default Access   The purpose of this setting is to determine the meaning of the list of network locations that follow. Your server will either allow access to any browser except one coming from any of the listed locations or deny access to any browser except one coming from one of the listed locations.

Exceptions   This list details the IP network and station addresses that are either specifically allowed or disallowed access to your Web server. (Whether they are allowed or disallowed depends on the setting of the previous option.)

Maximum Network Use   This setting allows you to limit how much bandwidth your Internet server will use. You can configure your IIS server to only use 500Kbps of your T1 leased line, for example. This setting is very useful when you need to use your network connection for purposes other than hosting Internet information.

The Maximum Network Use setting applies for all of the Internet services provided by IIS (WWW, FTP, and Gopher.)

In Exercise 6.2 you set limits on who may access your Web server and how much bandwidth the server will use.

FTP Properties

The FTP protocol is much older than HTTP (the protocol used by Web servers and browsers). While HTTP is still evolving (even IIS does not yet support all the new features of HTTP v1.1), FTP has been a stable protocol for years.

The purpose of FTP is to store and retrieve files on remote computers over the Internet. Although you can also use Web sites to make files available over the Internet, most Web sites providing files for download are one directional—you just download files, not upload them. In contrast, FTP is bidirectional—you can place files on a server (if you have permission) as well as retrieve them.

FTP and HTTP complement each other. Many Web administrators use FTP for remote management of files that make up a Web site. When you are familiar with the tools, you can easily FTP to a directory containing Web pages, download them to your local computer, modify them, and then put them back using FTP.

Like the WWW service, the Properties program window for the FTP service is divided into tabs, and the HTML pages for managing the FTP service has equivalent hyperlinks. The tabs are Messages, Directories, Logging, and Advanced.

EXERCISE 6.2

Limiting WWW Service Access

1. Log on to the Administrator account.

2. Start the Microsoft Internet Service Manager program. (Select Start ➤ Programs ➤ Microsoft Internet Server (Common) ➤ Internet Service Manager.)

3. Click the WWW service and then select Properties ➤ Service Properties.

4. Click the Advanced tab.

5. Click the Add button.

6. Type the IP address **10.10.10.34**.

7. Click the OK button.

8. Click the Add button.

9. Select the Group of computers option.

10. Type the IP address **10.10.11.0** and the subnet mask of **255.255.255.0**.

11. Click the OK button.

12. Click the Limit Network Use by all Internet Services on this computer option. The computer will remind you that this will limit the network use for all Internet services.

13. Click Yes.

14. Change the KB/S value to 1,024.

15. Click the Apply button and then click the OK button.

16. Click the Stop button to stop the WWW service.

17. Click the Start button to start the WWW service.

18. Exit the Microsoft Internet Service Manager.

Service

You configure the port, time-out, number of simultaneous connections, the anonymous account that IIS will use, and the comment for the service the same way you do for the WWW service. The only significant differences are in the default values.

FTP responds to port 21. (That low number is a reminder that FTP was developed way back in the dawn of Internet time.) You shouldn't change this value because nobody will be able to find your FTP server if you do.

The default time-out is also much longer than it is for the WWW service for two reasons:

- HTTP requests are made by Web browsers, which do not pause to think or to look up what they are requesting from your server.

- FTP sessions normally last much longer than HTTP connections do.

HTTP (as implemented by most Web browsers and servers) is a stateless protocol where the browser makes the connection, requests the Web page or other file, and then drops the connection. FTP sessions, in contrast, often involve multiple uploads and downloads before the connection is dropped. The time-out will not drop an active connection (one where data or commands are being transferred), but it will drop a connection that has been inactive for the length of the time-out.

You should also note that the number of simultaneous connections (set by default to 1,000) is much less than the number of HTTP connections, partly because FTP connections last longer than HTTP connections and the amount of data transferred in an FTP session is usually much greater. If you find that FTP requests are placing an excessive load on your server, you may wish to reduce this number.

Messages

You should provide three messages for users of your FTP server (configured from the Messages tab or Messages HTML page):

- Welcome message

- Exit message

- Maximum connection message

Welcome Message   This message is sent when a user first connects to your FTP server. It should include a description of your server and the usage policies of your FTP server.

Exit Message   This message is sent when a user chooses to disconnect from your server. You should keep this message short and sweet.

Maximum Connections Message   This message will be sent when too many people are already connected to your server. In this message you should explain the usage limits for your server and suggest other FTP sites that network clients can connect to get the same files.

In Exercise 6.3 you limit the number of simultaneous connections and configure the messages for the FTP service on your IIS server computer.

EXERCISE 6.3

Limiting FTP Connections and Configuring the FTP Messages

1. Log on to the Administrator account.

2. Start the Microsoft Internet Service Manager program. (Select Start ➤ Programs ➤ Microsoft Internet Server (Common) ➤ Internet Service Manager.)

3. Click the FTP service and then select Properties ➤ Service Properties.

4. Click the Service tab. Change the Maximum Connections field value to 100.

5. Click the Messages tab.

6. Type **Welcome to my FTP server.** in the Welcome Message field.

7. Type **Thank you and come again!** in the Exit Message field.

8. Type **We're so sorry, but we can only accept 100 simultaneous connections. Please try again later.** in the Maximum connections message field.

9. Click the Apply button and then the OK button.

10. Stop and then restart the FTP service.

11. Exit the Microsoft Internet Service Manager.

Directories

This tab of the FTP Service Properties window is similar to the Directory tab of the WWW Service Properties window. You add, edit, and remove directories the same way you do for the WWW service, and they have the same options (virtual, home, etc.) as WWW directories do. (FTP does not support virtual FTP Servers, however, so you can't associate an IP number with a directory.) If you make a directory that resides on a remote computer a part of your FTP site, then (just like the WWW directories) you will have to give a username and password for the FTP service to use to log on to that remote computer.

- **Directory**—This setting specifies the location of the directory (UNC path or path with a drive letter).

- **Alias**—This setting specifies where the directory will appear in the FTP site to FTP clients.

- **Error**—If the FTP server cannot serve the directory, an error message will be displayed here and a more detailed error report will be written to the Event log.

You edit the FTP directories just like you do the WWW directories. Click a directory and then click the Edit button or the Delete button, or click the Add button to bring up a new (blank) directory window.

Note that when you add, edit, or delete these entries you are not adding, editing, or deleting the actual directories, only IIS's use of them.

- **Directory Properties**—The Directory Properties window is *almost* identical to the Directory Properties window for the WWW service. However, you cannot limit access to the directory based on IP address (i.e., no virtual FTP servers), the FTP service does not support SSL and Certificates, and FTP supports Read and Write access instead of Read and Execute. Note that the FTP service does not support Secure Socket Layer communications, so you do not have an option to require Secure Socket Layer or enable client certificates for a directory.

- **Directory Listing Style**—When an FTP client requests a directory listing, you can specify whether to send it in UNIX or MS-DOS style.

Logging

Logging for the FTP service is configured the same way as for the WWW service. Refer to the previous section for a description of each field in this tab.

Advanced

The Advanced FTP Service features are also exactly the same as they are in the WWW service. Refer to the previous section for a description of the fields.

Gopher Properties

Gopher briefly (by just a few years) predates the World Wide Web. Gopher is an Internet service that allows you to provide information in a structured way. Gopher sites comprise links that are like directories (and implemented as directories in IIS) but that can also contain links to other Gopher servers over the Internet as well as text and data files.

The Gopher service is even easier to configure than the WWW and FTP services. You configure Gopher the same way, by using the Properties window for the service or by using the Gopher section of the Internet Service Manager HTML pages. The Gopher Service Properties window (and HTML pages) is divided into four sections (identified by tabs in the Internet Service Manger program and by hypertext buttons in the HTML pages): Service, Directories, Logging, and Advanced.

Service

You configure the general properties of the Gopher service just like you do the WWW and FTP services. The Service tab has almost all the same fields as WWW and FTP (plus two new ones, which identify the Service Administrator). However, the defaults are somewhat different.

- **Port, time-out, maximum**—The default port for Gopher is port 70. The default connection time-out is 900 seconds, and the default maximum number of simultaneous connections is 1,000. You shouldn't change these settings without good reason.

- **Service administrator**—Two fields identify the service administrator. Unlike the other user account fields in IIS, the service does not use these fields to log on to anything. These fields identify the name and e-mail address of the service administrator in case Gopher clients need to send a message reporting a problem with the service or with the data.

- **Anonymous logon**—The Gopher services use the anonymous logon fields (username and password) just as the other services do to provide access to the Gopher data when the user logs on anonymously. The account these fields describe does not have to be the same account as for the WWW and FTP services. If it is different, then a user accessing the Gopher tree anonymously may have different access privileges than a user accessing the WWW or FTP services anonymously.

- **Comment**—In this field you can place a comment that will appear when the server is listed in the Microsoft Internet Services Manager list of services.

Directories

Like WWW and FTP data, Gopher data is stored in directories, and you use the same interface (the Directories tab of the Gopher Service Properties window or of the Gopher Service Properties HTML page) to configure the directories.

When you select the Directories tab, you are presented with a list of the directories that are hosting Gopher data. To delete a directory entry, select that entry and click the Remove button. To Edit an entry, select that entry and click the Edit Properties button. To add a new entry, click the Add button.

The fields in the directories list are as follows:

- **Directory**—This field specifies the location of the directory (UNC path or path with a drive letter).

- **Alias**—This field specifies where the directory will appear in the FTP site to FTP clients.

- **Error**—If the FTP server cannot serve the directory, an error message will be displayed here and a more detailed report will be written to the Event Log.

Note that when you add, edit, or delete these entries, you are not adding, editing, or deleting the actual directories, only IIS's use of them.

- **Directory Properties**—When you click the Add or Edit button, you will see the Directory Properties window for that directory. For the Gopher service, you must provide the directory path (UNC path or regular path with a drive letter), whether it is the home or a virtual directory, an alias name, and if you entered a path to another computer for the directory, a username and password for that computer. Gopher does not support Secure Socket Layer or Client Certificates. Because Gopher clients can only read documents and links, you do not need to configure any security settings for the directories here. (On the NTFS directories themselves, though, you will set permissions for the anonymous user account.)

Logging

Logging for the Gopher service is configured the same way as logging is configured for the WWW service. Refer to the previous section for a description of each field in this tab.

Advanced

The advanced Gopher Service features are also exactly the same as they are in the WWW service. Refer to the previous section for a description of the fields.

Using Key Manager

Some functions of the IIS Web service (most notably, the option for requiring Secure Socket Layers on a directory) require you to install a certified key in your IIS server. You configure keys (and certificate requests and replies) from Key Manager, which is a separate program that you can run directly or start by selecting Tools ➤ Key Manager from the Key Manager program to create keys and use certificates. See Figure 6.6 for a view of Key Manager.

FIGURE 6.6

The Key Manager program is where you create keys and install certificates for the WWW service.

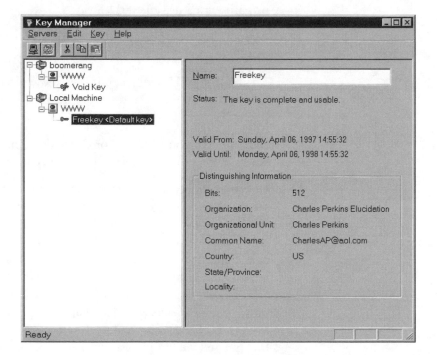

Keys and How They Work

IIS keys do for software what regular keys do in the physical world. They protect things by allowing only authorized people to access them. While a physical key might secure a house or a car, IIS keys secure the communications between the client Web browsers and your Web server.

When a client Web browser attempts to make a secure connection to your Web server (using the Secure Socket Layer mechanism and using the HTTPS protocol), the browser receives a key from the server to secure what it sends your Web server. The public key encryption mechanism uses this key to establish a secure communications channel.

The Secure Socket Layer uses public key encryption to protect the messages sent between the Web browser and the Web server. The algorithm is complex, but essentially it uses one key to scramble the message so that only the other key can unscramble it. Anyone eavesdropping on the exchange of information will see only random numbers—not messages. The private nature of encrypted communications is important if you want to be able to use the Web for commerce (i.e., to accept credit card numbers for purchases from your Web site).

A separate but related feature that IIS supports is Certificates and Certificate Authorities. With just Secure Socket Layer and HTTPS, client Web browsers can make secure connections to your Web server, but the users of those Web browsers have no assurance that you are who you say you are. When an individual visits your Web site, that person can assume that you are a legitimate business selling software or any other product over the Web, but you could just as well be an impostor with a bogus Web site, illicitly set up by unscrupulous individuals to capture credit card numbers.

Certificates and certificate authorities assure Web users that your Web site is registered with a responsible organization and is safe to visit. A certificate is a message from that responsible organization (the certificate authority) that identifies your server and resides on your server. Your server can give that message to Web browsers to identify itself.

Microsoft IIS requires a certificate from a certificate authority before you can require SSL on a directory. (The Require SSL option is grayed out in the WWW Service Properties Directory Properties windows until you install a valid certificate in a key for your Web server.)

Connecting to Servers and Viewing Keys

You can use Key Manager to manage the keys of several servers. When you start the Key Manager program, you will see the WWW server(s) on the local computer. You connect to additional servers using the Connect to Machine menu option of the Server menu.

The Key Manager main window has two panels. The left side shows the WWW servers you are connected to and the keys that are configured for those servers. You can expand or collapse the view of a particular server or computer by clicking the Plus icon next to the computer or WWW entry.

The right side of the window details a selected key. You can see the key's name, its status, the range of time it is valid for, and the distinguishing information for the key that you enter when you create the key.

When you double-click the key or select Properties from the Key menu, you see the Server Connection information for that key. This window specifies how your Web server uses the key. You can set the key use to None, in which case the key will not be sent to client Web browsers. You can set the key use to Default, in which case the key is visible to all Web browsers that connect to your site. The third option is to limit the use of the key to a certain (server) IP address. This third option links the use of this key to a virtual server. You would use this option with the virtual server options of your WWW service.

Generating Keys

You generate keys from the Create New Key menu option of the Key menu. (Select a WWW server to contain the key first.) The key name and the password identify the key. The Bits field sets the strength of the key. (Depending on the version, you may be limited to 512 bits, or you may be able to select a stronger length such as 1024 or greater bits.) The Request File field at the bottom of the window describes the file the key certificate request will be placed in when you click the OK button.

The Distinguishing Information fields in the middle of the window describe your organization. This information (plus the identity of your Web server) is what the certificate authority will be "signing."

After you click OK and verify the password for the key (by reentering it), you will be asked for an Administrator e-mail address and phone number. The certificate authority may use this information (along with other information that a certificate authority may require) to verify that the certificate request came from you. Once you enter this information, Key Manager will create a text file containing the certificate request.

You will then see a key with a hash through it, and the key status will report that the key still requires a certificate. In order to make the key complete and useable, you must send the key to a certificate authority. You can send your request to various certificate authorities, and certain software even enables you to be your own certificate authority. The certificate authority mentioned in the Microsoft Help information is VeriSign. (You can visit the VeriSign Web site at `http://www.verisign.com/microsoft` for more information.)

After you submit the request to the certificate authority (usually via e-mail, with other information and perhaps a fee sent via other means), you should receive a file containing a certificate you can install in the key you created. You install a certificate (in the form of a text file) by selecting Install Key Certificate from the Key menu and selecting the file that contains the certificate. You will have to enter the password for the key. After you do so, your key's status will change to complete and usable. You will then be able to require Secure Socket Layer on directories in your WWW service.

Moving, Importing, and Exporting Keys

Once you have installed a key, you can move the key between WWW servers using the cut, copy, and paste options in the Edit menu. You can also export the key to a backup file and import the key from a backup file or a keyset file. (Some security programs that create and manage keys store those keys in *keysets,* which are special files on the hard disk.)

Adding MIME Types, Registering ISAPI Applications, and Enabling CGI Scripts

The preceding sections on Microsoft Internet Service Manager and on Key Manager tell you all you need to know to manage a simple Internet site. Many Web administrators manage Web sites that are informational in nature and use only text and images. However, some Web designers and builders (yourself included, perhaps) will want to go beyond these simple static pages.

The strength of the World Wide Web is its flexibility. The original breakthrough of the Web was graphics. Arcane UNIX commands no longer barred all but the most technically inclined individuals from using the Internet. With the Web you can point and click your way around the world.

Now in addition to text and graphics, you can also embed sound and even video in your Web pages. You can include programs (written in Java or JavaScript), embed ActiveX controls, and encapsulate three-dimensional objects made with the Virtual Reality Markup Language.

To support the various elements that people embed in Web pages, and to make building dynamic Web pages easier, Microsoft has made IIS *extensible* (i.e., you can extend its functionality). You can add MIME (which stands for Multimedia Internet Mail Extensions) types so that IIS can inform Web browsers what they are downloading and how to handle it, and you can register extensions that will be recognized as ISAPI or CGI scripts that the server should handle itself rather than just sending as is to the client Web browser. The tool you use to configure the MIME types and the ISAPI or CGI extensions is the Registry Editor.

MIME Types

When a Web browser requests a file from the Web server, in addition to sending the file, IIS will also tell the Web browser what kind of file it is. If the browser understands the file type, then the browser can present the file to the user (embed a graphic in the page, play a sound, or launch another program that can display the file such as an Adobe Acrobat PDF viewer). To provide the necessary information to the Web browser, however, IIS has to know what kind of file it is dealing with. IIS gets this information by comparing the extension of the file to a list of extensions in the Windows NT registry. (See Figure 6.7 for a view of that list.) You can extend IIS to understand new file types by adding entries to that list.

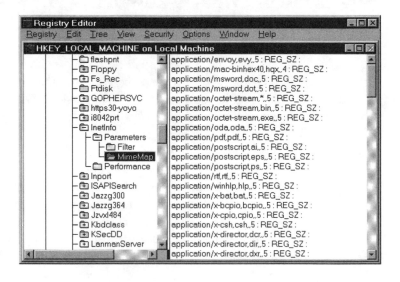

The list of MIME entries is stored in the location `HKEY_LOCAL_MACHINE\` `SYSTEM\CurrentControlSet\Services\Inetinfo\Parameters\MimeMap`. Each entry is the name of an empty REG_SZ value. The format of the MIME names follows: `<mime type>,<filename extens.>,<gopher type>`. The `<mime type>` is usually of two parts, separated by a slash, for example, `text/` `html` or `image/gif`.

ISAPI and CGI

MIME describes files that are handled differently than regular HTML pages by the Web browser. ISAPI and CGI describe files that are handled differently than regular HTML pages by your IIS server.

Sometimes you want to return dynamic data created by your server when the Web client asks for the Web page, for example, a Web page counter that tracks the number of accesses to the page. That counter will be different for each access to the page, and it requires the server to generate the HTML code dynamically when the page is accessed. This is a good example of what ISAPI and CGI do.

ISAPI and CGI do the same thing but in slightly different fashions—they allow you to write programs that run on your IIS server and generate Web pages dynamically. ISAPI describes how you can write Dynamic Link Libraries (DLLs) that IIS can call directly, and CGI describes how you can write programs that generate Web pages in C, Perl, or any other programming language. CGI is a standard feature of many WWW server software packages, while Microsoft developed ISAPI for IIS. The primary benefit of ISAPI is greater speed than CGI because ISAPI DLLs can be cached in memory, while CGI programs and scripts are usually stored on the hard drive and are loaded from the hard drive for each execution of a CGI script.

As with MIME, file extensions are the key to ISAPI DLLs and CGI scripts. IIS checks the extension against a list of extensions in the registry key `HKEY_LOCAL_MACHINE\SYSTEM\CurrentControlSet\Services\W3SVC\` `Parameters\Script Map`. The list contains REG_SZ values, with the extension for the name and the path to the interpreter or DLL as the value. (See Figure 6.8 for a view of a CGI and ISAPI list.) Note that most of the entries are for ISAPI DLLs, but the `.bat` entry points to the `cmd.exe` program (the command line) as a batch file script interpreter.

You add ISAPI and CGI entries just like you do MIME entries, by adding values to the list. However, for ISAPI and CGI you must also make sure that

FIGURE 6.8

IIS compares the file
extension of a requested
file to the list of extensions
in the registry to determine
whether to send the file to
the Web browser as-is
or to feed it through an
ISAPI DLL or a CGI
program first.

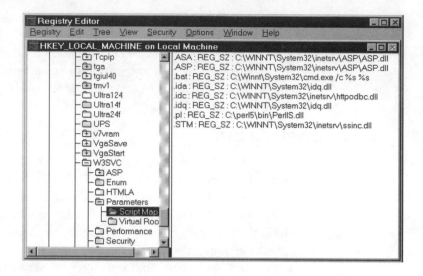

the Web user's user account has NTFS permission to run the DLL or CGI
interpreter—and (for DLLs) IIS directory Execute permission—for the directory that contains the DLL executable file. Also, if the DLL or CGI program
runs a script, then that user will need read access to the directory that contains
the script.

The actual creation of such dynamic Web pages is the subject of Chapters 10
through 13. The information in this chapter, however, should be sufficient for
you to manage the mechanisms (the CGI programs and the ISAPI DLLs) that
allow you to create that compelling dynamic content.

In Exercise 6.4 you register the .bat extension and the cmd.exe command
interpreter as a CGI scripting language.

WARNING

Don't leave this option enabled unless you really know what you are doing!
This exercise is an example only, so after you perform the exercise, you
should remove the CGI entry you just added. The Windows NT command
prompt is a powerful scripting tool, but it is too easily exploited by intruders
who may wish to access your system without your authorization.

EXERCISE 6.4

Configuring CMD.EXE as a CGI Interpreter

1. Log on to the Administrator account.

2. Start the Registry Editor. (Select Start ➤ Run and then type **Regedt32 .exe** in the Open: field. Click OK.)

3. Open the System key. (Double-click the plus sign.)

4. Open the Current Control Set key.

5. Open the Services key.

6. Open the W3SVC key.

7. Open the Parameters key.

8. Open the Script Map key.

9. Select Edit ➤ Add Value

10. Type **.bat** in the Value Name field. Click OK.

11. Type **C:\Winnt\System32\cmd.exe /c %s %s** in the String field and then click OK.

12. Close and exit the registry.

13. Stop and restart the IIS WWW Service.

Index Server

One ISAPI program that you have already installed (you did this in Chapter 4, believe it or not!) is Microsoft Index Server. Index Server is actually implemented as a set of DLLs that Microsoft IIS calls when a Web browser accesses a certain kind of Web page.

Indexing

Index Server (as you may have guessed) *indexes* your Web pages. It builds an index of the words in the files in your Web site and lists in that index which files contain each of those words. That sounds like a complex and tedious task, but it is the sort of thing that computers are good at.

Index Server actually creates a number of index files (the Master Index, shadow indexes, and so on, that you'll learn more about later) and keeps those index files in a directory called the `Catalog`. The default directory name for the `Catalog` is `Catalog.wci` in the `InetPub` directory.

The first time someone asks Index Server where to find a word or phrase (and periodically thereafter), Index Server goes through all of the files from the root of your Web server on down, creating (or updating) those index files. The words in the query are compared against the words in the indexes and references to those documents that satisfy the query are passed back to the person who requested the information.

Querying and Indexing

The query and search process gets a bit more complicated when you examine exactly how the user (via the Web browser) presents the query to the Index Server, how the Index Server satisfies the request, and how the results from Index Server are returned to the user in HTML form. The process is as follows:

1. The user enters a query phrase into a text field. The query may simply consist of words to be matched or perhaps a complex description of just what sort of documents the user wants to find.

2. The user presses the Enter key or clicks the Search button.

3. IIS passes the query string and the `.idq` file (indicated in the query string) to the Index Server DLL.

4. The Index Server DLL parses the `.idq` file to determine how Index Server should perform the search.

5. Index Server updates the indexes if necessary and then searches them to find documents that match the user's query.

6. Index Server formats results according to the description of how the results should be formatted in the .htx file that was specified in the .idq file.

7. Index Server returns the newly created HTML file to the user's Web browser.

When indexing your Web documents (also called your *corpus*), Index Server starts small and builds up. First, for each document, Index Server builds a word list. Those word lists exist in memory and are quickly built and searched. When the word lists get large enough, they are combined into structures on disk called *shadow indexes* in a process called a *shadow merge*. A shadow index is not very compressed because it is optimized for speed of indexing. The master index, in contrast, uses a compressed data structure that takes less disk space and is very fast to search. Shadow indexes can be combined in an *annealing merge,* and the process of combining all of the shadow indexes into a master index is called a *master merge*. After a master merge, all of the shadow indexes are deleted.

Several registry settings found in the following section of the Registry: HKEY_ LOCAL_MACHINE\SYSTEM\CurrentControlSet\Control\contentindex allow you to set criteria that will force a master merge. For example:

- MasterMergeTime sets a specific time each day for a master merge.

- MaxFreshCount causes a master merge when you have a large number of changed documents.

- MinDiskFreeForceMerge forces a merge when disk space gets low.

- MaxShadowIndexSize forces a master merge when the cumulative size of the indexes exceeds a threshold.

Interfacing Queries to Your Web Pages

Interfacing queries to your Web pages can be as simple or as complex as you want to make it. To allow simple queries of your whole site, all you have to do is provide a link on your Web pages to a sample Web page that was installed when you installed the IIS software—link to /samples/search/ query.htm on your own computer and you are done.

You can find out how to create custom search pages with your own graphics that search for particular types of information on your Web site in Chapters 10, 11, and 12. Chapter 12 also shows you how to create multiple master indexes.

Since the location of the master index is specified in the `.idq` file and creating Web pages (including `.idq` files) is the subject of Chapters 10, 11, and 12, you will be better prepared to customize how your Index Server Web pages at that point.

Using Filters

Index Server searches and indexes text, and many kinds of documents can contain text. An HTML file is just one kind of text file; another is Microsoft Word file, and Plain Text files also (obviously) contain text. Each kind of file stores text in a slightly different fashion, so Index Server needs to have some sort of mechanism to translate the different file formats in order to conduct a thorough search.

Index Server uses filters to perform the file format transformation. HTML, Microsoft Word, Excel, PowerPoint, and Plain Text are file formats that Index Server supports by default. Binary files are also a supported file type, but Index Server doesn't search them for words; only the file names and file attributes are indexed.

You can also add your own filter DLLs to Index Server, but the process is not easy. The HTML Help files for Index Server describe this process in some detail.

Administering Index Server

Now that you know what Microsoft Index Server does and a little bit about how it does it, you need to know how to administer Index Server. Unlike the Web server itself, Index Server does not have a program to manage it. You do all of the managing of Index Server from HTML pages.

You can reach the Index Server HTML pages by selecting Start ➤ Programs ➤ Microsoft Index Server (Common) ➤ Index Server Administration, or you can simply point your Web browser to the `/srchadm/admin.htm` page on your IIS server. (You can even put a link to this page on your home page or include it in your browser's hot list.)

Interestingly enough, the Index Server administrative pages introduce another type of Web page, with an `.ida` extension instead of `.idq`. Accessing an `.ida` Web page with the certain commands embedded in the page will cause Index Server to perform the administrative functions related to those commands.

The first Index Server Administration page (see Figure 6.9) has five buttons:

- View/Update indexing of virtual roots

- View unfiltered documents

- Index statistics

- Force merge now

- Force scan virtual roots

FIGURE 6.9

You administer Index Server from the srchadm HTML pages on your IIS server computer.

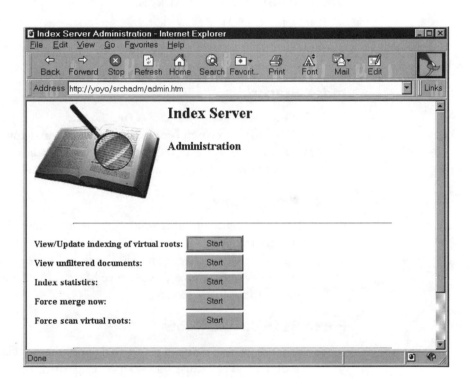

View/Update Indexing of Virtual Roots

This page (or pages, if the list has more than ten pages, it will be continued on the next page) shows you which directories are being indexed. By default, all Web directories that you define in the Directories tab of WWW Service Properties will be indexed. The check mark beside each entry controls whether or not that directory will be indexed. Since you probably don't want CGI scripts or the search administration pages to show up in searches, you can uncheck those entries. You should uncheck any other similar directories.

If you have set up security on your Web server properly, you don't have to worry about the search engine giving out references to pages that the Web user shouldn't have access to. Limiting the search engine is not a security measure—it is an action you can take to make searches on your site return better information.

View Unfiltered Documents

If Index Server has been unable to filter some documents, you can view them here. This page can help you diagnose indexing problems with Index Server filters.

Index Statistics

The Index Statistics page shows you the state of the indexes of your documents—that is, the number of queries pending and completed—as well as the number and total size of the documents (at least the ones that are indexed) in your Web site. This page is a very useful tool for keeping track of your Web site.

Force Merge Now

Clicking this button returns you to the Index Server Administration page. This option tells the Index Server DLL to start merging the indexes in the background. (Index Server knows to start merging indexes when it processes an .ida file that contains a merge command. The Force Merge Now button sends exactly such an .ida file to the Index server.)

Force Scan Virtual Roots

This page displays a list of the virtual roots that you configured Index Server to search. You can cause Index Server to perform an incremental or a full scan for each directory, or to ignore that virtual root directory.

A full scan examines and indexes all the files in the directory. An incremental scan examines only files that have been changed since the last scan or are new to the directory.

In Exercise 6.5 you review the virtual roots that are being indexed by Index Server and then force a Master Merge.

EXERCISE 6.5

Review Virtual Roots and Force Master Merge

1. Log on to the Administrator account.

2. Open the Index Server Administrator main administration page. (Select Start ➤ Programs ➤ Microsoft Index Server (Common) ➤ Index Server Administration.)

3. Click the Start button next to View/Update Indexing of Virtual Roots.

4. Remove the check next to /srchadm.

5. Remove the check next to /iisadmin.

6. Click the Submit Changes button.

7. Click the Start button next to Force merge now.

8. Close the Web browser.

Summary

Managing IIS can be very simple (just install it and let it go) if your Internet hosting requirements are light. Microsoft doesn't sacrifice any capability for that simplicity, though. This Internet server contains everything you need to host even the most frequently accessed and feature-rich Internet site.

The three Internet services that IIS supports are WWW, FTP, and Gopher. FTP is most often used to send and retrieve files over the Internet. WWW provides an easy-to-use Internet interface and makes organizing and providing information over the Internet easy. Gopher performs a similar role to WWW but is text based only and has been eclipsed by WWW.

You can perform most of the WWW, FTP, and Gopher administration from either the Microsoft Internet Service Manager program or HTML pages. Two exceptions are Key Manager, which does not have an HTML counterpart, and the Index Server Administration pages, which do not have a program counterpart.

WWW, FTP, and Gopher data are all stored in directories, and you structure your Internet site by managing these directories. A virtual directory may reside anywhere on the server computer or even on another computer over the network. Directories can also have IP addresses associated with them, and when a directory has an IP address associated with it, that directory will appear to exist only on the virtual server corresponding to that IP address. This IP mechanism is how IIS implements virtual WWW servers.

Indexing is automatic with Index Server. While performing a search, Index Server confirms that the user has sufficient privileges to access the item. Only those items that the user has sufficient privilege to access will be returned to the user. A simple search page comes with the Index Server installation, and you can customize searches by making your own search pages.

Review Questions

1. Your main business is selling aluminum siding, but you have a second business in aluminum recycling. You want to set up a separate Web site for each business. What is your best option?

   A. Buy two Windows NT Server computers and run IIS on each.

   B. Install IIS twice on your Windows NT Server computer. Configure the second copy to respond to port 8080 instead of port 80.

   C. Register two IP addresses for your Windows NT Server computer running IIS. Create two home directories and WWW Service directory entries for each. Then assign each directory a different IP address in the Directories tab of the WWW Service Properties window.

   D. Register two IP addresses for your Windows NT Server computer running IIS. Place the files for one business in the home directory (wwwroot). Create a new directory for the other business and in the Directories tab of the WWW Service Properties window make that directory a virtual directory (give it the alias /business2).

2. Your business is providing network support on retainer for professional firms that can usually handle their own computer problems, but you also compile shareware tools for network administration. You want to set up

two FTP sites: one for your business and one for your hobby. You do not want to purchase another computer, and Windows NT will not run multiple versions of the IIS services simultaneously. Select the best response:

A. The FTP service does not support virtual directories.

B. The FTP service does not support virtual servers.

C. Register two IP addresses for your Windows NT Server computer running IIS. Create two home directories and WWW Service directory entries for each and then assign each directory a different IP address in the Directories tab of the WWW Service Properties window.

D. Register two IP addresses for your Windows NT Server computer running IIS. Place the files for the business in the home directory (`wwwroot`). Create a new directory for the hobby, and in the Directories tab of the WWW Service Properties window, make that directory a virtual directory. (Give it the alias `/hobby`.)

3. You have created a key for your WWW server; sent, received back, and installed a certificate; and stopped and restarted your WWW service. The Require SSL option for WWW directories still remains gray, however. What is wrong?

A. WWW does not support the Secure Socket Layer protocol.

B. You have not given the WWW Service directory an IP address.

C. You have not checked the Windows NT Authentication/Response option.

D. You cannot require SSL on a home directory.

4. How do you configure IIS to run Perl CGI scripts? (Perl scripts have the extension `.pl`.)

A. Select Enable CGI Extensions in the Microsoft Internet Service Manger and select Perl (`.pl`) from the list of scripting languages.

B. Use the Registry Editor to add an entry for Perl to the `HKEY_LOCAL_MACHINE\SYSTEM\CurrentControlSet\Services\W3SVC\Parameters\Script Map` key.

    C. Use the Registry Editor to add an entry for Perl to the `HKEY_`
`LOCAL_MACHINE\SYSTEM\CurrentControlSet\Services\`
`Inetinfo\Parameters\MimeMap` key.

    D. You cannot add to the already supported CGI extensions.

5. How do you ensure that the Index Server search engine does not return a document that the user shouldn't see?

    A. Remove the Searchable option from WWW Service directories that the user should not access.

    B. Establish correct NTFS permissions so that the user doesn't have access to those directories or files.

    C. Create a CGI script that will parse the result of the query and remove any objectionable entries.

    D. Do not provide a search service if you are concerned about security.

CHAPTER

7

Files and Accounts

S ecurity is the most important issue you will face when you put a Web server on the Internet. Besides keeping hackers at bay, how do you keep the curious public away from data that you really want only your customers or coworkers to have access to?

The answer (at least for Internet Information Server) is to use the Windows NT built-in security mechanisms. Unlike other Internet service software that creates and maintains its own user account lists and access mechanisms, IIS simply relies upon the fortress of Windows NT for its security. Windows NT arguably has the strongest security mechanisms of any widely available operating system.

IIS piggybacks on top of Windows NT's inherent security mechanisms. When users log on to your site, they are logged on to a Windows NT account, not just an IIS account. Therefore, all the security mechanisms available on your Windows NT–based network are available to IIS.

Because you can use Windows NT security mechanisms to control access to the files and directories that make up your Web site, IIS doesn't really have to deal with security at all. The purpose of the few minor security mechanisms built into IIS is simply to make quick, sweeping changes to the way IIS serves data—IIS does not implement its own detailed security policy. The separate security mechanisms of IIS and Windows NT complement each other—neither replaces the other.

This chapter deals with the security mechanisms built into Windows NT. Chapter 8 covers the security mechanisms built into IIS. Study both rigorously—most of the test questions for the IIS exam deal with security.

You can control access to a Web site hosted by Windows NT Server running IIS in many ways. By far the easiest method is to use Windows NT file and directory security. This chapter provides a brief overview of four security constructs as they relate to IIS security:

- User accounts
- Groups

- Share permissions

- File and directory permissions

You will find more complete coverage of these constructs in the companion book *MCSE: NT Server 4 Study Guide.*

Using the security mechanisms built into Windows NT provides your Web site with the same level of protection as these mechanisms provide on your LAN. Basically, if your files can't be accessed from your LAN, they can't be accessed from the Internet.

Accounts are the basic mechanism by which Windows NT identifies who is accessing data. By securing data (such as your Web sites) by account, you are controlling who has access to that data. Groups make account management easy by granting or denying access to data to groups of accounts that have similar security requirements.

Accounts

To provide specific resources to specific users and to secure some resources against unauthorized disclosure, a network operating system has to know the identity of each attached user. This identification is provided by logon authentication. *Logon authentication* restricts access to computers and to the network until someone enters a valid account name and the correct password for that account name into a logon dialog. The logon name identifies each unique user and must be distinct for each account in a domain. A password keeps the use of that account private. Only individuals who know the password can use the account. In most instances, accounts are private to a single person.

Users log on to an Internet host running Windows NT through the client software, such as a Web browser or an FTP client. You can create accounts and groups on your Internet host to provide various levels of access to data on your intranet or Internet server. Visitors using Web browsers are secured through the anonymous logon account that was created when you installed IIS. Changing the permissions for this account will control what the general public can access on your Internet site. If you are logged on to a domain, some Web browsers (e.g., Internet Explorer) will automatically provide your domain credentials when you log on to an IIS Internet server. If you aren't logged on to an NT domain, these browsers will provide anonymous credentials as usual.

After you log on to a Windows NT security domain, the network knows what resources you are allowed to access and will not grant you access to resources to which you do not have specific permission.

User accounts can be grouped together for the assignment of permissions that apply to many people. For instance, access to financial information can be assigned to the Finance group, and then any member of the Finance group inherits permission from the group to access finance information. Groups allow administrators to effectively control security without being overwhelmed by the number of users in a Windows NT security domain, since permissions can be managed on a per group basis.

WARNING   On a Windows NT file server running IIS, users from the Internet are not logging on to the HTTP service. They are logging on to your Windows NT Server. They will have the full ability to act as a networked user unless your server is behind a firewall (most Internet servers are not) and you have properly implemented file and account security to prevent loss by Internet intrusion on an Internet server.

In a Windows NT security domain, user accounts are kept on the primary domain controller in the Security Accounts Manager portion of its registry. Users who appear as part of the security domain are called *global users* because they can log on to any computer attached to the security domain. Local user accounts are set up on individual computers for access to that specific machine only—local user accounts do not provide access to the domain.

In the same sense, local groups are groups of local user accounts. Global groups are groups of global users that are available to all computers logged on to the network.

Assigning users to groups allows you to keep track of who can access various resources. For example, your customers may need access to their own account information or to price lists, but not to internal company policy. You can assign appropriate permissions to a group called Customers and then in one action give the rights to an individual account by adding the account to the group.

Usually, intranet servers should simply be a normal part of your Windows NT domain, and you should use global accounts and groups to manage what is available to Windows NT security domain users. Internet servers, on the other hand, should be either stand-alone servers that use local accounts and groups (if you have only one) or on a security domain of their own (if you have more than one) so that you can create a totally separate security structure for users coming in on the Internet.

You can then create trust relationships so that users on your internal security domain are allowed to log on to the Internet security domain, but not vice versa. This method gives your coworkers full access to the Web site while protecting your internal network from users who should have access only to your Web site, such as customers and anonymous browsers. Your Internet security domain should also be separated from your internal network by a firewall for the most complete security. Figure 7.1 shows an ideal security structure for a company with multiple Web servers.

FIGURE 7.1

Implementing Internet
server security

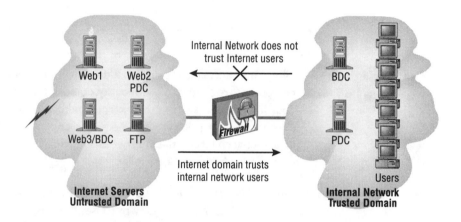

Windows NT security domains and global accounts and groups are covered in more detail in the companion book *MCSE: NT Server 4 Study Guide*. Local accounts and groups are covered in more detail in *MCSE: NT Workstation Study Guide*, and interdomain trust relationships are covered in more detail in *MCSE: NT Server 4 in the Enterprise Study Guide*.

Groups

Setting specific permissions for many users of an Internet server can be an error-prone and time-consuming exercise. Most organizations do not have security requirements that change for every user. Setting permissions is more manageable with the security groups concept, where permissions are assigned to groups rather than to individual users. Users who are members of a group have all the permissions assigned to that group.

Groups also make changing permissions easier. Permissions assigned to a group affect every member of the group, so changes can be made across the entire group. For instance, adding a new directory for the Finance group requires merely assigning the group permission to the directory to give each member access. This process is much easier than manually assigning permission to individual accounts.

The two basic types of groups in Windows NT are local groups and global groups. Local groups affect only the Windows NT computer they are created on. Global groups affect the entire network and are stored on the primary domain controller. If you have only one Internet server, consider using local groups on that server for your accounts that come in only from the Internet.

Global user accounts created on a domain controller are available to every computer participating in the security domain. User accounts that access only your Internet server from the Internet and don't require access to your internal network (such as customers or clients) should be implemented as local user accounts on the Internet server itself, rather than as global accounts on the primary domain controller.

One individual account can belong to many groups. This arrangement facilitates setting up groups for many purposes. For instance, you might define groups corresponding to the functional areas in your organization—administration, marketing, finance, manufacturing, and so on. You might create another group for supervisors, another for network support staff, and another for new employees.

For example, a member of the Finance group may have permission to access accounting information and financial statements, but a member of the New Users group may have No Access permission to accounting information. By assigning membership in both groups, you would be allowing access to financial statements without permitting access to accounting information until the new user becomes a trusted employee and is removed from the New Users group.

Windows NT networks have a default group called Domain Users that you can use to assign rights and permissions for every user on the domain. When accounts are created, they are automatically assigned membership in the default Domain Users group.

Changing permissions assigned to the default Domain Users group will change permissions for everyone who has access to the network. All users must be members of the Domain Users group—Windows NT Server will not allow you to remove this membership.

Built-In Groups

Windows NT has many built-in groups. These groups cover a wide array of typical functions and have permissions already assigned to support those functions. The Guests local group is included for complete compatibility with Windows NT Workstation and should be disabled on dedicated servers. Table 7.1 shows the groups built into Windows NT Server.

	Group	Type	Function
TABLE 7.1 Windows NT Server Built-In Groups	Account Operators	Local	Members can administer domain user and group accounts.
	Administrators	Local	Members can fully administer the server and the domain.
	Backup Operators	Local	Members can bypass file security to archive files.
	Domain Admins	Global	Members can administer domain accounts.
	Domain Guests	Global	Members have Guest rights to all domain resources.
	Domain Users	Global	All domain users are part of this group.
	Guests	Local	Members have guest access to the domain. This group should be disabled.
	Print Operators	Local	Members can administer domain printers.
	Replicator	Local	A special account for directory replication accounts.
	Server Operators	Local	Members can administer domain servers.
	Users	Local	Server users.

You create, modify, and delete groups with the User Manager for Domains (see Figure 7.2). Exercise 7.1 shows you how to create a global group. The process for making a local group is similar; you simply select the Local Group menu item instead of the Global Group menu item in step 2.

FIGURE 7.2

The User Manager
for Domains

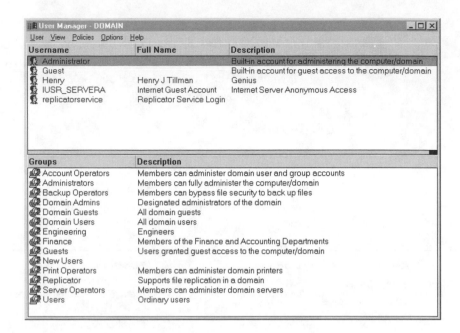

EXERCISE 7.1

Creating a Global Group

1. Select Start ➤ Programs ➤ Administrative Tools ➤ User Manager for Domains.

2. Select User ➤ New Global Group.

3. Type **Finance** in the Group Name input box.

4. Type **members of the finance and accounting departments** in the description input box.

5. Click OK.

6. Close the User Manager for Domains.

Special Groups

In addition to its many built-in groups, Windows NT has two groups that perform special functions: Everyone and Guests. You can use these two groups to create special sets of permissions without creating them yourself.

Everyone   In Windows NT, Everyone is a special group that applies not only to domain users (as does the global group Domain Users) but also to all members of any trusted domains. The Everyone group cannot be deleted or disabled, and it is the default permission group granted to any resource when you share it. You must specifically delete the Everyone permission and assign permissions to other groups if you do not want to allow global access to your shared resources.

Guests   Guests are accounts attached to the domain that could not provide a valid logon because they logged on remotely and they do not have an account, or because they did not provide logon credentials. Unlike other network operating systems such as NetWare or UNIX, where guests are specific accounts, a Windows NT guest is anyone who failed to properly log on to a Windows NT computer or domain, but was not denied access because of a bad password for a valid account. Therefore, users can log on remotely via the Internet, provide a bogus account name, and get Guest (and therefore, Everyone) access to your domain. You should never enable the Guest account unless you fully understand the security issues involved and have a valid reason to do so.

WARNING   Guests are members of the Everyone group. If you allow Everyone access permissions to a share (which is the default) and have Guest logons enabled, anyone with access to your network will have access to everything on that share. Do not leave access to the Everyone group enabled in your permissions—use Domain Users instead.

In addition to these two groups, some internal special groups appear in certain instances. You cannot assign permissions to these groups, so they are of little consequence, but they do reveal how Windows NT manages groups and connections internally. They are:

- **Interactive**—anyone using the computer locally, including users from the Internet logged on using anonymous or basic clear text authentication (because the HTTP service logs Internet users on to the Internet server rather than using the server service).

- **Network**—all users connected over the network, including Internet users who have logged on through the server service. Web users who log on using Windows NT Challenge/Response are network users.

- **System**—the operating system.

- **Creator/Owner**—an alias for the user who created the subdirectory, file, or print job in question.

You need not be concerned with the operation or effect of these groups as they are entirely internal to the function of Windows NT.

User Accounts

Managing users consists of creating and maintaining user accounts for the people who work on your network, including user accounts for Internet users who access your network using the services of IIS.

Local Users and Global Users

As with groups, Windows NT has two types of users: local and global. *Local users* are users who are allowed to log on to the computer itself. *Global users* are users who are allowed to log on to the network domain. You create local users with the User Manager included with Windows NT Workstation and with the User Manager for Domains included with Windows NT Server.

You create global users only with the User Manager for Domains included with Windows NT Server on servers designated as primary domain controllers, backup domain controllers, or member servers. Global user accounts are created on the primary domain controller. The primary domain controller replicates its account database to all Windows NT Servers designated as backup domain controllers in the domain. Backup domain controllers will respond to a logon attempt if the primary domain controller fails to log on the client after a short period of time, meaning that the primary domain controller is busy or temporarily unreachable.

Special Built-In Accounts

Windows NT creates two user accounts by default: the Administrator account and the Guest account.

The Administrator account is always present and should be protected with a strong password. This account manages the overall configuration of the computer and can be used for:

- Managing security policies

- Creating or changing users and groups

- Setting shared directories for networking

- Performing other hardware-maintenance tasks

This account can be renamed, but it cannot be deleted or disabled.

You should rename the Administrator account to make guessing its password harder, especially on a machine attached to the Internet. Hackers know that Windows NT defaults to an Administrator account that cannot be locked out, so they will attempt to hack the password of that account. Changing the Administrator account name closes this security loophole.

The Guest account enables one-time users or users with low or no security access to use the computer in a limited fashion. The Guest account does not save user preferences or configuration changes, so any changes that a guest user makes are lost when that user logs off. The Guest account is installed with a blank password. If the password is left blank, remote users can connect to the computer using the Guest account. The Guest account can be renamed and disabled, but it cannot be deleted.

You should leave the Guest account disabled unless you need to allow a specific service to users without passwords. Remember that the special group Everyone includes Guest users, and that shares give full control to Everyone by default. If you use the Guest account, be especially careful about share permissions.

Creating User Accounts

You can add user accounts to your NT network in two ways: You can create new user accounts, or you can make copies of existing user accounts. In either case you may make changes in three areas:

- User account information

- Group membership information

- User account profile information

To add a new user account, you will be working with the New User dialog box, as shown in Figure 7.3.

When you create users with the User Manager for Domains, you are creating global user accounts.

FIGURE 7.3

The New User dialog box

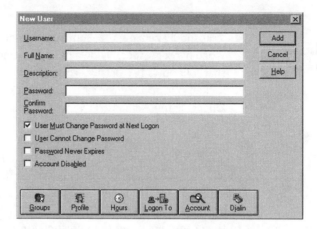

Table 7.2 describes the properties of the user account that are accessible from the New User dialog box.

	Field	Value
TABLE 7.2 User Account Properties	Username	A required text field of up to 20 characters. Uses both uppercase and lowercase letters except " / \ [ ] : ;	= , + * ? < > but is not case sensitive. This name must be unique among workstation users or among network domain members if attached to a network.
	Full Name	An optional text field typically used for the complete name of the user. For instance, a user whose full name is Mae West may have a username of mwest.
	Description	An optional text field used to more fully describe the user and his or her position in the firm, home office, etc. This field is limited to any 48 characters.
	Password	A required text field up to 14 characters; case sensitive. This field displays asterisks, rather than the characters typed to keep your password secure.

	Field	Value
TABLE 7.2 (cont.) User Account Properties	Confirm Password	A required text field used to confirm the password field. This method avoids typing errors, which result in unknown passwords. As with the Password field, the Confirm Password field also displays asterisks.
	User Must Change Password at Next Logon	A check box field used to force a password change at the next logon. Note that Windows NT will not allow you to apply changes to a user account if this field and User Cannot Change Password field are both checked.
	User Cannot Change Password	A check box field that makes it impossible for users to change their own password. This feature is used for shared accounts (such as the Guest account) where a user changing the account password would prevent other users of the account from logging on. You would normally not check this account for typical users.
	Password Never Expires	A check box field that prevents a password from expiring according to the password policy. This setting is normally used for automated software services that must be logged on as a user. Note that setting Password Never Expires overrides User Must Change Password at Next Logon.
	Account Disabled	A check box field that prevents users from logging on to the network with this account. This field provides an easy way to place an account out of service temporarily.
	Groups button	Assigns Group membership.
	Profile button	Activates the user environment profile information.
	Dialin button	Allows users to dial into this computer using Remote Access Service. See Chapter 14 for more information.

User accounts are administered with the User Manager administrative tool. Exercise 7.2 shows the process of creating new user accounts. (Subsequent exercises in this chapter assume that you have already opened the User Manager.)

EXERCISE 7.2

Creating a New User Account

1. Log on to the network as an administrator.

2. Click the Start menu and select Programs ➤ Administrative Tools ➤ User Manager.

3. Select User ➤ New User.

4. Type **mwest** in the Username field.

5. Type **Mae West** in the Full Name field.

6. Type **movie star/pop culture icon** in the Description field.

7. Type in any password you want in the Password field. A good password is at least eight characters long and includes at least one punctuation mark. Passwords are case sensitive.

8. Type exactly the same password in the confirm password field.

9. Leave the check boxes as they are for now.

10. Click Add.

11. Do not record this password anywhere. If you forget it, use the Administrator account to assign a new password to this account.

You should record the Administrator account password, seal it in an envelope, and keep it in a safe or other secure location. Make sure at least one other trusted individual knows where the password is stored in case you get hit by a meteor.

Copying User Accounts

If you have to create accounts for a large number of users, for instance, in an Internet-based computer-training Web server environment where hundreds of students come and go every year, you can create a few basic user account templates and copy them as needed. A user account template is a user account that provides all the features new users will need and has its Account Disabled field enabled. When you need to add a user account, you can copy the template. When you copy a user account, Windows NT automatically copies some of the user account field values from the template; you provide the remaining necessary information.

Windows NT copies these values from the template to the new user account:

- Description
- Group Account Memberships
- Profile Settings
- User Cannot Change Password
- Password Never Expires

Windows NT leaves the following fields blank in the new User account dialog box:

- Username
- Full Name
- User Must Change Password at Next Logon
- Account Disabled

The Username and Full Name fields are left blank for you to enter the new user information. The User Must Change Password at Next Logon check box is set by default. As a security precaution, leave this setting if you want to force new users to change from your assigned password when they first log on. Exercise 7.3 shows the process of copying a user account.

EXERCISE 7.3

Copying a User Account

1. Select the mwest user account in the User Manager.

2. Select User ➤ Copy or press F8.

3. Enter the following information into the Copy of mwest dialog box. Leave the check box fields in their default states.

4. Type **rvalentino** into the Username field.

5. Type **Rudolf Valentino** into the Full Name field.

6. Notice that the Description field is copied from the original New User dialog box. Although it remains correct in this example, it will usually change.

7. Type **ruvaruva!** in the Password field.

8. Type **ruvaruva!** in the Confirm Password field.

9. Explore the User accounts profile and group settings to note that the assignments for mwest have been automatically assigned to rvalentino. To do this inspection, click the Profile and Group buttons and then click OK to return to the Copy of User2 dialog box.

10. Click Add to complete the creation of the rvalentino account.

Notice we assigned an initial password loosely based on the user's name but mangled according to specific rules. This relatively secure initial password scheme keeps individuals outside your organization from easily guessing new user passwords. However, the only entirely secure initial password scheme is to assign randomly generated passwords, which are passed to the user through some physical means. Your security needs may require more rigorous precautions to keep initial passwords from creating a hole in your security measures.

Disabling and Deleting User Accounts

When access to the Internet server is no longer appropriate for a user, that account should be disabled. Leaving unused active accounts in the user accounts database permits potential intruders to continue logon attempts after accounts they've already tried lock them out. Disabling an account prevents it from being used, but retains the account information for future use.

This technique is useful for temporarily locking the accounts of employees who are absent or for temporarily denying access to an account that may have been compromised. Deleting an account removes all the user account information from the system. If a user account has been deleted and that user requires access again, you will have to set up a new account with all new permissions.

Creating a new user account with the same name will not restore previous account information, as a unique security identifier internally identifies each user account, not the username. Exercise 7.4 shows you how to disable a user account.

EXERCISE 7.4

Disabling a User Account

1. Double-click user account rvalentino in the User Manager.

2. Check the Account Disabled field.

3. Click OK to complete the operation.

4. Log off and attempt to log on as rvalentino.

If a user will no longer be using the system, you should delete his or her account, rather than disabling it. Deleting an account will destroy all user preferences and permissions, so be certain the user will never again require access before taking this step. Exercise 7.5 shows you how to delete a user account.

EXERCISE 7.5

Deleting a User Account

1. Log on to the network as an administrator. Go to the Start menu.

2. Select Programs ➤ Administrative Tools ➤ User Manager.

3. Click user account rvalentino.

4. Select User ➤ Delete (or hit the Del key).

5. Click OK in the Warning dialog.

6. Click Yes to confirm the deletion.

7. Log off and attempt to log on as rvalentino.

Renaming User Accounts

You can rename any user account, including the Administrator and Guest default accounts, with the User Manager. You may need to change an account username if an account that is associated with a specific job is passed on to another individual or if your organization changes its network naming policy.

Changing the name does not change any other properties of the account. You may want to change the names of the Administrator and Guest accounts so an intruder familiar with Windows NT default user account names cannot gain access to your system simply by guessing a password. Exercise 7.6 walks you through the steps.

EXERCISE 7.6

Rename a User Account

1. Log on to the network as an administrator and go to the Start menu.

2. Select Programs ➤ Administrative Tools ➤ User Manager.

3. Select mwest in the User Accounts list.

4. Select User ➤ Rename.

5. Type **wema** in the Change To box.

6. Click OK to complete the operation.

Anonymous Logon

Internet servers have traditionally allowed Anonymous logon—the World Wide Web is based on the ability to access information quickly without providing logon credentials. To satisfy the Windows NT requirement that all users log on but still allow Anonymous access to information, IIS implements a logon account for use in the absence of better credentials: the Anonymous user account.

IIS creates a user account when you install it. By default this name is IUSR_*servername*, where *servername* is the name of your Windows NT server. You can specify any other user account if you wish.

By assigning permissions to this user account, you can restrict or permit access to Internet information in the service root directories of your server.

File and Network Security

Security planning involves securing resources from unauthorized access. The two basic approaches to security are optimistic and pessimistic:

- **Optimistic**—Users are allowed maximum permission to access information except in specific cases where information should not be available to them.

- **Pessimistic**—Users are allowed permission to access only information they require to perform their jobs.

Both methods are equally valid approaches to security, and the method you choose will largely be determined by the nature of your organization and the work you perform. For instance, many government organizations use pessimistic security policies because access to the information they store could compromise the security of the country.

On the other hand, most medium-size and small businesses use optimistic security policies because they have not created information that would be useful to someone outside their organization, and it wouldn't be harmful even if an unauthorized user could gain access to it.

Pessimistic security policies take vastly more administrative effort than optimistic policies do, but pessimistic policies are far more secure and do not rely on users to safeguard data on their own. For instance, under a pessimistic security policy, any time a user needs access to information that is outside his or her need to know, a network administrator has to specifically allow permission for that user to access that information.

Optimistic security policies require very little administrative effort, but they are not very secure—nearly everyone on the network has access to most of the information on it. Therefore, it's usually not necessary to specifically assign permission to access a resource.

These two policies are the extremes—most network security policies are between the two. But deciding now which extreme policy is best for your organization will guide you through the rest of the security planning process.

Internet security is a security paradox: You are intentionally inviting the world into your server, but at the same time, you want to keep your network secure. The best (and most pessimistic) way to achieve both options is to keep them separated.

Should your internal network even be attached to the Internet? Many organizations choose to put their Web server and a few Internet browsing terminals in a central location attached to the Internet, but detached from the internal network. This method absolutely prevents intrusion into the internal network and forces users to move to another machine to access the Internet—thereby preventing long and unproductive sessions of random surfing.

The next most secure method is to put your Internet server on the outside of a firewall that protects the internal network from intrusion. This configuration allows maximum access to your Internet server from both the internal network and the Internet and also allows your users to use the Internet from their desktop machines.

A third (less secure) option that many organizations use is *filtered Internet connections,* where the Internet service provider filters TCP/IP traffic based on the port/socket information, thus allowing only the type of traffic you desire. By denying traffic types other than HTTP, SMTP, NNTP, and FTP, you can provide most of the functions of an Internet server and still keep your site reasonably secure.

Another (still less secure) method is to use a proxy server. Proxy servers act like Internet middlemen. Users actually don't browse the Web, they send requests to the proxy server, which actually retrieves the Web page and then forwards it to the user. The proxy server not only hides internal users from prying eyes on the Internet but also can be configured to cache frequently accessed pages.

The worst way to implement Internet security is simply through file permissions alone. This method is analogous to throwing a party for hackers and inviting them to try their hand at guessing a valid user's password at a directly connected LAN terminal. The TCP/IP connection that attaches your internal network to your file server is exactly the same as the TCP/IP connection that attaches the world to your Internet server. If both exist on the same network, you are exposing yourself to extreme risk.

WARNING   Never attach your internal network directly to the Internet without some sort of firewall or packet filtering service.

Nevertheless, file system permissions remain a very valid way to secure various Internet-based information sites such as Web pages specific to your customers from public dissemination—but only after you've implemented a firewall between your Internet server and your local network. With file system permissions, you can customize access to your Internet site based on a user's logon credentials.

Permissions

Windows NT implements security by keeping track of who has permission to access what. In other words, users identify themselves by providing logon credentials that the system compares to an access control list containing individual permission entries maintained for each object the user attempts to access. Permissions are applied to just about every operating system object, but the two most important objects are network shares and file system objects like files and directories.

Your access token is created when you log on. It contains your user identity and the identity of all groups you belong to. The system compares this access token to each secured resource (such as a share, file, or directory) you attempt to access. These resources contain access control lists, which list each security ID permitted to use the resource. If any of the identifiers in your access token match identifiers in a resource's access control list, you are allowed access as specified by that entry.

Share Permissions

Share permissions control access to shared resources. Table 7.3 shows the different share-level permissions that can be assigned and their effects.

Windows NT does not use share permissions to control access to the Internet host itself. Internet users are logged on locally on the Internet host, so share permissions for that machine do not affect them. However, that host may be logged on to other machines and serving data stored in those other machines. In that case, share permissions do affect which shares can be accessed. You will normally use file system permissions, rather than share permissions, to secure data on Internet hosts.

TABLE 7.3	Permission	Effect
Share Permissions	No Access	Prevents access to the shared directory.
	Read	Allows viewing of contained files and directories, loading of files, and the execution of software.
	Change	All read permissions plus creating, deleting, and changing contained directories and files.
	Full Control	All change permissions plus changing file system permissions and taking ownership.

File System Permissions

File system permissions complement the basic share-level permissions. Older file systems such as FAT do not have a set of file and directory attributes rich enough to implement security on a file or directory basis, so file system permissions are not available for these volumes. The server service implements share permissions to secure access to file systems that did not implement security.

WARNING File system permissions are available only for NTFS volumes, not for FAT volumes. You cannot properly secure your Web site without using file system permissions. Your Internet site files and system integrity could be compromised unless you use the NTFS file system and properly configure security for the Internet publication directories.

Modern file systems such as NTFS implement finer security control over the sharing of information with file system permissions, which are assigned to individual files and directories using file system attribute bits that are stored in the directory tables of the file system.

Consequently, file system permissions work even on stand-alone computers. For instance, if Jane creates a directory and assigns permissions for only herself, then no one else can access that directory (except administrators who take ownership of the directory) even when logged on to the same machine.

File system permissions can also be used to restrict which files are available to resource shares. Therefore, even though share permissions may allow access to a directory, file system permissions can still restrict it. Table 7.4 shows the effect of directory permissions.

	Permission	Effect
TABLE 7.4 Directory Permissions	No Access	Prevents any access to the directory and its files.
	List	Viewing filenames; browsing directories. Does not allow access to files unless overridden by other file or directory permissions.
	Read	Opening files and executing applications.
	Add	Adding files and subdirectories without Read access.
	Change	Incorporates Add and read permissions and adds the ability to delete files and directories.
	Full Control	Change plus taking ownership and assigning permissions.

Conflicting Permissions

With the myriad of shares, groups, files, and directories that can be created in a network environment, some resource permission conflicts are bound to occur. When a user is a member of many groups, some of those groups may specifically allow access to a resource while other group memberships deny it. Also, cumulative permissions may occur. For example, a user may have Read access to a directory because he's a domain user and also have Full Control because he's a member of the Engineers group. Windows NT determines access privileges in the following manner:

- Administrators always have full access to all resources.

- A specific denial (the No Access permission) always overrides specific access to a resource.

- When resolving conflicts between share permissions and file permissions, Windows NT chooses the most restrictive. For instance, if the share permission allows full control but the file permissions allow read-only, the file is read-only.

- When a user is a member of multiple groups, the user always has the combined permissions of all group memberships.

Choosing Permissions

Share permissions and file system permissions give you two ways to secure files, and you have to decide which one to use. Use the following criteria to guide your selection:

- If you are sharing from the FAT file system, you cannot use file system security, so you must use share permissions to secure each directory that needs unique permissions.

- If you need to secure access to files on a system that users will log on to locally, you must use file system security. Share security applies only to network connections, not to local users.

- Generally, you should create the fewest number of shares possible in your networking environment. For instance, rather than sharing each subdirectory on a server, consider sharing just the higher-level directory and then securing the subdirectories with file-level permissions. Shares should be reserved for sharing hardware devices such as entire hard disks and CD-ROMs.

- File system security allows a richer set of permissions and can be more finely controlled. You should use it whenever possible.

In sum, Internet users are usually logged on locally to your Internet server, so there's no way to use share security to restrict access to your site unless the files are actually located on other computers with share security set up and accessed through the virtual directory feature. This method is too silly to bother with. Use NTFS file system permissions on your Internet server. Set up most Internet publication directories (i.e., `Inetpub` and all of its subdirectories) with read-only permission for all Internet user accounts and for internal users who are not involved in site production. If you will be providing some special account-based service for customers, create a group (or groups) that maintain their security permissions, assign the customers to that group, and restrict Read access to those portions of your site that are for "members only" from the Anonymous Internet logon account.

Share Security

Sharing resources enables you to make a resource such as a directory or a printer that is available to a Windows NT server also available to clients. Sharing allows you to use another set of permissions, called *share permissions*, to restrict access to the shared resource if necessary. Share permissions work regardless of the file system security measures you may have implemented with either the FAT or NTFS file system, so you can use them on both NTFS and FAT shared volumes. If you have directory permissions set up on an NTFS volume, users will be restricted by both sets of permissions.

Windows NT selects the most restrictive permission when combining share permissions and file system permission.

Creating a share is simple. You simply select a directory, volume, or printer and then right-click it to select properties. Selecting the Sharing tab will allow you to create and name a new share and set the share permissions. Exercise 7.7 shows you how to create a network share.

EXERCISE 7.7

Creating a Network Share

1. Double-click My Computer.

2. Double-click the C: drive in the My Computer window. If your C: drive is not formatted with the NTFS file system, select a drive that is. If you don't have one, you can still follow along with these exercises, but you will not be able to complete Exercise 7.10.

3. Right-click a white area (an area where there are no icons or files).

4. Select New ➤ Folder in the pop-up menu that appears.

5. Type **Test Share** as the name of the folder. You must do this immediately or the focus will change. If the focus changes and you can't rename the file, right-click the folder and select the rename option.

6. Right-click your newly created Test Share folder.

7. Select Sharing.

8. Select Shared As:. The name of folder will automatically appear as the share name. You can change the share name if you wish.

9. Click OK.

10. Click Yes to acknowledge the warning about MS-DOS clients.

WARNING

MS-DOS users will not be able to access shares with names that violate the MS-DOS "8.3" file-naming conventions for length or characters not supported in MS-DOS file names.

NTFS File Security

When you use the Windows NT File System (NTFS) under Windows NT, you have many security options that you do not have with a DOS FAT file system. This section shows you how to set access permissions for files and directories in an NTFS partition.

NTFS Security Advantages

NTFS includes several features that you can use to provide a more secure environment for network and local users, including Internet users. Some of the features that NTFS provides that pertain to files and directories are:

- **Permissions**—NTFS keeps track of which users and groups can access certain files and directories, and it provides different levels of access for different users.

- **Auditing**—Windows NT can record NTFS security-related events to a log file for later review using the Event Viewer. The system administrator can set the events to audit and the degree of detail.

- **Transaction logging**—NTFS is a log-based file system, which means that it records changes to files and directories as they happen and also records how to undo or redo the changes in case of a system failure. This feature makes the NTFS file system much more robust than a FAT file system like DOS.

- **Ownership**—NTFS also tracks the ownership of files. A user who creates a file or directory is automatically the owner of it and has full rights to it. An administrator, or other individual with equivalent permissions, can take over ownership of a file or directory.

Using NTFS Permissions

In NTFS each file and each directory have permissions associated with it for users and groups. These permissions are in addition to the directory sharing permissions discussed in the previous section, and are the most restrictive set of permissions when the permission levels are not the same. For instance, if a directory is shared with Full Access, but the user accessing that directory has only Read access under NTFS, then that user will only be able to read in that directory.

Viewing Permissions   You can view the permissions that a file or directory has by selecting that file's icon and then selecting File ➤ Properties, or by right-clicking once on the file's icon and selecting the Properties item in the pop-up menu. When the file's Properties window appears, select the Security tab and then click the Permissions button. The Directory (or File) Permissions window will display the names of the users and groups that have access to the file (or directory). Figure 7.4 shows a File Permissions window.

FIGURE 7.4

The File Permissions window lists the names of users and groups that have access to the file.

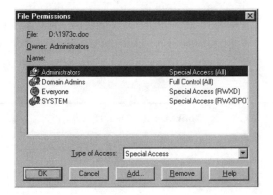

The permissions window for a directory allows you to specify additional permissions for subdirectories and files stored in the directory. Figure 7.5 shows a Directory Permissions window.

FIGURE 7.5

The Directory Permissions window lists the names of the users and groups that have access to the directory.

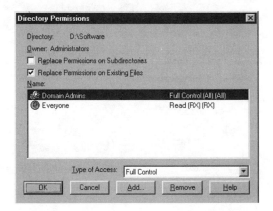

A user that is not explicitly listed in the File or Directory Permissions window may still have access to the file or directory because the user may belong to a group that is listed in the window. In fact, you should never assign access to files or directories to individual users. Instead, you should create a group, give access permissions to the group, and then assign users to that group. This method allows you to change access rights for whole groups of users without having to modify each individual user account.

NTFS defines access permissions based on file system operations. Because useful permissions usually require more than one file system operation, the file system permissions you can assign are actually combinations of permitted file system operations. Table 7.5 shows the file system operations that are allowed, and Table 7.6 shows the combinations that are formed to create actual permissions. The question marks in the Special Access row of Table 7.6 signify that special access provides a way to create your own combinations of file system operation permissions to create complex special accesses.

	Operation	Description
T A B L E 7.5 File System Operations	R	Read or display data, attributes, owner, and permissions.
	X	Run or execute the file or files in the directory.
	W	Write to the file or directory or change the attributes.
	D	Delete the file or directory.
	P	Change permissions.
	O	Take ownership.

	Permission	R	X	W	D	P	O
T A B L E 7.6 Access Permissions	No Access						
	List (Directory only)	X	X				
	Read	X	X				

TABLE 7.6 *(cont.)* Access Permissions	Permission	R	X	W	D	P	O
	Add (Directory only)		X	X			
	Add & Read (Directory Only)	X	X	X			
	Change	X	X	X	X		
	Full Control	X	X	X	X	X	X
	Special Access	?	?	?	?	?	?

Each access permission—except Special Access—can perform a specific set of operations on the file or directory, which can allow or disallow any combination of tasks.

The File Permissions and Directory Permissions windows are similar, but not exactly the same. The permissions for users and groups listed in the Directory Permissions window have two sets of parentheses after the description (e.g., Full Control (All) (All)). The first set of parentheses describes the permissions for that directory and subdirectories of that directory. Changing the Special Directory Access (see Figure 7.6) controls these permissions.

FIGURE 7.6

The Special Directory Access window contains special permissions for directories.

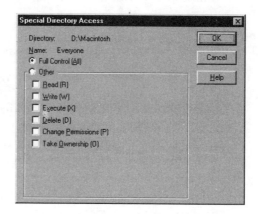

The second set of parentheses describes the permissions to be set on the current files in the directory and any new files. Changing Special File Access (see Figure 7.7) controls these permissions.

FIGURE 7.7

The Special File Access window contains special permissions for files.

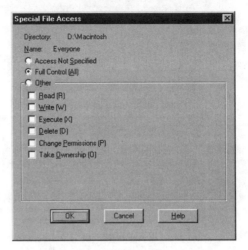

Changing Permissions   To change permissions on a file or directory, you must meet one of the following three conditions:

- You have Full Control access to the file or directory.

- You have the Change Permission permission.

- You are the owner of the file or directory.

Changing Permissions Graphically   You set permissions for directories and files graphically from the Directory (or File) Permissions window.

Exercise 7.8 shows you how to change the Dir_1 directory to add permission for June to access the directory and remove the permission for Everyone to access the directory. (This exercise assumes that the C: drive on your Windows NT computer is an NTFS partition. If your C: drive does not use NTFS, substitute a drive that does.)

EXERCISE 7.8

Changing Access Permissions for a Directory

1. Open the My Computer icon on your desktop.

2. Open the (C:) icon (or the icon for the NTFS partition in your computer) in the My Computer window.

3. Select the Dir_1 icon in the (C:) window (or other directory in the window corresponding to the NTFS drive on your computer) by clicking it once.

4. Select File ➤ Properties.

5. Select the Security tab.

6. Click the Permissions button.

7. Select the Everyone group in the Directory Permissions window and then click Remove.

8. Click Add.

9. Click the Show Users button. Select June. Click Add. Click OK.

10. Click OK in the directory permissions window and then click OK in the Properties window.

Default Permissions

The default permissions setting for a newly formatted NTFS partition is Full Control to the group Everyone. This setting makes an NTFS volume appear much like a FAT or an HPFS volume because any user can make any modification to any file. You should restrict access to the NTFS permission by removing the Everyone group and assigning access permissions to a group with a more restricted set of users. You should, of course, make sure that the Administrators group has Full Control of the partition by setting permissions on the root directory.

Copying and Moving Files with Permissions

When you copy a file (or a directory) from one directory on an NTFS partition to another directory, the file inherits the permissions and owner of the receiving directory.

Moving a file or directory from one directory to another does not change the permissions and owner of that file or directory.

The difference between copying and moving files is that when you copy a file, the original file still resides in its original location. You are essentially creating a new file in the new location that contains the same data as the old file. The new file (the copy) will have the receiving directory's new-file permissions.

When a directory is copied, it receives the directory and default new-file permissions of its new parent directory. As the new files are created within the new directory, they receive the new-file permissions of this directory.

Moving a file or directory, instead of copying it, merely changes pointers in the directory structure on the NTFS partition. The file or directory disappears from the old location and appears in the new location but does not physically move on the hard disk. The permissions and ownership of the file or directory remain the same. A file can be moved in this manner only between directories on the same NTFS partition.

Some programs perform a move command by actually copying the file or directory to the new location and then deleting it from the old location. In this case the file obtains new permissions from the receiving directory, just as it would in a regular copy operation. This effect is sometimes called the *container effect*.

Permissions for Users and Groups

Windows NT determines whether a user can access a resource by combining all the access permissions of the user and of the groups to which the user belongs.

If any one of the permissions is No Access for that resource, then access to that resource is denied the user. If the requested access is not specifically permitted by one of the permissions that the user has, then the user cannot perform that action.

For example, suppose that Bob is a member of the Marketing group and a member of the Management group. Marketing is allowed Change access to the Sales directory. Management is allowed Read access to the Sales group, and Full Control to the Projections directory. Management has Full Access to the Party_Plans directory, but Bob has No Access to the Party_Plans directory. Table 7.7 shows the combined access permissions that result for Bob from this combination.

TABLE 7.7

Combined Access
Permissions

	Bob	Marketing	Management	Result
Sales		Change	Read	Change
Projections			Full Access	Full Access
Party Plans	No Access		Full Access	No Access

When a user or program requests permissions to access a resource, either all of the permissions requested are granted or none of them are. For example, if a user requests Read and Write access to a directory, and the user has only Read access, no access will be granted. The user may request access only for resources that he or she has permission to access.

Ownership

By default, the creator of a file or directory has ownership of that file or directory. On an NTFS partition, Windows NT keeps track of the owners of files and directories. The owner has full control of the file or directory and can change any of its permissions.

The Owner dialog box (see Figure 7.8) shows the current owner and allows you to take ownership of it if you have the permissions to do so. An Administrator always has the permission to take ownership of a file or directory, even when the owner has restricted those rights.

FIGURE 7.8

The Owner dialog box
allows you to take
ownership of a file if you
have permission.

No user can *give* ownership of a file or directory to another user. You must *take* ownership to become the owner. For users other than the administrator, however, the owner must allow the user the permission to take ownership of the file or directory.

Distributed File System

The Distributed File System (Dfs—for some reason, Microsoft capitalizes only the first letter of this abbreviation) is an important new tool for Windows NT Server that allows administrators to simulate a single (or, if you prefer, many) coherent server share environment that actually exists across multiple servers. Dfs allows you to create links to other servers that look like subdirectories on a single server.

For instance, with Dfs you can create a facility very similar to the virtual directory facility described in Chapter 6, but without using the IIS virtual directory method. Dfs makes the share structure the same for local network users accessing the files directly as it is for Internet users accessing them through IIS.

Dfs allows you to graft a share located on any server into the directory hierarchy of any Dfs tree. You can make your share environment appear to be a single hierarchical environment. Dfs does not limit you to a single tree, however. You can provide multiple distributed trees for different users, groups, or purposes if you desire. Different trees allow you to provide different "views" of your network, customized for unique purposes. For instance, the Engineering department can use a tree that shows engineering and corporate resources, and the Finance department can use another tree that shows finance and corporate resources.

Although only Windows NT Servers can host Dfs trees, shares from Windows NT workstations and Windows 95 workstations (with the Dfs client software for Windows 95) can be grafted into Dfs trees.

One major benefit of the ability of Dfs to provide a single view of all the shares on your network is that by backing up the root share and all its subdirectories, your backup will actually span all the servers with shares grafted into the tree. Dfs makes backing up an entire network easy and painless.

Another benefit the Dfs tree structure is that you can create different trees for different departments that look exactly the same, but actually point to different servers—allowing you to replicate data to other servers and seamlessly split the load between them. This technique works best with read-only information (like most Web sites) because of the time delays involved with replication service of Windows NT Server.

Distributed file systems are called *trees,* and they are roughly analogous to the NetWare Directory Service (NDS) provided in NetWare 4.1.

In the case of Dfs, a picture is worth a thousand words, so take a close look at Figure 7.9. It looks like any regular network neighborhood view, right?

FIGURE 7.9

A Server hosting
a Dfs tree

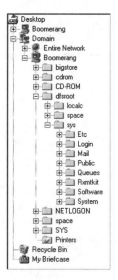

Here's what's actually going on:

- Server Boomerang is hosting a Dfs tree called **dfsroot**.

- The **localc** subdirectory is local to Boomerang.

- The **Space** subdirectory is actually located on another server called Yoyo.

- The **sys** subdirectory is actually a NetWare 4.1 server!

From a user's viewpoint, all these resources are simply available on a single server called Boomerang. Users don't have to know or care that other file servers are active on the network—Dfs provides the illusion of one large centralized store.

WARNING   Dfs currently works only with Windows NT 4 and Windows 95 computers running the Dfs client for Windows 95. If you are using other clients (such as MS-DOS or Macintoshes), the leaf shares inside the Dfs tree will appear empty. You can still access the shares on other computers by using their normal share names.

Using Dfs to Manage Growing Networks

Dfs really shines when it comes time to add servers to your network. Many networks start small and grow with the company. For instance, your company may start out with only 30 clients, with files located on a single server in four different shared directories, as shown in Figure 7.10.

FIGURE 7.10

The first server in a growing network

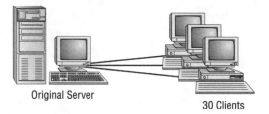

Original Server

30 Clients

By the time your network has grown to 100 users, that server has become quite strained trying to keep up with the load. So you purchase another server and decide to move half the files over to it, as shown in Figure 7.11.

If you don't use Dfs, you will have to go to about 50 different client stations and change all their share mappings to point to the new server. If you do use Dfs, you can simply graft the shares back into the original server's Dfs root. Fortunately, you don't have to start out using Dfs—you can add it at any time. You should start your servers with a single root share that you can later turn into a Dfs root—otherwise you will need multiple Dfs roots if you want to simulate multiple root shares.

FIGURE 7.11

The second server in a
growing network

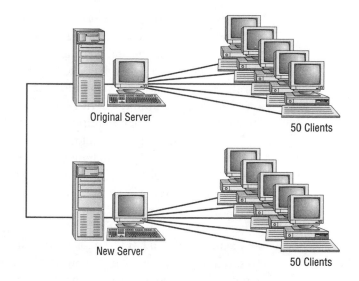

The next stage, a few years down the road, is where Dfs really makes your job easier. For example, suppose our hypothetical company has grown to 400 client computers, attached to eight different servers, as shown in Figure 7.12.

FIGURE 7.12

A larger hypothetical
company

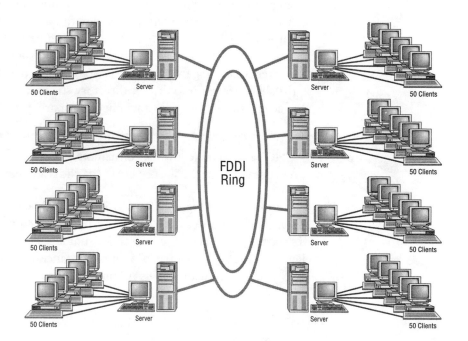

Without Dfs, each new server would require new share mappings throughout the company for users that need to attach to it. In this situation servers are usually brought online and given a specific purpose, such as the storage of financial data. When that data exceeds the capacity of a single server, administrators wind up with servers called FINANCE1 and FINANCE2. This process continues ad infinitum, with users becoming more and more frustrated as they have to dig through multiple servers to find data.

With Dfs, the company still looks like the good old days when everything fit nicely on the server. Even though financial data is spread across four servers, it still looks like subdirectories of a single finance folder in the original root share—just like it always has. You can use the network monitor and the performance monitor to determine which servers are loaded and which ones have excess capacity and then simply move shares from the loaded servers to those less loaded. All you have to do is update the Dfs tree using the Dfs administrator, and your users won't know anything happened at all. Best of all, you won't be spending weeks updating the share mappings of 400 computers.

How Dfs Works

So how does the distributed file system perform its magic? The answer is surprisingly simple. Dfs replaces Universal Naming Convention, or UNC (see *MSCE: NT Workstation Study Guide*) path names that point to grafted subdirectories in the Dfs root with the UNC path name of the actual network share. That's it—even though that explanation is a tad simplistic. The Dfs service on the server containing the Dfs root reports back to the client the true UNC path to the share grafted into the Dfs directory structure. The client then initiates a connection to that server in a manner transparent to the user.

UNC path names follow the convention:
`\\{servername}\{sharename}\{directory_path}`.

For example, in Figure 7.9 the UNC path `\\boomerang\dfsroot\sys` is actually `\\netware\sys`. When a user requests files from, say `\\boomerang\dfsroot\sys\public`, the Dfs service running on boomerang redirects the client to `\\netware\sys\public` in accordance with the Dfs structure mappings you created with the Dfs Administrator tool. That's all there is to it.

This process produces two important effects:

1. Dfs puts a slight load on the root server. Accordingly, you should make this server's file service load lighter than the load of the other servers on your network. Since most Dfs root servers actually started out as the only server on the network, it's a good bet that the server is also the primary domain controller, a service that also puts a slight load on the server.

2. You can't browse through the Dfs tree on the disk volume hosting the Dfs root because local disk requests go through the multiple provider router (which is not redirected by Dfs), rather than the multiple UNC provider (which is).

You can find more information on the inner workings of the multiple provider router and the multiple UNC provider in *MCSE: NT Workstation Study Guide.*

When a Dfs server receives a UNC request that resolves to a share actually located on another computer, the Dfs service sends a message back to the multiple UNC router on the client informing it to replace the Dfs root path with the actual UNC path of the server where the files are located.

Because the MPR that resolves local disk requests (like those issued using the My Computer icon) doesn't see these redirection messages, it can't browse through the Dfs tree. In addition, client computers that don't support Dfs will see only empty directories—the clients don't understand the redirection messages sent by the Dfs server. You can get around this problem by mapping the Dfs share as a local drive. You will then be able to browse the Dfs tree.

The multiple provider router sends requests for shares mapped as drives to the multiple UNC provider, which is redirected by Dfs.

Dfs can even redirect inbound requests for files and Web pages from the Internet. Therefore, your Web site can grow to multiple servers without changing your wwwroot directory structure if you create a dfstree containing your wwwroot and graft other server shares into it. However, Dfs cannot currently redirect share names that identify the server using IP addresses, such as \\128.110.121.13*sharename.*

Obtaining Dfs

Dfs was not finished in time for inclusion with the initial release of Windows NT Server 4, so if it is not on your CD-ROM, you may have to download it from the Microsoft Web site. Exercise 7.9 shows you how. The Dfs package is small, and it won't take you long to download.

EXERCISE 7.9

Downloading Dfs from the Microsoft Web Site

1. Use Dial-up Networking to connect to the Internet if your computer does not maintain a constant connection.

2. Launch Internet Explorer or your preferred Web browser.

3. Type **www.microsoft.com** in the location/URL input box of your Web browser.

4. Click the SEARCH link.

5. Type **distributed file system** in the search input box.

6. Find the link pointing to Microsoft Distributed File System Download Instructions and click it.

7. Read the instructions on the Web page, proceeding through each step until you are able to select the link pointing directly to the Dfs file. You will have to agree to a licensing statement, fill in a form asking about you and your network, and select the type of microprocessor you use.

8. Select the **dfs-v40-i386.exe** (differs for other processors) link to begin downloading the Dfs installation package.

9. Browse to the root of your system directory and create a new folder when the Save as prompt appears. Name the folder Dfs, and double-click to browse the new folder. Save the Dfs package in this folder. The file should take about five minutes to download. You may also want to download the Dfs client for Windows 95 computers that will allow you to treat Windows 95 shares as part of a Dfs tree.

10. Close your Web browser when the download completes.

EXERCISE 7.9 (CONTINUED FROM PREVIOUS PAGE)

11. Double-click My Computer ➤ C: drive ➤ Dfs ➤ dfs-v40-i386.exe (or to wherever you stored the Dfs package).

12. Click Yes to agree to the software license.

13. Click continue.

14. Click Exit.

15. Read the release notes and exit Write.

Installing Dfs

Once you've obtained Dfs, installing it is very simple. Exercise 7.10 walks you through the steps necessary to install Dfs assuming you've downloaded it from the Microsoft Web site. If it came on your Windows NT Server 4 CD-ROM, follow the installation instructions on the CD-ROM. It should install like any other network related service.

EXERCISE 7.10

Installing the Distributed File System Service

1. Right-click Network Neighborhood.

2. Select Properties.

3. Click the Services tab.

4. Click Add.

5. Click Have Disk. If Distributed File System appears in the Network Service list, do not select it; use Have Disk instead.

6. Type **C:\winnt\system32\dfs** (or wherever your Windows NT boot directory resides).

7. Press Enter.

8. Click OK to select Dfs for installation.

---

9. Check Host a Dfs on share.

10. Click New Share.

11. Type **C:\dfsroot** in the input box.

12. Click Yes to create the Dfs root directory.

13. Select Shared As.

14. Click OK.

15. Click OK.

16. Click Close.

17. Click Yes to restart the computer.

Creating Dfs Shares

Once Dfs is installed on your machine, you are ready to create a Dfs share. Dfs shares are created through the Dfs Administrator tool located in the Administrative tools group after you've installed the Dfs service. The administrator allows you to assign shared directories on any server to a subdirectory (called a graft) that the Dfs Administrator will create within your Dfs tree. Figure 7.13 shows the Dfs Administrator. Exercise 7.11 explains how to use the Dfs Administrator.

FIGURE 7.13

The Dfs Administrator

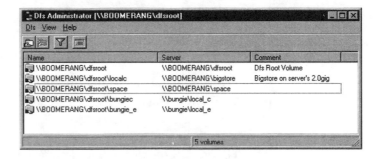

Don't just create Dfs shares on the fly—plan a coherent unified directory tree and create only the shares necessary to implement that tree. Then use the network and performance monitors to find out where you need to move directories to balance your file service load. No matter where resources actually exist on your network, your Dfs tree should remain the same—that's the point of Dfs.

EXERCISE 7.11

Creating and Managing Distributed File Systems

1. Select Start ➤ Programs ➤ Administrative Tools ➤ Dfs Administrator.

2. Select Dfs ➤ Add to Dfs (or click the yellow shared folder tool on the toolbar).

3. Type **localc** in the When a user references this path input box.

4. Click the Browse button next to the Send the user to this network path input box.

5. Click your computer to expand it. Notice that you could click any server, workstation, or Windows 95 computer running the Dfs client for Windows 95, in your domain.

6. Select the share you created in Exercise 7.7 to add to the Dfs volume.

7. Close the Dfs Administrator.

Exploring with Dfs

Now that you have a Dfs share grafted on, let's do a little exploring to see the behavior of Dfs under different circumstances. After you've played with Exercise 7.12, log on to your server from a client on the network and map a drive to the dfsroot share. Browse through that to see how Dfs looks from the client side.

EXERCISE 7.12

Exploring with Dfs

1. Double-click My Computer.

2. Double-click the C: drive (or the drive containing your Dfs root).

3. Double-click **dfsroot**. The folder called **localc** is a security object created to provide a presence in the file system that matches the distributed file system.

4. Double-click **localc**. Notice that it is empty, despite the fact that your share may not be.

5. Attempt to copy a file (any file will do) by right-dragging and dropping it onto the **localc** folder.

6. Click OK to acknowledge access is denied. The **localc** folder is not a true directory object, so you cannot copy files into it through the Explorer.

7. Close all the windows you have open on the desktop.

8. Double-click Network Neighborhood.

9. Double-click Dfs root.

10. Double-click localc.

11. Notice that your Browse window contains all the files and folders you would expect.

Exercise 7.12 highlights a very important aspect of Dfs. The difference in browser behavior between the My Computer directory browser and the Network Neighborhood share browser is caused by the services that provide pathname resolution to those browsers. The Network Neighborhood browses through the multiple UNC provider service, which is redirected by Dfs, whereas My Computer browses through the multiple provider router service, which is not redirected by Dfs.

When you double clicked localc this time, Dfs modified the UNC path to return the true UNC path name of the localc share. This behavior is invisible to the end user, thus providing the invisible redirection of shares anywhere on your network without the interaction of your users or the necessity to reconfigure clients when you move directory shares.

Summary

The easiest and most secure way to control access to data within your Internet site is to use the same basic account-based mechanisms that Windows NT provides to secure local area networks. Implementing user accounts beyond the default Anonymous account provided by the IIS service provides a simple and coherent way to control access to your site. Using groups to associate similar account requirements makes this process even easier.

Once the identity of an Internet user is known to your Internet host, you can use file permissions to restrict access a number of different ways. Share permissions provide a way to control access to other network shares based on the account name.

The distributed file system provides a generalized way to make multiple shares appear as a single directory structure.

Review Questions

1. You need to set up a Web and FTP site that will be available to the general public to download support files, and to your in-house engineers to upload files via FTP. You decide to use the Internet Service Manager to restrict your FTP and Web sites to read-only access rather than using NTFS file security. This option:

   A. Solves neither problem

   B. Solves both problems

   C. Solves the download problem but not the upload problem

   D. Solves the upload problem but not the download problem

2. You need to set up a Web and FTP site that will be available to the general public to download support files, and to your in-house engineers to upload files via FTP. You decide to use NTFS file system security to restrict your FTP and Web sites to read-only access for the Internet Anonymous user account. This option:

A. Solves neither problem

B. Solves both problems

C. Solves the download problem but not the upload problem

D. Solves the upload problem but not the download problem

3. You need to set up a Web and FTP site that will be available to the general public to download support files, and to your in-house engineers to upload files via FTP. You decide to use share-level security to restrict your FTP and Web sites to read-only access for the Internet Anonymous user account. This option:

A. Solves neither problem

B. Solves both problems

C. Solves the download problem but not the upload problem

D. Solves the upload problem but not the download problem

4. You've implemented a Web-site on your file server and intend to use NTFS file system security to secure the site. When you right-click the directory that you intend to secure and select properties, you notice that there's no Security tab so you can't set file system security. What's wrong?

A. The volume is formatted with the FAT file system.

B. You haven't turned on file auditing.

C. You haven't enabled file system security in the Internet Service Manager.

D. You aren't logged in as the administrator so you can't change security permissions.

5. You've implemented an intranet server and are using NTFS file system security to restrict permissions by department in your organization. You've made some information available to the Anonymous logon account. Your server is set to allow Anonymous logon for untrusted access from the Internet and basic text authentication to allow security domain account holders to log on from any operating system that provides logon credentials. Bob, a new hire, tells you he can access the site from his Windows 95 computer using Internet Explorer, but he can't get access to his department's area in the site. You check his group membership and verify that he is a member of his department's group. No one else is reporting any problems. What might be wrong? (Select all correct answers.)

A. Bob's account has a specific denial because he is a member of the New Hire group.

B. Bob is using a Web browser that does not support the security mechanism.

C. Bob's computer does not have the TCP/IP protocol stack correctly installed.

D. Bob's network adapter is malfunctioning.

E. Bob has not logged on to the domain, so his browser is automatically logging on as the Anonymous user.

CHAPTER

8

Securing Your Site

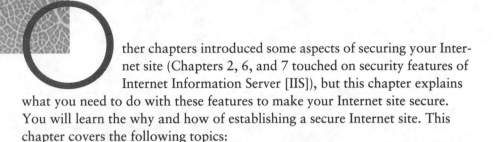

ther chapters introduced some aspects of securing your Internet site (Chapters 2, 6, and 7 touched on security features of Internet Information Server [IIS]), but this chapter explains what you need to do with these features to make your Internet site secure. You will learn the why and how of establishing a secure Internet site. This chapter covers the following topics:

- How your site may be compromised if you don't take sufficient security precautions

- IIS security features (some introduced in previous chapters)

- How IIS uses NT (and especially NTFS) security features

- Additional security measures you can take to secure your Internet site and your LAN

Why Secure Your Site?

The first question you might be asking is, Why should I worry about security? I want everyone to be able to access my Web (or FTP or Gopher) site anyway, so there's no point in securing it. Not so!

You should not dismiss security concerns even if all the material on your site is publicly available. Security is more than just what people can or cannot read. Internet security encompasses these factors:

- What information stored on your server is accessible and to which people

- The accessibility of your Internet server to Internet users

- Who has access to change specific information on your server, when, and from where

- Who has access to add new information to your server or remove information from your server, when, and from where

- The possibility of compromising the security of your entire network because of a poorly secured Web server

You should be concerned about more than the information you put on your Web site. You also need to be concerned about inappropriate use of your Web site by others. For example, if a security hole allows unauthorized users to store files on your server, you may find yourself unwittingly hosting pirated software and graphic images of questionable merit. This intrusion not only wastes your valuable disk space but also may expose you to legal action because of copyright infringements or offended parties.

You therefore need to be careful of two aspects of your Internet site security. You need to ensure that:

1. Information on your Internet site is stored with the appropriate security permissions. For example, make sure that a file meant for your sales force to view isn't actually stored with Read permissions for everyone.

2. Your Internet site does not have any security weaknesses that would allow unscrupulous individuals to gain control and use it for their own purposes.

How Security Can Be Compromised

The security of your Internet site can be compromised only if your Internet site has security loopholes or weaknesses. Unfortunately, it is almost impossible to remove all loopholes and weaknesses from Internet site software because often Internet site administrators do not recognize a loophole until someone exploits it to compromise security. Programmers and site administrators don't intentionally put loopholes in or weaken security; they are almost always an oversight, and how are you to know if you've overlooked something? If you know you've overlooked it, it's not an oversight!

Server administrators eventually find and fix these oversights in the server software, and Internet site security becomes much more difficult to penetrate. By choosing widely used Internet server software (and IIS is widely used!), you benefit from the experience of many other Internet server administrators who have found problems and fixed them.

The Computer Emergency Response Team at CMU (CERT) produces regular and timely advisory messages about weaknesses in Internet software. You should regularly check for CERT advisories that affect your Internet site, and you should swiftly move to close security holes identified in CERT advisories. (The nice thing about CERT advisories is that they tell you about the security holes and how to plug them.) The CERT home page is at www.cert.org (see Figure 8.1).

FIGURE 8.1

The CERT Coordination Center gives you timely warning of security holes in Internet software.

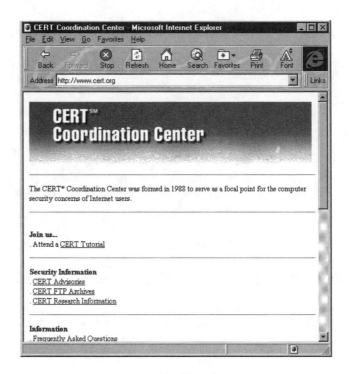

Incorrect Permissions Settings

The first thing you should make sure of is that the regular IIS and NTFS settings for the data you are hosting are correct. If you are not careful when you set up groups, you can unintentionally give people access to FTP files, Gopher files, and Web pages that they wouldn't otherwise have access to. You should, for example, make sure that the IUSER_<computername> account is not a member of groups that have access to files that you don't want anonymous users to access.

Incomplete Security on CGI Scripts and ISAPI Programs

You open up an entirely new can of security worms when you enable CGI scripts and ISAPI applications on your IIS. Every CGI script or ISAPI DLL is essentially a custom extension to your Web server, and you must make sure that the custom extension does not create a new security loophole.

If the CGI script or ISAPI component performs only a simple, well-defined function and returns data in a Web page, then you don't have much to worry about. Most CGI scripts and ISAPI components are carefully written so as not to be a security risk, but the more flexible the script or DLL, the more careful you must be when implementing it. A CGI script that accepts a command from the Web browser and executes that command on the server on behalf of the browser is an extremely flexible and useful extension, but it is also rife with peril. Such an extension could execute a command that would give unauthorized users access to your server computer.

CGI Scripts and ISAPI applications execute with the security permissions of the logged on user. Therefore, the IUSR_MACHINE account permissions will be used for anonymous users.

WARNING   Never create a CGI script that simply passes through commands to a command interpreter or a scripting language. This technique creates a security loophole that allows anyone smart enough to exploit it to remotely control your Web server.

Lax Username and Password Settings

If the passwords on your Internet server computer are simple and easy to guess, or if you or some of your network users use the same username and password on many different computer systems, then these weak usernames and passwords could be used to gain access to your system.

Bugs in Service Software

Many network services designed for a LAN environment will not stand up to the more intense security requirements of the Internet. E-mail server packages are especially vulnerable, but any service that runs on your server and engages in a network dialogue with a client computer can be a potential security hole. These security holes are most often exploited by causing the service software to execute a command provided by the unauthorized user, which will then give the unauthorized user more access to your Internet server.

Limit the number of applications that run on your Internet server to limit the number of potential security holes.

IIS Security Features

Maintaining Internet security is a constant process. Your job is to stay ahead of anyone who would like to gain access to your Web site. Your first defense is to set up an Internet site without any obvious security holes. Then as you discover weaknesses in your software or administrative practices, you must update your software or change those practices so that intruders can't gain access to your system.

Microsoft makes your job easier by providing security features both in IIS and in the underlying operating system and file system (Windows NT and NTFS.) You have a number of tools at your disposal to make your site secure and to detect when attempts are being made to compromise the security of your site. Many of these features were introduced in previous chapters (especially in Chapter 7 on NTFS security features and in Chapter 6 on managing IIS), but now you'll see how to put all these features together to make a secure Internet Web, FTP, and Gopher site.

This section shows you how to use the following IIS security features:

- Disabling directory browsing

- Disabling file uploads

- Using and requiring Secure Socket Layer

- Logging IIS activity

The later section on NTFS security explains how you can use NTFS security to make IIS secure. After that (in the section on additional security measures), you will see what else you can do to make your Internet site (and your LAN) secure from Internet malfeasants.

Disabling Directory Browsing

One of the easiest ways to secure your server is to disable directory browsing on Web directories. Unfortunately, you can only enable or disable browsing for the entire Web service, not just for individual directories.

You may want to leave directory browsing enabled if the purpose of your site is to provide information over the Internet. Sometimes smart users can find information based on the filenames of the Web pages when the links to those pages are broken or obscure. Search engines like AltaVista also rely on being able to search directories in order to index your site pages.

There is no sense, though, in giving intruders free information about files or scripts that network intruders can exploit to penetrate your security.

You disable directory browsing for the WWW service from the Directories tab of the WWW Service Properties window. There you simply remove the check from the Directory Browsing Enabled option.

WARNING   Disabling directory browsing does increase security, but only slightly. Security through obscurity is no real protection from a knowledgeable intruder. An observant intruder can determine what pages and scripts you have in your server merely by browsing your Web pages and observing the URLs that are used.

Disabling File Uploads (Write Access)

Most public access of FTP sites is anonymous. A username and e-mail address are often given in lieu of actual security credentials, and the name and address are written to the log files, but that process provides no real security. The user can enter anything, and the FTP server has no real way to verify the information.

Most experienced administrators disable file uploads (Write access) to all FTP directories but one and also remove Read access to that (incoming) directory. That common practice allows the administrators to check all files for viruses and appropriateness before placing the files in public portions of the FTP site.

Disabling file uploads is important especially for directories that contain scripts or programs because an intruder might upload a changed script or file that (when executed) would grant that intruder full access to your system. You should make sure that all CGI script and ISAPI application directories, as well as directories containing executable files for your system, have file uploads disabled.

You do not usually disable file uploads for users' home directories, though. Many Internet users use FTP to store and retrieve files from their home directories over the Internet. You would, however, use NTFS security to allow only authenticated (i.e., not anonymous) users access to their home directories. You should deny anonymous FTP access to all directories except those containing publicly accessible files for download only.

You disable file access by selecting the directory in question in the Directories tab of the FTP Service Properties window. You then click the Edit button and remove the check mark from the Write option. To remove FTP Read access for the same directory, you remove the check mark from the Read option in the same window.

Disabling Script Execution

You should be careful about which WWW Service directories you allow Execute permission on. You will probably want to give users of your Windows NT Server their own WWW directories for their Web pages. To allow the users to maintain their own pages, you have to give them at least NTFS Read and Write access to the directories, and if the users will be updating them remotely, you should give them FTP Read and Write access as well (see the earlier section on disabling file uploads). One reason that most companies won't allow users to maintain their own Web pages remotely is to avoid these security complications.

You do not, however, have to enable the Execute option on these WWW Service directories. Scripts and ISAPI DLLs are executed by the server, not downloaded to the user's browsing computer, and the user can place a compromising script or DLL in that directory. You should carefully consider what scripts and DLLs you will allow to be executed in your IIS-based Web site. You should place those scripts and DLLs in a protected directory that only authorized individuals can modify, and you should not allow the WWW Service Execute option on any other directories.

You select the WWW Service access permissions for a directory in the WWW Service Directory Properties window for that directory. Check the Execute option to enable it; clear the option to disable it.

You should also disable Read access to directories that have Execute access, especially for directories that contain Active Server Pages. This step prevents remote users from reading the scripts you've placed in those directories and figuring out how your scripts work, but it doesn't keep them from executing the scripts.

Secure Socket Layer

Secure Socket Layer (SSL) does not protect your Internet site from intrusion. Instead, it protects the communications between your Internet site and Web browsers from interception and eavesdropping. When a Web browser connects to your server using the HTTPS protocol, an encrypted link is established between the browser and the server, and sensitive information such as passwords and credit-card information can then be transferred back and forth.

When you install a key and a certificate into the WWW Service, you can then require SSL access to WWW Service directories. The Require SSL Channel option in the directory options for that virtual directory (which is grayed out otherwise) then becomes available. It is clear by default; you can check this option and require all accesses to the directory to be encrypted.

Encryption has its price, however. It takes more processing power, more bandwidth, and more time to send encrypted data than it does to send unencrypted data. You should therefore require SSL only on directories that contain sensitive data or Web pages that receive privileged information such as those credit card numbers we keep talking about.

Unfortunately, you can't enable SSL without buying a certificate from a security certificate vendor. If you need to use SSL, your security certificate provider can help you through the process of setting up secured directories.

Logging

The preceding IIS features and the Windows NT security features that appear in the next section help keep out intruders, much as a lock helps keep burglars out of your home. Logging helps keep intruders out by alerting you when someone has been testing your defenses. Logging is a bit like checking for scratches on the lock or footprints in the dust; it tells you if someone has been where they shouldn't be.

Logging also tells you which parts of your server are most popular and where bottlenecks are slowing down your IIS. But those uses for logging are the subject of Chapter15.

When you install IIS, the default configuration logs Internet server activity to the LogFiles subdirectory of the System32 subdirectory of the Windows NT system directory. You don't have to do anything to enable logging; it is set up to happen automatically. Every Web, FTP, and Gopher access of your Internet site is written by default to the log file.

The data stored to the log files are as follows (assuming that the log file is stored in the default, or Microsoft, format):

- **Client Host**—The computer that is making the Internet request (HTML page hit, FTP file transfer, etc.)

- **User Name**—The user account making the request, a dash (–) for anonymous

- **Log Date**—The date of the action

- **Log Time**—The time of the action

- **Service**—The service that is responding to the action; W3SVC for the WWW Service, MSFTPSVC for the FTP Service, and GopherSvc for the Gopher Service

- **Machine**—The computer name of the server

- **Server IP**—The IP address that the service is responding for

- **Processing Time**—How long it took for IIS to process the request

- **Bytes Received**—The size of the request in bytes

- **Bytes Sent**—The size of the response in bytes

- **Service Status**—A numerical value describing the status of the service

- **Wind32 Status**—A numerical value describing the status of the Win32 subsystem

- **Operation**—The command or request made by the Internet client

- **Target**—The target of the operation (e.g., the Web page requested or the FTP file transferred)

- **Parameters**—The parameters to the operation

- **Other Info**—Additional information

You can view the log files in various ways. You can pull a log file into a text editor and scan the entries visually, but this method is the least effective way to view the data. The data is stored in a comma-delimited file so that you can easily pull it into another program, such as a spreadsheet, database, or report generator, that has tools for manipulating and summarizing the data.

Internet Information Server comes with Crystal Reports, an application
that lets you query information from a set of IIS log files or from a database
(see Figure 8.2). When you install Crystal Reports, it is automatically configured with the following reports:

- Activity by day of week

- Activity by hour of day

- Most accessed directories

- Most requested pages

- Server errors

- Most downloaded file types and sizes

FIGURE 8.2

Crystal Reports can
organize the log data and
display important server
statistics.

You can generate these reports and view them in your Web browser by
going to the following page: `http://yoyo/logrpts/default.asp`; after you

install Crystal Reports, of course, and replace yoyo with the name of your computer. Be sure to select Refresh Report Data before you click the Generate Crystal Report button. To view other statistics, or to view the above statistics in greater detail, you will have to either create your own Crystal Reports forms or pull the log files into another tool to examine them.

You should regularly check the logs for unusual patterns of activity. You should be particularly concerned with a high proportion of Unauthorized, Forbidden, or Not Found access attempts, especially coming from one Internet address or user. This pattern of access could indicate that an intruder is attempting to find weaknesses in your security. If you determine that someone is indeed trying to circumvent your security, you might then disallow access altogether for that IP address in the Advanced tabs of the various Internet Server Properties pages.

Restricting Access

The Advanced tab of each service's Properties windows contains a list to which you can add computers that are expressly forbidden or expressly allowed access to your Web site. If you are using IIS to create an intranet, then you will know the identity of all the computers that should be allowed access to your site. You should list those computers and disallow all others.

If, however, you are creating an Internet site that will be publicly accessible to the whole world, then you should set it to allow access from everywhere but the specifically listed sites. Then you should add problem Internet addresses to the list as you discover them.

Exercise 8.1 shows you how to disable directory browsing in the WWW service and set up an incoming directory for the FTP service.

Windows NT Security Features

Chapter 7 explained how Windows NT user accounts, group accounts, NTFS file permissions, and the distributed file system all work. Although you may have wondered why you needed to know all about these Windows NT structures in a book about IIS, by now you have probably figured out that the Windows NT and NTFS security features are also the security features of IIS.

Some Internet servers (Netscape, for example) have their own lists of users and groups, independent of the operating system they run on. In contrast, IIS adopts Windows NT users and groups as IIS users and groups, and it adopts

EXERCISE 8.1

Making IIS Services More Secure

1. Log on as Administrator.

2. Open the ftpoot folder. (Open My Computer ➤ C: ➤ InetPub ➤ ftproot if you installed IIS with its default settings.)

3. Create a new folder in the directory and name it **Incoming**.

4. Start the Microsoft Internet Service Manager.

5. Right-click the WWW Service and then select Service Properties.

6. Click the Directories button and then uncheck the Directory Browsing Allowed button.

7. Click the Apply button and then the OK button.

8. Right-click the FTP Service and then select Service Properties.

9. Click the Directories tab and then click the Add button.

10. Type the path to the Incoming directory you created in step 3 in the Directory field (e.g., **C:\InetPub\ftproot\Incoming**).

11. Check the Write option and uncheck the Read option.

12. Click the OK button and then click the Apply button.

13. Click the OK button.

NTFS file security as the security for Web pages and FTP files. Therefore, you must know how to use these Windows NT features in their Windows NT environment to apply them to your Web site.

Chapter 7 gave you the tools to create a secure Windows NT environment. Now you will learn how to use these tools to make a secure Internet site using the same features. You'll look at each of the following in turn:

- User and group accounts

- File security

- Logging

- Dial-up security

User and Group Accounts

If you only care to allow anonymous Web, FTP, and Gopher access, then the IUSER_<computername> account that is installed by default will meet your needs. Otherwise, you will have to create user accounts and groups for Internet users who will access your site with anything other than anonymous access.

A number of accounts are already created for you. At least two—the Administrator and the Guest account were installed by default when you installed Windows NT Server. (The Guest account is disabled by default, though, and it is a good idea to leave it that way.) Any additional accounts you have created for regular file and print access in the Windows networking domain will be able to access your Internet server using their domain username and password. Depending on the NTFS security you have established, those accounts may have no more access than the anonymous account has. And if you have given them specific No Access permissions to directories that the WWW Service uses, some may have even less access to your Internet server.

For a Web server that is meant for access by members of your organization (an *intranet,* or at least part of one), this correspondence between Internet Server users and domain users is both convenient and appropriate. You can make Web pages and directories that are available only to certain groups of users or changeable only by certain groups of users—for example, the marketing department, all of your electrical engineers, or the computer help desk staff.

However, suppose you are creating a subscription Internet site where the Web user:

- Must enter a username and password in order to access the site

- Must not have access to log on to your domain

You can implement those subscription accounts as computer accounts on the Windows NT Server computer that is running IIS. Alternatively, you can create those subscription accounts using CGI scripts or ISAPI DLLs to accept the usernames and passwords and keep track of the users.

The problem with subscription accounts to Web sites is that (for most Web sites) just about anyone can ask for a subscription, and the site wants to acquire as many subscribers as possible. As a result, hundreds or thousands of individuals may have computer accounts for your network as well as for your Web site.

If you choose to implement these accounts using Windows NT security, then you will have to be particularly careful that no one will be able to actually log on and use the file and print services of your network (unless, of course, you want them to). In this case you should make your Internet server its own domain. This approach keeps Internet users separated from your internal users.

You can then establish trust relationships so that the Internet domain trusts your internal domain but not the reverse. The companion book *MCSE: NT Server in the Enterprise* covers trust relationships in more detail. Another complementary approach (meaning use both if you can) is to use a firewall that blocks all but FTP, Gopher, and WWW access (see the last section of this chapter on additional measures you may take to secure your Internet site). You may also use a clever combination of permissions and NT security settings to keep users from logging on to your server directly—but that's more difficult and error prone.

You may note that the anonymous account is implemented with a Windows NT user account (the IUSER_<computername> account), but users cannot use it to log on for file and print services. The anonymous account does not present the same problem as other user accounts you may create because the individual browsing your Web anonymously doesn't know the IUSER_<computername> password. Consequently, these users can't use the anonymous account to log on to and use the file and print services of your Internet server.

If properly defending your Internet site against the very user accounts you create within it seems daunting, you may choose to implement subscription users a different way. The CGI script or ISAPI DLL solution is perfectly adequate for most Web sites. Most Web sites provide essentially the same services to each customer and don't need elaborate group and file protection mechanisms. A CGI or ISAPI Web page can differentiate between users without using the NT or NTFS security features. Chapter 12 will show you how to create CGI- or ISAPI-based Web sites.

File Security

IIS seamlessly ties its security into the NTFS security mechanisms. Anonymous Web and FTP users, for example, have access only to files and directories that the IUSER_<computername> account has access to. Therefore, if you want to keep anonymous users from accessing a particular directory, all you have to do is give the IUSER_<computername> the No Access permission for that directory.

The first thing you will want to do (if you did not do it as a matter of course just after you installed Windows NT Server and formatted a volume with NTFS) is remove the Full Control for Everyone permission that is set by default when Windows NT Server formats a partition with NTFS. (Give the Administrators group Full Control before you do that, though! You don't want to make an entire file system unreadable to everyone. You can use the Administrator account to set security for other accounts later.) Then a safe permission to set for the root directory is Read for Everyone. You can later give specific users and groups (such as the anonymous account) more access to specific parts of the NTFS volume. To summarize:

- Set Domain Admins to Full Control for C: and all subdirectories

- Remove Everyone Full Control for C: and all subdirectories

- Set Local Group: WebAdministrators Full Control to `C:InetPub` and below

- Set Everyone Read to wwwroot, gopherroot, ftproot, and below

- Set Everyone NoRead / Yes Execute to wwwroot/scripts

Applying NTFS security to IIS Web pages and FTP directories is straightforward. The principles discussed in Chapter 7 apply to Web page access over the Internet as well as to file access from a regular network client. For example, an authenticated user accessing files in that user's home directory using FTP will be able to get and put files (i.e., read and write them) as well as rename them and delete them. That same user may have only Read access to a colleague's files (because that colleague set up the file permissions that way) and no access at all to the `Incoming` FTP directory.

The Index Server search engine also respects NTFS file permissions. A search performed on the behalf of a user who has accessed your Web site anonymously will show only references to Web pages and documents that are readable by the anonymous user account. A user who provides a username and password that has more permissions will be shown more than that anonymous user, but only what that authenticated user has NTFS permissions to read.

Auditing

NTFS also logs access attempts to files and directories, but the events it records can be reviewed in the Event Viewer rather than in the IIS log files or in an ODBC database. You can use NTFS log files just as you can use the IIS log files to determine which users are accessing what files and when.

Before you can audit NTFS events, however, you must enable auditing in User Manager for Domains. Then you can select specific events to audit for a directory or file from the Security tab of the Properties page for that directory or file.

Dial-Up Security

Finally, you should be careful about whom you allow to connect to your Internet server over the dial-up lines. The Remote Access Service (RAS) of Windows NT has a number of security features that you can use, including encrypted authentication, data encryption, and dial back (you dial the RAS server and it dials you back) that you can use to make the dial-up connections secure. (Chapter 14 covers dial-up security in more detail.)

In Exercise 8.2 you will set the NTFS permissions for the `ftproot` and `Incoming` subdirectories. These exercises assume that you have placed the `InetPub` subdirectory on an NTFS volume.

EXERCISE 8.2

Setting NTFS Security Permissions

1. Log on to the Administrator account.

2. Select the `ftproot` folder. (Open My Computer ➤ C: ➤ `InetPub` and then click the ftproot icon.)

3. Select Properties from the File menu.

4. Click the Security tab.

5. Click the Permissions button.

6. Click the Everyone entry and change the type of access to Read.

7. Click the OK button. Close the ftproot Properties window.

8. Double-click the `ftproot` folder.

9. Select the `Incoming` folder.

10. Select Properties from the File menu.

11. Click the Security tab.

12. Click the Permissions button.

13. Click the Everyone entry and change the type of access to Special Directory Access.

14. Uncheck the Read and Execute options. Check the Write option. Click OK.

15. Click the Everyone entry and change the type of access to Special File Access.

16. Uncheck the Read and Execute options. Check the Write option. Click OK.

17. Click the OK button. Close the Incoming Properties window.

Additional Security Measures

Keeping network intruders from breaking into your system is much easier if you can keep those intruders from even getting close to your system. You can use several mechanisms that are not a part of the Windows NT Server and Internet Information Server package to make your Internet server secure; you should consider these measures if making your site secure is a priority (and it should be):

- Firewalls

- Packet filters

- Proxy servers

Firewalls

A firewall is a dedicated computer that sits between two networks (one of the networks is usually the Internet, and the other is your LAN) and protects one of the networks from the other. Its function is to examine all the data flowing between the two networks and allowing to pass only the kinds of data it identifies as not harmful.

Firewalls can be configured to block network communications based on a number of different criteria, including:

- The source computer IP address or IP network

- The destination computer IP address or IP network

- The TCP/IP socket number (which can block specific services such as FTP, Gopher, WWW, DNS, Ping, and Telnet)

By allowing certain TCP port numbers and blocking the rest, you can ensure that only FTP, WWW, and Gopher data are going in and out of your network. Network intruders won't be able to use file and print services of your Windows NT server or log on to your domain because the NetBIOS communications over TCP/IP won't make it through the firewall. The companion volume *MCSE: TCP/IP Study Guide* has more information on TCP/IP ports.

Block *all* protocols with your firewall except HTTP, FTP, and outbound Ping. Then enable only those protocols you find are necessary later (when your users complain that something doesn't work!).

Packet Filters

Packet filters are simpler to implement than firewalls are, but they perform a similar function. Packet filters merely sit between networks (the Internet and your LAN, again) and examine each TCP/IP packet. If the packet meets a simple set of rules, then it is allowed to pass; otherwise, it is blocked. Compared to firewalls, packet filters are less complex and less secure, but they are faster and don't cause as much network latency.

Proxy Servers

A proxy server is a go-between for Web servers. A proxy server speeds up WWW access by caching Web pages, which reduces network bandwidth and hides the existence of client computers on your LAN.

When a proxy server sits between the client computer and the Web server, the Web browser on that client computer directs Web page requests to that proxy server rather than to the more distant Web server. The proxy server passes that page request to the actual Web server. The Web server replies to the proxy server, and the proxy server sends the resultant page to the Web browser. Meanwhile, the proxy server keeps a copy of that page for anyone else who is interested in it. If another Web browser comes along and asks for that page, the Proxy server can return the Web page immediately instead of waiting until the Web server can reply.

Proxy servers are most useful when your LAN is fast and your connection to the Internet is not as fast or is costly. By keeping a copy of the most commonly accessed Web pages, the proxy server saves you bandwidth and money.

Another significant benefit is that to the end Web server (and to the rest of the Internet as well) the proxy server alone seems to be the source of all Internet traffic on your LAN. The client computers are hidden behind it, which means that they won't be easy targets for intruders to find and examine (remotely, through the various Internet protocols) for weaknesses.

Proxy servers are often combined with firewalls to create a single point of access between your intranet and the Internet. They are also sometimes combined with Web servers when security is less important than software cost.

Summary

Maintaining security on your Internet site is an ongoing process. You must always be aware of the threats to your Internet site and the Windows NT server that hosts it. Making sure that the right permissions are set on the files and directories is only half the problem. You must also make sure that network intruders attempting to exploit weaknesses in network programs, operating system services, CGI scripts, and ISAPI DLLs have no weaknesses to exploit.

First you should make sure that the IIS security settings are correctly established:

- Disable directory browsing and enable FTP uploads in your FTP `Incoming` directory (and disable Read for that directory).

- Enable Execute only for WWW Service directories into which users cannot place their own CGI scripts or ISAPI DLLs.

- Allow only specified computers to access your Web site if you are establishing an intranet.

Next create users and groups for the Internet site and make sure that their access allows them to do only what they need to do. Set the NTFS permissions to support the IIS security. Enable auditing if you detect network intrusion and set proper RAS security for dial-in connections.

Finally, consider placing a firewall or at least a packet filter between your network and the Internet and think about establishing a proxy server to hide your network clients, speed network access, and reduce communications costs.

Review Questions

1. You suspect that someone on the Internet is trying to gain unauthorized access to files on your Windows NT Server. How can you verify your suspicions?

   A. Disconnect your Internet Server computer from the network.

   B. Assign only Read permission to all files and directories from the `InetPub` directory down.

C. Use Crystal Reports on the IIS log files data to show the percentage of Unauthorized, Forbidden, or Not Found access attempts per client IP address.

D. Examine the System Log portion of the Event Viewer for unauthorized access attempts.

2. You determine that most of the unauthorized access attempts on your server computer come from one Class C subnetwork. What can you do to make sure that this subnetwork cannot threaten your Internet Information Server?

A. Use Crystal Reports on the IIS log files data to show the percentage of Unauthorized, Forbidden, or Not Found access attempts per client IP address.

B. In the Advanced tab of each service, disallow access from that subnet.

C. In the Services tab of the Networking control panel, disallow access from that subnet.

D. Remove the TCP/IP default route to that subnet.

3. You need software to hide your client computers on your LAN from the Internet and to perform Web requests for them. Which software or hardware package will do what you want?

A. Internet Information Server

B. Index Server

C. A packet filter

D. A proxy server

CHAPTER

9

Seven Habits of Highly
Effective Webmasters

As the Internet has grown, Web sites have become more complex and difficult to maintain. Web browsers now support many types of content along with HTML, and Web users have come to expect professionally designed pages. Webmasters (the administrators of Web and Internet sites) combine the talents of writers, graphic designers, and network administrators to create coherent sites that are informative, well structured, and easy to use.

This chapter concentrates on the World Wide Web because, unlike FTP and Gopher sites, Web sites are more than simple collections of files with an index. Web sites can be extremely complex. Content such as real-time sound feeds and three-dimensional graphics expand the scope of Web sites far beyond the intent of the original architects of the Web.

The long-term maintenance and growth of a Web site are important factors to consider when you plan your site. Sites are never simply created and then left alone; visitors will not keep coming back to the same information over and over. Web sites change and evolve constantly. You will never be finished working on your Web site any more than you are ever finished with your day job—it goes on as long as the organization requires it.

Web sites tend to grow sporadically and sometimes incoherently. You'll often need to post information quickly, so you'll add a page and throw a link on your home page, regardless of whether that link has anything to do with the theme of your page. After just a few occurrences like this, your Web site will be a mass of spaghetti links and dead ends that make finding specific information difficult.

This first section of this chapter will help you organize the development of your Web site so that you can produce a coherent and useful source of information. The second section deals with long-term administration, and the final section considers legal issues such as copyright and IIS licensing. Pay special attention to the section on copyright and licensing—not understanding the legal issues surrounding the Web and software licensing can get you into a lot of trouble.

Seven Habits

The Webmaster makes the difference between an efficient and useful site, a pretty but difficult-to-navigate site, and a useless morass of pages that are easier to browse with a search engine than with the provided links. The work habits and techniques of different Webmasters are apparent when you browse their sites. A few rules of thumb will take you a long way in Web design:

- Be consistent.

- Keep your site fresh.

- Structure your site for clarity and efficiency.

- Work efficiently.

- Optimize content.

- Post changes in batches so your site remains consistent.

- Internationalize.

If you follow these rules, your Web site will be easier to manage and easier for visitors to browse.

Be Consistent

The Web has no borders, no edges, and no walls—there's no obvious way to tell when you've left one site and entered another. Consistency is what clues your visitors into the fact that they are still in your site. Consistency is the thematic design and decoration of your site. It is the signature that tells visitors when they are in your domain. (Pun intended.)

Consistency simply means using the same style, design, or theme throughout your site. You can achieve consistency by using the same background, logo, banner, or using some of the more advanced features of IIS to create a common header and footer throughout your pages.

Consistency is also an optimization. Because all Web browsers cache graphics, using the same graphical elements on all your pages ensures that the user will only need to wait for the first page to load. After that, all the buttons and banners will come from the cache, making your site appear to load very quickly indeed.

Create a Style Guide

A style guide is a single set of rules that defines the visual elements of a Web site so that many different designers can produce internally consistent pages. Have you noticed how every advertisement you've seen from Apple Computer looks like an ad from Apple? Familiarity registers in your mind partly because Apple uses the same typeface in every written document it produces.

Style guides are sets of written instructions or templates that define how the visual elements of a page should be presented. Your site development will progress very rapidly once you've created a style guide. The common elements, such as headers and footers, and the graphical elements, such as buttons, will be defined in your style guide. Development will be quick because you won't have to make style decisions for every page. Elements of a style guide include:

- Font usage for text and headers

- Logos and trademarks, and their location on pages

- Headers, footers, and backgrounds

- Graphics for buttons, bullets, and image maps

- Use of white space, frames, and breaking lines

- Grammar issues and linguistic style

Get together with other members of your organization to define the style guide. You may find that the marketing department (if you have one) already has a style guide for advertisements. Following it as closely as possible will make your site consistent with your organization's existing ad copy and brochures, which in turn will serve to further reinforce your company's image in the minds of your customers. You may also find that scanning camera-ready art is a quick way to get organizational logos and trademarks on your site and that current brochures about products and services can provide written content for your site.

Avoid the temptation to simply make your Web site a linked site of brochures—the Web has much more to offer than printed matter. Simply emulating printed matter electronically wastes a lot of potential.

Use Consistent Headers, Footers, and Toolbars

IIS and many other Web servers have a feature called *server-side includes* that automatically inserts the contents of a Web page in place of special HTML tags. This feature enables you to create a single page for headers, footers, navigation button bars, or any other set of common elements, and then include them in other pages. IIS will serve the HTML in the included file rather than the tag, so your page shows up on the browser as if you had simply cut and pasted the same information on every page.

You could actually cut and paste the same HTML code into your pages, but then if you needed to update the source, you'd have to cut and paste that code back into every page each time you updated the header.

Many visitors will be coming in from search engines and may not have seen your home page. Consistent headers and footers will tell them where they are, and a consistent toolbar with a link back to your home page will help them get to it.

Keep Your Site Fresh

Freshness refers to the delays between site updates. A site is fresh if the content is updated regularly; it is stale if it isn't updated much at all. The primary reason for updating your site frequently is to keep people coming back. Most sites exist as persistent advertisements for the hosting organization.

As with all forms of advertisement, repetition pays. Repetition pays. But unlike push forms of marketing like television, Web content has to pull the consumer in with some sort of compelling content. For software companies, this content is generally the lure of free software. Other companies typically provide freebies related to their market or informative content that changes on a regular basis.

A link to new product information and company events or press releases is also a good idea, but many smaller organizations don't have enough new releases in a year to really keep people coming back for that information alone. A good way to encourage repeat visits if you don't have much news is to provide a page of links to relevant information about your market or a tutorial about your market, products, organization, or methods used in your field. The primary reason people use the Web right now is to find information, so if that information is on your site, people will find your site.

Structure Your Site for Clarity and Efficiency

Have you ever browsed a Web site that was so poorly constructed that you couldn't find the information you knew it contained? Many Webmasters forget that people don't browse the Web to be fed information (that's what television is for); they browse the Web to find specific information. For instance, many companies (including Microsoft) post press releases and corporate news on their home page. This type of information is rarely what people want when they pull up a site.

The key to structuring your Web site clearly is an understanding of what your visitors want, what your organization wants to push, and balancing the two. Consider the following when you structure your site:

- If you sell products or services, always have a link to a single structure of product or service brochures from the home page. Most visitors will be interested in this information.

- Always have a navigation toolbar that allows visitors to at least return to the home page. Never provide a link to a page that contains no links—this is analogous to stranding the user in that page.

- Most Web site home pages would benefit from a home page consisting of a simple logo or banner and then a set of links to more specific pages. This type of page loads quickly and doesn't make any assumptions about what the user wants to see.

- Include a toolbar of links to major subsections of your site, such as your home page, products, customer support, and organizational information. Users should be able to find this information easily.

When your site is finished, ask a few people in your organization who did not participate in the site's development to navigate through it. Use their feedback to update or overhaul the site's organization. Remember that it is easier for people to comment on things they can see than on concepts, so the very people who were no help when you were planning the site are often very vocal about how you should change it. Accept this condition as a natural part of the design cycle and use these comments to improve the site accordingly.

Be Concise

Brevity is the soul of wit. With apologies to Shakespeare, brevity is also the soul of bandwidth optimization. Obviously, pages with less content take less time to load than pages that are packed. Edit your content thoroughly to reduce redundancy. Another important reason for brevity is that visitors are almost never going to read your entire page. Hypertext does not hold the reader hostage to a page the way traditional text does. Any link in your document is an invitation to skip out at that point in the document—and many users will. You have to get your point across before the user clicks out of your document for good.

Work Efficiently with Automated Content Tools

Few serious Webmasters still write HTML in a text editor—the process is simply too tedious and error prone. Tools such as FrontPage (see Chapter 10) speed Web development and maintenance. As pointed out earlier, stale sites don't attract repeat visitors.

Don't overuse sophisticated content types that are difficult to develop and maintain. As nifty as Java and ActiveX controls are, if you have to make a new control every month, you'll find yourself spending too much time on controls and widgets and not enough time keeping the information—the real point of your site—current. Save Java and ActiveX for the functionality that you cannot achieve with simpler content types like HTML, VB Script, or JavaScript. You'd be surprised how rarely you will actually need to resort to sophisticated content.

When you do need more sophisticated content, consider buying a package of controls that already does what you want or can be customized to do what you want. Serious programmers reuse all the code they can, and they buy libraries all the time because they realize that time saved is money saved.

Optimize Content

Optimizing the content of your pages is the process of reducing the complexity of your pages without reducing the information content. The two best ways to optimize content are to minimize the bandwidth required to load the page and to provide a text-only option for users who don't have graphical browsers or who are limited by slow connections to the Internet.

Remember that pages appear as they load. The design of the pages, then, is a key opportunity for optimization. If users find the information they need at the top of the page, they may be able to click and leave, thus eliminating the need to load the rest of the page entirely and saving the bandwidth the remaining page would have wasted. Therefore, you should always put your navigation link bars at the top of the page so users can navigate through if they aren't interested in the contents of that page. For the same reason, you should move complex graphics and content to the bottom of the page whenever possible.

Minimize Bandwidth

Minimizing bandwidth means making your site smaller so it can be transported in less time. Huge page-size image maps are very pretty—and painfully slow for users attached via typical modems.

Use tables of images rather than image maps. Tables of images with descriptive names allow users to read the text before the associated image graphic loads—and possibly to skip the image. Tables also don't require CGI scripts or server-side image-map support to determine where the user clicked.

Use small graphical images. An image that is half the size in each dimension loads four times faster. Make use of icons and buttons that are just large enough to convey the required information.

Reduce the color depth of your images. Color depth refers to the number of unique colors in an image. You can reduce many images that have thousands or millions of colors to 256 or less without losing much, if any, image quality. Reducing color depth can speed load times by a factor of two or three. Formats such as JPEG require you to save the image with 16-bit color or higher and then to use compression to reduce the size of the file based on the number of distinct colors in the image. You will still see the same dramatic reduction in bandwidth.

Use monochrome images. Large images can be very stylish using only a single color—and that color doesn't have to be black. Pencil-sketch style wallpaper is very graphically pleasing and loads quickly even on slow connections.

Use compressed graphics. Both JPEG and GIF file types are compressed by default. JPEG provides a high level of compression to any image, regardless of the number of colors in use. GIF is typically limited to images with 256 colors or less, but adds the option of interlacing the data in the image so that the image displays immediately and becomes increasingly clear as more data arrives, rather than simply filling in from the top down. Interlacing imparts a more sophisticated feel and begins conveying information immediately. GIF can also specify a "transparent" color, which will not hide information beneath it. You can use this color to hide the boundaries of an image if the image isn't square. Extensions to the GIF format also allow you to store multiple images (or frames) within a single graphic file. Rotating through the file provides a simple animation effect, which modern browsers will display. Early browsers that don't support this GIF format will still display the first frame. Browsers do not require extra code or special HTML to support this simple animation effect.

Provide Text-Only Pages for Simpler or Lower-Speed Browsers

Most books on Web development eschew the use of HTML code that doesn't conform to HTML 2.0 standards on the basis that many older Web browsers or users with low-speed links can't take advantage of these pages. Although that caution is justifiable, using only primitive HTML leaves a fairly limited set of functionality and often is far less efficient than using newer techniques.

Rather than limiting yourself by adhering to primitive standards, you are better off providing two entirely different versions of your site—one site with complex information types and the graphical elements you want and another text-only version. This method requires only slightly more development time and hosting space, provides the best of both worlds, and allows the visitor to choose the most appropriate version.

Text takes very little space compared to graphics or sound. If your site is graphically rich, the text version could take as little as a tenth of the space of your full site and will load ten times faster.

Post Changes in Batches

If you've ever browsed a site you've been to before but found that many links aren't behaving properly, only to come back days later and find everything working fine again, you've experienced a site where updates are made on the live version of the site.

Tools like FrontPage allow you to work on a live site while it's available for use. Unfortunately, this procedure makes navigating difficult for users who might be online while you are editing your site. You may have deleted pages that are linked on other pages or put up new links in advance of the pages that you are referencing. In either case, if users click a link and get an error message, your site will look unfinished or incomplete.

You are better off posting complete sites to your server. *Posting* refers to working on a copy of the site offline, performing all the testing and debugging on the offline site, and then copying the entire site to the Internet host directory. This approach minimizes the amount of time that inconsistencies can occur in your site and allows you to guarantee the site's coherence before it's live on the Internet.

FrontPage extensions to IIS allow you to perform remote updates to your live site while it is online. We don't recommend this procedure unless your site has limited traffic. If you are operating an intranet, you should perform live changes during periods when the site is not in use.

It's a Web Wide World: Internationalize

The World Wide Web is called the World Wide Web for a reason—it is world-wide. People from all over the world have access to your Web site. Your Web site will constitute the only access that many people have to information about your organization. Wouldn't it be nice if they could actually understand it?

In the real world, translating Web sites into foreign languages can be pro-hibitively expensive. Fortunately, most computer professionals have at least some English language fluency. This situation will change as the Web becomes available to more typical consumers around the world. If you can't afford to translate your site to another language, you can do some other things to inter-nationalize it. For example:

- Use graphically obvious buttons rather than words for links.

- Provide pictures of products and operational diagrams along with descriptions.

- Use technical language rather than literary descriptions and flowery ad copy—technical language is more universal.

- Survey other members of your organization for language skills. You may find people inside your organization who could perform translations with the help of a bilingual dictionary.

- When international users complain that you don't have a site in their language, enlist their support in translating it if they are bilingual. You will of course have to verify the translations, but you'll find that many people are more than happy to help.

Most of the popular anecdotes about unintentional mistranslation leading to all sorts of comedic results are fabrications or are overstated to exploit a humorous punch line. There's very little reason to fear translating your site without the help of a professional. The vast majority of computer users would be very appreciative of your attempt and will overlook (and even point out, if they can) the occasional slip up.

You don't have to worry about any international legal implications of a less-than-perfect translation unless your organization operates in the same country as anyone who would attempt to hold you responsible for a mistrans-lation. For instance, if you accidentally stated that you were selling computers for 2,000 *cents* instead of 2,000 *dollars,* no one can force you to sell a com-puter for 20 dollars. If you are actually operating in a foreign country, an employee in that country can translate your site.

Legal Issues

You need to be aware of two legal issues when you put up an Internet server: copyright and software licensing. Specifically, you must understand the software licensing for the Internet service software and operating systems you use, and you must understand the legal issues regarding the distribution of the content you publish on your server.

Understanding the legal issues surrounding the Internet will protect you from accidentally overstepping the bounds of the law. When you put up a site, you are inviting anyone on the planet to inspect your compliance with the law regarding copyright. Ignorance of the law is no protection in the event you accidentally publish copyrighted material on the Internet. Copyright owners have already rightfully claimed serious damage awards against unsuspecting Internet service providers for hosting copyrighted material on their servers. Understanding copyright law will protect you against accidental infringement, and more important, protect copyright holders against the uncontrolled distribution of their intellectual property.

Copyright

Copyright is a very misunderstood issue, especially in the realm of computer software and Internet publishing. As a Webmaster, you must understand the legal ramifications of Internet publishing to protect yourself from unintentional violation of the law. This section is only a brief survey of copyright law as it applies to the Internet. If you have any questions at all about the legal issues involved in publishing a specific work on your Internet servers, you should retain the services of a qualified legal expert.

Copyright is the legal right to control the distribution of an original work. Copyright is automatically granted by default to the person who creates (or is primarily responsible for the creation of) any work (the original author). The original author may sell the copyright or license its use in any way.

Copyright law protects anything you can post on an Internet server.

Generally, copyright applies to written works, software, music, video, photography, motion pictures, and most other forms of artistic expression. In most cases, parody is considered fair use of copyrighted material, and the right to paraphrase or quote to criticize a work is also legally protected and therefore a part of copyright law. However, excerpts longer than a sentence or two usually require permission from the copyright holder to reproduce.

Remember, a work still holds a copyright even if you can't find a specific claim to copyright on the work.

If you (or someone in your organization) didn't originally write a work, assume you must obtain permission to publish it on an Internet server. Without specific information to the contrary, always assume a work is subject to copyright even if you can't find a copyright date or the name of the author with the work.

To publish (or otherwise make publicly available) a work, you must have permission from the copyright holder unless the copyright holder has specifically made the work available in the public domain or the copyright has expired, generally sometime after the death of the original author. Works created under contract to (but not grant from) the government are usually in the public domain.

Making information available on the Internet is legally considered publication. Therefore, you must have permission to reproduce a work (be it software or written material) in order to make it available to the public on your server. Other restrictions may apply for private use in an intranet depending on the specific work in question—be sure to check with the copyright holder under any uncertain circumstance.

You can be held responsible for the accidental publication on the Internet of copyrighted material to which you have limited (intranet) publication rights. If you have obtained limited publication rights to a copyrighted work, be certain your network security structure limits access according to your limited rights.

Don't allow anonymous upload of information to your Internet server. If hackers use your server to store stolen software or information, you are legally liable for copyright violation.

Publishing works without the consent of the copyright holder not only is illegal but also can cause irreparable harm to the holder of a copyright. Small software companies have collapsed after their software has been pirated and made available on the Internet for free.

Once a work is published on the Internet, it is impossible to determine (or control) its electronic distribution. Although you can meter how often a work is downloaded or accessed from your site, you have no further control over how it is distributed by the downloading party. Since electronic data is easy to copy, a single download could be posted on a site in another country and ultimately be responsible for millions more copies without your permission.

Many people wrongly assume that anything appearing on a Web site does not have a copyright, so they will copy files and Web pages off your site and post them on their own without even realizing that they are breaking the law and violating your rights. Be certain you display an express claim to copyright on all your Web pages and all information you post on your site.

> You should assume that if you didn't create a work, you can't publish it on your Web site without the express written permission of the copyright holder. Exceptions to this basic rule are few and far between. You'll keep yourself out of trouble if you always follow this rule.

Licensing for Internet Servers

Licensing is essentially permission from the software publisher (Microsoft in the case of IIS, Windows NT Server, and FrontPage) to use software for a specific purpose. To maximize sales and profit, software vendors don't always charge all customers the same price for the same software. The rationale is that smaller customers require less service than larger customers do and cannot afford to pay for capacity they don't need.

Since IIS runs on Windows NT Server, many of its licensing restrictions are actually the licensing restrictions of Windows NT Server. Windows NT Server licensing has two components:

- **Server licenses** allow you to use the Windows NT Server operating system on one server. You must purchase a Windows NT Server license for every Windows NT server in your organization. Generally, the price of the software includes the license. Your Windows NT Server license is also your IIS server license and a license to use one copy of FrontPage on a Windows NT Server computer.

- **Clients Access licenses** allow you to attach a client to Windows NT servers to use file, print, remote access, or other non-Internet services.

The client access license is available on a per seat or a per server basis:

- **Per seat** licenses are purchased for each computer in your organization. Per seat licenses allow one computer to access any number of servers.

- **Per server** client access licenses allow you to connect a specific number of clients to a specific server, similar to the way Novell NetWare is licensed.

Although Microsoft recommends using per server licensing for a single server site, we recommend always using per seat licensing. There are very few circumstances in which per server licensing actually saves a significant amount of money. The exceptions include servers that provide a limited service that most of your clients don't use constantly, such as a RAS server or an application gateway like SNA server.

To scale Windows NT Server to fit any organization perfectly, Microsoft charges a fixed small amount for the server software and then a charge per computer that attaches to the server. This way, a customer with 10 computers pays only 20 percent of the amount a customer with 50 computers pays (excluding the cost of the Windows NT Server license). Essentially, with licensing, you are paying for use rather than availability.

Licensing can present a problem for public Internet servers running on Windows NT Server. Imagine if your Web server had 1,000 visitors at one time. You would technically be responsible for purchasing 1,000 client access licenses to support this use. This type of restriction would kill Windows NT Server as an Internet server platform because other operating systems manufacturers don't charge a per computer access license for HTTP connections. Therefore, to compete effectively, Microsoft has defined client access to mean clients that access the true server services of Windows NT Server such as file, print, and remote access. Microsoft does not consider connections through Internet protocols alone, such as HTTP, FTP, and Gopher, as client access.

However, attaching to a Windows NT Server via the Internet is not always license free because you can attach to the server services of a Windows NT Server over the Internet as easily as you can from within your own LAN. In this case you are still liable for a client access license.

The client access exemption applies only to access that does not make use of the Windows NT higher-level services such as file, print, or remote access.

Microsoft also faces another licensing problem. Windows NT Workstation is every bit as good an Internet server operating system as Windows NT Server; the two systems are essentially the same operating system, and the cost of NT Workstation is quite a bit lower than the cost of NT Server. Although Workstation has a license limit of ten clients, the above exclusion for Internet services on Windows NT Server would seem to pave the way for Workstation's unlimited use as an Internet Server, thus eating into the sales of Windows NT Server.

To solve this licensing dilemma, Microsoft limited the beta test version of Windows NT Workstation to a hard limit of ten inbound IP addresses, thus limiting Windows NT Workstation's usefulness as an Internet server. This restriction was a public relations fiasco for Microsoft, and the limitation was removed from the release version of the operating system.

The ten-user limit then showed up as a license restriction in IIS and its companion product Peer Web Services. You cannot use these products on Windows NT Workstation to serve more than ten inbound computers. Apparently, you are free to use third-party Web server software with Windows NT Workstation, but this issue is not entirely clear so you should research the (current) license restrictions for Windows NT Workstation before considering it for use as an Internet server operating system.

IIS license summary: You do not need to purchase a client access license for computers that attach to your server using only HTTP, FTP, Gopher, or most other Internet protocols.

Key points in the IIS and Windows NT Server licensing agreements:

- The IIS licensing agreement specifically limits IIS running on Windows NT Workstation to serving ten computers, but it does not limit the number of TCP sockets that those ten computers can use. You may not use aggregation or pooling (i.e., a proxy server) to bypass this limitation.

- The IIS does not limit the number of connections when running on Windows NT Server, nor does Personal Web Server running on Windows 95.

- You must purchase a Windows NT Server client access license for any computer attached to a Windows NT Server if that client uses higher-level services such as File, Print, RAS, or application services. This restriction applies even if that computer uses third-party client software not published by Microsoft or if the client connects to the server over the Internet.

- You do not need a client access license for computers that attach only through TCP sockets for protocols such as FTP, Telnet, or HTTP. Therefore, if you use your server solely as an Internet/intranet server, you do not need to purchase any client access licenses for it.

- You must purchase a client access license for computers that attach to your Internet server via the RAS, including computers that come in over the Internet using PPTP.

You can read the licensing agreement for Windows NT Server on Microsoft's Web site at www.microsoft.com/ntserver/info/licensing.htm. The licensing agreement for Internet Information Server 3.0 is located at www.microsoft.com/iis/GetIIS/DownloadIIS3/aseula.htm. Read these licensing agreements before setting up a specific Web site.

You are responsible for maintaining legal compliance with Microsoft's licensing requirements.

Summary

Effective and efficient Web sites are not difficult to produce and maintain if you truly understand why your customers visit your site and what will encourage them to visit more often. Here are the basic rules of thumb for Web site creation and management:

- Be consistent. Browsers can't tell where your Web site ends and the rest of the Internet begins unless your site is consistent.

- Keep your site fresh. If your site becomes stale, visitors have no reason to return.

- Structure your site for clarity and efficiency. Customers who get lost on your site when they are in a hurry to find something important will not return.

- Work efficiently. Web sites are difficult enough to maintain without adding complexity needlessly.

- Optimize content. Test your site with low-speed browsers to make sure it isn't painfully slow.

- Post changes in batches so your site remains consistent. Remember that your site is always available, and visitors are likely to be there at any time day or night.

- Internationalize. Nothing turns off potential customers more than ignoring their needs completely.

Copyright is an important issue for Webmasters to understand because in legal terms the Internet is a publication. Familiarize yourself with the law to be certain you don't stray outside it. Licensing can be a tricky issue as well. Microsoft does not require a client access license for computers that connect to IIS services, but it does require a license for clients that connect to higher-level file, print, and remote access services.

Creating Web sites is only the beginning. Web sites change constantly and present an ongoing maintenance challenge. But with a little planning and foresight, you'll have no trouble maintaining a compelling Web site indefinitely.

Review Questions

1. Four departments in your company maintain your Web site: marketing, engineering, information systems, and human resources. You've noticed that the different pages have very little stylistic similarity and in fact look more like four different Web sites. The CEO has also noticed this variation and asks you to do something to maintain a consistent company image across the Web site. What is the most efficient way to encourage a coherent and unified image on the Web?

   A. Use NTFS file permissions to control write access to the site. Have all departments submit all material to you for final production and posting on the site.

   B. Create a style guide and insist that all contributors follow it.

   C. Produce the Web site without input from the other departments.

   D. Use IIS security options to restrict the uploading of files to the site. Have all departments submit all material to you for final production and posting on the site.

2. You purchase Windows NT Server for use as an Internet/intranet server. You have 45 internal users and expect traffic of up to 100 Internet browsers at any one time. You install a 16-port multiport serial board with 16 modems attached so that your traveling sales force can dial

into the intranet site. You do not allow access to the server for file or print sharing. How many client access licenses must you purchase?

A. 59

B. 45

C. 145

D. 159

E. 16

F. 100

3. You set up a Windows NT server computer for a network of 50 users to provide the normal services of a file and print server. You also install IIS to host an intranet site for those users and another 150 intranet users attached to your organization's backbone. How many client access licenses must you purchase?

A. 50

B. 150

C. 200

4. You are setting up an Internet site with both HTTP and FTP services dedicated to promulgating Microsoft services and software for your clients. You want to host software that Microsoft gives away on its Web site, so you download the software from the Microsoft site and host it on your Web server. You are

A. Violating copyright law because you don't have Microsoft's permission to host the software.

B. Not violating copyright law because the software is publicly available and you can prove that by maintaining records of the Web URLs from which you downloaded the software.

C. Violating copyright law because you downloaded the software without paying for it.

D. Not violating copyright law because the software is freeware.

5. You are setting up an Internet site with both HTTP and FTP services dedicated to promulgating Microsoft services and software for your clients. You want to host software that Microsoft gives away on its Web site, so you include links directly to the pages inside Microsoft's Web site where the software is hosted. You are

  A. Violating copyright law because you don't have Microsoft's permission to host the software.

  B. Not violating copyright law because you aren't hosting the software.

  C. Violating copyright law because your site is set up as if the software were local to your machine and because you could potentially bypass Microsoft's copyright notices.

  D. Not violating copyright law because the software is freeware.

6. Customers are complaining that your Web site downloads too slowly. You've already reduced the color depth of your home page image map to the services on the rest of the site, but your customers still are not happy. Which solution is most effective?

  A. Tell your customers to get faster connections to the Internet.

  B. Increase your lease-line rate from T1 to T3.

  C. Use a Java applet instead of a large image map.

  D. Eliminate the image map in favor of a few graphical buttons and a monochrome background image.

CHAPTER

10

Creating Compelling Content

ost organizations implement Internet servers to host Web sites. Web sites use HTTP as a base from which to serve many protocols that in sum form a true client/server multimedia environment. HTML is used as a container document that embeds links to these different protocols. Special Web browser modular components called plug-ins interpret these different types of data, which are then (usually) displayed in the browser screen. This multimedia environment can consist of text, graphics, audio, video, virtual reality three-dimensional models, or any other form of information that a computer can process.

Putting simple text documents on the Web is easy; an ASCII text document on a Web site will display without modification on a Web browser. *Hypertext markup language* (HTML) documents embed markup codes called *tags* in the body of text documents to control how the text is displayed. The markup tags tell the browser how the marked up text should be displayed—for example, as a header, link, bulleted list, or body text. The markup tags also contain other information, such as the *uniform resource locator* (URL) of a link or the filename of an embedded picture.

Creating simple Web pages manually with a text editor is also easy. Keeping track of an entire site when pages refer to other pages with hypertext links becomes increasingly complex as the Web site grows. Graphically rich pages and pages with complicated markups can also be very difficult to debug manually because you must use two applications: a text editor to create the HTML and a Web browser to view your pages.

FrontPage

Microsoft provides a professional quality Web site creation tool called FrontPage to address the need for automated Web page editing and link maintenance. FrontPage ships with Windows NT Server, or you can purchase it separately if you are using another operating system (e.g., UNIX or other versions of Windows) to host your site.

FrontPage is to Web creation what Word is to writing. With FrontPage or a similar tool, creating Web pages is nearly as simple as using a word processor to write a brochure. FrontPage has two major components:

- **FrontPage Explorer** controls the links among Web pages.

- **FrontPage editor** creates the pages themselves.

FrontPage Explorer is shown in Figure 10.1. Pages appear as icons in the hyperlinks frame. Right-clicking a page brings up a menu of options for that page, and clicking the plus symbol in the corner of a page shows the pages that are linked to it.

FIGURE 10.1

FrontPage Explorer

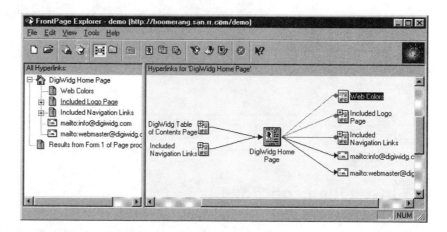

When you double-click any page, it opens in FrontPage Editor, shown in Figure 10.2.

FrontPage is missing a rather obvious component, however. It does not have a built-in utility to create, convert, or manage graphics. It will allow you to assign a default graphical editor, but the editor has to conform to the way FrontPage issues calls to work correctly. Many popular graphics editors don't work correctly with FrontPage, so when you double-click a graphics file, the editor will not open a file.

FIGURE 10.2

FrontPage Editor

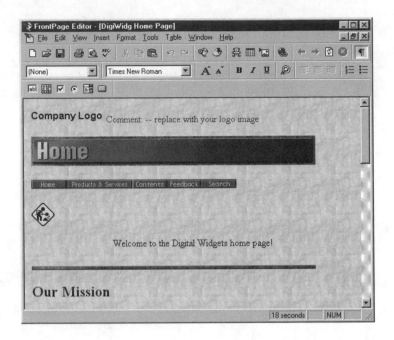

Microsoft is developing an image editor for FrontPage that may be available at www.microsoft.com/imagecomposer by the time you read this.

Installing FrontPage

To install FrontPage, you simply click through the installation wizard and select the obvious choices. Exercise 10.1 shows you how. FrontPage automatically installs FrontPage server extensions for IIS if it detects IIS running on the Web server.

The version of FrontPage that shipped on the early Windows NT Server 4 CD-ROM is version 1.1. The current version is FrontPage 97. The specific version of FrontPage 97 shipped on the Service Pack 2 and higher CD-ROM for Windows NT Server 4 will install only on computers running Windows NT Server 4. The retail version installs on Windows NT Server 4, Workstation 4, and Windows 95.

EXERCISE 10.1

Installing FrontPage

1. Launch the FrontPage setup program from your NT Server or service pack CD-ROM.

2. Click Next.

3. Correct the registration information if necessary.

4. Click Next.

5. Click Yes.

6. Click Next to accept the default file location, or click Browse to change it and then click Next.

7. Click Next to accept the typical installation options.

8. Ensure Internet Information Server is selected in the Installed Web Servers list box and click Next.

9. Click Next. The installation will now copy the FrontPage files to your hard disk.

10. Click OK to accept the default administration account name.

11. Click Yes to enable basic authentication if you will be using FrontPage 1.1 to edit Web pages on this site. Click OK to acknowledge the Log on locally right notice.

12. Click Yes to restart your computer.

Creating Webs with FrontPage

Working with FrontPage is very easy. FrontPage organizes your work into *webs,* collections of HTML pages and files that combine to accommodate a specific purpose. You should think of each web as a separate project.

FrontPage uses the templates similar to the templates used in the other Office applications to help jump-start your project. Microsoft has incorporated typical Web-site requirements into these templates so you can put together a Web site by simply filling in content unique to your organization.

Web templates are great for getting information onto the Internet in a hurry—but don't expect your site to look distinctive or unique. Web sites obviously based on FrontPage templates are cropping up all over the Net. If you want your site to be memorable, you'll have to do the hard work yourself.

Exercise 10.2 shows you how to create a new Web site based on one of the built-in Web templates.

EXERCISE 10.2

Creating a Web Site with FrontPage

1. Select Program ➤ Microsoft FrontPage ➤ FrontPage Explorer.

2. Select From a Wizard or Template in the Getting Started with Microsoft FrontPage window and then click OK.

3. Select Corporate Presence Wizard and click OK.

4. Type **demo** in the Name of New FrontPage Web input box.

5. Click OK.

   If you get a warning that port 80 of your Web server does not have Web server, launch the Internet Service Manager, start the www service, and repeat steps 3 through 5.

6. Click Next.

7. Check all available options except the What's New option.

8. Click Next.

9. Check all available options.

10. Click Next.

11. Click Next.

12. Check all the options for the services list.

13. Click Next.

14. Select all available options for the feedback form.

15. Click Next.

16. Click Next.

17. Check Keep Page up-to-date automatically.

18. Click Next.

19. Check Copyright notice.

20. Click Next.

21. Select Flashy.

22. Click Next.

23. Select Grey Texture 5 in the pattern pick box.

24. Click Next.

25. Click Next.

26. Type **Digital Widgets Corporation** in the What is the full name of your Company input box.

27. Type **DigiWidg** in the What is the One-word version of this name.

28. Click Next.

29. Type **webmaster@digiwidg.com** in the What is the e-mail address of your webmaster input box.

30. Type **info@digiwidg.com** in the What is the e-mail address for general info input box.

31. Click Finish.

32. Click Close on the FrontPage ToDo List.

Now that you have a template Web site in place, you're ready to work with FrontPage to modify the site for your requirements. Exercise 10.3 shows you how to work with the Web site you created in Exercise 10.2. You can finish working with this Web site at your leisure or begin working on your own.

Working with FrontPage

1. Launch FrontPage and open the demo Web if it is not running from the previous exercise.

2. Double-click the DigiWidg home page icon in the Hyperlinks for DigiWidgHome Page to launch the FrontPage editor with the Digi-Widg home page open.

3. Select the first instructional comment paragraph after the HOME block starting with the word *Comment*.

4. Type **Welcome to the Digital Widgets home page** to replace the instructive comment.

5. Select the paragraph starting under the Our Mission head.

6. Type **Digital Widgets serves as an example to show the proper techniques for rapid Web development.**

7. Select the first paragraph under the company profile head.

8. Type **Digital Widgets designs and manufactures digitally enhanced widgets, and assists customers in developing designs that incorporate digital widgets in their own products.**

9. Select the next paragraph and press the delete button twice.

10. Select the next paragraph.

11. Type **"Digital Widgets not only explained the purpose of widgets, they helped me justify purchasing thousands of them in my annual budget!"—N.S.**

12. Select the next paragraph.

13. Type **Henry Tillman, Ph.D., founded Digital Widgets to bring the benefits of digital semiconductor technology to the widget market.**

14. Click the Save Icon in the FrontPage Editor toolbar.

15. Select File ➤ Preview in Browser.

16. Select Internet Explorer.

EXERCISE 10.3 (CONTINUED FROM PREVIOUS PAGE)

17. Click Preview.

18. Close Internet Explorer.

19. Close FrontPage Editor.

20. Close FrontPage Explorer.

In Exercise 10.3, you opened the Web page you were editing in the FrontPage editor in an actual Web browser. You should always check your work in a browser before you post it for public display. Although the FrontPage editor is very close to the display of a Web browser, many minute differences affect the way your page displays. Contrast the page shown in Figure 10.3 with Figure 10.2 to compare a Web page shown in FrontPage Editor with the same page shown in Internet Explorer. Notice that the comments shown in FrontPage Editor do not appear in the actual Web page (which affects the spacing of text on the page) and that the spacing of the text differs slightly. You should always preview your site in all available Web browsers and platforms so you know how your customers will be seeing your site.

FIGURE 10.3

Internet Explorer previewing a Web page

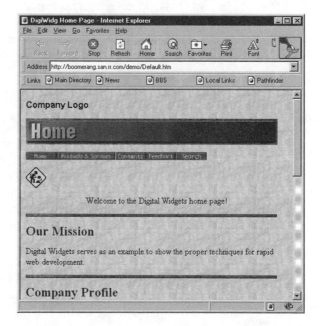

The comments you've been replacing in Exercise 10.3 are invisible to Web browsers—you can leave them in place as a note to yourself, or other Web developers who might work on your pages, without worrying about how they appear from the Internet.

FrontPage is an extraordinary tool for rapid Web site development, and because it comes free with Windows NT Server 4, there's little reason to use any other product for your site design.

Office Applications

After using FrontPage, you might wonder why you would use anything else to produce a Web site—and why all the other Microsoft Office 97 applications are capable of creating Web documents. The answer is simple: FrontPage can't do everything. Office 97 applications support the HTML file format to allow you to convert existing documents into pages for your Web site.

Some functions are more easily performed in a specialized application such as Excel than in FrontPage, and all Microsoft Office 97 applications can save their files as HTML documents. This feature allows you to publish a spreadsheet, word document, PowerPoint presentation, or access database on the Internet directly from the application that created the document. Using the source application to create HTML files directly loses less formatting information than converting the file to an intermediate format.

Word

Word documents are most closely related to HTML documents—in fact, the HTML facility in Word is simply an import/export filter like the one used to process WordPerfect documents. Because most HTML documents follow the basic format of a word processing document, and because Word uses heading styles and fonts that convert easily to and from HTML, Word is the best office application to use if you can't use FrontPage when creating a general purpose HTML document. Figure 10.4 shows a document in Word 97, and Figure 10.5 shows the same document being browsed in a Web browser.

Word has been extended to assist in the creation of HTML documents. When word recognizes a URL, it will automatically create a hot link in your document. Even without saving the file as HTML, you can click the link to

F I G U R E   10.4

A Word document

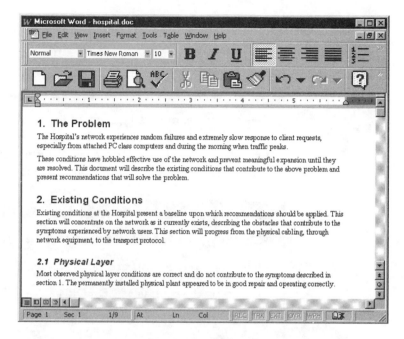

F I G U R E   10.5

Browsing a document
created with Word

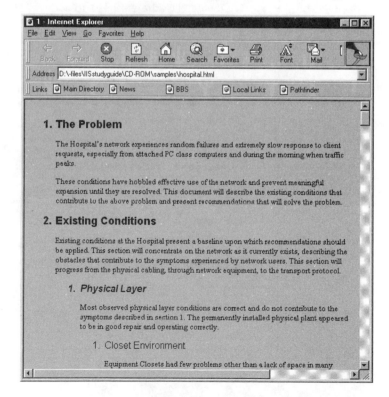

launch your Web browser and bring up that page. When you save your document in HTML format, Word will convert all the embedded links along with the rest of the document. Use Exercise 10.4 to practice creating an HTML document with Word.

Save two copies of Web pages you create in Word (especially if you will be using the word document somewhere other than on the Web): one in Word format and one in HTML format. HTML format isn't rich enough to describe a complete Word document without losing format information.

EXERCISE 10.4

Creating an HTML Document in Word

Note: This exercise works correctly only with Word 97.

1. Insert the companion CD-ROM in your CD-ROM drive.

2. Double-click your CD-ROM drive.

3. Double-click the `samples` folder.

4. Double-click the `hospital.doc` file. Word will launch and load the `hospital.doc` document.

5. Select File ➤ Save as HTML.

6. Browse to the location of your IIS www root directory. By default, this is `C:\InetPub\wwwroot`.

7. Click Save. Notice that when you are finished, Word automatically loads the HTML version of the document.

8. Close Word.

9. Browse to the location of your IIS www root directory using the desktop Explorer.

10. Double-click the `Hospital.htm` document.

11. Browse through the document. Notice the differences between the Word document and the HTML document.

12. Close Internet Explorer.

Excel

Like Word, Excel is capable of saving information in HTML format; and like Word, Excel is capable of loading HTML documents. Excel will load HTML tables as spreadsheets and will import the remainder of the page as text. You can use Excel to publish financial data on your intranet or to post price lists for your Internet catalog. Figure 10.6 shows a source Excel document in Excel.

F I G U R E   10.6

A typical Excel
spreadsheet

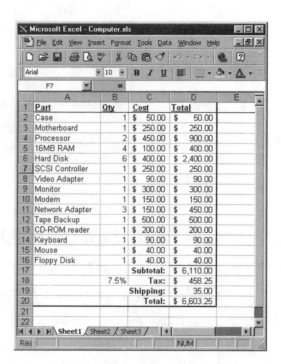

Figure 10.7 shows that file saved as an HTML file in a Web browser. Exercise 10.5 shows you how to save an Excel document as HTML and what happens when you import HTML documents from HTML.

WARNING   Always keep copies of your original Excel documents in Excel format. HTML is not sufficiently rich to maintain formulas and other important Excel information.

FIGURE 10.7

An Excel spreadsheet
saved as an HTML
document

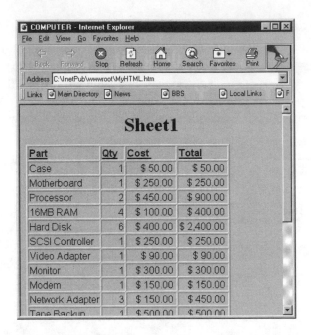

EXERCISE 10.5

Creating an HTML Document in Excel

Note: This exercise works correctly only with Excel 97.

1. Insert the companion CD-ROM in your CD-ROM drive.

2. Double-click your CD-ROM drive.

3. Double-click the `samples` folder.

4. Double-click the `Computer.xls` file. Excel will launch and load the `computer.xls` spreadsheet.

5. Select the range A1 through D20.

6. Select File ➤ Save as HTML.

7. Click Next.

8. Click Next to create a complete Web page.

9. Click Next to accept the page formatting defaults.

---

10. Click Browse.

11. Browse to the IIS www root directory. By default, this directory is `C:\InetPub\wwwroot`.

12. Click Finish to create the site. Although we aren't using the option in this example, notice the option to automatically insert the created page in a FrontPage Web.

13. Close Excel.

14. Double-click the drive containing your IIS www root directory and browse to the `Inetpub\wwwroot` directory.

15. Double-click the MyHTML`.htm` file.

16. View the output of the spreadsheet HTML converter.

17. Close your Web browser.

PowerPoint

PowerPoint is the tool of choice for people who like to fill up an entire 8.5-by-11-inch piece of paper with a single sentence and canned graphics. This feature makes it perfect for salespeople and executives. Now this amazing productivity tool can help you automatically create Web sites that violate most of the principles set forth in Chapter 9.

PowerPoint can load and save HTML documents, converting them into its own presentation format while they are loaded. PowerPoint treats level 1 headings as slides, and imports numbered and bulleted lists correctly. Other information may import strangely, so you shouldn't expect to be able to turn an HTML document into a PowerPoint presentation without some work.

Creating HTML documents with PowerPoint is very easy. When your presentation is finished, you simply save it as an HTML document in the manner described for the other Office applications. As with the other document types, you should always keep a copy of your PowerPoint-based HTML documents in the native file format because HTML is not as rich a format as PowerPoint supports.

Access

Access is the most powerful relational database software ever made for the LAN (non-client/server) database model. You can create tables in Access that store data for information-intensive purposes like contact management; accounting, purchasing, and billing; and cataloging. You control how that data is displayed by creating forms that can look like the traditional paperwork used to perform that task. Access can maintain millions of records and allows simultaneous access to that data by multiple users on a network. Access can even perform some convenience functions that are difficult, if not impossible, to implement on an SQL server. Databases can be easily migrated to Microsoft SQL Server when your data-handling problem outgrows the capability of Access.

Microsoft has made Access even more powerful by extending its data-handling capabilities over the Internet. You can now use HTML form fields or ActiveX controls in a Web page to control live data published by Access on your Internet server—thus providing full access to your database over the Internet. You can use Access's Internet publishing features to create a complete online store with a searchable catalog and online product ordering. Figure 10.8 shows a sample database published by Access running in an Internet browser. Exercise 10.6 shows you how to create an HTML document with Access.

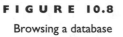

FIGURE 10.8

Browsing a database

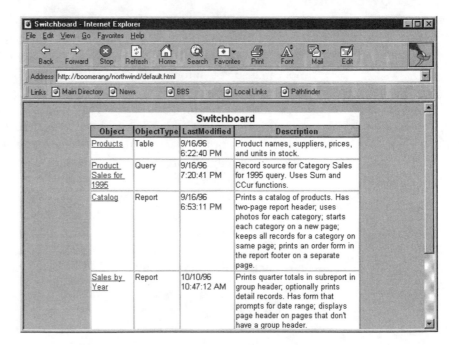

WARNING

Be certain you use strong security for Internet-published databases. Most online merchants require membership so they can restrict access to customers only. Don't even consider asking your customers for credit card numbers or other bearer instrument data over the Internet unless you are using an encryption service like Secure Socket Layer or a tunneling encryption protocol.

EXERCISE 10.6

Creating an HTML Document in Access

1. Select Start ➤ Find ➤ Files or Folders.

2. Type **Northwind.mdb** in the Named input box.

3. Select Local hard drives in the Look in pick box.

4. Click Find Now.

5. Double-click the Northwind.mdb file in the resulting pick box. If you have a choice of files in the box, select the file that is about 1510MB in size. (Smaller or larger files may have been created with an earlier version of Access.) If the pick box is empty, run the setup program on your Office 97 CD-ROM to install the Northwind sample database for Access.

6. Click OK to dismiss the Northwind splash screen.

7. Select File ➤ Save as HTML.

8. Click Next.

9. Select the All Objects tab.

10. Check Products.

11. Check Product Sales for 1995.

12. Check Catalog.

13. Check Sales by Year.

14. Check Summary of Sales by Quarter.

15. Click Next.

16. Click Browse.

17. Double-click Stones.

18. Click Next.

19. Select Static HTML.

20. Click Next.

21. Click Browse.

22. Browse to your IIS www root directory.

23. Click the New Folder icon in the browser toolbar.

24. Type **Northwind** as the name of the new folder and press Enter.

25. Double-click the Northwind folder.

26. Click Select.

27. Click Next.

28. Check Yes, I want to create a home page.

29. Click Finish.

30. Click OK on the Sales by Year dialog raised by the export wizard.

31. Exit Access.

Access will now create a static Web page of the data you selected from the database. Use Exercise 10.7 to see the contents of the Web site. Publishing static (unchanging) data from a database is certainly useful, but allowing users to browse and modify your database directly over the Internet is downright exciting—and too complex for this chapter. Chapter 13 discusses database connectivity in greater detail.

> **EXERCISE 10.7**
>
> ## Browsing a Web Site Created with Access
>
> 1. Double-click Internet Explorer.
>
> 2. Type `http://boomerang/northwind/default.html` into the Address input box, replacing *boomerang* with the name of your computer.
>
> 3. Click Products.
>
> 4. Click Back on the browser toolbar.
>
> 5. Click Product sales for 1995.
>
> 6. Click Back on the browser toolbar.
>
> 7. Click Catalog. Not quite what you expected, is it? This example shows why you must browse any files you create before you publish them.
>
> 8. Click Back on the browser toolbar.
>
> 9. Click Sales by Year.
>
> 10. Click Back on the browser toolbar.
>
> 11. Click Summary of Sales by Quarter.
>
> 12. Close Internet Explorer.

Summary

Although creating simple content for an Internet site is easy, managing the complexity of a growing site is very difficult. Microsoft's FrontPage is a specialized Web organization and creation tool that fills this need.

FrontPage provides a coherent way for individuals or teams to create, organize, and edit Web sites. FrontPage includes two components: FrontPage Explorer, which organizes related Web pages graphically, and FrontPage Editor, which makes creating Web pages as easy as using a word processor.

With the release of Microsoft Office 97, all the major Office applications support HTML as an optional file format. Word, Excel, PowerPoint, and Access are capable of importing and exporting HTML files. Because the HTML file format is not rich enough to contain all the information contained in the native formats of the Office applications, you cannot use HTML as a replacement for the native formats.

Review Questions

1. Your company has an open book policy. The controller wants to make some financial data available on the company's intranet, but doesn't want to bother learning the intricacies of Web design. Which solution is optimal for the controller?

    A. Create a link to a new document in FrontPage and have the controller save a copy of the financial data as an HTML document from within Excel.

    B. Have the controller import the financial data into FrontPage so it can be linked into the corporate intranet directly.

    C. Import the data into Word and use the Save as HTML feature to add a page to your FrontPage Web.

    D. Use Access to create the entire site, as it is the only Office application capable of maintaining tables of complex data.

2. You are designing an online catalog for a small company. Customers will need to view and browse a catalog, but the company is not yet willing to begin an online ordering service. You will export your catalog to HTML from an Office application that the company already owns. Which solution is optimal for this situation?

    A. Use Excel to maintain the catalog because it can automatically subtotal the products the customer selects.

    B. Use Word to maintain the catalog. Word is the best Office application to use for general HTML files because its internal format is similar to HTML.

C. Use FrontPage to maintain all Web data—it is far superior to the Office applications for HTML.

D. Use Access to maintain the catalog because it handles large data sets very well.

3. Customers are complaining that some of your Web pages are formatted strangely and are difficult to read. You created the Web pages using FrontPage and the Office applications, and they look fine in your version of Internet Explorer. What should you do?

A. The HTML code created by FrontPage and the Office applications work correctly only with Internet Explorer. Encourage the customers to upgrade.

B. The customers' Web browsers do not support Active Server Pages. Downgrade your site to older Web technology.

C. Check your public pages on all available Web browsers. Debug and tune your HTML code until it looks acceptable on as many browsers as possible.

D. Office applications create very primitive HTML documents. Use FrontPage to create all Web documents.

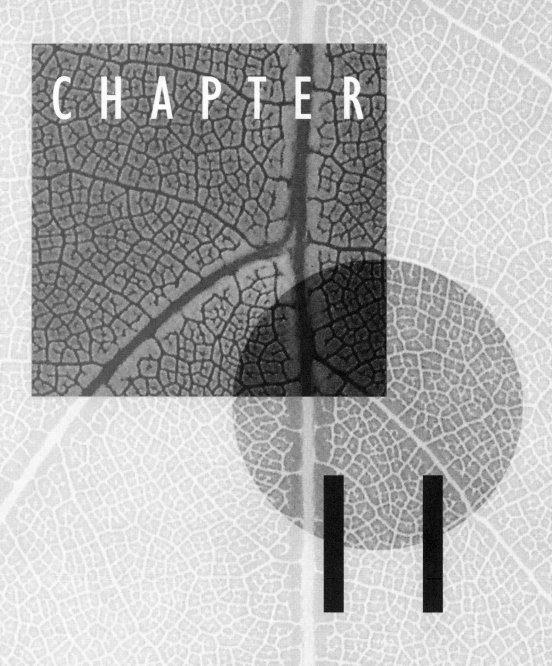

CHAPTER

11

Interactive Internet Clients

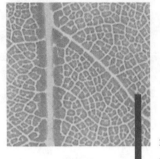

n Chapter 10 you learned how to create Web pages with FrontPage and with a number of Microsoft applications, including Word, Excel, and Access. Those HTML pages reside on your server and are sent to Web browsers when Internet users browse your site. This chapter examines the HTML pages from the Web browser's perspective and shows you how to use client-side plug-ins (such as VRML and Real Audio) as well as how to use client-side programming languages (such as JavaScript and VBScript) to enhance your Web pages.

These scripting languages provide the mechanisms to add animation and interactivity to Web pages. Any flashy Web page you've seen lately makes heavy use of scripting languages or Java. This chapter opens with a discussion of the general-purpose Web browsers that form the user interface for the World Wide Web and then considers the capabilities and features of Java and the scripting languages.

Web Browsers

Web browsers are applications that retrieve content in the form of HTML from Web servers, such as IIS, and format or interpret that content to create a graphical interface for the user. Browsers also keep track of the user input actions, for example, clicking buttons or selecting links, and execute those actions. When the user clicks inside forms or image maps, the Web browser returns that information to the Web server to be processed by a CGI script, ISAPI application, or an Active Server Page. (Server applications are covered in Chapter 12.)

Without Web browsers, the Web would not exist. So you might wonder why the companies that make Web browsers distribute them freely. If they are so powerful and they form the foundation of all user interface to the World Wide Web, why don't you always have to pay for them?

The answer lies in a strange new marketing phenomenon. The companies that make the powerful Web browsers (Microsoft and Netscape) are battling for control of the Internet. Both companies give away their browsers and are vigorously pursuing new technologies to embed in their browsers in an attempt to outclass the competition and make their browser the number one browser. Some companies (Netscape, for example) give away one version of their Web browser and sell another that has more features, may be more stable, or may be licensed for an entire organization's use instead of just personal use. Most companies that give away Web browsers, however, make their money from services that the Web browsers access (e.g., Netscape's Enterprise Server Web service software, or Microsoft's Windows NT Server operating system running IIS).

Read the licensing agreement for your Web browser. Even though you may not have to pay for browsers at the moment, you should be aware of licensing restrictions and conditions for which you could be held accountable.

NCSA Mosaic

The original graphical Web browser is Mosaic. The authors of Mosaic were college students fascinated by the potential of HTML and the newly formed Internet-based hypertext document distribution system known as the World Wide Web. Using the original text Web browser, Lynx, as a model, the students created a Web browser that could display graphical images as well as text. Mosaic was born, and the World Wide Web exploded on the university and scientific Internet scene. Because Mosaic was developed by a publicly funded university, the software was freely available to anyone who wanted it.

Mosaic also began filtering out into the business world, as the few (at the time) commercial organizations that had Internet links began using the World Wide Web.

The original versions of Mosaic are still freely available on the Web, but its popularity dwindled when the first commercial Web browsers with features like scripting languages and multithreaded downloading became available.

Netscape Navigator

Navigator is the traditional premium Web browser. In fact, Netscape developed many of the nice features you expect from Web browsers, such as downloads that don't hang your browser until they are finished.

Netscape was formed by some of the people who developed Mosaic and some businessmen who backed their efforts with financial support. After the release of Mosaic, the popularity of the World Wide Web exploded, and the developers knew they were on to something big. Of course, the student developers realized that they would not be able to put together a large enough programming team to create a compelling Web browser (not to mention make any money at it), so they formed their own company and released Netscape Navigator.

The original release version of Navigator was free because it had to compete with Mosaic, which offered similar functions. The only significant difference was that Navigator ran much faster than Mosaic ran (and crashed a little less frequently than Mosaic crashed). Navigator used multiple threads to download images, which kept images from blocking the download of text and links. Although Navigator was free, Netscape generated revenue from its Web server products. By giving away the browser, Netscape created demand for its server products, and the company expanded.

With the release of Netscape Navigator 2.0, Mosaic was clearly obsolete. Netscape 2.0 supported the JavaScript scripting language and frames, which enabled users to include animation in Web pages and to make Web pages look more like traditional media such as magazines. Netscape began charging for Netscape 2.0 because it was the clear leader in Web browser technology at that time.

Netscape 3.0 includes support for the Java programming language and Java applets, as well as plug-ins, which extend the browser to interpret specialized content like sound and streaming video. Figure 11.1 shows Netscape Navigator browsing the Netscape home page.

Version 4.0 of Netscape Navigator includes support for dynamicHTML (a client/server scripting facility) and Webcasting, which allows customers to receive content on their Web browsers automatically rather than as a result of clicking on links. Version 4.0 may also support ActiveX. Both Netscape and Microsoft support Webcasting and dynamicHTML technologies; however, their technologies are not compatible with one another.

Internet Explorer

After the release of Navigator 2.0, Microsoft woke up to the Internet and realized the vast potential of this entirely new market. In short order the company released Internet Explorer, which in its original version wasn't very compelling. Internet Explorer 2.0 was a vast improvement over 1.0, but it still lacked many of the features of the current version of Netscape Navigator. With the release of Internet Explorer 3.0, however, Microsoft has closed the gap.

FIGURE 11.1

Netscape Navigator

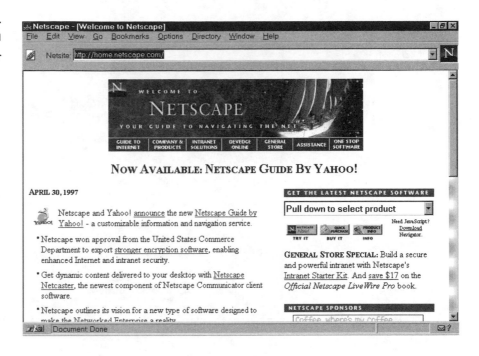

Internet Explorer 3.0 is now on par with Netscape Navigator; in addition, Internet Explorer includes support for VBScript, which Netscape does not support—and apparently never will. Navigator also does not yet support ActiveX controls or Windows NT Challenge/Response encrypted logon. Microsoft added these features to outcompete Netscape Navigator, which itself has a similar list of exclusive features. Figure 11.2 shows Internet Explorer browsing the Microsoft home page. Compare it to Figure 11.1 to see the similarities and differences in the interfaces of the two browsers.

Internet Explorer 4.0 will include support for DynamicHTML, Webcasting, and complete support for JavaScript (earlier versions had problems with some previously undocumented features of JavaScript).

Other Browsers

A whole slew of other browsers are available on the Web, most for free. Many of these browsers have evolved from the original Mosaic browser under license from NCSA; others were written for a specific purpose or application. You may recognize some of their names:

- **Spry Mosaic** is a licensed descendent of NCSA Mosaic. Spry has licensed it for use as the CompuServe Web browser.

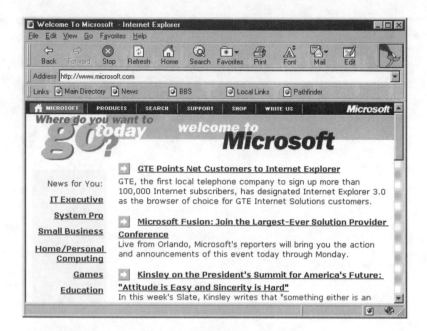

■ **Lynx** is the original text-only Web browser developed at CERN to support only pure HTML. Lynx is still used on many Web-enabled terminals and on slower computers that don't handle graphics well.

■ **HotJava** is a Web browser that Sun wrote entirely in Java as a demonstration of the programming power of the Java language. It was also the first Java-enabled Web browser. Since it's written entirely in Java, the same browser runs on all computers that support the Java API.

Plug-Ins

Plug-ins are code modules that extend the power of a Web browser without upgrading the main application. After the release of Netscape Navigator 2.0, Netscape realized that Internet software technology was simply moving too fast to keep up with. As a result, Netscape developed the plug-in API to allow other software companies to develop program modules that extend the capability of Netscape for a specific type of content. The browser calls plug-ins whenever it receives a link to the type of content that a specific plug-in handles. If a needed plug-in is not installed on your computer, the browser will pop up a dialog and ask you whether you want to go to the manufacturer's Web site and download the plug-in. Assuming you answer Yes, the browser will attach to the site, automatically download the plug-in, install it, link back to the source site, and then begin streaming the content to the plug-in for display. Internet Explorer also supports plug-ins written for Netscape Navigator.

Plug-ins are pretty cool, but they are difficult to develop properly. As Java interpreters and compilers get faster, Java will probably eliminate the need for custom plug-in development except in a few specialized areas where high speed is critical. Some examples of popular plug-ins are VRML, Shocked, and RealAudio.

- **Virtual Reality Modeling Language** (VRML) is a client/server 3-D rendering package that allows Web browsers to load a description of a 3-D space, which is then rendered inside their Web browser. You can then move through the VRML space using your browser. Your browser transmits your current location to the server and receives the data required to render that location.

- **Shocked** is a plug-in that supports frame-based video streaming. The Shocked plug-in receives video frames and displays them inside your browser. Shocked is based on Macromedia's Director product that evolved from HyperCard on the MacOS.

- **RealAudio** provides support for real-time audio over the Internet. By installing the plug-in and then browsing to a RealAudio server, you'll hear whatever content is being Webcast at that moment. Many radio stations use RealAudio to simulcast over the Internet to reach a larger audience than their broadcast area. You can even listen to radio stations from other countries over the Internet with RealAudio.

Plug-ins are really pretty cool, but to add them to your Web server, you typically must license a server product for that type of content from the plug-in manufacturer. You can then freely distribute the plug-in to your customers. Unless the function of their Web site absolutely requires the use of a plug-in, few Webmasters will actually pay a third-party for another server component just to make their Web site more animated.

Client-Side Dynamic Content

Plug-ins are a great idea, but they don't really fulfill the need for applications that can be quickly developed and delivered over the Web without additional cost—especially for simple content such as advertising banners and animation. As you know, the Web is based on a client/server protocol called HTTP. Modern Web browsers include interpreters for script languages that allow Webmasters to create all sorts of interactive content that would not be possible with simple Hypertext Markup Language documents. Four types of active content are now common on the Web:

- **JavaScript** is a scripting language created for Netscape Navigator based on the syntax of Java.

- **VBScript** is a scripting language created for Microsoft Internet Explorer based on the syntax of Visual Basic.

- **ActiveX** controls are compiled plug-ins that can be automatically downloaded and installed to provide application-like user interface controls on a Web page.

- **Java** is a complete interpreted programming language based on the syntax of C++.

You don't necessarily have to choose one form of active content over another—they all work together to some extent. In fact, the original purpose of JavaScript was to tie together different Java applets in the context of an HTML page, and the primary purpose of VBScript is to provide context for ActiveX controls on a page. You can use the scripting languages to mix and match active content types as required.

JavaScript

Netscape recognized the need for a client-based scripting language for its Web browsers to take care of many simple programmatic functions for the user, such as rotating graphic banners or scrolling messages across the screen. Sun had just released Java, but as a complete programming language with a development environment, Java was simply too complex for anyone who wasn't a professional programmer.

JavaScript is a simple but powerful language that does not have to be compiled or linked into applets that are downloaded. The JavaScript codes are simply inserted into the body of the HTML document, and when the page is fully read by the browser, the browser begins interpreting any embedded Java-Script codes.

JavaScript does not allow access to your computer outside your Web browser. It is not possible to create viruses or Trojan horses with JavaScript, nor is it possible to extract information about you with JavaScript.

JavaScript is best for Internet Web pages that need straightforward animation, scrolling text, or other simple programming requirements.

Exercise 11.1 shows you how to copy the JavaScript sample file from the CD-ROM to your Internet publication directory. Microsoft Internet Explorer did not fully support JavaScript until the release of Internet Explorer 4.0. For this reason, the examples shown in Exercises 11.1 and 11.2 cannot be run from Internet Explorer 3.0.

EXERCISE 11.1

Serving a JavaScript File

1. Insert the CD-ROM that came with this book.

2. Double-click My Computer.

3. Double-click your C: drive (or the drive containing your Internet publication directory).

4. Double-click InetPub (or the name of your Internet publication directory).

5. Double-click wwwroot.

6. Select File ➤ New ➤ Folder.

7. Type **TownRed** to change the name of the new folder.

8. Double-click My Computer.

9. Double-click your CD-ROM drive.

10. Double-click My Computer.

11. Double-click your CD-ROM drive.

12. Double-click Samples.

13. Double-click TownRed.

14. Select Edit ➤ Select All.

15. Drag one of the selected files from the CD-ROM TownRed directory and drop it on the TownRed directory in your wwwroot. This step copies the files into that directory.

Now that your server is serving the JavaScript example, browse to it with your Web browser to play the game. Figure 11.3 shows the JavaScript game running in Netscape Navigator. Because JavaScript files are executed entirely on the client, they add no processing load to the Web server.

You can find a complete JScript (Microsoft's implementation of JavaScript) tutorial and language reference from your Start menu by selecting Start ➤ Programs ➤ Microsoft Internet Server ➤ Active Server Pages Roadmap.

FIGURE 11.3

A game written entirely in JavaScript

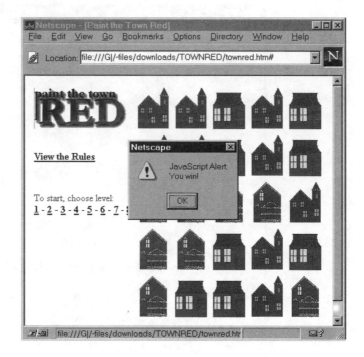

Now that you've seen what JavaScript can do, you might want to look behind the scenes. Programming in JavaScript is beyond the scope of this book, but many references are available if you are interested in using this simple programming language to add interactivity to your Web sites. Exercise 11.3 shows you how to load and edit a JavaScript Web page using Internet Explorer.

EXERCISE 11.2

Browsing a JavaScript Web Page

1. Launch Netscape Navigator 2.0 or higher or launch Internet Explorer 4.0 or higher. You can obtain any of these browsers at the Netscape (www.netscape.com) or Microsoft (www.microsoft.com) Web sites.

2. Type **//boomerang/townred/townred.htm** into the address line of your Web browser, replacing *boomerang* with the name of your server.

3. Click View the rules for an overview of the rules.

4. Play to your heart's content.

EXERCISE 11.3

Viewing and Editing JavaScript

1. Select Start ➤ Programs ➤ Microsoft FrontPage ➤ FrontPage Editor.

2. Select File ➤ Open.

3. Click Browse.

4. Browse to C:\boomerang\InetPub\wwwroot\townred\ (replacing *boomerang* with the name of your server).

5. Double-click townred.htm.

6. Double-click the small icon in the upper-left corner above the image map.

7. Use the vertical scroll bar to scroll through the code for the game. You can edit the text to change the way the game works if you are familiar with JavaScript using the FrontPage Editor or any text editor.

8. Click Cancel.

9. Close FrontPage Editor.

10. Click No when asked if you want to save changes on all open documents.

VB Script

Although JavaScript is a good interpreted object-oriented language for general Web browsing, it doesn't support many of the fundamental features of the Windows operating systems. This lack of support is intentional—JavaScript wasn't developed with just Windows in mind. It works perfectly well on any platform.

Microsoft created VBScript, which is comparable to JavaScript, primarily to assist in the creation of Internet-based client/server database applications. Like Visual Basic before it, its primary purpose is the rapid development of front ends for SQL database servers. VBScript doesn't run on the non-Windows versions of Internet Explorer (although a Macintosh edition will be released after the final release of ActiveX for the Macintosh), and no other Web browsers (e.g., Netscape Navigator) support it.

Like JavaScript, VBScript does not allow access to your machine, so you cannot use it to propagate malicious software or to extract information from your computer.

With those restrictions in mind, VBScript works seamlessly with ActiveX controls (which have a similar set of restrictions). If you are considering making strong use of ActiveX, you should probably use VBScript as your scripting language.

VBScript is perfect for intranet environments based on Microsoft operating systems and applications, as it interfaces well with Visual Basic for Applications and ActiveX controls.

The forms automatically created by Microsoft Access in Chapter 13 contain VBScript code. Use those exercises to get a feel for the capability of VBScript.

ActiveX

ActiveX is Microsoft's technology for extending the user interface capability of HTML and scripting languages. ActiveX controls such as buttons, pick lists, menus, and check boxes allow you to embed controls in your HTML forms that make them look like Windows applications. ActiveX was developed specifically to make Web browser–based database clients resemble database clients that can be created with Visual C++ or Visual Basic.

ActiveX controls are more similar to plug-ins than they are to Java applets or to scripts. ActiveX controls are compiled programs that are downloaded once and permanently installed into your browser.

ActiveX controls were originally supported only on PCs, but Microsoft has just released a Macintosh version of ActiveX (MactiveX?) that adds ActiveX support to all versions of Internet Explorer for the Macintosh after 2.1 and to Netscape Navigator 3.0 for the Macintosh. Controls must be developed separately for the Macintosh, however, as they are compiled to the native machine language of the computer. ActiveX controls for PCs will not operate on Macintoshes, but the controls are compatible. Therefore, a Macintosh browsing a Web site that references a PC ActiveX control will work properly if you have the Macintosh ActiveX control of the same functionality loaded. ActiveX controls are not supported on any platforms other than PCs and the Macintosh.

ActiveX technology is most appropriate for intranet or Internet servers where security isn't a major issue and similar software is in use.

Chapter 13 shows the use of ActiveX controls in database forms automatically created from an Access database.

Java

Java is a powerful new programming language for developing applets that run inside Web browsers or applications that run independently on your computer. Java is similar to many industrial programming languages (e.g., C or C++) except that it is not compiled to the native machine language of the target computer. Rather, Java is compiled to a "virtual machine," or a fictitious machine language. The resulting fictitious machine code is called Java byte code, which can then be interpreted by a Java run-time interpreter or compiled into the native machine language of your computer by a just-in-time (JIT) compiler.

The important difference between Java and more traditional languages is that the distribution of byte code—rather than machine code—allows the same application to run on any computer that has a Java run-time interpreter or compiler. For instance, a word processor written in 100 percent pure Java (i.e., Java that doesn't make use of any machine-specific libraries) could run on a Macintosh, a PC, or a UNIX workstation without any modification at all. In fact, two of the largest word processing and application development companies in the world are currently porting their application suites to the Java language for total cross-platform compatibility.

> Because Java can run on virtually any machine (sorry), it's the perfect language for developing active content in your Web pages if your customers are using a variety of computers. Like HTML, Java is the same on any computer.

Java may be the most important new programming language development in the past few decades. Although the factors that make Java important were not invented or developed specifically for Java, it is the first language to embody so many different factors. Although a single organization (JavaSoft) tightly controls the development of Java, it has gained wide acceptance among software and hardware developers. Here are Java's strong points:

- Truly object-oriented architecture.
- Syntactically similar to C and C++.
- Interpreted virtual machine is completely cross-platform.
- Easily speed optimized at both compile time and run time.
- Language-based object component model facilitates code reuse.
- Standard I/O libraries designed for Internet communication.
- Virtual machine can be embedded in applications like Web browsers to support the development of applets.
- Virtual machine byte code is dense, requires very little bandwidth, and can be just-in-time compiled for extra speed.
- Embedded virtual machines create safe environments that prevent security leaks in distributed applications.

As with all real languages, Java development is long and slow compared to development in scripting languages like JavaScript and VBScript. However, Java can do almost everything that any other language can do and is robust enough to handle any application you want to write for your Internet site. Exercise 11.4 shows you how to find some Java applications on the Web. Because the Web changes faster than books in print, you may find that these sites have changed considerably or moved, but you should be able to use a search engine like www.altavista.digital.com to find them or other interesting Java sites.

Because Java applets running in your Web browser are contained in security environments that don't allow access to your computer's hard drives or to other running applications, running Java applications embedded in Web sites poses very little security risk.

EXERCISE 11.4

Exploring Java Sites on the Web

These Web sites are best viewed with Internet Explorer 3.0 or higher.

   1. Double-click the Internet Explorer icon on your desktop.

   2. Type **http://langevin.usc.edu/Fred/** in the address line.

   3. Click the View Fred's World hypertext link. Wait for the Java game to load. It may take a while, depending on the speed of your connection to the Internet. When it is done loading, you will see a 3-D maze.

   4. Use your mouse or the arrow keys to walk through the 3-D maze. This 3-D full-motion game is written entirely in Java.

   5. Type **http://www.kona.lotus.com** in the address line of your Web browser.

   6. Click Demos.

   7. Click Start Demo.

   8. Fill in the marketing form and click Submit.

   9. Accept the software license agreement form.

  10. Click Sales Forecast.

  11. Change some of the numbers in one of the cells with a white background. Notice that all the related cells change. This fully functional spreadsheet is written entirely in Java.

  12. Close your Web browser when you are finished.

Although Java applets running in Web browsers have no access to your computer (they can only access files on the originating server), Java applications that you run on your computer (independent of the Web browser) can access files on any Internet server that allows Internet access. You can easily implement server services entirely in Java, which means that you can provide some custom services that IIS does not support (e.g., a Telnet client or a chat server). Running the Java server application (or *servlet*) on your IIS server allows users who download a client applet in their Web browser to connect to the Java server running on your Internet server. In this manner, you can create complete client/server applications written entirely in Java.

Active Content Security Issues

ActiveX controls and plug-ins are executable programs that are loaded onto your computer and run like any other program. As such, they can extract any information stored on your computer, and they can write information or programs to your hard disk. For this reason, ActiveX controls and plug-ins can be serious security risks.

It is possible for ActiveX controls and plug-ins to contain forms of computer viruses called "Trojan horses," which can scan your computer for information and return it to the Web site using the control. ActiveX controls have low-level access to your computer and can execute any code that any other program can. Don't set your browser to load ActiveX controls that aren't certified by an organization you trust (such as Microsoft) from the Internet unless you understand the security risks involved.

Java applets, on the other hand, are not executable machine language programs. They are interpreted by a special extension to your Web browser called a Java Virtual Machine (VM). Since the virtual machines in all Web browsers are limited from accessing your hard disk drive in any way, they cannot install software such as viruses or Trojan horses, nor can they extract information about you from your computer and transmit it back to an Internet server. For this reason, Java applications are not considered a security threat. However, undiscovered security holes can exist in the virtual machine (several have been discovered and closed in the past; more may exist), so you should make sure that you always have the latest virtual machine available for your browser.

> Although Java applets are safe to execute, your Java virtual machine may have security holes. Always stay up-to-date on active content security issues and use the most recent browser version.

To address the security risks involved with using ActiveX controls and plug-ins, Microsoft and other software vendors have implemented trust-based security. *Trust-based security* means that you decide whether or not to trust a certain vendor. If you do, software such as plug-ins and ActiveX controls from that vendor can be automatically downloaded and installed in your computer without your specific permission each time. If you don't, your standard security settings will determine how to handle the code. Figure 11.4 shows the security dialog when the high-security setting encounters potentially unsafe content.

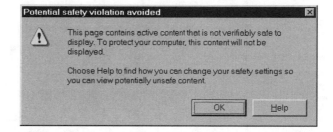

When a software company creates an ActiveX control, it can apply a digitally encrypted signature to the control. You can then set your Web browser to automatically accept ActiveX controls that are signed from certain companies, any companies, or to accept any controls whether they are signed or not.

This technology enables you to choose which software vendors you consider trustworthy. For instance, if you trust Microsoft not to transmit a virus to your computer or not to scan your computer for information, you can choose to automatically accept ActiveX controls from Microsoft. Forging digital signatures for active content is probably impossible, so you can be certain that controls actually come from the vendor whose signature is embedded in the control. Exercise 11.5 shows you how to change the active content security settings for your Web browser.

EXERCISE 11.5

Changing Active Content Security Settings

1. Double-click the Internet Explorer icon on your desktop.

2. Select View ➤ Options.

3. Select the Security tab.

4. Check Allow downloading of Active Content if you want to download content such as sound or video to your computer. This setting is relatively safe.

5. Check Enable ActiveX controls and plug-ins if you need to be able to use ActiveX controls. This setting causes a security risk.

6. Check Run ActiveX scripts if you wish to allow the use of ActiveX controls. This setting causes a security risk.

7. Check Enable Java programs if you wish to allow the execution of Java applets within your browser. There are no known serious security risks to running Java applets, but that may change in the future.

8. Click Safety Level.

9. Click High if you don't want to be allowed to download potentially unsafe content like ActiveX controls. Click Medium if you want to be warned and choose whether or not to download potentially unsafe content each time a security risk is encountered. Click low if you want to automatically download content without being warned or asked.

10. Click OK.

11. Click Publishers.

12. View the list of software publishers considered automatically trustworthy by your browser. Select any publishers you do not consider trustworthy and click the remove button.

> **EXERCISE 11.5 (CONTINUED FROM PREVIOUS PAGE)**
>
> 13. Check the Consider all commercial publishers trustworthy if you trust all commercial software publishers to keep their controls free of viruses and Trojan horses.
>
> 14. Click OK.
>
> 15. Click OK.
>
> 16. Close Internet Explorer.

ActiveX control security is a problem only when browsing the Web indiscriminately. Using ActiveX controls on your own server for an intranet- or Internet-based application is safe as long as the clients trust you—because you control the quality of ActiveX controls on your site.

Summary

Web browsers are your portal into the Internet. Two Web browsers in particular, Netscape Navigator and Microsoft Internet Explorer, are the premier Web browsers. They support all the features of standard HTML, as well as many open and proprietary types of active content. Both have strong support for plug-ins and scripting languages, as well as support for applets written in the Java programming language.

Table 11.1 summarizes the relative merits of each product. You can easily compare the different types of active content and determine which one is most appropriate for your Web site.

JavaScript is a scripting language supported by Netscape Navigator and Internet Explorer. VBScript is a version of Visual Basic included in Internet Explorer that supports easy integration with ActiveX controls. ActiveX controls are compiled plug-ins that allow you to simulate the controls used in regular applications in your Web browser–based client applications. Java is a complete cross-platform programming environment that allows you to create portable applets that run in most modern browsers on any platform.

	Feature	JavaScript	VBScript	ActiveX	Java
TABLE 11.1 Active Content Compared	Security	High	Medium	Low	High
	Development speed	Fast	Fast	Fast/Slow*	Medium
	Capability	Low	Low	High	High
	Execution speed	Slow	Slow	Fast	Medium
	Portability	Medium	Low	Low	High
	C/S Communication	Medium	Medium	Medium	High
	Browser support	Most	Few	Few	Most

*Using ActiveX controls: Fast. Developing ActiveX controls: Slow.

Review Questions

1. You are creating a client/server database application that will interface your customers to a private database stored on your server. Security is not a concern because none of your customers will be using the Web browser to browse other sites. You can dictate which browser they use to attach to your site, and you need the shortest possible development cycle. Which Web browser and active content solution for the client application fits your needs best?

   A. Internet Explorer with VBScript and ActiveX controls that access data on your SQL server directly.

   B. Either Internet Explorer or Netscape Navigator running a custom Java applet that responds to a Java server running on the same machine as your SQL server.

   C. Either Internet Explorer or Netscape Navigator running a purely JavaScript client application.

D. This application is too complex for the standard client-side active content tools.

2. You are developing an Internet public debate forum Web server that will include a custom written chat client and links to other resources on the Web. Security is a requirement, and you want to support the widest variety of browsers and platforms. Which client-side active content tool will best fit your needs?

   A. JavaScript

   B. VBScript

   C. ActiveX

   D. Java

3. You are creating a Web site containing links to Internet gaming resources on the Web and want to be able to include animated banners from your sponsors. You aren't a programmer, so simplicity is a big requirement, and you don't want to force people to use a specific Web-browser to see the ads. Which client-side content tool will work best for you?

   A. JavaScript

   B. VBScript

   C. ActiveX

   D. Java

4. Your company is considering developing an Internet-based client for its database so that data entry clerks can work from home. Security is the most important factor, but keeping costs down is always important. What solution do you recommend?

   A. Internet Explorer with VBScript and ActiveX controls that access data on your SQL server directly via an Secure Socket Layer connection.

   B. Either Internet Explorer or Netscape Navigator running a custom Java applet that responds to a Java server running on the same machine as your SQL server via an SSL connection.

C. Either Internet Explorer or Netscape Navigator running a purely JavaScript client application via PPTP.

D. This application is too complex for the standard client-side active content tools.

CHAPTER

12

Interactive Internet Servers

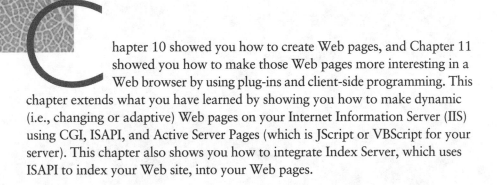

hapter 10 showed you how to create Web pages, and Chapter 11 showed you how to make those Web pages more interesting in a Web browser by using plug-ins and client-side programming. This chapter extends what you have learned by showing you how to make dynamic (i.e., changing or adaptive) Web pages on your Internet Information Server (IIS) using CGI, ISAPI, and Active Server Pages (which is JScript or VBScript for your server). This chapter also shows you how to integrate Index Server, which uses ISAPI to index your Web site, into your Web pages.

Dynamically Created Web Pages

Even though you now know how to create Web pages that interact with the user, you still don't know how to create a Web page that can tailor the data it sends based on who is accessing the Web site, the status of the Web site, or the user's interest. Dynamic Web pages are created in response to specific browser requests. Here are some examples of dynamic Web pages:

- "Catalog" Web pages that display the contents of a database

- "Shopping cart" and product ordering Web pages that allow users to browse catalog items and select items for purchasing

- Search pages

- Web pages with counters in them

- Confirmation Web pages that confirm data input in other Web pages

- Web pages that customize their appearance for whichever Web browser the user is using

- "Gateway" Web pages that act as an interface to another service such as e-mail or the UNIX "finger" program (which shows you information about a user such as the user's phone number)

- Secured Web pages that do not use the Lightweight Directory Access Protocol or Windows networking security

- Web pages that interface to hardware devices or operating system components

You can use CGI, ISAPI, or Active Server Pages (ASP) to do on the server computer just about anything that IIS doesn't already do for you. (JavaScript, VBScript, Java, and ActiveX controls similarly extend the client Web browser's functionality.)

Dynamic Web pages are Web pages that do not exist in HTML form on the Web server before they are accessed. Instead IIS generates the HTML Web document when the Web browser or Server-Side Include requests that HTML document. The created HTML document does not persist either; each time the document is requested, it is generated again by the CGI executable, ISAPI DLL, or ASP program.

The Web browser and the Web server cooperate to create dynamic Web pages. This chapter will first look at how the Web browser requests a dynamically created Web page and how it sends parameters to the CGI, ISAPI, or ASP program that creates it. Then we explore how CGI, ISAPI, and ASP work. At the end of the chapter, you will see how Index Server uses ISAPI to index your Web site.

Activating CGI, ISAPI, and Active Server Pages

Dynamic Web pages require two things: (1) a way for IIS to recognize that the Web page must be dynamically created rather than just presented to the Web browser or included in a Web page as-is and (2) a way for the Web browser request (or server-side include) to pass parameters to the CGI program, ISAPI DLL, or ASP program.

IIS meets these requirements by maintaining a list of filename extensions that it associates with CGI executables or ISAPI DLLs. When IIS is asked to return a file to a Web browser or to include a file in an HTML page to return to the Web browser, it checks the extension of the file. If the extension is in its list of CGI or ISAPI extensions, then IIS passes the file (along with any parameters) to the CGI executable or ISAPI DLL. The executable or DLL then produces HTML text, which it returns to IIS. IIS sends the new HTML document to the Web browsers for the user to view.

The two ways that CGI executables and ISAPI DLLs are most often referenced are from the following:

- Web browser hypertext links

- HTML forms in Web pages

Activating Dynamic Web Pages from Web Browser Hypertext Links

You can activate a CGI executable, an ISAPI DLL, or an ASP program directly from the Address field of your Web browser. Typing **http://www .starlingtech.com/quotes/randquote.cgi?file=wright&number=3** into your browser, for example, will display three random quotes from Stephen Wright (see Figure 12.1). Your Web browser and the Web server go through the following steps to bring those quotes to your screen:

1. The Web browser sends a request for the page http://www.starlingtech .com/quotes/randquote.cgi with the parameters file=wright&number =3 to the WWW server.

2. The WWW server compares the file extension .cgi with its list of registered file extensions and discovers that it is associated with the perl.exe program.

3. The WWW server passes the randquote.cgi file (in this example, randquote.cgi is a Perl script) to the perl.exe program along with the file=wright&number=3 parameters.

4. The perl.exe program interprets the randquote.cgi file and performs the scripted commands within it.

5. The script reads three random quotes from the wright text file, which contains many quotations of Stephen Wright. It converts the quotes to HTML format and presents the resulting HTML document to IIS.

6. IIS sends the HTML file to the Web browser.

Later in this chapter (in the sections on CGI scripts and ISAPI DLLs), you will read about this process in greater detail. The preceding example is just a cursory view of the complex operations involved in running a CGI script, ISAPI DLL, or ASP program.

You can also embed a hypertext link to a dynamically created Web page in your HTML Web pages. For example, embedding the following link in a Web page will create a hypertext link that refers to the above random quotes CGI page:

```
<A HREF="http://www.starlingtech.com/quotes/randquote
.cgi?file=wright&number=3"> Follow this link to the Random
Quotes page </A>
```

FIGURE 12.1

The quotes in this Web page are randomly selected when a CGI script creates the Web page.

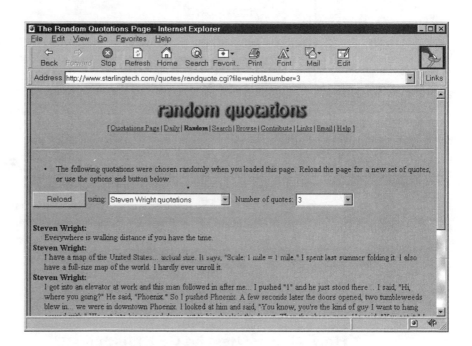

In Exercise 12.1 you will activate a CGI program directly, and you will also create a hypertext link to the same CGI program.

Activating a CGI Script from the Web Browser Directly

1. Start your Web browser.

2. Type `http://www.starlingtech.com/quotes/randquote.cgi?file=wright&number=3` into the Address field. Press Enter.

3. Open the Notepad utility.

4. Type the following lines into the Notepad:

   `<HTML><HEAD><TITLE> Link Test </TITLE></HEAD><BODY>`

   `<A HREF="http://www.starlingtech.com/quotes/randquote.cgi?file=wright&number=3"> Follow this link to the Random Quotes page </A>`

   `</BODY></HTML>`

5. Save the file as `linktest.htm` in the wwwroot directory for IIS.

6. Type `http://localhost/linktest.htm` into the Address field of your Web browser and press Enter.

7. Click the Follow this link to the Random Quotes Page link.

Activating Dynamic Web Pages from HTML Forms

Sometimes when you are designing Web pages, you need to pass more data to a CGI, ISAPI, or ASP page than you can fit in the parameters part of a URL. You may want to allow the user of the Web browser to type in the parameter data instead of having that data fixed in the hypertext link. HTML forms are a bit more complicated than simple hypertext links are, but they allow you to both send more parameter data and have the user enter that data. Forms pass data to the Web server in two ways: using the GET method and using the POST method.

How a Form Uses the GET Method

You can view an HTML form in the Web page in Figure 12.1. This form uses the GET method, which instructs the Web browser to pass all the fields displayed to the user, and optionally some fields that are hidden from the user, (along with the field names) to the WWW server as parameters to a CGI, ISAPI, or ASP page. For example, if you were to select Dave Barry Quotations from the Using pick list in the form, select 4 from the Number of Quotes pick list, and then click the Reload button, the form in the Web page will ask the Web browser for the Web page http://www.starlingtech.com/quotes/ randquote.cgi?file=barry&number=4 and display the HTML text that the Web server returns (in this case, four very funny Dave Barry quotations).

The following HTML form inserted in a Web page allows people browsing your Web page to select and view a number of quotations from Michael Moncur's quotations page:

```
<form method="get" action="http://www.starlingtech.com/
quotes/randquote.cgi">

<input type="submit" value="Go">

 using: <select name=file>

<option value=altq>alt.quotations archives

<option value=barry>Dave Barry Quotations

<option value=bywomen>Quotations by Women

<option value=mgm selected>michael moncur's collection

<option value=usenet>The USENET fortune file

<option value=wright>Steven Wright quotations

</select> Number of quotes: <select name=number>

<option value=1>1

<option value=2>2

<option value=3 selected>3

</select>
```

This example returns a Web page similar to the one you got when you typed the URL directly into your Web browser or embedded a hypertext link into a Web page. The GET method works well when your HTML form has to send only a few parameters to the Web server, such as some search criteria or the type and number of widgets you want to order. If your HTML form must send a larger amount of data, then you should use the POST method in your HTML forms instead.

How a Form Uses the POST Method

The POST method does not send the parameters as a part of the URL. Instead, this method sends the parameters in a separate part of the HTTP communication. This technique allows the POST method to send more parameter data than would fit in a hypertext URL. The following example uses the POST method to send search parameters to a CGI search script:

```
<FORM METHOD="POST" ACTION="http://www.starlingtech.com/
quotes/qsearch.cgi">

<strong>Search for:</strong><INPUT TYPE="text" NAME="Search"
SIZE="30">

<br>

<strong> in collection: </strong>

<select name=file>

<option value="mgm" selected>michael moncur's collection

<option value="coles">Cole's Quotables

<option value="usenet">The USENET fortune file

<option value="altq">alt.quotations archives

<option value="poorc">*Poor Man's College

<option value="devils">The Devil's Dictionary

<option value="wright">Steven Wright quotations

<option value="deep">Deep Thoughts - Jack Handey

<option value="barry">Dave Barry Quotations

<option value="20thcent">20th Century Quotations

<option value="bywomen">Quotations by Women

</select>

<BR>

<input type="hidden" name="type" value="b">

<INPUT TYPE="submit" VALUE="Start the Search">

</FORM>
```

One way that you can tell the difference between a Web page generated from a form using the GET command and a page generated from a form using the POST command is that the page with the GET command includes the parameters to the Address field of the Web browser. (The parameters follow the question mark that comes after the page name.) The preceding POST example does not show you the parameters in the Address field when you receive the CGI-generated page from the Web server, because the parameters are sent separately, rather than as part of the URL.

Because you can use two methods to send parameters to CGI, ISAPI, or ASP programs, your CGI, ISAPI, or ASP program must be written to accept either or both methods. Exercise 12.2 shows you how to create a Web page with an embedded form that calls a Perl CGI script on a Web server.

The preceding examples of forms are not the only way you can present structured information and request data from the Web browser user. You can create forms with editable text fields, check boxes, pick lists (like these examples), radio buttons, and even clickable images. With Java, JavaScript, Visual Basic, and ActiveX controls, you can have the Web browser calculate parameters for you. The purpose of this book, however, is not to teach you the basics of HTML or how to write programs. Our purpose is to teach you the features and capabilities of IIS. You should refer to one of the many excellent books on HTML and the various Internet programming languages to expand your knowledge and skills in those areas.

The Common Gateway Interface (CGI)

Chapter 6 showed you how to associate a CGI program with a file extension type (using the Registry Editor), and Chapter 8 warned you about the security implications of using CGI scripts in your Web site. Here you will learn how to use a CGI script in your World Wide Web site.

CGI stands for Common Gateway Interface, and CGI is the way WWW servers on most other operating systems such as UNIX and the MacOS are extended to support dynamically created Web pages. CGI specifies two things:

- How a WWW server can recognize a CGI script or CGI executable

- How a Web browser can send parameter information to the CGI script or executable

---

EXERCISE 12.2

Using Forms to Activate a Perl Script

1. Open the Notepad utility.

2. Type the following text into the Notepad:

   ```
   <HTML><HEAD><TITLE> Form Test </TITLE></HEAD><BODY>
   <FORM METHOD="POST" ACTION="http://www.starlingtech
   .com/quotes/qsearch.cgi">
   <strong>Search for:</strong><INPUT TYPE="text"
   NAME="Search"
   SIZE="30">
   <br>
   <strong> in collection: </strong>
   <select name=file>
   <option value="mgm" selected>michael moncur's
   collection
   <option value="coles">Cole's Quotables
   <option value="usenet">The USENET fortune file
   <option value="barry">Dave Barry Quotations
   <option value="20thcent">20th Century Quotations
   <option value="bywomen">Quotations by Women
   </select>
   <BR>
   <input type="hidden" name="type" value="b">
   <INPUT TYPE="submit" VALUE="Start the Search">
   </FORM>
   </BODY></HTML>
   ```

3. Save the file as formtest.htm in the wwwroot directory of your Web site.

4. Open your Web browser.

5. Type `http://localhost/formtest.htm` into the Address field of your Web browser and press Enter.

6. Select Cole's Quotables and then click the Search button.

Because the running program environment for Windows and Windows NT is not the same as UNIX, the CGI for IIS is more properly called WIN-CGI.

Although most UNIX CGI scripts and programs written for the UNIX version of CGI can be run from IIS on Windows NT (or recompiled and run, in the case of programs written in C or C++), some scripts that rely on particular features of the UNIX environment (for example, the sendmail program being available) will not work properly. The same restriction applies to CGI scripts written for the MacOS. And, of course, if you write CGI scripts that depend on features of the Windows programming environment, then you won't be able to run those CGI scripts on Mac or UNIX Web servers.

How the CGI programs are recognized by the Web server, how the Web server starts them running, and how parameter information is provided to the CGI programs are basically the same for Mac, UNIX, and Windows NT Web servers, including IIS. The process is as follows:

1. The Web server recognizes the file requested by the Web browser to be a CGI script because the extension of the file matches an extension reserved for CGI programs. (Win-dows NT lists registered extensions in the registry. See Chapter 6 for details on how the extensions are stored in the registry.)

2. IIS retrieves from the registry setting for that extension the path and file-name of the executable program associated with that extension.

3. IIS creates an environment for that application that includes setting environment variables for such things as the IP address and Internet name of the Web browser requesting the Web page, the remote username, the request method (i.e., POST or GET), the query string, and the content length. See Figure 12.2 for a view of some of the environment variables that are passed to a WIN-CGI program.

4. IIS runs the program listed in the registry setting. The program is run in a separate memory space from IIS because it is a completely separate program, not a dynamically linked library to IIS (see Figure 12.3). You should note that the registry setting provides the full path to the executable program and that two question marks follow the program name. These question marks are placeholders for the two command-line parameters that are sent to the CGI application. (See Figure 12.4 in the section on ISAPI applications later in this chapter for a view of the registry with two CGI entries in the list of registered extensions.)

■ The first parameter is the translated path of the browser's request. (This parameter usually identifies either the CGI script that will be interpreted by the CGI executable or the executable itself, if the executable is not an interpreter.) However, this path is from the root of Windows NT's file system, not from the Web root, because CGI scripts run in the environment of Windows NT directories, not in the restricted environment of the Web tree of directories. This first parameter corresponds to the PATH_TRANSLATED environment variable set up by IIS.

■ The second parameter is the query string (the information that comes after the question mark in the URL). This parameter corresponds to the QUERY_STRING environment variable set up by IIS.

5. The CGI executable runs according to this scheme:

■ If the CGI executable is a simple (or even a complex) program and not an interpreter of a scripting language, then the CGI executable runs in that environment, performs the functions it is programmed to do, produces HTML text output, and returns control back to IIS.

■ If the CGI executable is an interpreter, such as Perl, TCL, BASIC, or even the Windows NT CMD batch file interpreter, it loads the program script identified in the first parameter (and the PATH_TRANSLATED environment variable). The CGI executable then runs the script. The script performs the functions it was programmed to do, produces HTML text output, and then terminates. The CGI executable then returns control to IIS.

6. IIS processes the result. (It may, for example, prepend or append HTML text to all HTML pages, including those generated by CGI scripts. See the section on ISAPI for the details.) Finally, IIS sends the HTML text to the Web browser.

FIGURE 12.2

Internet Information
Server creates
environment variables for
the CGI program.

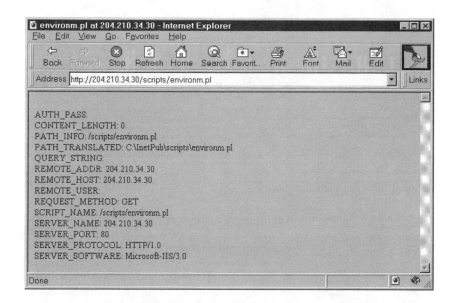

FIGURE 12.2

Internet Information
Server creates
environment variables for
the CGI program.

FIGURE 12.3

A CGI program does not
run in the same memory
space as the Internet
Information Server.

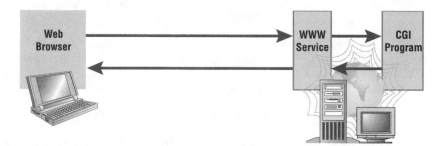

When to Use CGI

You can use any executable program that accepts command-line input and
produces console (i.e., text-screen, or standard-out for you programmer types)
output as a CGI program. Because the text output of the program will be sent
to a Web browser, the program you use should produce HTML-formatted
text. Otherwise, the Web browser might complain that your CGI program is
returning badly formatted Web pages.

Because you can configure IIS to use any program for CGI, you can write
executable programs in C or any other compiled language. Consequently, you
can interface your Web pages to applications, hardware, and software that
might not yet be supported by ISAPI DLLs or the JScript or VBScript interpreters built into IIS. For example, you can write a C program that interfaces

to the Windows NT operating system and shows you the Event Viewer log files in a Web page.

You can also use CGI for the following functions:

- E-mail gateways

- User feedback to Web pages

- WWW access to e-mail archives

- Page hit counters

- Imagemaps

- Internet chat rooms

- Cryptographic security

- Web order selection and total calculation

- User feedback to e-mail

- Multiple-player Internet games

- Web control of hardware devices such as cameras, robots, beverage machines, and hot tubs

- Security restrictions to private Web pages

- Random selection from text files

- Integrating data from multiple sources, such as several database query results or separate text files

- Converting data output from older programs into HTML text

- Searching of specialized text databases such as bibliographies

These, of course, are not the only uses for CGI, just a representative sample. You can use CGI to do almost anything you can write a regular program to do. To fully explore what you can do with CGI, you should see how other Web sites use CGI, check Web pages and Usenet newsgroups on CGI programming, and get a good book on programming your Web site with CGI.

Creating CGI executables for use in your Web site is easier than creating ISAPI applications because you can create CGI applications in any development environment, such as Microsoft, Borland, or Symantec's C compilers; Visual Basic; less popular languages such as Pascal, Modula 2, and Oberon; and even interpreted QBasic. Using CGI applications is easier than using ASPs because CGI applications may be compiled to the machine language of the server computer.

Many CGI executables are actually interpreters for CGI scripts. Programming in Perl, TCL, and other interpreted languages (i.e., scripting languages) is much easier than programming in compiled languages such as C and C++ because you can just type in the program and run it. You don't have to compile it and link it before you can see if it works. Interpreted languages do not depend on specific features of the operating system or computer they are written to run on, which makes interpreted languages much more portable than compiled languages.

If you are using a CGI executable that is an interpreter, you should see if an ISAPI version of the executable is available because the ISAPI version is likely to run faster than the CGI version. An interpreter can be written as either a CGI executable or an ISAPI application. Writing the interpreter is easier, but the ISAPI application will run faster.

NTFS Security and CGI

CGI executables (such as a C program that accesses the Event log or a Perl interpreter that runs Perl scripts) are programs just like any other program on your Windows NT server computer and are subject to the same restrictions and permissions. The environment that CGI programs run in is subtly different from the Web environment IIS creates for normal HTML pages. Instead of working within WWW Service directories, CGI programs work within the standard Windows NT directory structure.

Since the CGI program uses Windows NT directories instead of WWW Service directories, you must make sure that the CGI programs still access the right information. CGI programs will not see the virtual directories in the same place that you put them with the WWW Service, for example. Also, a CGI program may have access to directories that a Web browser cannot access. Although the Web browser can access only the root directory and virtual directories established in the Directories tab of the WWW Service Properties window, the CGI script may have permission to access any directory on your hard drive.

Because a CGI program may access more than the WWW Service will normally permit, you must be careful to construct CGI programs that will access only the data you want accessed, or you should make sure that the users with permission to run the CGI program (including the IUSER_<computer name> anonymous user account) have NTFS permissions to access only the files and directories that you determine are safe.

The user of a CGI program must have Execute permission for the directory containing the application executable (.exe) program. The user doesn't need Read access to that directory, however, unless the executable itself has some reason to read a file in that directory. If the CGI program is a script interpreter, however, the user must have read permission to the directory containing the script.

The script interpreters should never go in a directory that is readable by a Web browser. Scripts go in the /scripts directory, not in the executable program that interprets the scripts.

A CGI Example

In Exercise 12.3 you install a sample C program that you can use as a CGI executable to show you the contents of the Event Log. This program was written using Visual C++ version 4.0 and compiled as a command-line application. You can also run it from the command line, but the Event Viewer that comes with Windows NT is much friendlier to use.

EXERCISE 12.3

Installing a CGI Program

1. Copy the files log2html.exe, g1.gif, g2.gif, g3.gif, g4.gif, and g5.gif from the samples\log2html subdirectory of the CD-ROM to the cgi-bin subdirectory of IIS.

2. With the Internet Service Manager program, create a new virtual directory for this cgi-bin directory. Set Read and Execute permissions for the virtual directory.

3. Enable NT Challenge/Response authentication and disable the other two logon authentication options.

4. Open your Web browser.

5. Type **http://localhost/cgi-bin/log2html.exe**.

The Internet Server Applications Programming Interface (ISAPI)

Microsoft developed Internet Server Applications Programming Interface (ISAPI) to make it easier to customize IIS and to provide a faster interface than CGI for making dynamically generated Web pages. The two general types of ISAPI DLLs are ISAPI applications and ISAPI filters. ISAPI applications work much as CGI executables do. You will take a look at ISAPI applications first, and then you will see how ISAPI filters can extend the capability of IIS.

ISAPI Applications

ISAPI applications are DLLs that are activated when the WWW Service is asked to return a page whose file extension is recorded in the registry as an ISAPI file type. (See "Adding MIME Types," "Registering ISAPI Applications," and "Enabling CGI Scripts" in Chapter 6.) If the recorded entry points to an executable program (i.e., one that ends in .exe and has the %s %s parameters after it), then IIS starts that program as a CGI executable. If the recorded entry points to a file that ends in .dll, then ISAPI loads the dynamic link library into its own memory space and passes control to it. See Figure 12.4 for a view of the ScriptMap registry key with 11 extensions defined (two of them for CGI executables; the rest for ISAPI applications).

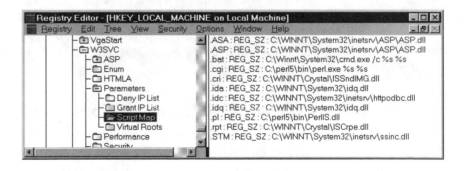

FIGURE 12.4

The ScriptMap registry key registers extensions that IIS identifies with CGI scripts (paths to files that end in .exe %s %s) and ISAPI applications (paths to files that end in .dll).

ISAPI DLLs are usually quite a bit faster than CGI executables because the DLLs are loaded into the same memory space as the IIS program (see Figure 12.5). Also, ISAPI DLLs do not have to be loaded and run each time a Web page using them is accessed, because the IIS ISAPI mechanism can use the same copy of the DLL in memory for each access. This arrangement reduces the data transfer time between IIS and the ISAPI DLL and allows the DLL to respond faster than a CGI executable that performs the same function. ISAPI DLLs are more difficult to write, however, because they require a specialized programming environment (most commonly Microsoft C++ with the Win32 SDK, although some people have had success using other compiler environments).

FIGURE 12.5

An ISAPI DLL runs in the same memory space as IIS.

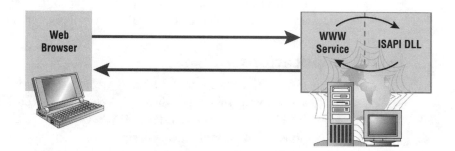

An ISAPI application can do anything that a CGI executable can do, including running scripts. Many scripting languages have been implemented as ISAPI DLLs; one example is Perl, which is currently the most popular server-side scripting language for developing Web pages. (However, JScript and VBScript, which are also implemented by Microsoft as ISAPI DLLs, may soon eclipse Perl.)

After you configure IIS to activate the ISAPI DLL when a file with its extension is accessed, you can treat the ISAPI application just like a CGI executable. You interface to an ISAPI application (i.e., pass parameters) the same way as you interface to a CGI executable (via a URL, from a hypertext link, or from a HTML form).

NTFS Security and ISAPI Applications

ISAPI DLLs extend the functionality of the WWW Service of IIS. ISAPI DLLs respect the same NTFS restrictions as IIS; that is, if a user is logged on anonymously, the ISAPI DLL will be able to access only resources available to the IUSER_<comptuer name>; but if the user has attached to the WWW Service using the Administrator account, then the ISAPI DLL will be able to access any resources that the Administrator account can access.

Because an ISAPI program may access more than the WWW Service will normally permit (i.e., it can access directories that are not in the list of home or virtual directories for the WWW Service), you must be careful to construct ISAPI programs that access only the data you want accessed. Or you should make sure that the users with permission to run the ISAPI program (including the IUSER_<computer name> anonymous user account) have NTFS permissions to access only the files and directories that you determine are safe.

The user of an ISAPI application must have Execute permission for the directory containing the application (.dll) program. The user doesn't need Read access to that directory unless the DLL itself has some reason to read a file in that directory. If the ISAPI application is a script interpreter, however, the user must have NTFS Read permission to the directory containing the script.

An ISAPI Application Example

In Exercise 12.4 you will install the PerlIS ISAPI application which implements an interpreter for Perl scripts. You will then install a Perl script in your IIS Web pages that displays a randomly selected image link.

EXERCISE 12.4

Installing an ISAPI Application and a Perl Script

1. Run the `setup.exe` program in the `\software\Perl5` subdirectory of the CD-ROM.

2. Follow the Install Shield prompts and accept the default values when given a choice.

3. Stop and start the WWW Service.

4. Copy the `randpix.pl` file from the `\samples\Perlpix` subdirectory of the CD-ROM to the `/Scripts` subdirectory of IIS.

5. Copy the `randpix` directory from the `\samples\Perlpix` subdirectory of the CD-ROM to the `wwwroot` subdirectory of IIS.

6. Open your Web browser.

7. Type **http://localhost/randpix.pl**.

8. Click Reload on your Web browser several times.

9. Click the image in the Web page.

ISAPI Filters

The other use for ISAPI DLLs is to directly extend the functionality of the WWW Service of IIS. ISAPI DLLs can be written to preprocess the HTTP requests and to postprocess the HTTP responses of IIS. You can use filters for the following purposes:

- Authentication (for other than Windows NT security)

- Specialized encryption or compression

- More elaborate access restrictions (such as by Internet name as well as by IP address)

- Implementation of HTTP commands that IIS does not yet support

- Additional specialized server-side include commands that execute faster because they do not require file access

- Additional logging and traffic analyses beyond what the built-in logging features provide

When you develop an ISAPI filter, you register which server actions the filter will respond to. It can, for example, preprocess the raw data sent from the client, the headers sent by the client, the data that will be sent to an CGI executable or ISAPI application, the data returned by an application, and final data that will be sent to the Web browser.

In order for ISAPI to load and use the filter, it must be registered in the HKEY_LOCAL_MACHINE\System\CurrentControlSet\Services\W3SVC\Parameters\FilterDLLs registry key. A correctly written filter will, when initialized by IIS, register which WWW Service events it will process.

Configuring IIS to use an ISAPI filter is a simple matter of installing the filter in a directory with appropriate permissions and then registering the DLL in the registry key. Using the ISAPI filter, however, requires that you know what the filter does and how it is used. There is no standard as to what filters may do to your IIS server. The whole point of filters is to extend the capabilities of IIS in new and unexpected (to Microsoft programmers, at least) ways.

Active Server Pages (ASP)

ASPs are HTML pages that contain scripts written in VBScript or Jscript, as well as regular HTML text. ASPs have the extension .asp, which is listed in the extensions that are associated with CGI and ISAPI applications. The .asp extension is associated with the `asp.dll` ISAPI application.

When IIS is asked to return a file ending in .asp, it recognizes that the file must first be processed by the ASP DLL. The ASP DLL processes the .asp file sequentially until it encounters a scripting language portion of the .asp page. (The special symbols <% and %> surround the scripting language portions of the .asp document.)

ASP.DLL interprets the scripting language portion(s) of the document using the default scripting language for the page, which is VBScript unless the DefaultScriptLanguage registry key is changed, or unless the command `<%@ LANGUAGE = JScript %>` appears at the beginning of the document.

You can also include scripts in .asp files using the SCRIPT LANGUAGE and RUNAT HTML tags. For example, `<SCRIPT LANGUAGE=JScript RUNAT=Server>` identifies the start of a JScript code segment that will run on the server. A script code segment defined in this manner ends with the `</SCRIPT>` HTML tag.

The environment available to JScript and VBScript is similar to that provided by a Web browser except for user-interface functions and objects. Because the server may not have a user at the console—and because that user is probably not the user that the script should be communicating with anyway—those features have been disabled for both JScript and VBScript running on the file server.

Just as it is not the purpose of this book to teach you HTML, it also is not the purpose of this book to teach you JScript and VBScript programming. You should refer to other books, to the Internet, and to Microsoft's documentation for information on how to develop useful ASP programs.

You can use ASP scripts to do many of the HTML text generation functions that you can do with CGI executables and ISAPI applications. (In fact, ASPs are implemented as ISAPI applications.) The primary advantage of ASP scripts, however, is that you can embed them right in with regular HTML text. In Exercise 12.5 you will create an ASP that uses VBScript, and in Chapter 13 you will use ASP and VBScript to connect to databases.

EXERCISE 12.5

Creating an Active Server Page with VBScript

1. Open the Notepad utility.

2. Type the following text in the Notepad:

```
<HTML><HEAD><TITLE> ASP Script Test </TITLE>
</HEAD><BODY>
This is a test of Active Server Pages Scripting.<p>
The date is: <% Call PrintDate %> <p>
The above text came from a VBScript program!<p>
</BODY></HTML>
<SCRIPT LANGUAGE=JScript RUNAT=Server>
function PrintDate()
{
 var x
 x = new Date()
 Response.Write(x.toString())
}
</SCRIPT>
```

3. Save the file as `testasp.asp` in the wwwroot directory of the WWW Service.

4. Open your Web browser.

5. Type **http://localhost/testasp.asp** in the Address field.

Index Server

In Chapter 6 you saw how to install and configure Index Server and even how to connect your Web pages to a sample Index Server search page. This section shows you how to customize the way that Index Server queries your WWW Internet site.

Index Server, like ASP, is actually a set of Microsoft ISAPI applications. The Index Server DLL (`idq.dll`) registers two file extensions: .ida and .idq for use with Index Server. Index server also uses a third file type—.htx. To understand how Index Server works and to customize it for your site, you must know how these files interact. You should understand how the following components work:

- Query forms

- Internet Data Query (.idq) files

- HTML extension (.htx) files

- Internet Database Administration (.ida) files

Query Forms

Database queries start from query forms that look just like any other HTML form. Once you install Index Server on your Web site, you can embed the following form to any of your Web pages. The following form uses the sample search pages installed by Index Server in your scripts directory.

```
<FORM ACTION="/scripts/samples/search/query.idq"
METHOD="POST">

Enter your query:

<INPUT TYPE="TEXT" NAME="CiRestriction" SIZE="60"
MAXLENGTH="100" VALUE=" ">

<INPUT TYPE="SUBMIT" VALUE="Execute Query">

<INPUT TYPE="RESET" VALUE="Clear">

<INPUT TYPE="HIDDEN" NAME="CiMaxRecordsPerPage" VALUE="10">

<INPUT TYPE="HIDDEN" NAME="CiScope" VALUE="/">

<INPUT TYPE="HIDDEN" NAME="TemplateName" VALUE="query">

<INPUT TYPE="HIDDEN" NAME="CiSort" VALUE="rank[d]">

<INPUT TYPE="HIDDEN" NAME="HTMLQueryForm" VALUE="/samples/
search/query.htm">

</FORM>
```

In contrast to the first form we examined in this chapter, which had no hidden fields, and the second form, which had only one field, this form has five fields. The information in these five fields is passed on to the .idq file identified in the FORM ACTION field. You should also notice that query forms to the Index Server use the POST method.

This HTML text is not interpreted by IIS or by Index Server—the HTML form listed above instructs your Web browser to display the form to you. When you click the Execute Query button, the form data (the input fields with names, hidden or otherwise) are sent to the Web server with the request that the `query.idq` file be used to process it.

In Exercise 12.6 you will add a search page to a demonstration Help pages Web site.

Internet Data Query (.idq) files

When IIS is asked to access an .idq file, it looks up the file extension in the registry and associates it with the `idq.dll` ISAPI application. If that DLL is not already loaded into the IIS memory space, it is loaded now. Then control passes to `idq.dll`, along with the location of the .idq file and the query data sent by the Web browser.

The `idq.dll` application uses the .idq file to guide its processing of the query data. The .idq file contains parameters about the query such as the scope of the search, how many records (maximum) will be returned, how many will be returned in each query result page, the HTML template that will be used, and how the results will be sorted.

Paths within the .idq files are from the virtual root of the server and cannot backtrack (i.e., they contain . or ..).

The .idq file consists of two sections:

- **Names** defines nonstandard properties that this query may be limited on or display in the result. You can use this feature to index on special properties of documents that are indexed using document filters such as the filter for Microsoft Office applications. This section is optional.

- **Query** specifies the parameters of the query, such as the scope, columns, restrictions, and template. (These four parameters are required.) Parameters can (and some should) be passed from the HTML query form; for example, `%Restriction%` takes the restriction value—what you are searching for—from the field named Restriction in the HTML form.

EXERCISE 12.6

Add a Search Page to an Existing Web Site

1. Open the Notepad utility.

2. Copy the nethelp subdirectory and all its contents from the \samples subdirectory of the CD-ROM to the wwwroot directory of IIS.

3. Open the default.html Web page in the /nethelp subdirectory of your Web site.

4. Type the following text at the end of the page just before the </BODY> HTML tag:

```
<FORM ACTION="/scripts/samples/search/query.idq"
METHOD="POST">

Enter your query:

<INPUT TYPE="TEXT" NAME="CiRestriction" SIZE="60"
MAXLENGTH="100" VALUE=" ">

<INPUT TYPE="SUBMIT" VALUE="Excecute Query">

<INPUT TYPE="RESET" VALUE="Clear">

<INPUT TYPE="HIDDEN" NAME="CiMaxRecordsPerPage"
VALUE="10">

<INPUT TYPE="HIDDEN" NAME="CiScope" VALUE="/
nethelp">

<INPUT TYPE="HIDDEN" NAME="TemplateName"
VALUE="query">

<INPUT TYPE="HIDDEN" NAME="CiSort" VALUE="rank[d]">

<INPUT TYPE="HIDDEN" NAME="HTMLQueryForm" VALUE=
"/samples/search/query.htm">

</FORM>
```

5. Save the modified HTML file.

6. Open your Web browser.

7. Type **http://localhost/default.htm** in the Address field.

8. Type **printer** in the search field and then click Execute Query.

Here is an example of an .idq file:

```
[QUERY]

CiRestriction=%CiRestriction%

CiColumns=filename,size,characterization,vpath,DocTitle,
write

CiScope=%CiScope%

CiFlags=DEEP

CiTemplate=/scripts/result.htx

CiSort=%CiSort%
```

To use the preceding .idq file, you must place the `result.htx` file in the `/scripts` subdirectory, of course. You can use the .idq files to create multiple catalogs simply by creating multiple .idq files, each with a separate CiCatalog setting. For example, if one .idc had the settings:

```
CiCatalog=C:\Inetpub\Catalog1\

CiScope=\firstroot
```

and another .idc was identical except for the settings:

```
CiCatalog=C:\Inetpub\Catalog2\

CiScope=\secondroot
```

then you would have two catalogs: one in the `Catalog1` subdirectory, which allows the user to find files from the `firstroot` subdirectory, and the other in the `Catalog2` subdirectory, which allows the user to find files from the `secondroot` subdirectory. Note, however, that the preceding example doesn't keep both catalogs from indexing your entire Web site. It just establishes two roots and allows both to be searched with a restriction on each.

A better use for the CiScope parameter is to limit queries to certain parts of your Web site when the network user is looking for particular information. For example, if you have separate subdirectories for new products, current products, press releases, device drivers, and technical documentation, then you can create specialized .idq files for each area of your Web site. That way browsers of your Web site won't have to wade through extraneous information that just happens to match the search criteria the user types in.

HTML Extension (.htx) Files

The ASP DLL uses the parameters from the .idq page to search its database. It needs another file to tell it how to format the resulting data so that IIS can send it to the Web browser, and .htx files are Microsoft's answer to that problem.

The .htx documents are almost like programming languages because they must be able to respond to various conditions; for example, no files match your query, one page worth of files match, or many HTML pages worth of files match. Other than the special conditional constructs (i.e., the %if statement and %endif statement) and the commands to insert data returned from the query (i.e., %filename% and %DocTitle%), the .htx document contains regular HTML formatted text.

The following .htx file is very simple; it is merely an example of how an .htx file is formatted. You should use the more complicated query sample files installed with Index Server—or edit them to suit the needs of your Web site.

```
<HTML>
<!--
  <%CiTemplate%>
-->
<HEAD>
<TITLE>SEARCH</TITLE>
</HEAD>
<%begindetail%>
  <p>
  <dt>
    <%CiCurrentRecordNumber%>.
    <%if DocTitle isempty%>
      <b><a href="<%EscapeURL vpath%>"><%filename%></a></b>
    <%else%>
      <b><a href="<%EscapeURL vpath%>"><%DocTitle%></a></b>
    <%endif%>
```

```
<dd>

  <b><i>Abstract: </i></b><%characterization%>

  <br>

  <cite>

    <a href="<%EscapeURL vpath%>">http://
    <%server_name%><%vpath%></a>

    <font size=-1> - <%if size eq ""%>(size and time
    unknown)<%else%>size <%size%> bytes - <%write%>
    GMT<%endif%></font>

  </cite>

<%enddetail%>

</HTML>
```

Internet Database Administration (.ida) Files

One more type of file that you should be familiar with to customize Index Server for your Web site is the .ida file type. .ida files are like .idq files except that .ida files accept only four parameters:

- **CiCatalog** specifies where the catalog is located. If it is missing, the default location specified in the registry is used.

- **CiTemplate** specifies the template file (i.e., .htx file) that will be used to format the data that results from execution of the .ida command.

- **CiAdministration** specifies the administrative command, which must be one of the following: UpdateRoots, GetState, ForceMerge, or ScanRoots. If nothing is specified, the administrative action will default to GetState.

- **CiLocale** specifies locale information such as the character set or time zone in use.

The administration .ida file for updating the virtual roots that is installed when you install Index Server is as follows:

```
[Admin]

CiCatalog=C:\Inetpub\
```

```
CiTemplate=/srchadm/admin.htm

CiAdminOperation=UpdateRoots
```

The administration .ida file for forcing a master merge that is installed when you install Index Server is as follows:

```
[Admin]

CiCatalog=C:\Inetpub\

CiTemplate=/srchadm/admin.htm

CiAdminOperation=ForceMerge
```

The administration .ida file for forcing a scan of the virtual roots that is installed when you install Index Server is as follows:

```
[Admin]

CiCatalog=C:\Inetpub\

CiTemplate=/srchadm/admin.htm

CiAdminOperation=ScanRoots
```

The administration .ida file for getting statistics on Index Server that is installed when you install Index Server is as follows:

```
[Admin]

CiCatalog=C:\Inetpub\

CiTemplate=/Scripts/srchadm/state.htx

CiAdminOperation=GetState
```

These four administrative files don't seem like much for the results they produce. Most of the work is actually done in the `idq.dll` program, and the results are formatted using the `admin.htm` and `state.htx` files. You should have no reason to modify the `admin.htm` and the `state.htx` files, but you may want to modify the .ida files to customize the functionality of Index Server for your site.

For example, you might want to create .ida files that allow you to manage separate master catalogs. You could create two sets of .ida files, like those shown in the example, except that the CiCatalog entry for one would point to the `C:\InetPub\Catalog1` and the other set would point to `C:\InetPub\Catalog2`.

You could then use these administration pages (using the UpdateRoots .ida command) to limit the virtual roots that each will index. You will end up with two (or more) catalogs that index different portions of your Web site. You can then use specialized .idq files (as described in the section on Internet Data Query files) to search these limited catalogs.

Summary

Internet Information Server by itself is a fast and secure platform for serving HTML files to Web browsers. CGI, ISAPI, and ASP programs, however, give IIS its flexibility and power. CGI, ISAPI, and ASP programs allow IIS to generate Web pages dynamically—that is, only when the Web pages are needed.

Dynamic Web pages (i.e., Web pages created using CGI, ISAPI, and ASP) can be activated a number of ways, including directly from the Address field of a Web browser, from a hypertext link, and from a form. When dynamic Web pages are activated from forms, data can be sent to the CGI, ISAPI, or ASP program using the GET method or the POST method.

CGI executables run in an address space separate from the IIS program. CGI executables can be written in any language that produces Windows .exe files. The Windows CGI environment (WIN-CGI) is also very much like the UNIX CGI environment, but the environments are not identical.

CGI executables are often program interpreters, which means that they read in and execute a scripting language such as Perl, TCL, or BASIC. The term *CGI script* describes a text file containing commands that are interpreted by such a CGI executable.

ISAPI applications are very much like CGI executables except for two things. ISAPI applications run in the same address space as IIS and are therefore faster than CGI executables, and they are written to a specialized interface in a compiled programming language such as C++. ISAPI applications like CGI scripts can perform complex operations on their own or can be interpreters for scripting languages such as Perl and TCL.

ISAPI can also be used to implement filters, which extend the functionality of IIS and can affect how all communications stream in and out of IIS.

ASPs use an ISAPI DLL to implement the VBScript and JScript scripting languages within HTML pages. VBScript and JScript are also used in Web browsers. Some commands are not available for VBScript and JScript when the scripts are run on the server, however, because there is no user to interact with.

An ISAPI DLL also implements Index Server. You customize how searches occur from within .idq files and prepare the output of searches with .htx files. .ida files contain commands that control Index Server's indexing function.

Review Questions

1. You expect a heavy load on your Web server and you need the fastest way to implement custom Web-based data logging (to a special file on the Web server) and results reporting interactive Web page. Which is your best option?

    A. Implement the routine in Java on the Web browser.

    B. Implement the routine as a custom-written (in C++) ISAPI DLL on the Web server.

    C. Implement the routine using C++ and install it as a CGI executable on your Web server.

    D. Implement the routine in Perl using the PerlIS ISAPI DLL.

2. You wish to efficiently extend IIS to support encrypted communications for all Web pages using the BLOWFISH cipher. Which environment best fits your needs?

    A. JScript

    B. An ISAPI application

    C. CGI

    D. An ISAPI filter

3. Which of the following IIS extension mechanisms allows you to accept input from HTML forms and process that information? (Choose all that apply.)

    A. CGI scripts

    B. ISAPI applications

    C. JScript

    D. VBScript

4. You want to limit the scope of queries from within the /Products/ Software/Downloads section of your Web site to just the that section of your Web site. You want to be able to query your whole site from the home page, however. How can you do this most easily?

   A. Set the CiScope value in the .idq file to /Products/Software/ Downloads.

   B. Remove Read permission for the IUSER_SEARCH user from all directories except for the /Products/Software/Downloads directory.

   C. Disable indexing on all virtual directory except for the /Products/ Software/Downloads virtual directory.

   D. You cannot limit the scope of a query.

CHAPTER

13

Database Connectivity

Nearly all commercial transactions are processed by databases; databases are the software engines of our economy. The business use of the Internet, for more than ad brochure Web pages and e-mail, depends on the ability to interface Web sites with databases. Most important commercial information is stored in databases, and the ability to interface with these databases over the Internet allows consumers to find and purchase the products they need without involving a human operator or making a phone call.

Databases are also useful for reporting tables of information, such as portions of phone books or catalogs of product information. Databases are appropriate for any application that requires the storage or retrieval of data.

This chapter covers the database connectivity options that IIS and the Microsoft database products Access and SQL Server support. IIS supports any standard database solution, but Access support for Internet integration makes publishing databases on the Web especially easy.

This chapter covers the following topics:

- How databases work

- The differences between databases

- The criteria you should use to select a database product

- How IIS supports the connection of databases to the Internet

You will also learn how to create Web pages to support database connectivity, using a sample Contacts database.

The Dao of Database

If you work with computers, you've probably heard a lot about databases. Often they are presented as mysterious solutions to problems as widely disparate as manufacturing control, workflow, order entry, and document management. You've probably heard many different software systems described as databases (like the DNS system presented in Chapter 5). Trying to find a common thread among these different uses might be a bit confusing.

Databases are nothing more than organized collections of data. Your telephone book is a perfect example of a manual database, one that contains four elements of data:

- Last Name or Business Name

- First Name

- Address (optional)

- Telephone number

In a database, these elements are called *fields* or *columns* (because when laid out as a table, they form the columns). Entries in the phone book (e.g., Valentino, Rudolph, 555-1212) are called *records* or *rows* (because when laid out as a table, they form the rows). If we printed a portion of a telephone database, it might look something like Table 13.1.

	Entry	Last Name	First	Name	Phone
TABLE 13.1 A Fictitious Phone Book	1	Foot	B.	13 Forest Way	555-9192
	2	Kringle	Kristopher	34th St.	555-4242
	3	Kruger	Frederick	683 Elm St.	555-1234
	4	Valentino	Rudolph	3434 Hollywood Blvd.	555-3452
	5	West	Mae	789 Vine St.	555-6547

Table 13.1 represents a *table*. A table contains lists of information of the same structure. A *relational database* comprises one or more related tables. Relational databases keep track of how a record in one table (say, a list of customers) relates to records in another table (say, orders).

Suppose you order books from a company on the Web. If you had to reenter your name and address every time you ordered a book, you'd quickly tire of their system. Relational databases allow you to enter your address information once into an address table. Later, when you place an order, the company can simply look up your address from the address table using some key information like your name or a customer ID, which it issued when you started using the service. A *key* is a field that is stored in both tables that relates (or *joins*) the information in the two tables. When you place an order, your customer ID is stored in the order table. When it comes time to print the shipping label, the database *queries* (or asks for the record or records that satisfy the search criteria) the address table by your customer ID. Your address is the result of the query, which is printed on the shipping label. Because you can have only one address, but you can place many orders, this type of data relationship is called a *one-to-many* relationship.

Now lets say the company wanted to offer a discount to its best customers. A relational database allows the merchant to query the orders table by customer ID. This query will return all the orders you've made. If the number of orders you've made satisfies the cutoff for the discount program, you'll automatically receive a discount on your next order.

After you enter your order, the database will automatically run your credit card for the required amount and print an order to ship the book (with a mailing label) in the shipping department. The only human intervention required is the person who looks at the order printouts, retrieves the specific book from the warehouse, and sticks the mailing label to it—and even these steps can be automated.

Database Products

In the early days of database management (before 1990), two distinct types of database management applications existed:

- **Relational** client/server databases (structured query language databases such as Oracle, DB2, or Informix) tracked millions of records and supported thousands of simultaneous users. The software was expensive; the hardware even more so.

- **Flat-file** PC LAN databases (dBase, FoxPro, Pick, or Clarion) were based on proprietary scripting languages and did not support real data relationships. These databases were intended for small workgroups or businesses with limited data processing needs. The software was cheap and ran on PCs.

These two database camps had very little to do with one another. Client/server relational databases were the acknowledged solution for medium to large databases that supported large numbers of simultaneous users, and PC LAN databases were the acknowledged solution for single computer or workgroup databases for small businesses. Entirely different groups developed software solutions for each, and very little cross-development occurred. The programming and information management skills for the two types were very different, so there wasn't much point in trying to make them work together. PCs simply didn't have the computing power available to resolve relational queries or to manage large amounts of information.

That situation has, of course, changed. PCs are now as powerful as the minicomputers of ten years ago; they can run fully relational database management software and can act as the client, the server, or both in the distributed database model. Nearly all current PC LAN database software packages support interoperation with SQL servers, and most of them are either truly relational or will automatically generate code that makes them work like relational databases. In addition, SQL servers can now be run on standard PCs to support thousands of simultaneous users.

This merging of technology can make choosing a database somewhat confusing.

LAN Databases

Low-end, LAN-based nonrelational (or *flat file*) databases are stored on file servers (not application servers) or on PCs. The database and the application are stored together in the same directory. Data is retrieved programmatically through written scripts, rather than automatically with defined relationships. If more than one client uses the same database at the same time, simple record locks prevent data corruption.

Microsoft Access

Microsoft Access has blurred the line between application servers and LAN-based application packages. Access is truly relational and supports SQL queries. Access 97 supports a distinct split between the client application and the server-based data. However, it supports neither as many simultaneous client connections nor the robust fault-tolerance mechanisms that true client/server database servers support.

Access Licensing Issues   Microsoft Access is licensed per copy of Access in use. For instance, if you have five people using Microsoft Access at the same time, you must have five licenses to use Microsoft Access. However, you do not have to pay for concurrent use of an Access database. If you publish your Access database using the Publish to the Internet Wizard, you don't have to pay a licensing fee or a client access license for computers that attach to an Access database without using Access, such as those coming in over the Internet.

Consequently, you can create your database with a single copy of Access, publish it to your Internet server, and have many people legally access it via their Web browsers. The Jet database engine (upon which Access is built) does have a hard limit of 64 concurrent accesses to the same database, but it will probably not work very well past 25 concurrent users, as it is designed for lighter workloads.

Client/Server Databases

High-end, client/server relational databases run on database application servers and serve queries to thousands of clients simultaneously. The database files are stored on the server, and clients send query requests using the *structured query language* (SQL) to the server. The server responds with the record or records that fulfill the query, which are then edited or processed on the client. A single computer processes all changes, which eliminates the need for intercomputer communication of record locks. Client software packages use the data stored on the database server. These client packages are usually custom written in Visual C++, Visual Basic, Access, or Delphi (Borland's rapid application design tool based on an object-oriented version of the Pascal programming language).

SQL Server

SQL Server is Microsoft's database application server software package. SQL Server runs on a server (generally a server of its own) and responds to query requests for the data it stores from clients. SQL Server is a strong contender in the SQL server market, but it runs only on Windows NT. (Most other SQL server packages run on VMS, UNIX, or other traditional mainframe and minicomputer operating systems.)

SQL Server does not come with client access software beyond a few tools to test your database. You must create your own client software to access an SQL server. Perhaps the fastest way to create a client for SQL Server is to use Microsoft Access with linked tables to a data source provided by an SQL server. You can then use the publish to the Internet wizard built into Access to create Active Server Pages for IIS. Web browsers will then be able to connect directly to your SQL server through Web pages stored on your Web server. (Access is used only to create the Active Server Pages automatically, so it's out of the process at this point.) This approach means that you won't have to pay much for custom client software development and that your client interface can access the SQL server from anywhere on the planet.

The SQL Server Internet License   SQL Server requires a client access license for every concurrent user that attaches to the SQL data source by any means. Therefore, if 1,000 people are accessing your SQL server over the Internet and 200 people are accessing it directly via your in-house LAN, you will need 1,200 client access licenses. At current prices, your cost would be about $6,000.

More important, you may not even know how many people will access your site via the Internet, so you won't really know how many licenses to buy. Microsoft provides a solution: For a reasonable sum (currently about $4,000), you can get an SQL Server license that allows unlimited use via the Internet. Once you have this license, you won't need to worry about the number of simultaneous Internet users on your site.

The unlimited Internet access license does not clearly state if it covers intranet use, nor is it clear on whether the license covers client software on your local network. You should check with Microsoft regarding these licensing issues if you intend to use the SQL Server Internet license on your intranet.

You do not have to purchase the Internet unlimited access license if you don't mind limiting your SQL server to a smaller number of concurrent users. If you intend to provide service to fewer than about 100 users, it makes more sense to simply purchase the number of licenses you need and limit the server to that number. You can add licenses as you please, and Microsoft will give a credit toward an unlimited license based on the number you've already purchased. Contact a Microsoft sales representative to determine exactly what level of licensing is most cost-effective for your application.

Internet Databases

Publishing data on the Internet can be easy or difficult depending on the tools you use and your needs. If you simply want to report data or produce a static catalog or product listing, you can generate a report in HTML format (or even text) and store it on your Web server. If you need current information every time a database is accessed, you can create query files that generate reports automatically from your database and convert the reports to HTML output files using CGI scripts or the Internet Database Connector for your database product. Finally, if you want to interact with your client/server database over the Internet as a full-fledged database client, you'll need to create a sophisticated set of Web pages. Three styles of database publications appear on the Internet:

- **Static** HTML databases are unchanging HTML pages that are produced as output reports from a live database manually. Static HTML databases do not reflect changes to the database since the last production of the page, and they do not put much processing load on the Internet server. Static pages are useful for catalogs that don't change much, are heavily accessed, or are located on servers that you do not own (because they don't require execute permissions).

- **Dynamic** HTML databases are output-only databases that are produced automatically each time the page is accessed, providing complete snapshots of the database at any time. Producing the HTML output puts some processing load on the Web server and requires the Web server to run software to interface to the database.

- **Interactive** HTML databases are input/output databases that are controlled through ISAPI applications, CGI scripts, or Active Server Pages. Interactive HTML databases can be viewed and updated live over the Internet. Interactive HTML databases put a serious load on the Internet server, which should actually be configured as a database server because of the traffic load involved and because it will have to run or connect to the database server software.

Each level of interactivity is appropriate in different circumstances and for different types of data. Some data doesn't change often, so it doesn't make sense to go to a lot of trouble to make an interactive HTML database site to support it. Other information (like stock quotes) is worthless if it isn't current, so you really need to make it dynamic if you publish it at all. If you are looking at the Internet as an inexpensive way to extend your company's wide area networked database, you will require true interactivity.

A Database Example

The companion CD-ROM contains a sample Access database that stores addresses and phone numbers. This type of database is easy to create with a tool like Access, and many organizations use similar databases to maintain a unified company directory of contacts.

Maintaining a unified directory between branch offices, however, rarely makes much sense because the difficulty involved in setting up a wide area network and creating a complex self-replicating database between the sites isn't justified for this simple database. This level of effort is usually worthwhile only for order-entry databases or other mission-critical database applications.

Access includes convenient Publish to the Web wizards with which you can create a true client/server database application that uses Access's Jet database engine, IIS as the server, and a Web browser as the client. This easy method makes providing even the simplest database worthwhile—it's so easy that you'll actually spend more time tweaking the results to look good than you will generating the pages.

Combined with Active Server Pages technology to create the views, publishing databases on the Web can be as interactive as working with them locally. Earlier versions of Access could create static HTML pages of information, useful for publishing catalogs and phone lists on the Web, but you really couldn't add new data to the site without a lot of work. ActiveX and Active Server Pages make truly interacting with a database easy.

Figure 13.1 shows the form used to add or edit a phone book entry in Access 97, the application used to create the database.

FIGURE 13.1

An Access database form

Compare this form to Figure 13.2, which shows Internet Explorer browsing an Active Server Page Web site that was automatically created by Access 97 from the same database.

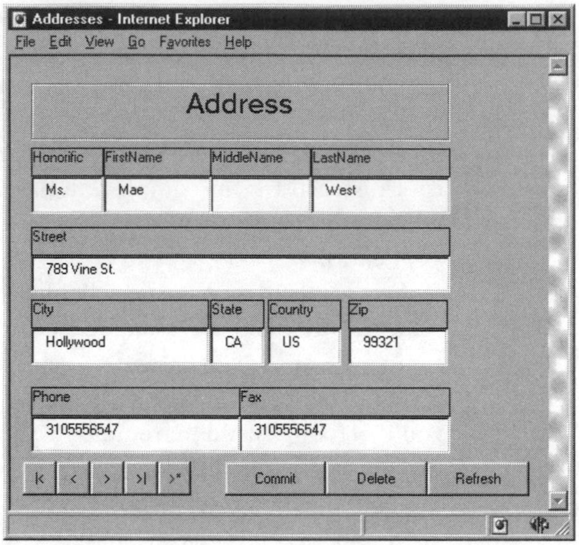

FIGURE 13.2

An Internet view of an
Access database

The two are obviously different, yet they share the same structure and feel.
Anyone familiar with the first form will have no problem adapting to the
Internet-based form. The phone book database is a simple example—any
complex database can be published as a complex Web site. You may find
you'll have to correct some of the automatically generated Web pages, and
some more complex access controls do not work the same way when published to the Web. More information about these issues is available in the
Access online help.

The exercises in the rest of this chapter use the phone book database to introduce the steps you need to take to publish an existing database on the Internet.
In the following examples we show you how to create interactive Internet databases. Static and dynamic Internet databases are easier to produce, so you'll be
able to figure them out on your own after completing these exercises.

Exercise 13.1 sets up the sample phone book database for publication on
the Internet. You will copy the sample database to a folder on your computer,
and then create another folder in your **wwwroot** to hold the Active Server
Pages automatically generated by the Access Publish to the Internet wizard
in Exercise 13.2.

EXERCISE 13.1

Preparing the Phone Book Database for Publication

This exercise requires the companion CD.

1. Insert the companion CD-ROM in your CD-ROM drive.

2. Double-click My Computer.

3. Double-click your CD-ROM drive.

4. Double-click the Samples folder. Close any other windows that may be open.

5. Double-click My Computer again.

6. Drag the My Computer window to another portion of the screen so that it does not obscure the Samples folder window.

7. Double-click your C: drive.

8. Right-click the white background and select New ➤ Folder.

9. Change the name of the folder to **phonebook**.

10. Drag the phonebook.mdb file from the Samples window to the phonebook folder in the C: drive window.

11. Double-click My computer.

12. Double-click your C: drive or the drive containing your http root directory.

13. Browse to **\InetPub\wwwroot** or the http root on your computer.

14. Right-click on the background of the wwwroot window.

15. Select New ➤ Folder.

16. Change the name of the new folder to **phonebook**.

Database Publication with IIS

Because IIS controls the services that actually publish your database on the Internet, you will have to tell IIS how you want to deal with the data. You should create a folder to contain the site, create a virtual directory or virtual server to support it, and set the access permissions as appropriate. Remember that Active Server Page scripts must have Execute permission assigned in IIS to function properly. Exercise 13.2 shows you how to set up the Internet Service Manager to serve the sample database.

EXERCISE 13.2

Setting Up the Phone Book Directory with the Internet Service Manager

1. Select Start ➤ Programs ➤ Microsoft Internet Server ➤ Internet Service Manager.

2. Double-click the name of your server on the WWW service line.

3. Select the Directories tab.

4. Click Add.

5. Click Browse.

6. Browse to C:\InetPub\wwwroot\phonebook or its equivalent on your system.

7. Select Virtual Directory.

8. Type **phonebook** in the Alias input line.

9. Check the Execute permission in the Access control group.

10. Click OK.

11. Click OK.

12. Close the Internet Service Manager.

Open Database Connectivity

The Open Database Connectivity (ODBC) interface is the standard database interface that allows databases to access or link to other software products. ODBC provides a standard method to configure a database as a *data source,* or a publisher of database information. Other software products (like IIS) can then link to those data sources to request (query) information or store information to the database. Most database products that run under Windows support ODBC, so they can function as database engines for IIS. Exercise 13.3 shows you how to configure the Access ODBC driver to publish an Access database.

EXERCISE 13.3

Defining an ODBC Data Source

This exercise requires a complete installation of Microsoft Access 97.

1. Select Start ➤ Settings ➤ Control Panel.

2. Double-click the ODBC Control Panel Program.

3. Click System DSN.

4. Click Add.

5. Double-click the Microsoft Access Driver. If the Microsoft Access Driver does not appear, reinstall Microsoft Access 97 with the complete installation option.

6. Type **phonebook** in the Data Source Name input line.

7. Type **A Web-enabled access phone book** in the Description input line.

8. Click Select to select a database.

9. Browse to the C:\phonebook\phonebook.mdb database and click OK.

10. Click OK.

11. Click OK.

12. Close the control panel window.

Internet Database Connector

The Internet Database Connector (IDC) is an add-on to IIS that allows the dynamic publication of databases. Dynamic HTML databases are databases that are updated every time a Web browser requests them, so they contain up-to-the minute snapshots of the database in question. This method of publication is different from simple static HTML databases, which are published manually whenever the database administrator gets around to it and do not contain changes more recent than the last publication.

IDC works as a plug-in to IIS (actually, it's an ISAPI application). When a browser requests a dynamic database, IIS reads the IDC file and performs the database connection and query instructions contained within it to create an HTML page. This HTML page contains the results of the database query stored in the IDC file and is formatted according to HTML format instructions contained in an associated HTX file. Since the database is required and a new HTML page is created each time a connection is made, data on the Web site is always in sync with data in the actual database.

Remember: The IDC file contains the query for retrieving the database information from the database server. The HTX file contains the instructions for formatting the data as HTML.

Some database products contain wizards to automatically create the IDC and HTX files required by the IDC. When you select the Dynamic HTML option in Microsoft's Publish to the Internet wizard in Access, you are creating the IDC and HTX files required by the IDC.

The IDC has no provisions for accepting database input from the Web, however—it is a one-way publication medium. You will have to use CGI scripts, ISAPI applications, or Active Server Pages if you want to update a database over the Internet.

Before Active Server Pages existed, IDC was created to allow dynamic publication to the Web. Because Active Server Pages supersedes the functionality of IDC and allows far more query and format options, you should use it for any new custom development that is more extensive than simply publishing data with Access. If you want more information on the format of IDC and HTX files, consult the help files that come with IIS or perform a search for documentation on the Microsoft Web site.

Publishing Access Data with Active Server Pages

Dynamic HTML databases are convenient for their purpose, but they still don't allow remote users to add or edit the information they provide. Interactive HTML databases provide this functionality by running code on the Web server to extract information from the remote Web browser and push it into the ODBC-linked database driver running on the Web server. This ODBC driver may simply provide an interface to an existing SQL server, or it may start a database engine to store data into a database file. In either case, the key is the software running on the Web server that retrieves the client data and stores it into the database.

This process used to require quite a bit of trick programming with complex CGI scripts or the use of ISAPI applications dedicated to the task. With Active Server Pages and Access 97's Publish to the Internet wizard, the process of publishing an interactive HTML database is easy. Exercise 13.4 walks you through using Access to publish a sample database on the Internet. This exercise creates the Active Server Web pages that provide access to your ODBC data source. This data source could just as easily be an SQL server, a FoxPro database, or even an Excel spreadsheet—although those products don't automatically produce the Active Server Page code to publish the data.

WARNING The directory containing your .asp files must have Execute permission set in the Internet Service Manager, or browsers will simply see your ASP code.

EXERCISE 13.4

Creating an Internet-Enabled Access Database

1. Select File ➤ Save As HTML and then click Next.

2. Click the All Objects tab.

3. Click Select All and then click Next.

4. Click Browse.

5. Double-click Default.htm and then click Next.

6. Click Dynamic ASP and then click Next.

7. Type **phonebook** in the ODBC data source name.

8. Delete all the text in the server URL input line.

9. Click Browse.

10. Browse through the directory selector to C:\InetPub\wwwroot\ phonebook.

11. Click Select.

12. Click Next to publish locally.

13. Check Yes, I want to create a home page and then click Next.

14. Click Finish. The Access Internet publication wizard will create the site files to attach to your ODBC data source.

Internet Database Client

Now that your database is published on the Internet, you should examine it with your Web browser. When you pull up your browser and connect to your Web site, you'll see a form that looks somewhat like the Access form you used to create it. Access automatically generates these forms using ActiveX controls that simulate the controls embedded in Access.

Browsing your site also gives you a chance to debug it. If you don't see anything at all, Active Server Pages probably can't find the ActiveX controls required to build the HTML output page. You won't get an error message because your browser gets the Web page it asked for, but the page contains no information. When Active Server Pages can't find ActiveX controls, it displays nothing, so chances are your Web pages contain references to controls that Active Server Pages can't find. Try running the publication wizard and providing a different server URL (or none at all) to produce correct HTML output pages.

Using Web browsers and Active Server Pages to automatically create database clients that can be distributed anywhere in the world is very exciting. The Internet is finally fulfilling the real promise of client/server computing, where the computational load can be balanced on the server and on the client to minimize the amount of data sent, thus optimizing the use of high-cost long-distance network links and performing the computational workload where it makes the most sense. Because just about any computer can run a Web browser without problems, you may find that converting your database applications to run through Web browsers over an Intranet is a great way to extend the life of older computers. You'll only have to upgrade one computer (the server) as the workload increases.

Unfortunately (there's always a down side), ActiveX works only on PCs running Windows and Internet Explorer. A Macintosh version is in the works, but support for other platforms such as UNIX, and for other browsers such as Netscape Navigator, will depend on the support of developers other than Microsoft—and may never develop. If you need cross-platform database client support, look to Java and the Java Database Connectivity (JDBC) standard for development. These clients unfortunately will take quite a bit more effort to develop.

Exercise 13.5 shows you how to attach to your Web site. Internet Explorer will warn you about downloading ActiveX controls unless you configure your browser for low security.

EXERCISE 13.5

Browsing the Phone Book Site Files

1. Launch Internet Explorer or any other Web browser.

2. Type `http:\\`*boomerang*`\phonebook\default.htm` in the address line, replacing *boomerang* with the name of your server.

3. Click the Address object.

4. Click Yes to continue if your Web browser warns you that an ActiveX control is being downloaded. You may want to disable warnings about ActiveX controls for your browsing session, as a warning will come up between each page.

5. Click the >* button at the bottom of the Web page.

6. Enter your honorific (Mr/Ms/Mrs) in the Honorific input box and then press tab.

7. Enter your first name in the FirstName input box and then press tab.

8. Enter your middle name or initial in the MiddleName input box and then press tab.

9. Enter your last name in the LastName input box and then press tab.

10. Enter your street address in the Street input box and then press tab.

11. Enter your city in the City input box and then press tab.

12. Enter your state in the State input box and then press tab.

13. Enter your country in the Country input box and then press tab.

14. Enter your postal code in the Zip input box and then press tab.

15. Click the Commit button.

16. Double-click the C: drive.

17. Double-click the phonebook directory.

18. Double-click the phonebook.mdb database file.

19. Click the Forms tab.

20. Double-click the Address form.

21. Click the >| (last record) button.

22. View the record you just added through your Web browser.

23. Close Microsoft Access.

Summary

Databases power modern commerce. Any serious attempt to use the Internet for direct commerce requires live access to these databases and the information they store. IIS supports attaching to databases through the Internet Database Connector and, more important, through Active Server Pages.

Microsoft has provided a number of database tools and utilities to allow access to databases over the Internet using Internet Information Server. The three distinct types of Internet database publications are

- **Static**—Databases are manually published as simple HTML files.

- **Dynamic**—HTML files containing snapshots of current database tables are automatically produced.

- **Interactive**—Editing and updating live database information is supported over the Internet.

These three models vary in their level of usefulness and server load based upon the type of information being served.

IIS supports the ODBC interface, allowing nearly all database products to function interactively over the Internet. Microsoft Access is capable of automatically producing an entire Web site of Active Server Pages that simulate the forms used to interact with the database.

Review Questions

1. You are running a small public service Web site detailing treatment options for athlete's foot. You have a database of health care providers and doctors in your area who specialize in the treatment of athlete's foot that you'd like to publish on your site. You update your database perhaps once every three months or so. What database publication method is most appropriate for this type of data?

    A. Static

    B. Dynamic

    C. Interactive

2. You've set up an offshore bookmaking operation. You'll be taking bets online using credit cards, publishing horse racing and sporting results as they become available from your online news feeds, and creating queries of winners and losers so you can credit and debit their card accounts as appropriate. The entire operation must be automatic because you expect a police raid at any time and you don't want to be present when it happens. What database publication method is most appropriate for this type of data?

    A. Static

    B. Dynamic

    C. Interactive

3. You've created an Interactive database using Microsoft Access and Active Server Pages, but when you browse to the site, you get garbage on

your screen that looks like a computer programming language rather than the database forms you expected. What's wrong?

A. You haven't enabled Active Server Pages output in the IIS Manager.

B. You selected the wrong type of output in the publish to the Internet wizard in Microsoft Access.

C. Your Web browser doesn't support Active Server Pages.

D. You didn't set Execute permissions on the directory containing your database Web files.

4. You've decided to set up an intranet database for manufacturing process reporting at your semiconductor fabrication facility. This database will extract information from many internal manufacturing control data sources and summarize it automatically so that corporate managers and top-level distributors from anywhere in the world can check current yield rates, expected inventory levels, and current manufacturing costs. What database publication method is most appropriate for this type of data?

A. Static

B. Dynamic

C. Interactive

5. You want to set up an Internet interactive gaming site that relies on a database to store the current game state for all your connected users. You expect about 100 simultaneous users. You decide to use Microsoft Access as your database engine and Active Server Pages to interface game data in and out of the Access database. This approach means that you will only have to pay for a single Access license. This solution:

A. Is legal and will work fine.

B. Is legal, but won't work because Access isn't powerful enough to support that many concurrent connections.

C. Is illegal, as Access requires a client access license for all concurrent users regardless of the client software used.

6. You will be setting up an SQL server with an order-entry database. The database will have 200 internal data entry clerks who will be entering orders from phone calls to the company's 800 number, and 100 work-at-home data entry clerks who will be entering data from reply mail post cards. The internal data entry clerks will use a custom Visual C++ client that operates quickly (because the customer is on the phone with them) and directly attaches to the SQL server. The work-at-home data entry clerks will be connected via the Internet using IIS and an ODBC data source. How many SQL client access licenses are required?

   A. 100

   B. 200

   C. 201

   D. 300

CHAPTER

14

Remote Access Service

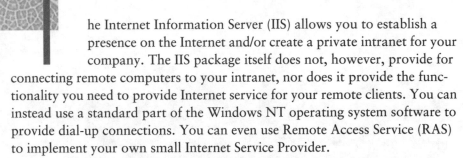

he Internet Information Server (IIS) allows you to establish a presence on the Internet and/or create a private intranet for your company. The IIS package itself does not, however, provide for connecting remote computers to your intranet, nor does it provide the functionality you need to provide Internet service for your remote clients. You can instead use a standard part of the Windows NT operating system software to provide dial-up connections. You can even use Remote Access Service (RAS) to implement your own small Internet Service Provider.

This chapter starts with a survey of how RAS works and then shows you how to install and configure RAS on your network. You learn how to make RAS secure, connect client computers to a RAS server, and troubleshoot RAS connections. Most important, you'll learn how to use a RAS connection on your Internet server to profile the performance of your Web site at the speed most users will experience.

This chapter also serves to explain the "last mile" of the Internet—the road to your house. Understanding how IP forwards packets between Internet hosts that are constantly connected to the Internet doesn't really explain the dial-up connection most Internet users actually experience. That final portion is provided by Internet hosts running RAS or a service like RAS to answer inbound calls and route data to hosts connected only through dial-up modems.

Remote Access Service Overview

The purpose of RAS is to provide temporary Internet links over regular telephone lines. You can also set up RAS to use other types of connections such as ISDN and X.25, but in most networks RAS controls a bank of modems attached to telephone lines so that remote users can dial in and access network resources, including the Internet. Figure 14.1 illustrates a typical RAS setup.

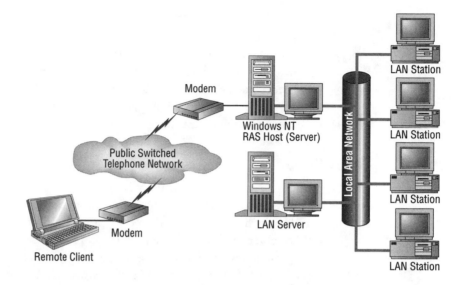

FIGURE 14.1

In a typical RAS setup, remote client computers connect to a central network via RAS and the telephone lines.

RAS Clients

In order for you to use RAS in a client computer, you must install networking on that computer. If your computer is configured for IIS, you've already done that. You do not need a network interface adapter (such as an Ethernet or a token-ring card), but you do need a transport protocol such as TCP/IP or NetBEUI, and you need the components that use networking such as the Workstation component in Windows NT Workstation and the Client for Microsoft Networks component in Windows 95. If you will be using RAS to connect to Internet services you will need to use the TCP/IP transport protocol.

RAS on the client computer will allow you to use the modem to dial to and establish a connection with a RAS server on your organization's network. Then RAS will emulate a network interface adapter for the transport protocol and allow the network services component (Workstation or Client for Microsoft Networks) to operate just as if your client computer were directly connected to the network. The network connection, however, will be slower than a direct connection would be because most network adapters are much faster than modems.

> A regular Ethernet adapter can (theoretically) transmit 10 megabits of information in one second. Modems can (theoretically) transmit 56 kilobits of information in one second, which makes Ethernet almost 200 times faster than the fastest modems. However, Ethernet networks seldom achieve more than 50 percent of their theoretical limit, so in practice Ethernet is only 100 times faster than the fastest analog modems.

The RAS Server

The RAS server, which usually runs on a Windows NT Server, uses modems attached to the server computer to accept connections from client computers and to exchange network data over those connections. You can configure the RAS server to allow the client to access resources on the RAS server only, or you can configure it as a router or gateway so that the client computer can access any of the resources on the network. RAS supports the TCP/IP, NetBEUI, and IPX/SPX transport protocols. For Internet services, you will need to support only the TCP/IP protocol.

To the server computer the RAS server modems look like network interface adapters. A RAS server, like a RAS client, must have networking components installed to use RAS.

Analog Modems or ISDN?

What is the difference between an analog modem (that is, Public Switched Telephone Network [PSTN] modem, the type in most common use today and that you are probably most familiar with) and an Integrated Services Digital Network (ISDN) modem? The best way to explain the difference is to first explain what a modem does, how the telephone company works, and why modems are inefficient. Then we'll explain how ISDN makes networking via telephone lines more efficient.

- **How modems work**—Modem stands for MODulator/DEModulator, and modems traditionally have operated by converting the serial data from your computer's serial port (digitally encoded using the RS-232 serial communications standard) to an analog signal in the acoustic range that can be transmitted over the public telephone system. Most modem communications involve two modems—one at either end of a telephone call. The modem at the other end of the call takes the analog signal and converts it back into a digital signal (RS-232) that is sent to the receiving computer's serial port.

- **How the telephone company works**—In early telephone technology someone making a phone call was physically "patched through" to the receiving party by an operator who made the connection with patch cords. The two parties of the phone call would then have a circuit over which the analog electrical signal of their voices could travel. Later the telephone companies automated the connection process with relays, allowing people to establish their own connections. The relays replaced the operators. With the advent of digital communications, the phone companies learned to digitize the analog signals and use digital electronics to squeeze more phone calls into the telephone lines between branch offices (for instance, New York and Chicago). Because solid state integrated circuits can switch digital data (essentially making the phone company a vast computer network), there is no need for physically moving relays.

- **Why modems are inefficient**—When you use a regular (or PSTN) modem to communicate with another computer, the modem encodes the digital serial signal from your computer into analog form. (These are the sounds that you hear when your modem connects.) Your telephone company is encoding that analog signal into digital form. The telephone company branch office (called a central office by the telephone company) at the other end of the call decodes that digital signal back to analog form, and the resulting analog signal is encoded back to the original digital serial signal sent by your computer. That serial signal finally enters the serial port of the receiving computer. Data flowing the other way undergoes the same process.

- **What ISDN does**—An ISDN "modem" does not modulate or demodulate a signal. Instead it delivers the digital serial signal from your computer's RS-232 port in its original form to the telephone company. (This process requires a special phone connection, which is why a telephone company technician may have to make changes to your phone line.) Because the signal is already digital, the phone company does not have to transform it into a digital signal. The phone company routes the digital information through its digital network to the other phone company branch office, which provides the signal to the ISDN modem at that end of the connection. The ISDN modem there sends the digital signal to the receiving computer's serial port. Figure 14.2 illustrates the difference between regular modems and ISDN *adapters*.

Although many vendors refer to ISDN adapters as modems, they really aren't because they don't modulate or demodulate. The correct term is ISDN adapter.

FIGURE 14.2

In a typical RAS setup, remote client computers connect to a central network via RAS and the telephone lines.

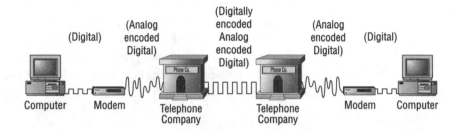

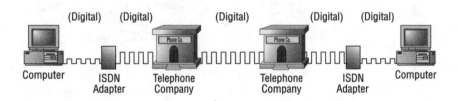

ISDN adapters allow you to take advantage of the phone companies' digital networks to send digital information. ISDN is faster than regular analog modems because it doesn't waste any capacity of the telephone line with encoding schemes that are less than 100 percent efficient. Many ISDN connections are even faster than the optimal analog modem encoding schemes because the telephone company allows you to use additional voice channels to transmit information. (Essentially, you are using two telephone lines to send your data.)

Unfortunately ISDN is not available to every telephone company customer. Some telephone company installations have not upgraded to equipment capable of accepting ISDN connections. In other places ISDN is prohibitively expensive. ISDN is, however, both available and affordable in many areas of the United States. You should check with your local phone company as to the availability and cost of ISDN in your area.

RAS Capabilities and Limitations

RAS performs both dial-out and the dial-in service. RAS can host clients from many operating systems and can support all Windows NT interprocess communications mechanisms. RAS supports all true Windows NT transport protocols loaded on your machine and is capable of operating over any dial-up public network medium. RAS supports software compression to maximize bandwidth over low-speed connections.

Dial-In Operating Systems

RAS can host any computer running the following operating systems:

- LAN Manager

- Windows for Workgroups

- Windows NT 3.1 and higher

- Windows 95

- PPP-based TCP/IP clients such as the Apple Newton, Macintoshes, UNIX computers, or most other operating systems.

In addition to the Windows-based operating systems capable of using NetBEUI or NWLink, RAS can support any computer using a TCP/IP protocol stack and capable of dialing in via Point-to-Point Protocol (PPP), but these clients will not be able to use many domain resources such as print and file services. These clients can be as esoteric as personal digital assistants, mainframes, UNIX X-terminals, and remote data acquisition devices. Although Windows NT Server can dial out to SLIP servers, it will provide dial-in connections only to client computers using the PPP protocol.

Network Interfaces

RAS supports all Windows NT interprocess communications mechanisms. Therefore, the client side of any client/server application capable of running under Windows NT can run over a RAS connection. These mechanisms include

- Windows Sockets

- NetBIOS

- Mailslots

- Named Pipes

- Remote Procedure Call (RPC)

- Win32 and LAN Manager APIs

RAS Limitations

RAS for Windows NT Server supports up to 256 simultaneous inbound sessions. Setting RAS to receive calls will dedicate the COM port and modem you are using. The port will not be available for non-RAS communication software such as terminal emulators or fax software. However, you can stop the RAS service through the Services control panel if you need to dial out using the COM port that RAS dedicates. When you are finished, simply start the RAS service the same way to again receive RAS calls.

Installing RAS

Installing RAS is no more difficult than installing any other service in Windows NT. Because the purpose of RAS is to connect computers over a low-speed dial-up line, you should have access to another computer running RAS or RAS client software (such as Windows NT Workstation or Windows 95) and using the same transport protocol (such as TCP/IP or NWLink).

Without access to another computer to which you can attach, you will have difficulty understanding the operational nuances of RAS. You really need to *use* the software in order to understand it.

Before you install RAS you need to install modems or other WAN connection adapters (such as ISDN or X.25) for RAS to use. If you have two computers next to each other, you can use the Dial-Up Networking serial cable between 2 PCs option provided in the RAS device selector. You can also select this option if you want to install RAS but don't yet have a modem for it, since RAS requires you to select a device when you install. We explain how to install a modem in Windows NT first, then we show you the more complicated process of configuring an ISDN adapter, and finally in this section we guide you through the steps of installing and configuring RAS.

RAS and PSTN Modems

If you have a modem, but have not installed it through the Modem control panel, do so now. You need to identify a free COM port in your computer and configure the modem to use that port if you have not already done so. Use Exercise 14.1 to perform this step if you have an internal modem. You should have your modem documentation available to show you how to change the COM and IRQ settings for that device. (Follow the steps in Exercise 14.2 to install RAS.) If you are using an external modem, you only need to know the COM port to which it is attached. If you are using an external modem or if your modem is already installed in the Windows NT system, you can skip Exercise 14.1.

EXERCISE 14.1

Finding an Available COM Port

1. Select Start ➤ Programs ➤ Administrative Tools ➤ Windows NT Diagnostics.

2. Select the Resources tab.

3. Click the IRQ button.

4. Note the state of interrupt requests (IRQ) 03 and 04. If either does not appear in the list, you need to configure your modem to use that IRQ.

5. Select a free IRQ.

   - If IRQ 04 is available (not in the resource list), set your modem to use IRQ 04 and COM 1.

   - If IRQ 03 is available, set your modem to use IRQ 03 and COM 2.

   - If both are in use, you will need to set your modem to use another unused IRQ. Check your modem documentation to see if it supports IRQ 05, 07, or 09. Set the modem IRQ to any IRQ your modem supports that is not shown in the resource list.

6. Set your modem to use either COM 1 or COM 2. Make sure that no other serial port in your system is using the COM port you select. Most computers do not.

7. Shut down your Windows NT Server and physically install the modem. When you restart, your modem should be available for use. If you have any difficulties or encounter new error messages, call the technical support number provided by your modem manufacturer for assistance.

Once your modem is in place, you need to tell Windows NT about it. Follow Exercise 14.2 to make your modem available to Windows NT. Before going through this exercise, make certain that your modem is physically installed on a free COM port and IRQ.

EXERCISE 14.2

Modem Installation

1. Double-click the My Computer Icon on the Desktop.

2. Double-click Control Panel.

3. Double-click the Modems control panel.

4. Click the Next button to detect your modem. Letting Windows NT automatically detect allows you to confirm that your modem is answering as it should. Detecting will take up to five minutes, depending upon the speed of your computer.

5. Accept the settings shown in the detected modem window by clicking the Next button unless you are absolutely certain they will not work with your modem. (Windows NT will usually work correctly with a modem it has identified, even if the model shown in the window doesn't match the brand name of the modem.)

6. Click Finish to complete the installation process.

7. Click the Dialing Properties button in the Modem Properties dialog box.

8. Enter the country and area code information that is appropriate for you.

9. Add the appropriate information if you need to add outside line access or disable call waiting. If you have call waiting and someone calls while a RAS session is active, your RAS connection can be abruptly terminated.

10. Click OK.

11. Click the Close button.

Your modem is now available to Windows NT programs such as RAS.

Multiport Serial Adapters

RAS can support up to 256 connections in Windows NT Server. But most computers come with only four serial ports. So how in the world do you attach more than four modems? You can use multiport serial adapters to add serial ports to your computer. Multiport serial adapters are interface cards that plug into your motherboard and provide a number of serial ports.

These multiport serial adapters are similar to all other hardware adapters in that they require the hardware installation and the installation of a driver. Some boards are compatible with the Windows NT built-in serial drivers and need only to have some registry settings changed to support the additional serial ports. In either case, you simply run the setup program provided by the manufacturer to install the driver or modify the registry settings for the Windows serial driver. Multiport serial adapters usually come in sizes of 4, 8, 16, 24, and 32 ports. Many adapters can be cascaded or daisy-chained to expand the number of serial ports available on a single adapter. Multiport serial adapters typically cost about $100 per port. Including the cost of the attached modem and cabling, you should figure on spending about $250 per port.

Higher-density (more than four ports) multiport adapters connect to an external device that breaks out the actual serial ports you plug your serial devices into because the card itself is too small for the ports to be connected to it directly. This device is entirely passive—it simply matches serial ports to an adapter on the multiport adapter.

Once you install the adapter and the driver, you can simply plug external modems into the serial ports, plug each modem into its own phone line, and you are ready to answer up to 256 in-bound dial-up connections.

Each modem is addressed with a COM port number, just like the first four serial ports built into your computer. Multiport serial adapters use only a single interrupt to exchange data with your processor. The drivers that come with the multiport serial adapter will poll each port in turn, buffer the incoming (and outgoing data), and signal an interrupt to transfer all the data in one batch.

You can modify the serial port adapter built into Windows NT through certain registry settings to support the use of multiple serial ports on the same interrupt in the same manner as long as the multiport serial adapter is compatible with the method used by the Windows NT serial driver. If this is the case, your adapter will come with instructions on how to set the registry for that adapter or with a setup program that will do it for you. Although the ports on a multiport serial adapter share a single interrupt, each requires a unique port address (8 bytes usually) and a COM number (i.e., COM 1 through COM 256!).

Modem Banks

Setting up more than 20 telephone lines and modems is a lot of trouble. Of course, the purveyors of serial equipment have come up with a solution: the integrated multiport serial adapter, modem bank, and CSU/DSU. With these devices, you simply install the adapter in your computer, attach a cable to the modem bank, and plug in a T1 line. The CSU/DSU digital interface to the T1 line is built in, and it automatically attaches the 24 digital voice channels that make up the T1 circuit to 24 modems. Essentially, you plug the T1 into the modem bank and the serial cable into the multiport serial adapter in your computer. Once you install the operating system driver, you will be up and running. These solutions typically cost about $800 per modem.

Installing RAS

Installing RAS is similar to installing all other network services. If you are using X.25, ISDN, or a multiport serial adapter connection, follow the device manufacturer's instructions to install those adapters before proceeding with the RAS installation. Exercise 14.3 shows the standard procedure for installing a RAS server with a regular modem. (You should already have installed your modem to work with Windows NT through the Modems control panel.)

Configuring Network Protocols for RAS

RAS can use any of the three primary Windows NT protocols to provide network services over a dial-up connection. However, you must install the protocol for Windows NT before you can use it with RAS.

RAS uses a framing protocol (SLIP or PPP) to provide a network layer protocol in addition to the transport protocols it uses for local area network communication. SLIP and PPP perform the same function in a dial-up networking

Installing the Remote Access Service

1. Right-click the Network Neighborhood icon on the desktop.

2. Select the Properties menu item to open the Network control panel.

3. Click the Services tab.

4. Click the Add button.

5. Select Remote Access Service from the Services list.

6. Click OK.

7. Enter the path to your Windows NT Server CD-ROM and the directory containing the source files for your microprocessor. For most users, this will be D:\i386.

8. Select the modem you wish to use for RAS and click OK in the Add RAS Device dialog box. If your modem does not appear in the Modem list, click the Install Modem button and follow the prompts to install your modem.

9. Click Configure.

10. Select the Dial Out and Receive Calls option if you wish to dial out using the modem line. (We will use this setting for later exercises.) Otherwise, select Receive Calls Only and click OK.

11. Click Add and then repeat steps 8 through 10 if you want to configure another modem or serial port for RAS.

12. Click Continue when you are finished adding your modem(s). We will accept the default protocols for now and show you how to choose specific transport protocols in Exercise 14.4.

13. Close the Network dialog box.

14. Answer Yes when asked if you want to restart your computer.

connection that Ethernet or token ring perform in a local area network environment—they provide an access protocol for the media (the serial link) that the transport protocol (TCP/IP, NWLink, or NetBEUI) uses to transport information.

For each device you configure for use with RAS (usually a modem), you can select the transport protocols you want to use. For Internet/intranet services, you must at least select TCP/IP.

You enable the protocols a modem will use from the RAS item in the Services tab of the Network control panel. You can enable or disable TCP/IP, NWLink, and NetBEUI for a modem for dialing out and/or calling in.

Each protocol is configured for dial-in in a slightly different manner. When you click the Configure button for a protocol, a window prompts you for the specific settings for that protocol. The next section of this chapter examines the settings for TCP/IP, and Exercise 14.4 explains how to configure the TCP/IP protocol for a typical RAS installation.

TCP/IP

TCP/IP is the transport protocol of the Internet. You can also use TCP/IP to connect remote computers to your network. TCP/IP is a very robust protocol, and if you cannot guarantee that the telephone connection will be free of extraneous noise, then the error detection and correction characteristics of TCP/IP may make it a better protocol than faster transport protocols such as NWLink and NetBEUI for this purpose.

With TCP/IP you can allow an incoming call to access only the RAS server computer, or you can allow the computer making the incoming call to access the rest of the network as well. In addition, you can configure the incoming connection to get an IP address via the Dynamic Host Configuration Protocol (DHCP), you can configure the IP address to come from a pool of addresses maintained on the RAS server, or you can allow the incoming connection to request its own IP address. Figure 14.3 shows the RAS Server TCP/IP Configuration window.

RAS and SLIP   Serial Line Internet Protocol (SLIP) is an early protocol for the transfer of Internet Protocol (IP) packets over serial connections such as modems and T1 leased lines. Until recently SLIP was the most common method of making an Internet modem connection. PPP is now more popular than SLIP.

Although you can configure RAS to dial out and make a connection to another computer using the SLIP protocol, you cannot configure RAS to accept a connection using the SLIP protocol. Consequently, you cannot use SLIP to connect two computers running RAS, nor can you provide Internet service to SLIP clients. Instead you will have to use PPP.

FIGURE 14.3

You configure TCP/IP
dial-up settings from the
RAS Server TCP/IP
Configuration window

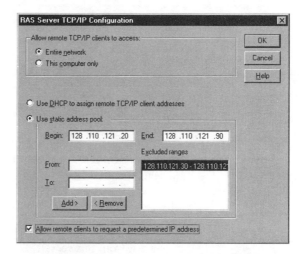

RAS and PPP   PPP stands for Point-to-Point Protocol. PPP addresses some deficiencies in the SLIP protocol, for example, providing mechanisms for encrypting logon requests and for supporting transport protocols other than TCP/IP. PPP is optimized for low-bandwidth communications and conveys data between communicating computers more efficiently than SLIP does.

PPP is the default method of making connections to and from a RAS server. PPP is automatically installed when you install the RAS server component, and there is little you can do to directly configure how RAS uses PPP. You do, however, indirectly configure PPP when you select and use PPP security options (explained in the section on security later in the chapter).

Configuring TCP/IP for RAS

Windows NT automatically provides settings for the protocols that should work properly in most dial-in situations. In most cases you can simply accept the values and selections that appear in the configuration windows. In Exercise 14.4 you will configure your RAS server to allow access to your network via RAS using TCP/IP.

RAS Security

Before RAS connects your remote client computers to your network, it must ensure that the client computers are not intruders masquerading as regular client connections. RAS security features, including permissions, callback, encrypted passwords, and PPTP, protect your RAS connections against intrusion and eavesdropping.

EXERCISE 14.4

Configuring RAS Protocols

1. Select Start ➤ Settings ➤ Control Panel.

2. Double-click the Network Control Panel program.

3. Select the Services Tab.

4. Select the Remote Access Services entry from the list and then click the Properties button.

5. Click Configure.

6. Select Receive calls only or Dial out and Receive calls if you will be dialing out from this server.

7. Click OK.

8. Select the modem you wish to configure TCP/IP for and then click the Network button.

9. Check TCP/IP in the Allow remote clients running section.

10. Click the Configure button next to TCP/IP. Select Entire network. Select Use DHCP and select Allow clients to request a predetermined IP address. Click OK.

11. Click OK in the Network Configuration window and then click Continue in the Remote Access Setup window.

12. Click Close in the Network window. You must restart your computer before the changes take effect—select Yes to restart your computer.

Permissions

If your network is not connected to the Internet and if it does not provide dial-up connections, then you do not have to be concerned about electronic intrusion. Your primary security concerns will be unauthorized physical access to your network and network users who may exceed their authority to read or modify network data.

If, however, you do provide dial-up lines (or Internet connections), then you must ensure that only authorized users access your network. Internet security is discussed in Chapter 8. Figure 14.4 shows RAS permissions for users of dial-up connections.

F I G U R E   14.4

You select which users have dial-up permissions in the Remote Access Permissions window of the Remote Access Admin program.

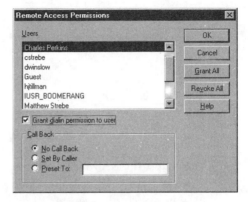

 You can also set dial-in permissions with the Dial-up button in the User Manager for Domains.

The RAS permissions you establish for dial-up connections are your first line of defense against network intruders. You should pay careful attention to how you set up the dial-in permissions of your RAS server so that only users that should access your network over dial-up lines can access your network that way. In addition, if your network contains sensitive information, you should consider disallowing dial-up access for user accounts with extensive permissions to the system (such as the Administrator account) and requiring the users of those accounts, if they require dial-up access, to use an account with fewer privileges when connecting via RAS.

You may notice that when you start the Remote Access Admin program, you see only user accounts local to the server that RAS is running on, not domain accounts. In order to view and set permissions for domain users, you must click Server ➤ Set Domain or Server from within the Remote Access Admin window and then select the domain (not a server within the domain) that you wish to view. Click OK. This procedure displays the users for the domain as a whole. If you provide Internet service, you should use dial-up accounts local to your Internet server. In this case you will not need to view domain accounts.

 You can set permissions only for individual users, not for groups.

Network intrusion is a serious threat to any network that is connected to the Internet or that allows dial-up access via telephone lines. This section discusses dial-up security. Chapter 8 introduces the concept of firewalls for Internet security and outlines steps you should take to protect your network from unauthorized access from the Internet.

Callback

The RAS callback feature provides additional security to your network by ensuring that the calling computer is at the phone number it says it is at or that the calling computer is at a predetermined number configured from RAS.

Callback functions by calling back the client computer after the client computer calls the RAS server and requests a network connection. You use the Remote Access Permissions window (shown in Figure 14.4) to enable callback in your system. Just as you set dial-in permissions for each user, you also set callback features for each user account that has dial-in permissions. You do not set callback features for groups of users or for specific modems.

Encrypted Passwords and Data Encryption

When you log on to your network using RAS, you must provide a username and a password. That password must travel over the telephone lines to your RAS server so that it can determine whether that username has dial-in privileges and whether the connection requires using the RAS callback feature.

The way the RAS client and the RAS server exchange the username and password (and some other information such as the temporary network address allocated to the client) is called the *authentication protocol*. RAS Server supports only PPP for dial-in connections, and it supports three authentication protocols for PPP:

- Password Authentication Protocol (PAP)

- Challenge Handshake Authentication Protocol (CHAP)

- Microsoft extensions to CHAP (MS-CHAP)

The default setting for RAS password authentication is to Require Microsoft encrypted authentication. When you enable this option for a RAS device (such as a particular modem or ISDN adapter), the clients connecting via that device must encrypt the password with the MS-CHAP protocol. When you select this option, only Microsoft clients (such as Windows 95, Windows NT Workstation, or other Windows NT Server computers) can connect to your RAS server.

If you use the MS-CHAP protocol, then you can also set the RAS device to Require data encryption. This option encrypts the data exchanged between the RAS server and client as well as the password exchanged to establish the connection. Windows NT handles the details of establishing the encrypted communications channel, such as selecting and exchanging encryption keys. You simply have to select the feature.

If you want to allow computers running other operating systems (such as UNIX) to connect to your RAS server but you also want to require encrypted passwords, then select the Require encrypted authentication option, which will enable the CHAP authentication protocol. CHAP implements the RAS Data Security MD5 algorithm over PPP.

Some client operating systems do not support encrypted password authentication. For these computers you can select the option Allow any authentication including clear text. This option allows users to connect using the PAP protocol, which does not require encryption.

If you use computers that run anything other than Microsoft operating systems and UNIX (such as Macintosh computers), you will have to use the Allow any authentication protocol including clear text. Microsoft does not support encrypted passwords on clients from other operating systems.

Multilink

Multilink combines multiple serial data streams into one aggregate bundle. The most common use of Multilink is to combine the multiple ISDN channels into one aggregate total, but it can also combine regular modems. For instance, if you have two 14.4Kbps modems with Multilink enabled, your bandwidth could be aggregated to 28.8Kbps.

To use Multilink, both the server and client must be Windows NT computers and both must have Multilink enabled. ISDN jargon sometimes refers to Multilink as "bonding" because you are bonding together multiple data streams.

For example, say you have four 33.6Kbps modems in your RAS/Internet server and you have four matching modems in your computer at home. You could then dial into your Internet server and communicate at a blinding (well, slightly blurry, anyway) 134.4Kbps—more than twice the speed of a 56K leased line. And your line costs would simply be four times the basic rate for a phone line. In most areas this charge is less expensive than dial-up ISDN lines, and the technology works in rural areas where ISDN is not yet available (although you may not be able to squeeze 33.6Kbps out of your telephone lines in rural areas).

Point-to-Point Tunneling Protocol

A new feature of Windows NT 4 is RAS support for the Point-to-Point Tunneling Protocol (PPTP). PPTP allows you to exploit the Internet to allow secure connection to your RAS server from anywhere you can get an Internet connection.

PPTP uses a two-step process to connect the client computer to your RAS server. First, connect the client computer to the Internet (usually by making a regular connection to an Internet service provider) and then use the PPTP service on the client to make an encrypted link to the RAS server on your network. (The RAS server must therefore be connected to the Internet; otherwise, the client would not be able to make a connection to it.) The RAS server will encrypt the traffic that it would normally send over a modem connection to the client and instead send it over the Internet to the client. The client and the RAS server can continue to exchange information in this manner, "tunneling" the stream of information through the Internet.

PPTP works on any network technology that supports the IP protocol—for instance, on Ethernet, over T1 lines, or over serial links. PPTP is typically used to provide a secure IP tunnel between two computers on the Internet. PPTP uses the RAS service as its serial entry into the computer—but it does not require a RAS dial-up connection to work. Think of it as simulating a secure dial-up connection via the Internet.

PPTP is currently available only on Windows NT. Windows 95 support may be available by the time you read this book. However, you probably won't find PPTP support for earlier Microsoft operating systems, and support on other platforms will probably come only from the OS vendors.

You enable PPTP access via the Services tab of the Network control panel. Exercise 14.5 sets up PPTP for RAS.

RAS Clients

The previous section showed you how to set up a RAS server. That, however, is only half the problem of enabling remote access to your network. The other half entails the configuration of clients to connect to your RAS server.

RAS supports the connection of any operating system that supports PPP; one of the three authentication protocols (PAP, CHAP, or MS-CHAP); and one of the three transports (TCP/IP, NWLink, or NetBEUI). If the client is going to access services on the Windows NT Server, then the client must support a service protocol of Windows NT (such as NetBIOS for file access or HTTP for access to Internet Information Server Web pages).

These "limitations" effectively mean that just about any computer can connect to your network via Remote Access Services. Each operating system has its own methods of configuring the various protocols it supports.

EXERCISE 14.5

Configuring PPTP for RAS

1. Select Start ➤ Settings ➤ Control Panel.

2. Double-click the Network control panel program.

3. Select the protocols Tab.

4. Click the Add button.

5. Select Point to Point Tunneling Protocol and then click OK.

6. Enter the location of the Windows NT Server setup files. (If the CD is in drive F and you are running Server on an Intel-based computer, then you would enter `F:\I386\`.)

7. Accept 1 as the number of virtual private networks and then click OK. The setup process will invoke RAS so that you can configure it to accept PPTP connections. Click OK.

8. Click the Add button and then select VPN1 - RASPPTPM from the list of RAS capable devices. Click OK to continue.

9. Click Continue and then click Close at the Network window.

Explaining how to configure these protocols is well beyond the scope of this book. Other books in this series (*MCSE: Windows 95 Study Guide* and *MCSE: NT Workstation Study Guide*) explain how to connect Windows 95 and Windows NT Workstation computers to RAS in some detail.

You can connect Windows NT Server as a client to another Windows NT Server using RAS exactly the same way you connect Windows NT Workstation. The following section describes how to use RAS as a client to connect a Windows NT computer to a RAS server on another computer.

Installing RAS Client Software

On a Windows NT Workstation computer or on a Windows NT Server computer that does not already have RAS loaded to allow RAS dial-in connections, you may need to install RAS services to connect to a RAS server. If you already have RAS configured for dial-in, you do not have to install it again for dial-out; you can simply check the Dial Out and Receive Calls or the Dial Out Only options from the Configure Port Usage window.

(Refer to Exercise 14.3 to review the process of installing RAS on a Windows NT server or workstation computer.)

Creating a Dial-Up Connection

After installing RAS, you will need to create a dial-up network connection in the RAS phone book that contains the dialing and network information for each dial-up server to which you will attach. This process is basically the same for Windows RAS servers and UNIX/Internet servers. Follow Exercise 14.6 to create a dial-up networking connection. Repeat this process for each dial-up server to which you need access. The RAS Edit Phonebook Entry screen appears in Figure 14.5.

FIGURE 14.5

The RAS Edit Phonebook Entry screen

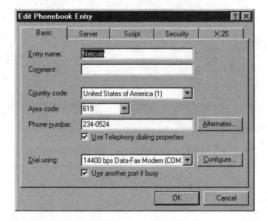

Security

The RAS client complement to the RAS server security options resides in the Security tab of the phone book entry. From there you can specify the kind of dial-up authentication you will use to connect your RAS client computer to the remote server. The same options are available from both the client and server side:

- PAP—Accept any authentication including clear text

- CHAP—Accept Only (require) encrypted authentication

- MS-CHAP—Accept Only (require) Microsoft encrypted authentication

EXERCISE 14.6

Creating a Dial-Up Networking Connection

1. Double-click the My Computer icon on the Desktop.

2. Double-click the Dial-Up Networking icon.

3. Click OK to pass "The phone book is empty" notice if it appears. If it does not appear, you already have at least one RAS entry. Click New to display the New Phonebook Entry Wizard dialog box.

4. Type the name of the new phone book entry, check the I know all about phone book entries box, and click the Finish button. (If you choose to enter the phone book information without the wizard, you must use More ➤ User Preferences ➤ Appearance ➤ Use Wizard to Create New Phonebook Entries to use the wizard again.)

5. Enter the name of the server to which you will be attaching in the Entry name text box.

6. Select your modem in the Dial Using drop-down box. If you are using a null modem cable to connect two computers, select Dial-Up Networking Serial Cable between 2 PCs on the appropriate COM port.

7. Click the Use Telephony dialing properties option.

8. Enter the area code and phone number of your RAS server in the Phone number input lines. If you are using a null modem cable, leave these lines blank.

9. Click the Alternates button if your RAS server has alternate phone numbers. Add the alternate phone numbers.

10. Click the Server tab.

11. Select TCP/IP.

12. Click the Security tab.

13. Select Allow any authentication including clear text.

14. Click OK to accept your settings.

15. Click Close. Restarting your computer is not necessary.

You can also specify that data passing over the RAS connection will be encrypted if you select the MS-CHAP protocol.

The security you select must match the security selected on the remote server. However, if either side selects Allow any authentication including clear text, then it doesn't matter which protocol the other uses (except from a security standpoint).

Multilink

You can select Multiple Lines in the Dial Using selection box of the Basic tab of the phone book entry screen. The Configure button then will allow you to check each modem you want to use for the Multilink connection. You can use several modems to connect to the same RAS server, providing you with more bandwidth for your dial-up connection. You must configure your RAS server to accept Multilink connections to use this feature.

Scripting

Windows NT Server and Workstation version 4 include a powerful new scripting language, which you can use to automate connections to non-RAS dial-up servers. (The scripting language is not necessary for connecting to RAS servers because the authentication protocols already do all the work of connecting the client to the RAS server.)

Using the scripting language is not difficult, but it is beyond the scope of this book to show you how to program in it. Look at the examples provided with the Windows NT Server CD-ROM and read the documentation about the scripting language (<Winnt>\system32\ras\Script.doc).

Testing a RAS Installation

Testing a RAS installation requires two computers running a compatible dial-up service such as Microsoft RAS. You may need to ask your network administrator for the phone number of your company's RAS server and what protocols it supports. You can test both a client and a server installation using the procedure shown in Exercise 14.7.

After running this procedure, you are connected to the remote server. You will have access to all the resources on the remote network that your security permissions allow.

EXERCISE 14.7

Testing a RAS Connection

1. Double-click the My Computer Icon on the Desktop.

2. Double-click the Dial-Up Networking Icon.

3. Check whether the server you entered in the previous section appears as the default phone book entry. If it does not, select the entry from the list box. If it does not appear in the list box, repeat Exercise 14.6 to add a phone book entry.

4. Click the Dial button.

5. Enter your user name, password, and domain for the remote server in the Connect to window. Click the Save Password checkbox.

6. Click OK.

7. Listen for the modem to dial and connect. RAS will beep if the connection went through correctly.

Disconnecting a RAS Session

You can disconnect a RAS session through the RAS session dialog box. Exercise 14.8 shows this simple procedure.

EXERCISE 14.8

Disconnecting a RAS Session

1. Right-click the RAS monitor that looks like a small external modem next to the Time in the Taskbar. (If you already changed the icon into a status window, right-click the window.)

2. Select the Hang up option.

3. Select the name of the server or service provider from which you wish to disconnect.

4. Answer Yes to the Disconnect dialog box.

5. Listen for a beep to confirm the disconnect.

Troubleshooting RAS Connections

RAS is easy to set up, but it sometimes can be difficult to troubleshoot because any of a number of incorrect settings can cause your RAS connection to fail. The most important part of troubleshooting RAS, like troubleshooting any other part of Windows NT, is knowing where to start, and as in most other troubleshooting situations, you should check your cables first. Exercise 14.9 will help you find the trouble spot in a failed RAS communication.

EXERCISE 14.9

Troubleshooting RAS Connections

1. Check your telephone cord and make sure that it is securely connected to the telephone outlet and to your modem.

2. Check the modem cable (for external modems) and make sure it is securely fastened to both the modem and the serial port of your computer.

3. Plug a regular telephone into the telephone jack of the modem if it has one. (Most do—if it does not, plug the telephone into the phone jack in your wall for testing purposes, then replace the modem phone line.) If you do not hear a dial tone through the telephone handset, then you have either a telephone service problem, in which you need to contact the telephone company, or a wiring problem at your location.

4. Make sure that the modem (internal modems only) is securely fastened in the expansion slot of your computer.

5. Verify that the modem itself is working properly and that the Windows Modem Properties settings reflect the IRQ and port address settings of the modem. Port addresses and Base I/O addresses are the same thing.

6. Do one of the following:

   ▪ If you are using an external modem, ensure that the COM port that the modem is using is enabled in the BIOS of your computer.

   ▪ If you are using an internal modem, verify that the IRQ and port address of your modem do not conflict with other devices in your computer, including the built-in serial ports of your computer.

7. Verify that RAS is installed in your computer and that it is configured to use your modem as a RAS device.

8. Do one of the following:

- If you plan only to place calls, verify that Dial Out Only is selected in the RAS configuration panel of the network control panel program.

- If you plan only to receive RAS calls, verify that Receive calls Only is selected.

- If you want to do both, verify that Dial Out and Receive calls is selected.

9. Verify that you have installed the same transport protocols on both the client computer and the RAS server computer and that both computers are configured to use those protocols from within RAS.

10. Verify that both computers allow the same type of authentication or that the server has selected Allow any authentication including clear text.

11. Verify that the user account you will be using to connect to the RAS server has dial-in privileges and that the call-back feature is properly set.

12. Verify that you are using the correct username, password, and domain name when making the connection.

The RAS Monitor

The RAS Monitor is a useful way to keep track of the occasionally unreliable status of modem connections over the public network. The RAS Monitor appears by default in the Taskbar, but you can change it to a window that constantly shows the connection status. If you use Exercise 14.10 to change the RAS Monitor icon into a window, remember that clicking the window has the same effect as clicking the icon. Figure 14.6 shows the Dial-Up Networking Monitor screen.

FIGURE 14.6

The Dial-Up Networking
Monitor screen controls
the RAS Monitor.

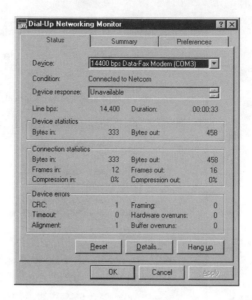

EXERCISE 14.10

Checking the Status of a RAS Connection

1. Establish a RAS session using the procedure shown in Exercise 14.7.

2. Double-click the RAS Monitor (it looks like a small external modem) icon next to the time system tray on the Taskbar.

3. Notice the count of incoming bytes and frames in the status page.

4. Select the Preferences tab.

5. Select the As a window on the desktop in the Show status lights control group.

6. Check Display the windows title bar.

7. Check Always on top.

8. Click OK.

9. Notice that the RAS monitor now shows up as a window on the desktop.

Testing Your Web Site with RAS

Although RAS is important if you want to set up a small Internet Service Provider, or if you want to allow dial-up access to your intranet, it's also very important for Webmasters who will attach their servers only to the Internet. Often, especially at companies where a fast Internet connection is available, you won't have any access to a low-speed dial-up Internet provider. Under most circumstances, that's perfectly fine—you don't want a slow connection if you already have a fast link.

But if you've ever browsed a Web site from home and had to go to lunch while an image map loaded, you understand why browsing your own site with a low-speed modem is a crucial step in the design and implementation of a Web site. More than 95 percent of the traffic on an Internet site occurs from modems that operate at 28.8Kbps or less. The Web pages that blaze in on your local area network can seem to take forever on the wrong end of a 14.4Kbps modem.

You should always use a low-speed dial-up connection to browse the Web sites you create. If you don't, you won't understand the customers' perspective of your site, and therefore, of your organization. Many Web surfers simply get fed up with slow loads and leave before the site even has a chance to come up on their screen. You'll still register a hit in your site logs, but you will not make an impact on the user. And if your site is slow to load, most users probably won't bother.

RAS allows you to test your site with a dial-up connection without setting up an account with a dial-up Internet Service Provider. You simply attach a modem to your Internet server and set up RAS to accept calls as shown in the exercises in the previous sections. Because you won't be providing public dial-up support, you should require MS-CHAP authentication—and it wouldn't hurt to turn on encryption.

Once you've dialed in to your site, take note of which content takes a long time to appear or download. Use the methods detailed in Chapter 9 to optimize your site content so that the core information appears more quickly.

You can now dial in from any computer you want to test your site. Remember that if you dial in via a computer with a high-speed connection to your local area network or the Internet, the site will still probably load over the network, not over your dial-up link. You must disable the network TCP/IP connection during your test sessions to ensure that the IP traffic doesn't route over the higher-speed connection.

You have two options: You can disable the network adapter's access to TCP/IP in software, or you can simply unplug your network adapter from the network. Unplugging your network adapter is easier, but that option may not be available if you are working on one of the many network physical plant architectures that don't like intermittent connection and disconnection. For instance, Ethernet over twisted pair or fiber supports disconnection, but disconnecting an Ethernet over thin or thick coaxial cable is fraught with peril.

Always check with your network integrator or system administrator before modifying any hardware on your network.

As an alternative, you can simply disable TCP/IP access over your high-speed adapter. Exercise 14.11 is an interesting workaround that removes the default gateway address from your default adapter and changes your IP address to an address that routers won't pass. This approach forces all IP traffic to route through your dial-up connection. When you are finished, you can simply restore the settings for your high-speed adapter. You can safely ignore any warnings to restart your computer, but you may have to log back on to your local area network domain controller or servers.

In addition to disabling high-speed access to your site for testing, remember to clear your Web browser's cache if you've been browsing your site on the high-speed link. If you don't clear your cache, Web pages will load from your own machine rather than over the dial-up link. Each Web browser is unique, so refer to Chapter 10 or your Web browser's Help file for assistance in clearing its cache.

The procedure shown in the next exercise will result in a loss of network services. Make sure to save everything you are working on before you perform this exercise. Also be certain you are not running any software that is relying upon a TCP/IP connection to your network. To be safe, you should close all running applications.

EXERCISE 14.11

Disabling Network TCP/IP Access

1. Right-click the Network Neighborhood icon.

2. Select Properties.

3. Select the Protocols tab.

4. Double-click the TCP/IP protocol in the Protocols list.

5. Select your network adapter in the Adapters list box. If you only have one, it is already selected.

6. Select the Specify an IP address radio button. If data already appears in the IP address, subnet mask and default gateway input boxes, record this information so you can restore it later in the exercise.

7. Type **10.1.1.1** (or **.2** for your second adapter, and so forth) in the IP address field.

8. Type **255.255.255.0.** in the subnet mask field. (The subnet mask actually doesn't matter, but this setting will cause less of a delay.)

9. Leave the default gateway address empty.

10. Repeat steps 5 through 9 for each adapter in your computer.

11. Click OK.

12. Click OK.

13. Click No if a dialog appears stating that you must restart your computer for the changes to take effect. In this case the dialog is not correct.

14. Launch your Web browser and browse your Web site. All IP traffic will now be routed through dial-up connections. When you finish, close your Web browser.

15. Right-click the Network Neighborhood icon.

16. Select Properties.

17. Select the Protocols tab.

---

18. Double-click the TCP/IP protocol in the Protocols list.

19. Select your network adapter in the Adapters list box. If you only have one, it is already selected.

20. Do one of the following:

    ■ Select the Specify an IP address radio button.

    ■ If no information appeared in the IP address field previously, select Obtain an IP address from a DHCP server and skip to step 25.

21. Type the IP address you recorded for this adapter in step 6 in the IP address field.

22. Enter the subnet mask that you recorded in step 6 in the subnet mask field.

23. Enter the default gateway you recorded in step 6 in the default gateway field.

24. Repeat steps 19 through 22 for each adapter in your computer.

25. Click OK.

26. Click OK.

27. Click No if a dialog appears stating that you must restart your computer for the changes to take effect. In this case the dialog is not correct.

28. Reestablish any network connections that may have dropped while your network adapter was not responding. You may wish to restart your computer if that is easiest.

Summary

Remote Access Service for Windows NT extends the advantages of networking to computers that cannot be directly connected to your network. RAS uses modems or other devices that attach to telephone company lines to call in and share files and services.

Regular Ethernet can transfer data 100 times faster than the fastest regular modems can. Fast Ethernet (which can be 10 times faster than regular Ethernet) can transfer data 1,000 times faster than regular modems can.

A RAS server can connect to a client computer using any of the three primary transport protocols of Windows NT (TCP/IP, NWLink, and NetBEUI). It supports PPP for dial in and supports both SLIP and PPP for dial out. It supports PAP, CHAP, and MS-CHAP for password authentication, and if you use MS-CHAP, you can also encrypt the data transferred over a RAS link. Internet services are supported only over the TCP/IP protocol.

RAS permissions are established on a per user basis and include a callback feature. You cannot assign permissions for RAS using Windows NT server or domain groups.

The Multilink protocol allows you to use more than one modem for the same dial-up connection. Using multiple modems allows you to transfer data faster than if you had only one modem. The Point-to-Point Tunneling Protocol allows remote clients to access your network in a secure manner over the Internet using an Internet service provider.

RAS provides a way for users of regular modems to attach to your Internet or intranet site from anyplace where telephone service is available. Additionally, RAS provides a mechanism for testing your Internet Web site using the same connection method that most browsers will be using. By dialing into your own site, you'll be able to ferret out pages, graphics, and embedded scripts or code that operate slowly on client connections and then to optimize them to provide a less frustrating experience for your users.

Review Questions

1. You are providing a dial-in connection to the Internet for remote computers in your organization. Some of the remote computers do not use Windows 95 or Windows NT. (Some are UNIX computers, and some run the MacOS.) Which authentication protocol should you use?

   A. MS-CHAP

   B. CHAP

   C. PAP

   D. SLIP

2. You need to provide secure communications over the Internet so that remote computers can use an Internet Service Provider local to them to connect to Microsoft networking services on your local area network. Which protocol will provide that secure connection over the Internet?

    A. TCP/IP

    B. PPTP

    C. PPP

    D. SLIP

3. Windows 95 and Windows NT client computers (which have only the TCP/IP transport protocol installed) are able to connect to your RAS server on your network and are able to access resources on that computer but cannot access any other resources on the network or on the Internet. What is most likely to be the problem?

    A. You do not have the TCP/IP to NetBEUI bridge configured to route IP over your local area network.

    B. You have not selected Entire Network in the RAS Server TCP/IP configuration window.

    C. You have not configured your authentication protocol to Allow any authentication including clear text.

    D. Your client computers have not been configured with or dynamically assigned an IP address.

4. Which of the following transport protocols will provide the most efficient connection to Internet services over dial-up lines, even when you have routers in your network?

    A. NetBEUI

    B. NWLink

    C. TCP/IP

    D. DLC

5. You wish to encrypt both the logon authentication (password exchange) portion of a dial-up connection and the data that is transferred over the connection. Which type of authentication should you choose?

   A. PAP

   B. CHAP

   C. MS-CHAP

   D. TCP/IP

6. You have created a Web site that tests out very well through your network connection and now you want to test it using RAS and a dial-up connection. You disable TCP/IP on your network adapter by changing the IP address and removing the default gateway information, but Web pages still load faster than you think they would over your modem. What is wrong?

   A. You didn't restart your computer, so the new TCP/IP settings have not taken effect.

   B. You must also unplug your network adapter cable.

   C. You must also remove the network adapter from the Adapters list in the Networking control panel.

   D. You must clear your Web browser's cache to prevent pages from being displayed out of it.

CHAPTER

15

Maintaining Internet
Information Services

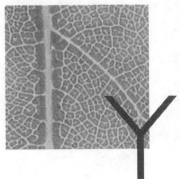

You have Windows NT installed, IIS humming along, and a nice Web site stuffed with compelling content available on the Internet. Security is set up in accordance with your company's security policy and everything works correctly.

For a while. Then users start complaining that Web pages are taking too long to download. Or that suddenly they can't log on. Or they can log on from work, but no longer from home. Or you find the tracks of an intruder on your site—or any one of a myriad of problems that can suddenly afflict a seemingly well-groomed Web server.

The server was probably set up correctly, but the company has now outgrown its capability. Or a new security feature was installed that has an unexpected side effect. Or someone's password was compromised when the user logged on to a nonsecure server.

Performance tuning and troubleshooting keep your server running correctly for the long haul. You can't expect the same computer to keep up with the workload in the year 2000 as it kept up with in 1995 unless your organization is actually getting smaller. And don't think someone won't exploit new-found bugs in software to bypass the security on your site. For example, Microsoft recently uncovered a new security hole in the FrontPage Server extensions that allow knowledgeable users (a.k.a. hackers) to bypass your IIS security settings and actually change your site content remotely. New updates to Web browsers that fix security holes are practically a monthly occurrence. Firewalls are currently the only way to prevent these sorts of intrusions when programming oversights allow security loopholes to slip into production software.

This chapter covers both performance tuning to keep your Internet server running optimally and troubleshooting to repair it. These two skills separate the IIS Webmasters from the IIS Webgrasshoppers, so pay careful attention.

Performance Tuning

Performance tuning is finding the resource that most drastically slows your network, speeding it up until something else has the most impact on speed, and then starting over by finding the new slowest resource. This cycle of finding the speed-limiting factor, eliminating it, and starting over allows you to reach the natural performance limit of your network in a simple, methodical way.

Bottlenecks are factors that limit performance in a computer. For instance, slow memory limits the speed at which a processor can manipulate data—thus limiting the computers processing performance to the speed that the processor can access memory. If the memory can respond faster than the processor, the processor is the bottleneck.

System performance is always affected by a bottleneck. You may not notice it because your computer may run faster than the work you perform requires. Chances are, if you use your computer only for Web service attached to the Internet via a T1 line, the speed of your machine has never limited how fast you can work. On the other hand, if you use your computer as an SQL server for a large organization, chances are you've spent a lot of time waiting for the server to catch up to you.

Your pipe to the Internet should be your bottleneck in an Internet server. If your server can keep all its connections to the Internet loaded, you're getting all the performance you possibly can out of your Internet server.

Performance tuning Internet servers is the systematic process of finding the resource experiencing the most load and then relieving that load. You can almost always optimize a server to make it more responsive. Understanding how Internet Information Server (IIS) performs and how you can increase its performance is important. Even if you don't need to make your servers any faster, understanding performance tuning can help you diagnose problems when they arise.

If it's not broken, don't fix it. Windows NT, IIS, and Index Server are highly tuned and factory optimized to work well in most situations. You should perform rigorous performance monitoring only when a problem that is obviously load-related occurs on your server. You should be especially careful not to cause more harm than good with your performance tuning. Avoid changing any settings or options that you don't fully understand.

Performance tuning is a very complex topic. If you need additional information about performance monitoring beyond its use with IIS, check out *MCSE: NT Server 4 Study Guide* and *MCSE: NT Workstation Study Guide*, both from Sybex, or *Optimizing Windows NT*, from Microsoft Press and included as part of the Windows NT Resource Kit.

Monitoring IIS Performance

The Performance Monitor is the tool built into Windows NT that monitors all facets of its performance. IIS extends the Windows NT Performance Monitor to include performance counters for each of the Internet services and for IIS as a whole. This extension of the Performance Monitor's functionality enables you to compare IIS performance counters with Windows NT system counters to find coincidental performance characteristics.

Exercise 15.1 shows you how to load the Performance Monitor and view different Internet-related performance counters. Figure 15.1 shows the Performance Monitor monitoring an IIS load.

FIGURE 15.1

The Performance Monitor

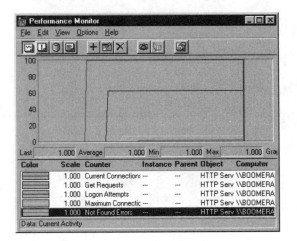

IIS services such as the HTTP, Gopher, and FTP services will appear in the Performance Monitor only when the services are running. If you don't see the counter object for the service in the object pick box, close the Performance Monitor, start the service, and restart the Performance Monitor.

EXERCISE 15.1

Monitoring IIS Performance with the Performance Monitor

1. Select Start ➤ Programs ➤ Administrative Tools ➤ Performance Monitor.

2. Select Edit ➤ Add to Chart or click the large + button on the toolbar.

3. Select HTTP Service in the Object pick box.

4. Select Current Connections in the Counter list box.

5. Click Add. Note that a colored line has begun moving from right to left in the Performance Monitor main window.

6. Select HTTP Service in the Object pick box.

7. Select Bytes Total/sec in the Counter list box.

8. Click Add.

9. Click Done. You are now monitoring the number of current connections and the total throughput to the IIS HTTP service using the Performance Monitor.

IIS extensions to the Performance Monitor allow you to track the following objects:

- Active Server Pages
- FTP Server
- Gopher Service
- HTTP Service
- Internet Information Services Global

In addition to the performance counters added by IIS, numerous objects contain counters that particularly pertain to Internet services. These counters are the Windows NT objects that provide the services upon which IIS rests—therefore, they bear the load that IIS causes. You can examine these objects to quickly narrow down where bottlenecks are occurring and then examine IIS counters to determine which IIS services are causing the load on these services of Windows NT:

- **IP**—The basic network layer transport upon which Internet services rely. Network I/O bottlenecks will show up here.

- **Logical Disk**—Disk speed–based bottlenecks will show up here.

- **Memory**—Do you have enough? Excessive pages/sec means you don't.

- **Processor**—Is it fast enough? If your average %Processor time is higher than 80 percent, it's either time to upgrade or lighten the load.

- **TCP**—Shows the number of concurrent TCP sockets in use and network activity by sockets.

Understanding Performance Counters

The IIS services (HTTP, Gopher, and FTP) provide a very similar set of counters that measure the same things for each service. However, because the services differ, some counters are service specific.

In the following set of counters, each counter counts from the time the service was started unless otherwise noted by some sort of rate indicator like per second (/sec), current, or percentage (%).

Per second counters measure the number of counts that occur in one second and provide a good indicator of load relative to earlier loads on the same counter. These counters are good for determining the thresholds at which bottlenecks occur and how often those thresholds happen.

Current counters tell you how many instances of a certain load factor are currently occurring—these counters are especially useful for comparing against processor, disk, and memory counters to identify processes that cause bottlenecks to occur. Try putting them on the same charts as processor, disk, and memory counters to find obvious similarities. Using the Performance Monitor this way will help you determine how and when to upgrade your server.

Counters that don't have a current or per second indicator simply rate the number of times the measured event has occurred since the service was started. Because there's no indication of how long the service has been running, these counters don't mean much in terms of Performance Monitoring or optimization—but they are a good source for marketing and usage statistics, or as a metric upon which to base fees for services rendered.

Counters Relevant to IIS

Some performance counters are far more important than others. They track factors that greatly affect the performance of the Internet services, so they are the most important counters to keep an eye on. The purpose of each of these counters should be relatively obvious if you understand how the service works. The following counters are especially important for most IIS administrators:

- **Aborted Connections** caused by errors or service maximums. Look for sudden spurts indicating hardware problems or compare to network throughput counters to find network I/O bottlenecks.

- **Bytes Total/sec** shows overall throughput of the service. Compare this value to network I/O counters to see how much of your network bandwidth is consumed by Internet services.

- **Current Connections** shows the number of connections currently logged on to the server, which is a good indicator of relative use by hour, day, week, and so on.

- **Maximum Connections** shows the most load the server has ever been under. Check this value to determine when you might need to upgrade your server.

- **Not Found Errors** are requests that failed because of file-not-found-on-this-site errors.

Service Performance Counters

The services also have other, more esoteric counters, which will be of interest in certain situations. You will have to use your knowledge of your system and special circumstances to determine when these counters are appropriate to track. For instance, if you are making heavy use of CGI or ISAPI, you may want to track the counters specific to them. The standard performance counters are:

- Bytes Received/sec

- Bytes Sent/sec

- Connection Attempts

- Current Anonymous Users

- Current Nonanonymous Users

- Files Sent

- Logon Attempts

- Maximum Anonymous Users

- Maximum Nonanonymous Users

- Total Anonymous Users

- Total Nonanonymous Users

HTTP Service Counters

The preceding counters profiled are applicable to all three Internet services (WWW, Gopher, and FTP). The following counters are specific to the HTTP service:

- **Connections /sec**—Shows the number of connections initiated per second, which is another good measure of server load.

- **CGI Requests**

- **Current CGI Requests**—Compare peaks in this counter to peaks in %Processor time, %Disk time, or PageFaults/sec to see if your CGI scripts are causing a processor, disk, or memory bottleneck.

- **Current ISAPI Extension Requests**—Compare peaks in this counter to peaks in %Processor time, %Disk time, or PageFaults/sec to see if your ISAPI applications requests are causing a processor, disk, or memory bottleneck.

- **Files Received**

- **ISAPI Extension Requests**

- **Head Requests**—Shows browsers checking for page changes against their cached copies.

- **Post Requests**

- **Other Request Methods**—Identifies requests other than the GET, POST, or HEAD methods. Used to indicate less common requests.

- **Get Requests**
- **Maximum CGI Requests**
- **Maximum ISAPI Extension Requests**

Gopher Counters

The following counters are specific to or specifically not included in the Gopher Service:

- Connections in Error
- Gopher Plus Requests

The following counters are not available in the Gopher service because files cannot be uploaded to it:

- Files Received
- Files Total

IIS Global Counters

Counters are also provided for the functions of IIS as a whole. Those functions that either can't be measured separately or that have little meaning when measured separately are combined. For the most part, these counters measure cache effectiveness and service blocking because of bandwidth throttling. They aren't usually very useful when looking for straightforward performance problems, although you may want to check the effectiveness of your bandwidth throttling. The IIS global counters are

- Cache Flushes
- Cache Hits
- Cache Hits%
- Cache Misses
- Cache Size
- Cache Used
- Cached File Handles

- Current Blocked Async I/O Requests

- Directory Listings

- Measured Async I/O Bandwidth usage

- Objects

- Total Allowed Async I/O Requests

- Total Blocked Async Requests

- Total Rejected Async I/O Requests

Active Server Pages Performance Counters

The Active Server Pages object allows you to track counters related to the execution of Active Server Pages content on your server. This measurement allows you to determine how much load your Active Server Pages puts on your server. The meaning of these counters is not documented, although some are quite obvious. The Active Server Pages counters are

- Allocated Memory in Free List

- Allocated Memory in Used List

- Browser Requests Executing

- Communication Failed

- Free Script Engines in Cache

- Memory Allocated

- Request Errors/Sec

- Request Execution Time

- Request Total Bytes In

- Request Total Bytes Out

- Request Wait Time

- Requests Current

- Requests Executed

- Requests Failed

- Requests Rejected

- Requests Timed Out

- Requests Total

- Requests/Sec

- Session Timed Out Requests Executed

- Session Timed Out Requests in Queue

- Sessions Current

- Sessions Timed Out

- Thread Pool Count

- Total Queue Length

Optimizing Performance

Now that the Performance Monitor has armed you with knowledge of the internal workings of the IIS services, it's time to actually compare these counters with other performance counters to determine the impact of the services on the operation of the server. This process is called *performance analysis*.

Since IIS isn't the only software running on your computer, many other factors will affect the computer's performance. However, if your server is primarily an Internet or intranet server, most of the performance affecting software will be engaged in activities directly related to Internet service. If IIS is merely an add-on to a general purpose server that performs everything from file and print service to light SQL duties, you'll have trouble determining which services impact speed the most. If this is the case, perform your testing at night or when the server is mostly idle.

Generate synthetic (i.e., made up or nonreal) loads to put the server under a specific sort of strain. For instance, if you want to measure the impact of HTTP service on a general purpose server, isolate the server from other sources of load and then connect a Web browser to a complex Web page 20 or 30 times. This test will put the server under a known load, and you'll be able to filter out how much that specific factor impacts server performance.

Synthetic loads show you how much a specific service loads your system, but they won't ferret out all your performance problems by themselves. Many performance problems don't show up unless the server is under a full load. For instance, let's say you are running an Internet database that has both an Active Server Pages IIS component and an SQL Server component running on the same machine.

Once the server load reaches a certain point, connections start timing out. But which service is causing the problem? A synthetic load won't tell you unless it's designed to exercise both components the same way a real connection would. Even then, you need to determine whether the bottleneck is caused by network I/O, disk, processor, or memory constraints by using performance counters appropriate to those subsystems. You may not be able to overcome a disk bottleneck if both services compete for time on the same disk array—but moving the SQL Server to another machine attached via a fast network fixes the problem completely.

To analyze performance quickly, select the counters that are most relevant to the aspect of performance that you wish to measure (e.g., Memory Allocated if you suspect you are low on memory; Communication Failed and Session Timed Out if you are diagnosing bad connections; or Requests/Second, Requests Current, and Total Queue Length if your server is heavily loaded) and add to the same graph counters for %Processor Time, %Disk time, and Page faults/sec. Now when you put the server under a synthetic Internet service load, you'll see spikes in these counters that correspond directly to the service counters you added. This measurement gives you a good indication of the relative load IIS is causing on your machine for a specific level of concurrent use.

Many serious performance problems are sporadic. You may have to use the Alerting or logging features of IIS to track down strange or infrequent problems or problems that tend to occur when you aren't around. These features are beyond the scope of this book, but you should be able to figure out how to use them with the help file built into the Performance Monitor.

Exercise 15.2 generates a small load on the counters you started in Exercise 15.1.

EXERCISE 15.2

Generating a Performance Load

1. Double-click the Internet Explorer icon on your desktop.

2. Arrange the positions of Internet Explorer and the Performance Monitor on your desktop so that you can see the content windows of both of them at the same time. You may need to make Internet Explorer very small.

3. Type **//boomerang/**default.htm in the Address input line, replacing *boomerang* with the name of your Internet server.

4. Notice the slight load this procedure creates on your server. Also notice that the load drops back down after the initial connection once the page is loaded. This example shows the "bursty" nature of HTTP transmissions.

Performance-Tuning Logs

The logs created by IIS are a gold mine of information on how your server is used. Chapters 6 and 8 discuss logs in a security context, but they are also useful for figuring out how well your server performs over time.

Unfortunately, these logs create an enormous amount of information. You can log to an ODBC data source like a Microsoft Access database or an SQL Server, query the data, and then create reports to view any statistics you want, but that process takes a lot of setup effort. IIS 3 provides a third-party product called *Crystal Reports* that can perform much of this work for you.

Crystal Reports is actually a very broad-based, drill-down, data-mining tool for use with different types of databases to quickly extract complex sets of data and report on them. The Crystal Reports program itself is totally oriented toward database reporting—its interface for loading IIS forms even simulates an SQL server so that Crystal Reports won't know the difference. Exercise 15.3 shows how you can use Crystal Reports to get details of Web server usage in a compact form.

EXERCISE 15.3

Using Crystal Reports to Extract Internet Information Server Log Data

1. Select Start ➤ Programs ➤ Crystal Reports 4.5 ➤ Crystal Reports 4.5.

2. Click Cancel if a dialog appears asking you to fill in registration information. You can do this later.

3. Select Databases ➤ Log On Server.

4. Double-click MS IIS Log Files.

5. Click OK if your log files are stored in the location shown in the log files location input box.

6. Click OK.

7. Select File ➤ New.

8. Click Listing.

9. Click SQL/ODBC.

10. Click Add. This step adds all log files to the report.

11. Click Done.

12. Click Next.

13. Double-click the Client Host field.

14. Double-click the User Name field.

15. Double-click the Log Date field.

16. Double-click the Log Time field.

17. Click Next.

18. Select the User Name field in the Report fields list box. You may have to use the horizontal scroll bar to see all the field names.

19. Click Add.

20. Select Is and then Equal To in the criteria pick boxes.

21. Click the Selector in the next empty pick box that appeared. You may have to wait while Crystal Reports selects unique data from the specified reporting field.

22. Select the name of a user that interests you in the User Name pick box.

23. Click Preview Report.

24. Click Print.

25. Select File ➤ Exit.

26. Click No when asked whether or not you want to save the report.

As you can see, Crystal Reports provides a very detailed reporting interface for the IIS log files. You can create summary reports that compare the total number of connections to your Web server by username to identify your heaviest users, for instance.

An easier interface to the Crystal Reports reporting engine for IIS is provided through HTML engines that use ActiveX controls to send queries to the Crystal Reports engine. The Crystal Reports engine then processes the query, uses its IIS Log Reports data source DLL to extract information from the log files, generates the report, and then uses its Publish to HTML component to create new Web pages that contain the results of your query. For many typical log-based queries, this method is far faster—especially if you need to access this information from a computer other than the Internet server itself. Exercise 15.4 shows you how to use the HTML interface to the Crystal Reports reporting engine. Figure 15.2 shows a Crystal Reports–generated graph.

Now that you have an easy-to-use interface that shows the most-accessed pages, you can spend your time optimizing those pages. Your optimization efforts will now bear the most fruit. For instance, the most accessed file on your site might be a logo graphic that occurs in many different Web pages. By reducing the size of that single file and converting it to a monochrome image, you can dramatically reduce the load on your server.

Crystal Reports is a complex piece of software. You can find out quite a bit about it by reading through the relevant help files and the Crystal Web Engine Docs HTML files stored with the application.

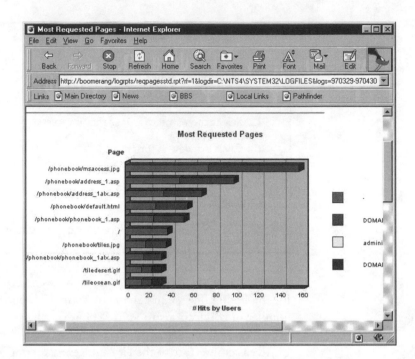

EXERCISE 15.4

Using Crystal Reports for Performance Optmization

1. Select Start ➤ Programs ➤ Crystal Reports 4.5 ➤ Sample Log Reports.

2. Select Most Requested Pages in the Select the report to generate list box.

3. Select Refresh Report Data. This step uses the actual IIS logs your server creates as it runs.

4. Enter a date one month prior to the current date in the Start Date input box.

5. Click Generate Crystal Report.

6. Note the top three accessed files shown in the graph.

7. Close Internet Explorer.

Optimizing performance is the ultimate goal of performance monitoring. Essentially, when you understand how your server is operating, you can make reasonable improvements to the process. Chapter 9 discusses various methods of optimizing content in considerable detail. This section details a few specific ways to optimize how IIS runs on a specific server regardless of the content stored.

Metering Bandwidth

Metering bandwidth is not really a performance optimization because it doesn't make IIS perform better. In fact, metering bandwidth impedes performance by restricting load times to a certain level. However, if you are using IIS on a server that does double duty as a file server and the IIS traffic is simply not as important as the regular network traffic, you may have to use bandwidth metering to prevent Internet traffic from stealing time away from more important uses of your machine. Exercise 15.5 shows you how to implement bandwidth metering if you need to.

Your pipe to the Internet is an automatic bandwidth meter. If you have a 56K leased line, your Internet traffic will never account for more than 56K of network I/O. You don't have to set anything for inherent bottlenecks like this to limit the flow of information to and from your server. Bandwidth metering is more suited for intranet use than it is for Internet use.

Optimizing Index Server

The Index Server search engine is designed for speed efficiency. When indexed documents change on a server, they are added to a change queue. The change queue is processed in first-in, first-out order very quickly after the documents are stored.

When documents are first indexed, the resulting index of words is stored in RAM in a buffer called a *word list*. Word lists are not compressed, and they are stored only in RAM, so they can be stored very quickly. When the size of a word list reaches a certain point, it is compressed and stored into a shadow index on the disk. *Shadow indexes* serve as disk buffers for word lists that have not yet been added to the monolithic master index. Shadow indexes are easy to create but do cause a small amount of disk and processor load. A *shadow merge* combines all the shadow indexes and word lists into a single shadow index whenever the number of word lists or shadow indexes passes a

---

EXERCISE 15.5

Metering IIS Network Bandwidth

1. Select Start ➤ Programs ➤ Microsoft Internet Server ➤ Internet Service Manager.

2. Double-click the name of your server in the WWW service line.

3. Select the Advanced tab.

4. Check the Limit Network Use by all Internet Services on this computer.

5. Click Yes.

6. Enter the value you want to restrict total bandwidth to. The default value is reasonable for many circumstances.

7. Click OK.

8. Click the Service Stop button. Wait for the service to stop.

9. Click the Service Start button. Wait for the service to start.

10. Close the Internet Service Manger.

---

certain threshold. Shadow merges are generally very quick because the indexes are small.

The *master index* is the main index for all the documents indexed by the search engine. Every night at midnight (by default) a shadow merge occurs to combine all the word lists and indexes into a single shadow index. Then a *master merge* occurs to add the shadow index changes to the master index.

All this effort with word lists, shadow indexes, and merges is an important optimization because adding words to the master index is very time-consuming. If every document index was master merged after each indexing during the day, the load on your server would be tremendous. Word lists and shadow indexes serve as caches for the master merge so that the load-intensive master merge can be delayed until the server is under a light load.

The trade-off for this load optimization is query speed. Every query has to first search all existing word lists, then all shadow indexes, and then the master index each time a query is performed. Searching only the master index is far faster, so queries are quicker after a master merge.

The Performance Monitor determines how your Index Server is loaded using the following objects:

- Content Index

- Content Index Filter

- Http Content Index

These objects show you the current state of merges, the number of persistent indexes in your system, and the number and size of word lists. By watching these values compared to the disk, memory, and processor loads in your system, you can determine how much load Index Server puts on your system. Try staying up one night and monitoring your servers performance during a master merge. You will learn a lot about the indexing load your server is subject to, which will help you make determinations about how to optimize index speed.

If your server spends more time on queries than on merges, you should tighten up the registry values to force merges more often. On the other hand, if your server is spending too much time on merges, you should loosen up the intervals to master merges. Exercise 15.6 shows you how to edit some important registry values for Index Server to change the timing of different merges. Examine the Registry Settings page in the Index Server online documentation for a complete list of registry keys that can be modified to tune the performance of Index Server.

Do not modify Index Server registry keys unless you are certain you understand the impact of the changes you make. Improperly modified registry keys might disable your IIS server. You should be able to remove and then reinstall IIS and Index Server to restore default values in any event.

If Index Server is returning strange files (e.g., not .htm, .html, .doc, or .txt) and you don't want files of these other types to be returned, then you should set the FIlterFilesWithUnknownExtensions key (as shown in the next exercise) to 0. Setting the key to 0 will cause Index Server not to index files when it does not recognize the extension.

EXERCISE 15.6

Modifying the Index Server Registry Keys

1. Select Start ➤ Run.

2. Type **regedit** and press Enter. You may also use Regedt32 if you want better protection from accidentally changed registry keys.

3. Double-click HKEY_LOCAL_MACHINE.

4. Double-click SYSTEM.

5. Double-click CurrentControlSet.

6. Double-click Control.

7. Double-click contentindex.

8. Double-click MasterMergeTime.

9. Select the Decimal radio button.

10. Type **240** in the Value Data input box. This entry specifies 240 minutes after midnight (4:00 A.M.).

11. Double-click MaxIndexes.

12. Select the Decimal radio button.

13. Type **10** in the Value Data input box. This entry specifies that no more than 10 persistent indexes (master index plus shadow indexes) can exist before a shadow merge occurs. Lower this value to optimize query time on lightly loaded systems; increase it on heavily loaded systems.

14. Double-click FilterFilesWithUnknownExtensions.

15. Type **0** in the Value Data input box. This entry specifies that only files with registered file types should be indexed. This option prevents strange system files from showing up in your queries and reduces the size of your index dramatically.

16. Close the Registry Editor.

The following Index Server optimizations are especially effective. You should check out the Index Server online documentation for specific information on how to perform some of these optimizations:

- Move a catalog to a different hard disk than the corpus. (The *corpus* is all the files that are indexed in a catalog. See Chapters 6 and 12 for an explanation of catalogs.) This optimization splits the I/O traffic during the master merge among two disks and eliminates the need to seek the disk head between the areas containing the corpus and the areas containing the index.

- Use the standard Windows NT speed optimizations like striped hard disks or hardware RAID arrays to improve disk I/O speed.

- Increase the amount of RAM in your computer. You can edit registry settings to allow larger word lists in RAM, thus staving off the time to the next shadow merge.

- Create multiple catalogs if you don't need the ability to query everything at once. For instance, you may want to create separate catalogs for office documents than you will for HTML files because users will generally know what type of document they are searching for. Smaller indexes mean a faster search.

- Narrow the scope of your queries by eliminating virtual roots that don't contain useful query information, such as scripts directories and directories that contain ISAPI applications or Java code.

- Change the time that the daily master merge takes place to coincide with the time of day when your server is under the least load. If you are running a public Internet server, this time is most likely in the early morning between 4 A.M. and 9 A.M.; however, if you get browsers from all over the world, there may be no good time.

- Set Index Server to filter only files with known file types. This setting keeps a lot of garbage files out of your query indexes and makes everything run quite a bit faster.

Check out the registry settings in the Index Server online documentation for a complete list of the registry settings that you can modify to optimize Index Server.

Troubleshooting Index Server

Index Server works very well and is almost completely automatic. However, its behavior may not be what you expect. Sometimes the results of a query can seem strange. Index Server problems fall into four categories, all but one of which are actually optimization problems:

- **Queries return files that shouldn't be returned.** This problem can be caused by NTFS file permissions that are not correctly set up or by filtering files of all types when you should be restricting filtering to known types. See Chapters 7 and 8 for help on file security and the section on optimizing Index Server earlier in this chapter on restricting filtered types.

- **Queries don't return files that they should.** This problem can be caused because the catalog may be restricted to certain virtual directories, because not all files are being filtered and some extensions are not registered for filtration, or because file permissions are limiting the files that the query returns.

- **Queries take too long to fulfill.** You might be able to correct this optimization problem by forcing master merges more often. Or you may simply have too many users. Consider creating more catalogs if your data doesn't need to be searched in a single index or moving data to another server.

- **Queries time out or fail to return any data.** If the cause of this problem is an overloaded Index Server, outright failure will be foreshadowed by queries that take too long to fulfill. Other causes of this problem are network connectivity problems or corrupted Index Server files. If you've verified the connection between the host and the server, try reinstalling Index Server.

Troubleshooting IIS

Troubleshooting is the systematic process of isolating faults in a system and correcting them. Most IIS faults occur in two general categories: connectivity and security.

IIS must operate on a properly operating computer with a functional installation of Windows NT Server. This troubleshooting section assumes that your computer is working correctly and that it boots normally. If you suspect a hardware fault or an operating system configuration problem, fix those problems before proceeding with IIS troubleshooting.

Connectivity

Connectivity issues account for the vast majority of IIS problems. Connectivity issues encompass all the problems that a client might have when connecting to a host. Although connectivity problems can occur in a number of places in a connected system, you can do a few things to determine where connectivity problems lie.

Follow these three steps to troubleshoot the connection to a Web server:

- Verify the network connection to the host.

- Verify proper domain name resolution.

- Verify that the service (Gopher, FTP, or HTTP) is responding.

If your troubleshooting session passes these three phases, then your server is reachable, domain name resolution is working properly, and the service is running on the server. At that point any problems you encounter are security problems, not connectivity problems.

Verifying the Network Connection

Ping the remote host's IP address. This step validates the physical network link between the two computers and verifies that a routable path exists. Exercise 15.7 shows you how to Ping a remote hosts IP address. If you get the message that the request timed out, then either no host exists with that address (but the route was valid) or the time taken to respond is too long. If you get a message that the destination host is not reachable, then no valid route exists between the two networks. If you know the host is working correctly on the Internet or is reachable from other computers, check your default gateway settings to make sure packets are being forwarded correctly.

> ### EXERCISE 15.7
>
> ## Pinging a Remote Host to Verify Connectivity
>
> 1. Select Start ➤ Programs ➤ Command Prompt.
>
> 2. Type **ping 204.210.7.21** and press Enter.
>
> 3. Verify that Reply from 204.210.7.21 appears at the beginning of the four response lines.

Verifying Proper Domain Name Resolution

Ping the remote host's DNS name. This test verifies that name resolutions are happening correctly. Make sure the response IP address is the address you expect. Exercise 15.8 shows you how to use Ping to verify name services.

> ### EXERCISE 15.8
>
> ## Verifying Name Services
>
> 1. Select Start ➤ Programs ➤ Command Prompt.
>
> 2. Type **ping www.microsoft.com** and press Enter.
>
> 3. Verify that the four response lines all start with Reply from. This entry verifies that the name is actually resolving to a server on the Internet.

Verifying Service Response

If you can't get your browser to attach to a Web site that you think is running, Telnet into the HTTP port to verify that IIS is responding. Telnet simply attaches to the port, so you won't see anything useful, but it will tell you if a service is listening on the port or not. Exercise 15.9 allows you to determine if the service is running and you have a security problem, or if the service is shut down for some reason. You can use the method shown in Exercise 15.9 to check for any service listening on any port of any Internet server. If the port fails to respond, but you know the service is available to hosts on other networks, you can also use the same method to determine whether a firewall or proxy server between your client and the host is not forwarding access to the port in question.

EXERCISE 15.9

Using Telnet to Verify an Operational Service

1. Select Start ➤ Run.

2. Type **telnet** *boomerang* **80**, replacing *boomerang* with the name of your server. The Telnet window will pop up and nothing will appear if the service is active.

3. Close the Telnet window.

4. Type **telnet** *boomerang* **78**, replacing *boomerang* with the name of your server.

5. Notice the Connect Failed dialog box that pops up a moment after the window appears. This message indicates that no service is listening on port 78 of your server. Click OK.

6. Close the Telnet Window.

After you verify that a route exists between your computer and the Internet host in question, that the domain name resolves properly, and that the service to which you are attempting to attach is running correctly, you've eliminated all possible connectivity problems. The problem is either a security problem or a configuration problem on the Internet server.

Security

Security issues account for most IIS problems. The myriad of security mechanisms available to IIS and Windows NT means that tracking down which security mechanism is causing the problem can be a fairly time-consuming procedure.

Steps to checking security issues:

- Verify that any firewalls or proxy servers between the client and the server are configured to pass the correct types of traffic.

- Verify that the logon method supported by the browser is enabled in IIS.

- Verify that the logged-on user has sufficient permissions to access the directories and files.

- Verify that the paths to the various files are correct.

Firewalls and Proxy Servers

Firewalls and proxy servers are designed to prevent unlimited network access, and they do a good job of it. Many basic problems with Internet connectivity are actually caused by overly restrictive firewalls and proxy servers, which is not necessarily a bad thing. In fact, a good pessimistic security policy is simply to restrict all network traffic through a firewall except obvious types like FTP and HTTP and then to begin opening up only the types of traffic that users complain about not having access to.

If you have a firewall and certain types of content don't load correctly in your Web browser, determine which ports that content type relies upon and open your firewall to pass that type of traffic.

Logon Authentication

Logon authentication problems are probably the biggest source of problems for secure sites. The three types of logon authentication are

- Anonymous

- Basic (clear text)

- Windows NT Challenge/Response

If you allow only Windows NT Challenge/Response authentication, be aware that people using Web browsers other than Internet Explorer will not be able to connect to your site. If you need broad access to your site for all types of browsers but still require strong password security, consider using Secure Socket Layer (SSL) with Basic (clear text) passwords. By establishing the connection through SSL, the link is encrypted so your plain text password is not compromised on the network.

If you can't use SSL or Windows NT Challenge/Response, your best bet is to allow anonymous logon. This method prevents plain text passwords of valid Windows NT accounts on your network from being compromised.

File System Security

If a logged-on user can't get access to certain portions of your Web site, but anonymous users can, you've got a file system security problem. Windows NT is denying access to Web files on your site because the logged-on user doesn't have the same permissions that an anonymous user has. Study Chapter 7 on file system and account security to determine how best to solve these problems.

Anonymous Logon Account Permissions

All anonymous users are logged on through the single Windows NT account created by IIS when you installed it. Controlling access permissions and group memberships for this account allows you to secure or open up portions of your Web site for all anonymous users. Chapter 7 has more information on account and file system-based security. Check account and file system security if you are having access problems with anonymous users that don't occur with users who log on with valid accounts.

IIS Configuration

The configuration of IIS through the Internet Service Manager also accounts for a number of common problems. The Internet Service Manager controls many different settings that can cause strange errors. After you've determined that you don't have a connectivity problem and that file and account security are not the problem, you should take the following steps:

- Verify that virtual directory paths are correctly set up.
- Enable default documents.
- Check service-based access or denial for computers or networks.
- Check directory executable/readable settings.
- Check keys and certificates for SSL.
- Check registry settings for executable script DLLs.

Virtual Directories

Make sure your virtual directories are named and set up the way you think they should be. Remember that the URL to a virtual directory has the form:

```
//<computername>/<alias>
```

The location of the files on your computer doesn't matter—virtual directories are always accessed this way.

Default Document

If "not found" errors occur when you access WWW service directories without specifying a Web page (i.e., the URL ends with the name of a directory, not with an HTML file name), check your default document settings. Make sure you actually have a home page on the server or in the virtual directory that matches the name entered in the default document field of the directories tab.

Service-Based Denial

If no one is able to access your site, or if only some computers can't, make sure you aren't denying access by default under the advanced settings for the service in question. If you have a firewall, you should use its security mechanisms, rather than IIS, to prohibit or allow access to your Internet Server if possible. Many public Internet servers are outside firewalls, however, so you may want to specifically deny access to certain computers, especially if your server has been subjected to attacks by hackers.

Directory Executable/Readable Settings

If your Active Server Pages or Java applets are showing up as garbled code in Web pages, you need to activate the executable service property for the virtual directory in which they are stored. If you can't read files you know exist in a directory, check the readable setting for the virtual directory to make sure they're available. In general, all HTML, JavaScript, and VBScript content files should be in directories that have the Read WWW Service option set, whereas all Active Server Pages, CGI, and ISAPI applications should be stored in directories that have the executable option set, but not the Read option.

Secure Socket Layer

If you've installed Secure Socket Layer, but people are able to attach to your site without using it, you need to check the Require Secure Socket Layer settings under the service property for the specific virtual directory in question. You must have a certificate in order to require Secure Socket Layer.

IIS General Errors

The error messages presented in Table 15.1 are configuration errors you may run into when setting up IIS or virtual directories. Most of them are obscure, so you will probably never see them. You may need to reinstall IIS to fix many of these problems.

TABLE 15.1 Internet Information Server Error Messages	**Error Message**	**Meaning**
	A home directory already exists for this service. Creating a new home directory will cause the existing directory to no longer be a home directory. An alias will be created for the existing home directory.	You have chosen the Home directory option for a virtual server when one already exists. You can continue if you want to replace the home directory with the new directory.
	Invalid Server Name	The server name you entered does not resolve to a valid host.
	More than 1 home directory was found. An automatic alias will be generated instead.	Duplicate directory entries exist in the virtual directories table. Delete both, then recreate one.
	No administerable services found.	IIS is not running on the target machine. IIS may not be started or may not be installed.
	The alias you have given is invalid for a non-home directory.	The '/' alias is automatically assigned to the home directory and cannot be reassigned.
	The connection attempt failed because there's a version conflict between the server and client software.	IIS does not match the administration tool you are attempting to use. Make sure the tool is compatible with your version of IIS.
	The service configuration DLL 'filename' failed to load correctly.	An IIS configuration DLL is corrupt, has been replaced by a DLL of the same name from another application, or is an incompatible version. Uninstall and then reinstall IIS.
	Unable to connect to target machine.	The target computer is offline or unreachable.
	Unable to create directory.	The directory name is invalid or already exists.

Summary

The maintenance of IIS over a period of time involves performance optimization and troubleshooting. Performance optimization is the systematic process of eliminating performance limitations in a system until an inherent bottleneck like network I/O is the only limiting factor.

IIS and Index Server both add numerous performance counters to the Performance Monitor built into Windows NT. These counters enable you to determine exactly what sort of usage is limiting the performance of your Internet Server, and armed with that knowledge you can take measures to fix the problem.

Using the logs that IIS generates automatically will help you profile the use of your server over time. Crystal Reports can help you mine valuable statistics about your server's use and report on them in various useful ways.

Index Server is largely self-tuning and automatic—but there are still a few ways to optimize its performance. Limiting the indexing of files to only registered types is a great way to keep your indexes small and your queries relevant and fast, as long as your files conform to the use of standard file extensions. You can also change the timing of merges to correspond more closely to the actual use of your machine and move the index to other hard disks to relieve the burden on your primary storage volumes.

Most IIS problems are either connectivity or security related. Using a few simple tricks, you can verify the path to an Internet host and make sure it is serving the protocols to which you wish to attach. After that, any problems you may have will either be security related or related to the configuration of the Internet host.

Review Questions

1. Users are complaining that Web pages are taking a lot longer to load than they used to. Using the Performance Monitor, you determine that your intranet server is bandwidth limited because it is attached to your network via a single Ethernet network adapter. Which repairs are appropriate? (Choose all that apply.)

    A. Use throttling to restrict bandwidth to the amount supported by the network link.

    B. Upgrade the link technology to fast Ethernet.

    C. Implement disk striping to speed access to the Web pages.

    D. Upgrade to the latest version of IIS, which is faster than previous versions.

    E. Optimize the content on your site by making images smaller, eliminating graphical content when possible, and providing text-only pages for people who don't care to see images.

2. Index Server queries are taking too long. You've already restricted queries to types you actually want queried, but because of heavy usage, the Index Server is still not able to keep up. Using the Performance Monitor, you determine that shadow merges and master merges are happening far too often because new documents are being updated frequently. Which optimizations will help? (Choose all that apply.)

    A. Increase the amount of disk space allocated for shadow merges.

    B. Change the default master merge time to occur at 4:00 A.M. when the network is less loaded.

    C. Increase the amount of disk space allocated to catalogs.

    D. Implement bandwidth throttling to limit the number of simultaneous queries.

    E. Install more RAM and increase the amount of memory reserved for word lists to stave off shadow merges and master merges.

    F. Move the catalog to a disk different than the corpus to reduce the time that merges take to execute.

3. Your Index Server queries are returning CGI scripts as well as normal documents. How can you prevent this?

    A. Use NTFS file system permissions to disallow access to CGI files for anonymous Internet users.

B. Allow only Execute permissions to the CGI directories in the directory permissions dialog for all virtual directories.

C. Uncheck the CGI script virtual roots in the Index Server Administrator.

D. Create multiple catalogs so that all CGI scripts appear in one catalog and all other content appears in another.

4. You've noticed that special HTML files created by FrontPage for administration purposes keep showing up in Index Server queries along with your published Web pages. You want to keep these files from showing up in your customer's searches, but you still need to be able to use FrontPage to edit your site. Which methods can you use? (Choose all that apply.)

A. Use NTFS security features to restrict access to the directories that contain FrontPage special files, allowing access only to those accounts that modify the FrontPage Webs.

B. Edit the Index Server registry settings to restrict query filtering to published Web page types.

C. Uncheck the virtual roots that contain the FrontPage Web directories in the Index Server Administration pages.

D. Delete the FrontPage Web directories and special files.

E. Move published Web pages to "production" virtual roots, then uncheck indexing of the virtual roots that contain the FrontPage Webs.

5. You want to optimize the content of your Web server, but you don't have a lot of time to spend on the problem. How can you determine which pages deserve the most attention?

A. Use the Performance Monitor to determine which directories are hit most often.

B. Use Crystal Reports to find the ten most accessed Web pages. Optimize these pages first.

C. Use Crystal Reports to identify the most frequent users. Send them e-mail asking which portions of the site deserve the most attention.

D. Use the Performance Monitor to analyze network performance. When network throughput peaks, use the server manager to determine which files are open.

6. Some external customers cannot log on to your Internet Web site, while others have no problem. You've checked to make sure that no firewall or specific service-based restrictions are in effect. Logon authentication is set to allow only Windows NT Challenge/Response and to require Secure Socket Layer because you don't want the general public using your system. Which of the following are possible problems? (Choose all that apply.)

A. Some users are using Netscape 3.0, which doesn't support Windows NT Challenge/Response authentication.

B. Some users may not have the Windows NT domain account set up correctly, so they can't log on to IIS.

C. Some customers may be behind firewalls that don't pass SSL traffic.

D. Some users may have forgotten their passwords.

APPENDIX

A

Answers to Review Questions

Chapter 1

1. You need a computer (and operating system) to serve as a World Wide Web server for your company's Web site. Which of the following can you use to host the Web site? (Choose all that apply.)

   A. UNIX

   B. MacOS

   C. Windows NT Server

   D. Novell NetWare

   Answer: A, B, C, D. All the above operating systems can host World Wide Web sites.

2. You have created a simple company Web site that contains information about your company and brochures about your company's products. You would like to put this Web site on the Internet with the minimum of fuss and cost, but you want a large number of people to be able to access it simultaneously. You want customers to connect to the Web site using the address www.yourcompany.com. What is your best option?

   A. Lease a T1 line and purchase a UNIX workstation. Set up the workstation to host the Web site and connect it to the Internet with the T1.

   B. Put a 33.6Kbps modem into a PC running Windows NT Workstation. Dial in to your local Internet service provider and leave the PC constantly connected. Serve your Web site using Peer Web Services.

   C. Contract with your Internet service provider to host your Web site. Place the Web pages on the Internet service provider's Web server.

   D. Get a personal account on an online information service such as AOL. Place the Web pages under your personal account.

   Answer: C. Your Internet service provider will host your Web site and make it look like you have a computer of your own responding to that Internet address.

3. Your company sells garden tools. You would like customers to be able to browse your Web site, select tools and supplies, have the selections itemized and totaled, and then order and pay for the items over the Internet using a credit card. You have a database containing tools and prices and

customer information. You don't want anyone outside of your company to be able to access those credit card numbers. What is your best option for fast and secure hosting of this kind of Web site?

A. Lease a T1 line and install Windows NT on a computer. Set up the computer with Internet Information Server to host the Web site and connect it to the Internet with the T1.

B. Put a 33.6Kbps modem into a PC running Windows NT Workstation. Dial in to your local Internet service provider and leave the PC constantly connected. Serve your Web site using Peer Web Services.

C. Contract with your Internet service provider to host your Web site. Place the Web pages on the Internet service provider's Web server.

D. Get a personal account on an online information service such as AOL. Place the Web pages under your personal account.

Answer: A. Windows NT Server with Internet Information Server can host a secure Web site with encrypted communications and database access.

4. Which of the following Internet services would you use to get files off the Internet? (Choose two.)

A. FTP

B. Telnet

C. Usenet News

D. World Wide Web

Answer: A, D. The FTP protocol is designed to store and retrieve files on remote computers, and through the World Wide Web you can both access FTP sites and download files from Web sites.

Chapter 2

1. After having your Web site hosted for six months, your Internet service provider tells you that your site on average consumes 400Kb/s during business hours. You've decided to move the Web site onto your own server to support running some CGI scripts to take customer orders.

You estimate this switch may double or triple the bandwidth required for your site. Which data link technology should you use?

A. 56K frame relay service from the local telephone company (cost: $500/mo).

B. T1 frame relay service from the local telephone company (cost: $2,000/mo).

C. T3 frame relay service from the local telephone company (cost: $15,000/mo).

D. Access to an FDDI metropolitan area network provided by an alternate carrier (cost: $5,000/mo).

Answer: B. T1 covers the bit rate with room to spare and is less expensive than C and D. 56K is inadequate.

2. After running a public access Web site about treatment options for athlete's foot for a few months, you notice some files are missing in the wwwroot directory. You suspect someone may have gained access through the Internet and somehow deleted the files. How can you prevent this kind of intrusion in the future without inhibiting normal access?

A. Require a logon to the server and use NTFS file permissions to restrict the files to read only.

B. Disconnect the Web server from the Internet and make it an intranet.

C. Implement PPTP or Secure Socket Layer to encrypt the data.

D. Put in a firewall.

Answer: D. Options A and B restrict access, Option C won't work.

3. You are considering using your Pentium-150 desktop computer as an Internet server. It has 16 megabytes of RAM and a 420 MB hard disk drive. You load Windows NT Server 4 and Internet Information Server and configure all the services. You also will be using the server to route traffic to the T1 circuit from your Ethernet LAN and to resolve Internet and NetBIOS names. This computer:

A. Won't work.

B. Will work, but will be very slow because the hard disk is small.

C. Will work, but will be slow because it doesn't have enough RAM.

D. Will work very well.

Answer: C. This computer will work but will be extremely slow because it doesn't have enough RAM.

4. You've just installed a leased 56K circuit and an Ethernet router to allow Internet access for all the clients on your 30-computer LAN. Your network is segmented into four networks each attached to the server through a network adapter. After adding TCP/IP services to each client computer, you remove the NWLink service from the server to increase efficiency. Users now complain that they can't see some network printers and computers in their Network Neighborhood windows. You verify that you can PING the computers and printers from computers on different subnets, so the server must be routing properly. No one is having problems accessing the server or the Internet. What is wrong?

A. You need to implement the WINS service.

B. You haven't properly configured the default gateway setting.

C. You haven't configured the server to forward TCP/IP broadcasts.

D. You need to implement the DNS service.

Answer: A. WINS allows a server to maintain a master browse list and resolve NetBIOS names to IP addresses.

Chapter 3

1. You need a Web server for your Windows NT Server computer that will allow you to establish virtual Web sites. Select the most correct observation.

A. Windows NT will run any Web server software, and all Web server software packages support virtual servers.

B. Only Microsoft IIS both runs on Windows NT Server and allows you to create virtual servers.

    C. Both IIS and Netscape Enterprise Server run on Windows NT Server and support virtual Web servers.

    D. Both IIS and Novell Web Server run on Windows NT Server and support virtual directories.

Answer: C

2. If the Web server you select does not support direct database access via ODBC, which Web server mechanism can you use to provide database access?

    A. You can use LDAP to access database information.

    B. You cannot access database information if you do not have direct support for ODBC in your Web server.

    C. You can use server-side includes to access database information.

    D. You can use CGI scripts to access database information.

Answer: D

3. You need to support the FTP and Gopher Internet services as well as the World Wide Web. Which of the following observations are true?

    A. IIS, Peer Web Services, Netscape Enterprise Server, and NCSA HTTPd all support all three Internet services.

    B. You can use IIS and Peer Web Services to provide all three Internet services.

    C. Only IIS provides all three Internet services.

    D. FTP and Gopher services are always provided by separate software packages.

Answer: B

4. You need a Windows NT Server Web Server package with search capability. Which of the following fits your needs? (Choose all that apply.)

    A. Peer Web Services

    B. NCSA HTTPd

    C. IIS with Index Server

D. Netscape Enterprise Server

Answer: C, D

Chapter 4

1. One of your users is having trouble attaching to your Web site. From your Internet Explorer browser, you have no problem attaching with your test user account. You try attaching at the server and also have no difficulty. But when you try attaching from that user's computer running Netscape 3.0 with your account, you get an Access Denied message. You check the Advanced options in the Internet Service Manager and determine that all computers are by default allowed access and no specific exclusions are listed. What is wrong?

A. The HTML page is protected with NTFS security restrictions for that user.

B. The computer does not have the TCP/IP protocol stack installed.

C. The user is using the wrong password.

D. The HTTP service is only using Windows NT Challenge/Response security.

Answer: D. No other answer explains why your account cannot attach from that user's computer given that the service is running, that the Access denied response is being served, and that the computer is not specifically denied access.

2. You want to provide FTP file access to some documents stored on an older NetWare server at your site. Your Web server doesn't have enough storage space for them, you have no budget for upgrades, and the users that own them don't want you to move the files from their current location. What should you do?

A. Create a virtual server that is configured to access the NetWare server.

B. Create a virtual directory that specifies the network drive attached to the NetWare server.

    C. Create a virtual root and index it using Index Server. This step will create a local catalog that can be browsed on the Web server.

    D. Convert the NetWare server to Windows NT Server 4, install IIS, and specify the file location as the `wwwroot` directory.

    E. You cannot provide this type of file access because of the restrictions in the system.

Answer: B. Virtual directories can load files from shares on other computers.

3. Your company purchases a small competitor and wants to retain that company's brands, logos, trademarks, and other image-related properties. The acquisition's Internet site is closed, and its employees move to your facility. You copy the Web site files onto your server but want that site to appear as it always has on the Internet. What should you do?

    A. Put a link on your company's home page to the `default.htm` file of the newly acquired company.

    B. Inform InterNIC that the company's IP address has changed to your company's IP address. This action will forward requests to `www.them.com` to your server.

    C. Create a virtual server, update the IP address for the company's domain name to reflect a new unique IP address in your subnet, and install the original site files in the virtual server root.

    D. Create a virtual directory, update the IP address for the company's domain name to reflect a new unique IP address in your subnet, and install the original site files in the virtual server root.

Answer: C. B is incorrect because your home page will appear when users attach to the acquired company's Web site. Answer A does not satisfy the criteria of no apparent changes, and D simply doesn't work.

4. You install a new content filter in Index Server designed to display PostScript files. When you run a query using words that you know appear in Display PostScript Documents in your `wwwroot` directory, no Display PostScript files appear in the query. What should you do?

    A. Force a scan to activate the new content filter.

B. Add the `wwwroot` directory to the Index Server list of scanned directories—it's not included by default.

C. Force a Master Merge to include the catalog created for PostScript files.

D. Create a new catalog for displaying PostScript files.

Answer: A. Forcing a scan assures that newly installed content filters index files of their respective type.

Chapter 5

1. You have a multihomed server with two network interfaces installed. All client computers can communicate with the server correctly, but you can attach only to resources shared by peers on the same physical data link; in addition, your browser does not show computers on the other network. What service should you install to correct the problem?

   A. DCHP

   B. DNS

   C. WINS

   D. TCP/IP

   Answer: C. WINS allows Windows name resolution across networks.

2. You've set up a single Fast Ethernet network based on TCP/IP. Your file server and primary domain controller also acts as a DHCP server. Everything works fine until you attach a router that connects to a T1 line attached to your new Internet Service Provider. You find that none of your clients seem to be able to attach to servers on the Internet. When you try to Ping an address you know exists on the Internet, you get an error message stating that the destination is unreachable. What is wrong?

   A. The WINS service is not correctly configured.

   B. You need to enable IP forwarding on the server.

   C. Your ISP is not providing DNS.

D. The DHCP server did not assign a default gateway.

Answer: D. You must assign a default gateway so clients can route to other networks.

3. You are responsible for a network of 358 clients and 16 servers. You expect to add about 50 computers over the next two years to keep up with normal company growth. You are about to start the process of attaching your network to the Internet. How many bits of local address space should you request when you request your domain?

A. 7

B. 8

C. 9

D. 10

Answer: C. Nine bits allows 510 IP addresses ($2^9 = 512 - 2 = 510$).

4. You are responsible for a TCP/IP domain of 3,488 computers. Assuming that you have not subnetted your original 12-bit local address space, what should your subnet mask be?

A. 255.255.240.0

B. 255.255.248.0

C. 255.255.254.0

D. 255.255.255.0

Answer: A. A 12-bit subnet mask equals 11111111.11111111 .11110000.00000000 (255.255.240.0).

5. You have a multihomed server that serves three Ethernets. For some reason, only clients on the same data link as your Ethernet-to-T1 router can attach to the Internet. You check your server and verify that IP forwarding is set up, no conflicting IP addresses exist, and that every network adapter in the server shows the address of the router as the default route. What is wrong?

A. You must install DNS to resolve names across the network.

B. You need to install WINS for clients on other data links to see the router.

C. The DHCP server did not assign a default gateway.

D. You've specified more than one default route, but only one exists.

Answer: D. You must assign the default route only to the adapter actually attached to the Internet.

6. You have a 50-computer network, and you want to use a single server with three network adapters to attach to three different Ethernet network hubs so you can maximize your network bandwidth. One Ethernet network has 12 computers, one has 22 computers, and one has 16 computers. What is the smallest subnet mask that will work with your network?

A. 255.255.255.248

B. 255.255.255.240

C. 255.255.255.224

D. 255.255.255.192

Answer: C. This subnet mask allows 30 IP addresses per subnet—enough for the 22-computer network without wasting a large range of IP addresses.

Chapter 6

1. Your main business is selling aluminum siding, but you have a second business in aluminum recycling. You want to set up a separate Web site for each business. What is your best option?

A. Buy two Windows NT Server computers and run IIS on each.

B. Install IIS twice on your Windows NT Server computer. Configure the second copy to respond to port 8080 instead of port 80.

C. Register two IP addresses for your Windows NT Server computer running IIS. Create two home directories and WWW Service directory entries for each. Then assign each directory a different IP address in the Directories tab of the WWW Service Properties window.

D. Register two IP addresses for your Windows NT Server computer running IIS. Place the files for one business in the home directory (`wwwroot`). Create a new directory for the other business and in the Directories tab of the WWW Service Properties window make that directory a virtual directory (give it the alias `/business2`).

Answer: C. Each virtual server (not virtual directory!) gets its own home directory.

2. Your business is providing network support on retainer for professional firms that can usually handle their own computer problems, but you also compile shareware tools for network administration. You want to set up two FTP sites: one for your business and one for your hobby. You do not want to purchase another computer, and Windows NT will not run multiple versions of the IIS services simultaneously. Select the best response:

A. The FTP service does not support virtual directories.

B. The FTP service does not support virtual servers.

C. Register two IP addresses for your Windows NT Server computer running IIS. Create two home directories and WWW Service directory entries for each and then assign each directory a different IP address in the Directories tab of the WWW Service Properties window.

D. Register two IP addresses for your Windows NT Server computer running IIS. Place the files for the business in the home directory (`wwwroot`). Create a new directory for the hobby, and in the Directories tab of the WWW Service Properties window, make that directory a virtual directory. (Give it the alias `/hobby`.)

Answer: B. Only WWW Service directories support virtual servers.

3. You have created a key for your WWW server; sent, received back, and installed a certificate; and stopped and restarted your WWW service. The Require SSL option for WWW directories still remains gray, however. What is wrong?

A. WWW does not support the Secure Socket Layer protocol.

B. You have not given the WWW Service directory an IP address.

C. You have not checked the Windows NT Authentication/Response option.

D. You cannot require SSL on a home directory.

Answer: C. Before you can require Secure Socket Layer connections in IIS, you must enable Windows NT Challenge/Response.

4. How do you configure IIS to run Perl CGI scripts? (Perl scripts have the extension `.pl`.)

A. Select Enable CGI Extensions in the Microsoft Internet Service Manger and select Perl (`.pl`) from the list of scripting languages.

B. Use the Registry Editor to add an entry for Perl to the `HKEY_ LOCAL_MACHINE\SYSTEM\CurrentControlSet\Services\W3SVC\ Parameters\Script Map` key.

C. Use the Registry Editor to add an entry for Perl to the `HKEY_ LOCAL_MACHINE\SYSTEM\CurrentControlSet\Services\ Inetinfo\Parameters\MimeMap` key.

D. You cannot add to the already supported CGI extensions.

Answer: B. The `W3SVC\Parameters\Script Map` key contains the list of extensions for CGI scripts and where to find the programs that process files with those extensions.

5. How do you ensure that the Index Server search engine does not return a document that the user shouldn't see?

A. Remove the Searchable option from WWW Service directories that the user should not access.

B. Establish correct NTFS permissions so that the user doesn't have access to those directories or files.

C. Create a CGI script that will parse the result of the query and remove any objectionable entries.

D. Do not provide a search service if you are concerned about security.

Answer: B. If you establish appropriate security for the user account that actually accesses the files (IUSER_<computername> for anonymous access or the user name of the individual for authenticated access), then Index Server will not return entries that the user shouldn't see. Index Server checks each entry against the files that the user is permitted to view.

Chapter 7

1. You need to set up a Web and FTP site that will be available to the general public to download support files and to your in-house engineers to upload files via FTP. You decide to use the Internet Service Manager to restrict your FTP and Web sites to read-only access rather than using NTFS file security. This option:

   A. Solves neither problem

   B. Solves both problems

   C. Solves the download problem but not the upload problem

   D. Solves the upload problem but not the download problem

   Answer: C. File uploading requires write access, so the IIS read-only restriction is not appropriate.

2. You need to set up a Web and FTP site that will be available to the general public to download support files and to your in-house engineers to upload files via FTP. You decide to use NTFS file system security to restrict your FTP and Web sites to read-only access for the Internet Anonymous user account. This option:

   A. Solves neither problem

   B. Solves both problems

   C. Solves the download problem but not the upload problem

   D. Solves the upload problem but not the download problem

   Answer: B. NTFS security is both more flexible and more secure than IIS service restrictions.

3. You need to set up a Web and FTP site that will be available to the general public to download support files and to your in-house engineers to upload files via FTP. You decide to use share-level security to restrict your FTP and Web sites to read-only access for the Internet Anonymous user account. This option:

   A. Solves neither problem

B. Solves both problems

C. Solves the download problem but not the upload problem

D. Solves the upload problem but not the download problem

Answer: A. Share permissions normally have no effect on Internet users because they are usually logged on locally to the Web server.

4. You've implemented a Web site on your file server and intend to use NTFS file system security to secure the site. When you right-click the directory that you intend to secure and select properties, you notice that there's no Security tab so you can't set file system security. What's wrong?

   A. The volume is formatted with the FAT file system.

   B. You haven't turned on file auditing.

   C. You haven't enabled file system security in the Internet Service Manager.

   D. You aren't logged in as the administrator so you can't change security permissions.

   Answer: A. FAT volumes have no security options.

5. You've implemented an intranet server and are using NTFS file system security to restrict permissions by department in your organization. You've made some information available to the Anonymous logon account. Your server is set to allow Anonymous logon for untrusted access from the Internet and basic text authentication to allow security domain account holders to log on from any operating system that provides logon credentials. Bob, a new hire, tells you he can access the site from his Windows 95 computer using Internet Explorer, but he can't get access to his department's area in the site. You check his group membership and verify that he is a member of his department's group. No one else is reporting any problems. What might be wrong? (Select all correct answers.)

   A. Bob's account has a specific denial because he is a member of the New Hire group.

   B. Bob is using a Web browser that does not support the security mechanism.

C. Bob's computer does not have the TCP/IP protocol stack correctly installed.

D. Bob's network adapter is malfunctioning.

E. Bob has not logged on to the domain, so his browser is automatically logging on as the Anonymous user.

Answers: A, E. Both specific denial and lack of permission could cause this problem.

Chapter 8

I. You suspect that someone on the Internet is trying to gain unauthorized access to files on your Windows NT Server. How can you verify your suspicions?

A. Disconnect your Internet Server computer from the network.

B. Assign only Read permission to all files and directories from the InetPub directory down.

C. Use Crystal Reports on the IIS log files data to show the percentage of Unauthorized, Forbidden, or Not Found access attempts per client IP address.

D. Examine the System Log portion of the Event Viewer for unauthorized access attempts.

Answer: C. If you find an IP address that is the source of an unusually large number of bad access attempts, then someone may be trying to compromise your security.

2. You determine that most of the unauthorized access attempts on your server computer come from one Class C subnetwork. What can you do to make sure that this subnetwork cannot threaten your Internet Information Server?

A. Use Crystal Reports on the IIS log files data to show the percentage of Unauthorized, Forbidden, or Not Found access attempts per client IP address.

B. In the Advanced tab of each service, disallow access from that subnet.

C. In the Services tab of the Networking control panel, disallow access from that subnet.

D. Remove the TCP/IP default route to that subnet.

Answer: B. You can cause IIS to ignore network requests or commands from any IP address or set of addresses from the Advanced tab of each service.

3. You need software to hide your client computers on your LAN from the Internet and to perform Web requests for them. Which software or hardware package will do what you want?

A. Internet Information Server

B. Index Server

C. A packet filter

D. A proxy server

Answer: D. A proxy server stands between your LAN and the Internet and makes Web requests on behalf of your client Web browsers.

Chapter 9

1. Four departments in your company maintain your Web site: marketing, engineering, information systems, and human resources. You've noticed that the different pages have very little stylistic similarity and in fact look more like four different Web sites. The CEO has also noticed this variation and asks you to do something to maintain a consistent company image across the Web site. What is the most efficient way to encourage a coherent and unified image on the Web?

A. Use NTFS file permissions to control write access to the site. Have all departments submit all material to you for final production and posting on the site.

B. Create a style guide and insist that all contributors follow it.

C. Produce the Web site without input from the other departments.

D. Use IIS security options to restrict the uploading of files to the site. Have all departments submit all material to you for final production and posting on the site.

Answer: B. A style guide is the most efficient way to encourage a unified image.

2. You purchase Windows NT Server for use as an Internet/intranet server. You have 45 internal users and expect traffic of up to 100 Internet browsers at any one time. You install a 16-port multiport serial board with 16 modems attached so that your traveling sales force can dial into the intranet site. You do not allow access to the server for file or print sharing. How many client access licenses must you purchase?

A. 59

B. 45

C. 145

D. 159

E. 16

F. 100

Answer: E. You only need client access licenses to support the 16 dial-in RAS users in this configuration.

3. You set up a Windows NT server computer for a network of 50 users to provide the normal services of a file and print server. You also install IIS to host an intranet site for those users and another 150 intranet users attached to your organization's backbone. How many client access licenses must you purchase?

A. 50

B. 150

C. 200

Answer: A. You do not need client access licenses for intranet users using services based entirely on Internet protocols, so you need only 50 licenses (for the users using file and print services).

4. You are setting up an Internet site with both HTTP and FTP services dedicated to promulgating Microsoft services and software for your clients. You want to host software that Microsoft gives away on its Web site, so you download the software from the Microsoft site and host it on your Web server. You are

   A. Violating copyright law because you don't have Microsoft's permission to host the software.

   B. Not violating copyright law because the software is publicly available and you can prove that by maintaining records of the Web URLs from which you downloaded the software.

   C. Violating copyright law because you downloaded the software without paying for it.

   D. Not violating copyright law because the software is freeware.

   Answer: A. You must obtain permission from the copyright owner to distribute original works.

5. You are setting up an Internet site with both HTTP and FTP services dedicated to promulgating Microsoft services and software for your clients. You want to host software that Microsoft gives away on its Web site, so you include links directly to the pages inside Microsoft's Web site where the software is hosted. You are

   A. Violating copyright law because you don't have Microsoft's permission to host the software.

   B. Not violating copyright law because you aren't hosting the software.

   C. Violating copyright law because your site is set up as if the software were local to your machine and because you could potentially bypass Microsoft's copyright notices.

   D. Not violating copyright law because the software is freeware.

   Answer: B. Links to other servers cannot be construed as copyright violation.

6. Customers are complaining that your Web site downloads too slowly. You've already reduced the color depth of your home page image map to the services on the rest of the site, but your customers still are not happy. Which solution is most effective?

   A. Tell your customers to get faster connections to the Internet.

   B. Increase your lease-line rate from T1 to T3.

   C. Use a Java applet instead of a large image map.

   D. Eliminate the image map in favor of a few graphical buttons and a monochrome background image.

   Answer: D. Reducing the required bandwidth is always the optimal solution.

Chapter 10

1. Your company has an open book policy. The controller wants to make some financial data available on the company's intranet, but doesn't want to bother learning the intricacies of Web design. Which solution is optimal for the controller?

   A. Create a link to a new document in FrontPage and have the controller save a copy of the financial data as an HTML document from within Excel.

   B. Have the controller import the financial data into FrontPage so it can be linked into the corporate intranet directly.

   C. Import the data into Word and use the Save as HTML feature to add a page to your FrontPage Web.

   D. Use Access to create the entire site, as it is the only Office application capable of maintaining tables of complex data.

   Answer: A. Finance professionals are very familiar with spreadsheets, and this method doesn't require knowledge of another product.

2. You are designing an online catalog for a small company. Customers will need to view and browse a catalog, but the company is not yet willing to begin an online ordering service. You will export your catalog to HTML from an Office application that the company already owns. Which solution is optimal for this situation?

A. Use Excel to maintain the catalog because it can automatically sub-total the products the customer selects.

B. Use Word to maintain the catalog. Word is the best Office application to use for general HTML files because its internal format is similar to HTML.

C. Use FrontPage to maintain all Web data—it is far superior to the Office applications for HTML.

D. Use Access to maintain the catalog because it handles large data sets very well.

Answer: D. Access is the best Office application for maintaining large data sets such as catalogs.

3. Customers are complaining that some of your Web pages are formatted strangely and are difficult to read. You created the Web pages using FrontPage and the Office applications, and they look fine in your version of Internet Explorer. What should you do?

A. The HTML code created by FrontPage and the Office applications work correctly only with Internet Explorer. Encourage the customers to upgrade.

B. The customers' Web browsers do not support Active Server Pages. Downgrade your site to older Web technology.

C. Check your public pages on all available Web browsers. Debug and tune your HTML code until it looks acceptable on as many browsers as possible.

D. Office applications create very primitive HTML documents. Use FrontPage to create all Web documents.

Answer: C. All Web browsers are slightly different, and variables such as screen size and color depth will affect the way your site appears. Always check your pages using all available browsers and platforms.

Chapter 11

1. You are creating a client/server database application that will interface your customers to a private database stored on your server. Security is not a concern because none of your customers will be using the Web browser to browse other sites. You can dictate which browser they use to attach to your site, and you need the shortest possible development cycle. Which Web browser and active content solution for the client application fits your needs best?

   A. Internet Explorer with VBScript and ActiveX controls that access data on your SQL server directly.

   B. Either Internet Explorer or Netscape Navigator running a custom Java applet that responds to a Java server running on the same machine as your SQL server.

   C. Either Internet Explorer or Netscape Navigator running a purely JavaScript client application.

   D. This application is too complex for the standard client-side active content tools.

   Answer: A. In this application ActiveX and VBScript offer the fastest development cycle.

2. You are developing an Internet public debate forum Web server that will include a custom written chat client and links to other resources on the Web. Security is a requirement, and you want to support the widest variety of browsers and platforms. Which client-side active content tool will best fit your needs?

   A. JavaScript

   B. VBScript

C. ActiveX

D. Java

Answer: D. Only Java meets these requirements.

3. You are creating a Web site containing links to Internet gaming resources on the Web and want to be able to include animated banners from your sponsors. You aren't a programmer, so simplicity is a big requirement, and you don't want to force people to use a specific Web-browser to see the ads. Which client-side content tool will work best for you?

A. JavaScript

B. VBScript

C. ActiveX

D. Java

Answer: A. JavaScript is the most widely supported simple scripting language for Web browsers.

4. Your company is considering developing an Internet-based client for its database so that data entry clerks can work from home. Security is the most important factor, but keeping costs down is always important. What solution do you recommend?

A. Internet Explorer with VBScript and ActiveX controls that access data on your SQL server directly via an Secure Socket Layer connection.

B. Either Internet Explorer or Netscape Navigator running a custom Java applet that responds to a Java server running on the same machine as your SQL server via an SSL connection.

C. Either Internet Explorer or Netscape Navigator running a purely JavaScript client application via PPTP.

D. This application is too complex for the standard client-side active content tools.

Answer: A or B will work, but A is better. In this application ActiveX and VBScript offer the fastest development cycle. ActiveX security is not a problem because you control the quality of ActiveX controls on your own site.

Chapter 12

1. You expect a heavy load on your Web server and you need the fastest way to implement custom Web-based data logging (to a special file on the Web server) and results reporting interactive Web page. Which is your best option?

   A. Implement the routine in Java on the Web browser.

   B. Implement the routine as a custom-written (in C++) ISAPI DLL on the Web server.

   C. Implement the routine using C++ and install it as a CGI executable on your Web server.

   D. Implement the routine in Perl using the PerlIS ISAPI DLL.

   Answer: B. A custom-written ISAPI DLL will have less overhead than the other solutions.

2. You wish to efficiently extend IIS to support encrypted communications for all Web pages using the BLOWFISH cipher. Which environment best fits your needs?

   A. JScript

   B. An ISAPI application

   C. CGI

   D. An ISAPI filter

   Answer: D. An ISAPI filter is an excellent way to control or extend how IIS handles its communications.

3. Which of the following IIS extension mechanisms allows you to accept input from HTML forms and process that information? (Choose all that apply.)

  A. CGI scripts

  B. ISAPI applications

  C. JScript

  D. VBScript

  Answer: A, B, C, D. All the options can accept input from forms and perform calculations on that input.

4. You want to limit the scope of queries from within the /Products/ Software/Downloads section of your Web site to just the that section of your Web site. You want to be able to query your whole site from the home page, however. How can you do this most easily?

  A. Set the CiScope value in the .idq file to /Products/Software/ Downloads.

  B. Remove Read permission for the IUSER_SEARCH user from all directories except for the /Products/Software/Downloads directory.

  C. Disable indexing on all virtual directory except for the /Products/ Software/Downloads virtual directory.

  D. You cannot limit the scope of a query.

  Answer: A. The CiScope value limits the scope of the query.

Chapter 13

1. You are running a small public service Web site detailing treatment options for athlete's foot. You have a database of health care providers and doctors in your area who specialize in the treatment of athlete's foot that you'd like to publish on your site. You update your database perhaps once every three months or so. What database publication method is most appropriate for this type of data?

A. Static

B. Dynamic

C. Interactive

Answer: A. Because your data doesn't change much, there's no point in putting a load on the server every time your database is accessed.

2. You've set up an offshore bookmaking operation. You'll be taking bets online using credit cards, publishing horse racing and sporting results as they become available from your online news feeds, and creating queries of winners and losers so you can credit and debit their card accounts as appropriate. The entire operation must be automatic because you expect a police raid at any time and you don't want to be present when it happens. What database publication method is most appropriate for this type of data?

A. Static

B. Dynamic

C. Interactive

Answer: C. You must use interactive database publication to support this type of interactivity and real-time responsiveness.

3. You've created an Interactive database using Microsoft Access and Active Server Pages, but when you browse to the site, you get garbage on your screen that looks like a computer programming language rather than the database forms you expected. What's wrong?

A. You haven't enabled Active Server Pages output in the IIS Manager.

B. You selected the wrong type of output in the publish to the Internet wizard in Microsoft Access.

C. Your Web browser doesn't support Active Server Pages.

D. You didn't set Execute permissions on the directory containing your database Web files.

Answer: D. Active Server Pages requires Execute permissions.

4. You've decided to set up an intranet database for manufacturing process reporting at your semiconductor fabrication facility. This database will extract information from many internal manufacturing control data sources and summarize it automatically so that corporate managers and top-level distributors from anywhere in the world can check current yield rates, expected inventory levels, and current manufacturing costs. What database publication method is most appropriate for this type of data?

A. Static

B. Dynamic

C. Interactive

Answer: B. The data changes all the time, but there's no requirement for input from remote sources; so dynamic HTML database publication is most appropriate.

5. You want to set up an Internet interactive gaming site that relies on a database to store the current game state for all your connected users. You expect about 100 simultaneous users. You decide to use Microsoft Access as your database engine and Active Server Pages to interface game data in and out of the Access database. This approach means that you will only have to pay for a single Access license. This solution:

A. Is legal and will work fine.

B. Is legal, but won't work because Access isn't powerful enough to support that many concurrent connections.

C. Is illegal, as Access requires a client access license for all concurrent users regardless of the client software used.

Answer: B. You don't need additional licenses for concurrent use with Microsoft Access, but it only supports a maximum of 64 concurrent connections.

6. You will be setting up an SQL server with an order-entry database. The database will have 200 internal data entry clerks who will be entering orders from phone calls to the company's 800 number, and 100 work-at-home data entry clerks who will be entering data from reply mail post cards. The internal data entry clerks will use a custom Visual C++ client that operates quickly (because the customer is on the phone with them)

and directly attaches to the SQL server. The work-at-home data entry clerks will be connected via the Internet using IIS and an ODBC data source. How many SQL client access licenses are required?

A. 100

B. 200

C. 201

D. 300

Answer: D. You must have a client access license for all concurrent users of a Microsoft SQL Server database, no matter how they connect to it (or an unlimited use license).

Chapter 14

1. You are providing a dial-in connection to the Internet for remote computers in your organization. Some of the remote computers do not use Windows 95 or Windows NT. (Some are UNIX computers, and some run the MacOS.) Which authentication protocol should you use?

A. MS-CHAP

B. CHAP

C. PAP

D. SLIP

Answer: C. The Password Authentication Protocol (selected when you choose Allow any authentication including clear text) allows computers that do not support the newer CHAP and MS-CHAP protocols to log on.

2. You need to provide secure communications over the Internet so that remote computers can use an Internet Service Provider local to them to connect to Microsoft networking services on your local area network. Which protocol will provide that secure connection over the Internet?

A. TCP/IP

B. PPTP

C. PPP

D. SLIP

Answer: B. PPTP provides a secure connection using IP over an unsecured network.

3. Windows 95 and Windows NT client computers (which have only the TCP/IP transport protocol installed) are able to connect to your RAS server on your network and are able to access resources on that computer but cannot access any other resources on the network or on the Internet. What is most likely to be the problem?

   A. You do not have the TCP/IP to NetBEUI bridge configured to route IP over your local area network.

   B. You have not selected Entire Network in the RAS Server TCP/IP configuration window.

   C. You have not configured your authentication protocol to Allow any authentication including clear text.

   D. Your client computers have not been configured with or dynamically assigned an IP address.

   Answer: B. The Entire Network option must be enabled for your dial-in computers' communications to be routed over your network.

4. Which of the following transport protocols will provide the most efficient connection to Internet services over dial-up lines, even when you have routers in your network?

   A. NetBEUI

   B. NWLink

   C. TCP/IP

   D. DLC

   Answer: C. Only the TCP/IP transport protocol allows you to connect to the Internet.

5. You wish to encrypt both the logon authentication (password exchange) portion of a dial-up connection and the data that is transferred over the connection. Which type of authentication should you choose?

   A. PAP

   B. CHAP

   C. MS-CHAP

   D. TCP/IP

   Answer: C. The MS-CHAP option (Require Microsoft encrypted authentication) provides you with the option to require data encryption.

6. You have created a Web site that tests out very well through your network connection and now you want to test it using RAS and a dial-up connection. You disable TCP/IP on your network adapter by changing the IP address and removing the default gateway information, but Web pages still load faster than you think they would over your modem. What is wrong?

   A. You didn't restart your computer, so the new TCP/IP settings have not taken effect.

   B. You must also unplug your network adapter cable.

   C. You must also remove the network adapter from the Adapters list in the Networking control panel.

   D. You must clear your Web browser's cache to prevent pages from being displayed out of it.

   Answer: D. If you don't clear the cache, Web pages will load from your own machine, rather than over the dial-up link.

Chapter 15

1. Users are complaining that Web pages are taking a lot longer to load than they used to. Using the Performance Monitor, you determine that your intranet server is bandwidth limited because it is attached to your

network via a single Ethernet network adapter. Which repairs are appropriate? (Choose all that apply.)

A. Use throttling to restrict bandwidth to the amount supported by the network link.

B. Upgrade the link technology to fast Ethernet.

C. Implement disk striping to speed access to the Web pages.

D. Upgrade to the latest version of IIS, which is faster than previous versions.

E. Optimize the content on your site by making images smaller, eliminating graphical content when possible, and providing text-only pages for people who don't care to see images.

Answers: B and E. If you are bandwidth limited, you can either speed up the connection or transmit less information.

2. Index Server queries are taking too long. You've already restricted queries to types you actually want queried, but because of heavy usage, the Index Server is still not able to keep up. Using the Performance Monitor, you determine that shadow merges and master merges are happening far too often because new documents are being updated frequently. Which optimizations will help? (Choose all that apply.)

A. Increase the amount of disk space allocated for shadow merges.

B. Change the default master merge time to occur at 4:00 A.M. when the network is less loaded.

C. Increase the amount of disk space allocated to catalogs.

D. Implement bandwidth throttling to limit the number of simultaneous queries.

E. Install more RAM and increase the amount of memory reserved for word lists to stave off shadow merges and master merges.

F. Move the catalog to a disk different than the corpus to reduce the time that merges take to execute.

Answers: E and F. Increasing the amount of RAM allocated to word lists will stave off merges, and moving the catalog will reduce the time that merges take to execute.

3. Your Index Server queries are returning CGI scripts as well as normal documents. How can you prevent this?

   A. Use NTFS file system permissions to disallow access to CGI files for anonymous Internet users.

   B. Allow only Execute permissions to the CGI directories in the directory permissions dialog for all virtual directories.

   C. Uncheck the CGI script virtual roots in the Index Server Administrator.

   D. Create multiple catalogs so that all CGI scripts appear in one catalog and all other content appears in another.

   Answer: C. All other options either won't work or will restrict normal use of the CGI scripts.

4. You've noticed that special HTML files created by FrontPage for administration purposes keep showing up in Index Server queries along with your published Web pages. You want to keep these files from showing up in your customer's searches, but you still need to be able to use FrontPage to edit your site. Which methods can you use? (Choose all that apply.)

   A. Use NTFS security features to restrict access to the directories that contain FrontPage special files, allowing access only to those accounts that modify the FrontPage Webs.

   B. Edit the Index Server registry settings to restrict query filtering to published Web page types.

   C. Uncheck the virtual roots that contain the FrontPage Web directories in the Index Server Administration pages.

   D. Delete the FrontPage Web directories and special files.

   E. Move published Web pages to "production" virtual roots, then uncheck indexing of the virtual roots that contain the FrontPage Webs.

   Answers: A and E. Both methods will work. **A** is most efficient, but **E** is a good idea if you post changes to your site anyway.

5. You want to optimize the content of your Web server, but you don't have a lot of time to spend on the problem. How can you determine which pages deserve the most attention?

A. Use the Performance Monitor to determine which directories are hit most often.

B. Use Crystal Reports to find the ten most accessed Web pages. Optimize these pages first.

C. Use Crystal Reports to identify the most frequent users. Send them e-mail asking which portions of the site deserve the most attention.

D. Use the Performance Monitor to analyze network performance. When network throughput peaks, use the server manager to determine which files are open.

Answer: B. Crystal Reports is the fastest way to get summary information about the use of your site.

6. Some external customers cannot log on to your Internet Web site, while others have no problem. You've checked to make sure that no firewall or specific service-based restrictions are in effect. Logon authentication is set to allow only Windows NT Challenge/Response and to require Secure Socket Layer because you don't want the general public using your system. Which of the following are possible problems? (Choose all that apply.)

A. Some users are using Netscape 3.0, which doesn't support Windows NT Challenge/Response authentication.

B. Some users may not have the Windows NT domain account set up correctly, so they can't log on to IIS.

C. Some customers may be behind firewalls that don't pass SSL traffic.

D. Some users may have forgotten their passwords.

Answers: A, B, C, and D. All these problems afflict secure Internet sites.

APPENDIX

B

Glossary

A

Access   Microsoft's relational database manager for small workgroups or individual use. See *Database, SQL*.

Access Control Entries (ACE)   Each ACL has an associated ACE which lists the permissions that have been granted or denied to the users and groups listed in the ACL. See *Access Control List*.

Access Control List (ACL)   Lists of security identifiers contained by objects that allow only those processes identified in the list as having the appropriate permission to activate the services of that object. See *Object, Permissions, Security Identifier*.

Access Tokens   Objects containing the security identifier of a running process. A process started by another process inherits the starting process's access token. The access token is checked against each object's ACL to determine whether or not appropriate permissions are granted to perform any requested service. See *Access Control Entries, Access Control List, Object, Permissions, Process, Security Identifier*.

Account Lockout   Specifies how many invalid logon attempts should be tolerated before a user account is locked out. Account lockout is set through User Manager for Domains. See *Security, User Manager for Domains*.

Account Policies   Account policies determine password and logon requirements. Account policies are set through User Manager for Domains. *See User Manager for Domains*.

Accounts   Containers for security identifiers, passwords, permissions, group associations, and preferences for each user of a system. The User Manager for Domains utility is used to administer accounts. See *Groups, Passwords, Permissions, Preferences, Security Identifier*.

ACE   See *Access Control Entries*.

ACL   See *Access Control List*.

Active Server Pages   An extension to Internet Information Server that enables you to run server-side scripts written in JScript or VBScript; those scripts return dynamically created HTML documents based on user input or other variables. See *Internet Information Server*.

ActiveX   Microsoft's control plug-in technology for Web browsers that allows HTML documents to reference compiled controls and to automatically download and install them if they are not already plugged into the Web browser.

Adapter   Any hardware device that allows communications to occur through physically dissimilar systems. This term usually refers to peripheral cards permanently mounted inside computers that provide an interface from the computer's bus to another medium such as a hard disk or a network. See *Network Interface Card, SCSI.*

Address Resolution Protocol (ARP)   An Internet protocol for resolving an IP address into a physical layer address (such as an Ethernet media access controller address). See *Internet Protocol, Physical Layer.*

Administrator Account   A special account in Windows NT that has the ultimate set of security permissions and can assign any permission to any user or group. The Administrator account is used to correct security problems. See *Permissions.*

Administrators   Users who are part of the Administrators group. This group has the ultimate set of security permissions. See *Administrator Account, Groups, Permissions.*

Advanced Projects Agency Network (ARPANET)   Predecessor to the Internet that was developed by the Department of Defense in the late 1960s.

Alias   The reference name of a virtual directory, which appears as a subdirectory in the www root directory. See *Virtual Directory.*

Applet   A small application (typically written in Java) that runs inside another application, such as a Web browser. See *Java.*

Applications   Large software packages that perform specific functions, such as word processing, Web browsing, or database management. Applications typically consist of more than one program. See *Programs.*

Application Layer   The layer of the OSI model that interfaces with User mode programs called applications by providing high-level network services based upon lower-level network layers. Network file systems like named pipes are an example of application layer software. See *Application, Named Pipes, OSI Model.*

ARP   See *Address Resolution Protocol.*

ARPANET   See *Advanced Research Projects Agency Network.*

ASP   See *Active Server Pages.*

Asymmetrical Multiprocessing   A multiple processor architecture in which certain processors are designated to run certain threads or in which scheduling is not done on a fair-share basis. Asymmetrical multiprocessing is easier to implement than symmetrical multiprocessing, but does not scale well as processors are added. See *Microprocessor, Symmetrical Multiprocessing.*

Asynchronous Transfer Mode (ATM)   A wide area transport protocol that runs at many different speeds and supports real-time, guaranteed packet delivery in hardware, as well as lower-quality levels of service on a bandwidth-available basis. ATM will eventually replace all other wide-area protocols, as most worldwide PTSN providers have declared their support for the international standard. See *Public Switched Telephone Network, Wide Area Network.*

Audit Policy   Audit policy determines which user events you wish to track for security reasons. Audit policy can track the success or failure of specified security events; it is set in the User Manager for Domains. See *Security, User Manager for Domains.*

B

Back End   The server side of a client/server application.

Backing Up   The process of writing all the data contained in online mass storage devices to off-line mass storage devices for the purpose of safe keeping. Backups are usually performed from hard disk drives to tape drives. Also referred to as archiving. See *Hard Disk Drive.*

Backup Domain Controllers   Servers that contain accurate replications of the security and user databases; servers can authenticate workstations in the absence of a primary domain controller. See *Primary Domain Controller.*

Baseline   A snapshot of your computer's current performance statistics that can be used for analysis and planning purposes.

Basic Input/Output System (BIOS)   A set of routines in firmware that provides the most basic software interface drivers for hardware attached to the computer. The BIOS contains the bootstrap routine. See *Boot, Driver, Firmware.*

Binding   The process of linking network services to network service providers. The binding facility allows users to define exactly how network services operate in order to optimize the performance of the system. By default, Windows enables all possible bindings. The Network control panel is used to change bindings. See *Data Link Layer, Network Layer*.

BIOS   See *Basic Input/Output System*.

Bit   A binary digit. A numeral having only two possible values, 0 or 1. Computers represent these two values as high (voltage present) or low (no voltage present) state on a control line. Bits are accumulated in sets of certain sizes to represent higher values.

Boot   The process of loading a computer's operating system. Booting usually occurs in multiple phases, each successively more complex until the entire operating system and all its services are running. Also called bootstrap. The computer's BIOS must contain the first level of booting. See *Basic Input/ Output System*.

Boot Partition   The boot partition is the partition that contains the system files. The system files are located in C:\WINNT by default. See *Partition, System Partition*.

BOOTP   See *Bootstrap Protocol*.

Bootstrap Protocol (BOOTP)   Predecessor to the DHCP protocol. BOOTP was used to assign IP addresses to disk-less workstations. See *Dynamic Host Configuration Protocol*.

Bottlenecks   Components operating at their peak capacity that restrict the flow of information through a system. Used singularly, the term indicates the most restrictive component in a system.

Bridge   A device that connects two networks of the same data link protocol by forwarding those packets destined for computers on the other side of the bridge. See *Data Link Layer, Router*.

Browser   A Web browser application or a person using a web browser to retrieve information from the Internet. Also refers to a computer on a Microsoft network that maintains a list of computers and services available on the network. See *Web Browsers*.

C

Caching   A speed optimization technique that keeps a copy of the most recently used data in a fast, high-cost, low-capacity storage device rather than in the device upon which the actual data resides. Caching assumes that recently used data is likely to be used again. Fetching data from the cache is faster than fetching data from the slower, larger storage device. Most caching algorithms also copy next-most-likely to be used data and perform write caching to further improve the speed.

CD-ROM   See *Compact Disk–Read-Only Memory*.

CGI   See *Common Gateway Interface*.

Central Processing Unit (CPU)   The central processing unit of a computer. In microcomputers such as IBM PC compatible machines, the CPU is the microprocessor. See *Microprocessor*.

Certificates   Encrypted electronic documents that attest to authenticity of a service, provider, or vendor of a product. Forgery of certificates is not possible, so users can trust the information the encrypted documents contain. A prerequisite to using the Secure Socket Layer is installation of a key with a valid certificate. See *Key, Secure Socket Layer*.

CIX   See *Commercial Internet Exchange*.

Channel Service Unit/Digital Service Unit   A device used to interface a digital telephony trunk to a serial I/O port.

Client   A computer on a network that subscribes to the services provided by a server. See *Server*.

Client/Server   A network architecture that dedicates certain computers, called *servers,* to act as service providers to other computers, called *clients*, which users operate to perform work. Servers can be dedicated to providing one or more network services such as file storage, shared printing, communications, e-mail, and Web response. See *Peer, Share*.

Client/Server Applications   Applications that split large applications into two components: computer intensive processes that run on application servers and user interfaces that run on clients. Client/server applications communicate over the network through interprocess communication mechanisms. See *Client, Interprocess Communications, Server*.

Code   Synonymous with software but used when the software is the object of discussion, rather than the utility it provides. See *Software*.

Commercial Internet Exchange   Locations where top-tier ISPs maintain routers to route IP packets between their respective networks. CIX locations connect ISPs to form the Internet from discrete TCP/IP wide area networks. See *Internet*.

Common Gateway Interface   A standard for starting programs on the Web server computer that returns dynamically created HTML documents to the HTTP service for transmission to the remote client. A new instance of the CGI application starts each time a connection is made, which can put excessive load on an Internet server.

COM Port   Communications port. A serial hardware interface conforming to the RS-232 standard for low-speed serial communications. See *Modem, Serial*.

Compact Disk–Read-Only Memory (CD-ROM)   A medium for storing extremely large software packages on optical read-only discs. CD-ROM is an adaptation of the CD medium used for distributing digitized music. CD-ROM discs can hold up to 650MB of information and cost very little to produce in large quantities. See *Hard Disk Drive*.

Components   Interchangeable elements of a complex software or hardware system. See *Module*.

Compression   A space optimization scheme that reduces the size (length) of a data set by exploiting the fact that most useful data contains a great deal of redundancy. Compression reduces redundancy by creating symbols smaller than the data they represent and an index that defines the value of the symbols for each compressed set of data.

Computer   A device capable of performing automatic calculations based upon lists of instructions called programs. The computer feeds the results of these calculations (output) to peripheral devices that can represent them in useful ways, such as graphics on a screen or ink on paper. See *Microprocessor*.

Computer Name   A 1- to 15-character NetBIOS name used to uniquely identify a computer on the network. See *Network Basic Input/Output System*.

Control Panel   A software utility that controls the function of specific operating system services by allowing users to change default settings for the service to match their preferences. The registry contains the Control Panel settings on a system and/or per-user basis. See *Account, Registry*.

Cooperative Multitasking   A multitasking scheme in which each process must voluntarily return time to a central scheduling process. If any single process fails to return to the central scheduler, the computer will lock up. Both Windows and the Macintosh operating system use this scheme. See *Preemptive Multitasking, Windows for Workgroups 3.11*.

CPU   See *Microprocessor*.

Crystal Reports   A drill-down data-reporting tool used to extract and report on disparate information contained in many documents. A version is included with IIS to report on IIS log data.

CSU/DSU   See *Channel Service Unit/Digital Service Unit*.

D

Data Link Layer   In the OSI model, the layer that provides the digital interconnection of network devices and the software that directly operates these devices, such as network interface adapters. See *Network Layer, OSI Model, Physical Layer*.

Database   A related set of data organized by type and purpose. The term also can include the application software that manipulates the data. The Windows NT registry (a database itself)contains a number of utility databases such as user account and security information. See *Access, Registry, SQL*.

Datagram   A discrete packet of information that is not a part of a larger data stream.

Default Document   The HTML document returned when no specific page is referenced on a Web server.

Default Shares   Resources shared by default when Windows NT is installed. See *Resource, Share.*

Desktop   A directory that the background of the Windows Explorer shell represents. The default desktop contains objects that contain the local storage devices and available network shares. Also a key operating part of the Windows GUI. See *Explorer.*

Dfs   See *Distributed File System.*

DHCP   See *Dynamic Host Configuration Protocol.*

Dial-Up Connections   Data link layer digital connections made via modems over regular telephone lines. The term *dial-up* refers to temporary digital connections, as opposed to leased telephone lines, which provide permanent connections. See *Data Link Layer, Modem, Public Switched Telephone Network.*

Directories   In a file system directories are containers that store files or other directories. Mass storage devices have a root directory that contains all other directories, thus creating a hierarchy of directories sometimes referred to as a *directory tree.* See *File, File System.*

Directory Replication   The process of copying a directory structure from an import computer to an export computer(s). Any time changes are made to the export computer, the import computer(s) is automatically updated with the changes.

Distributed File System   A method for aliasing directory shares on a network so they show up as subdirectories of other shares in Windows NT.

DNS   See *Domain Name Service.*

Domain   In Microsoft networks a domain is an arrangement of client and server computers referenced by a specific name that share a security permissions database. On the Internet a domain is a named collection of hosts and subdomains, registered with a unique name by the InterNIC. See *InterNIC, Workgroup.*

Domain Controllers   Servers that authenticate workstation network logon requests by comparing a username and password against account information stored in the user accounts database. A user cannot access a domain without authentication from a domain controller. See *Backup Domain Controller, Domain, Primary Domain Controller.*

Domain Name   The textual identifier of a specific Internet Host. Domain names are in the form server.organization.type (`www.microsoft.com`) and are resolved to Internet address by Domain Name servers.

Domain Name Server   An Internet host dedicated to the function of translating fully qualified domain names into IP addresses.

Domain Name Service (DNS)   The TCP/IP network service that translates textual Internet network addresses into numerical Internet network addresses. See *Domain Name, Internet, TCP/IP.*

Drive   See *Hard Disk Drive.*

Drive Letters   Single letters assigned as abbreviations to the mass storage volumes available to a computer. See *Volumes.*

Driver   A program that provides a software interface to a hardware device. Drivers are written for the specific device they control, but they present a common software interface to the computer's operating system, allowing all devices (of a similar type) to be controlled as if they were the same. See *Data Link Layer, Operating System.*

Dynamic Host Configuration Protocol (DHCP)   DHCP is a method of automatically assigning IP addresses to client computers on a network.

E

Electronic Mail (E-Mail)   A type of client/server application that provides a routed, stored-message service between any two user e-mail accounts. E-mail accounts are not the same as user accounts, but a one-to-one relationship usually exists between them. Because all modern computers can attach to the Internet, users can send e-mail over the Internet to any location that has telephone or wireless digital service. See *Internet.*

Encryption   The process of obscuring information by modifying it according to a mathematical function known only to the intended recipient. Encryption secures information being transmitted over nonsecure or untrusted media. See *Security.*

Ethernet   The most popular data link layer standard for local area networking. Ethernet implements the carrier sense multiple access with collision detection (CSMA/CD) method of arbitrating multiple computer access to the same network. This standard supports the use of Ethernet over any type of media including wireless broadcast. Standard Ethernet operates as 10 megabits per second. Fast Ethernet operates at 100 megabits per second. See *Data Link Layer*.

Exchange   Microsoft's messaging application. Exchange implements Microsoft's mail application programming interface (MAPI) as well as other messaging protocols such as POP, SNMP, and faxing to provide a flexible message composition and reception service. See *Electronic Mail, Fax Modems*.

Explorer   The default shell for Windows 95 and Windows NT 4.0. Explorer implements the more flexible desktop objects paradigm, rather than the Program Manager paradigm used in earlier versions of Windows. See *Desktop*.

F

FAT   See *File Allocation Table*.

Fault Tolerance   Any method that prevents system failure by tolerating single faults, usually through hardware redundancy.

Fax Modems   Special modems that include hardware to allow the transmission and reception of facsimiles. See *Exchange, Modem*.

Fiber Distributed Data Interface (FDDI)   A data link layer that implements two counter-rotating token rings at 100 megabits per second. FDDI was a popular standard for interconnecting campus and metropolitan area networks because it allows distant digital connections at high speed, but ATM is replacing FDDI in many sites. See *Asynchronous Transfer Mode, Data Link Layer*.

File Allocation Table (FAT)   The file system used by MS-DOS and available to other operating systems such as Windows (all variations), OS/2, and the Macintosh. FAT has become something of a mass storage compatibility standard because of its simplicity and wide availability. FAT has few fault tolerance features and can become corrupted through normal use over time. See *File System*.

File Attributes   Bits stored along with the name and location of a file in a directory entry that shows status of a file, such as archived, hidden, read-only, etc. Different operating systems use different file attributes to implement such services as sharing, compression, and security.

File System   A software component that manages the storage of files on a mass storage device by providing services that can create, read, write, and delete files. File systems impose an ordered database of files on the mass storage device, called volumes, that use hierarchies of directories to organize files. See *Database, Directories, Files, Mass Storage Device, Volumes.*

File Transfer Protocol (FTP)   A simple Internet protocol that transfers complete files from an FTP server to a client running the FTP client. FTP provides a simple no-overhead method of transferring files between computers, but cannot perform browsing functions. You must know the URL of the FTP server to which you wish to attach. See *Internet, Uniform Resource Locator.*

Files   A set of data stored on a mass storage device identified by a directory entry containing a name, file attributes, and the physical location of the file in the volume. See *Directory, File Attributes, Mass Storage Device, Volume.*

Filter (ISAPI)   A program (DLL) used to extend the capabilities of IIS. See *Internet Information Server.*

Filter (Index Server)   A program (DLL) that can parse documents of a specific format to return a list of index terms for that document.

Firewall   A dual-homed computer attached to both the Internet and an intranet that protects the computers on the intranet from intrusion by blocking connections from untrusted sources and on specific protocols. Firewalls are the strongest form of Internet security yet implemented.

Firmware   Software stored permanently in nonvolatile memory and built into a computer to provide its BIOS and a bootstrap routine. Simple computers may have their entire operating system built into firmware. See *BIOS, Boot, Software.*

Form   A collection of input fields processed by a scripting language or passed to a back-end service.

Format   The process of preparing a mass storage device for use with a file system. There are actually two levels of formatting. Low-level formatting writes a structure of sectors and tracks to the disk with bits used by the mass storage controller hardware. The controller hardware requires this format, and it is independent of the file system. High-level formatting creates file system structures such as an allocation table and a root directory in a partition, thus creating a volume. See *Mass Storage Device, Volume.*

Frame   A data structure that network hardware devices use to transmit data between computers. Frames consist of the addresses of the sending and receiving computers, size information, and a check sum. Frames are envelopes around packets of data that allow them to be addressed to specific computers on a shared media network. See *Ethernet, FDDI, Token Ring.*

Front End   The client side of a client/server application.

FrontPage   Microsoft's Web site organization and Web page content creation application.

FTP   See *File Transfer Protocol.*

G

Gateway   A computer that serves as a router, a format translator, or a security filter for an entire network.

Global Group   A special group that exists only on NT Server domain controllers. A global group's members must be from within its domain. See *Local Group.*

Gopher   Serves text and links to other Gopher sites. Gopher predates HTTP by about a year but has been made obsolete by the richer format provided by HTTP. *See Hypertext Transfer Protocol.*

Graphical User Interface (GUI)   A computer shell program that represents mass storage devices, directories, and files as graphical objects on a screen. A cursor driven by a pointing device such as a mouse manipulates the objects. Typically, icons that can be opened into windows that show the data contained by the object represent the objects. See *Explorer.*

Group Identifiers Security identifiers that contain the set of permissions allowed to a group. When a user account is part of a group, the group identifier is appended to that user's security identifier, thus granting the individual user all the permissions assigned to the group. See *Accounts, Permissions, Security Identifier*.

Groups Security entities to which users can be assigned membership for the purpose of applying the broad set of group permissions to the user. By managing permissions for groups and assigning users to groups, rather than assigning permissions to users, security administrators can keep coherent control of very large security environments. See *Accounts, Global Group, Permissions, Security Local Group*.

GUI See *Graphical User Interface*.

H

HAL See *Hardware Abstraction Layer*.

Hard Disk Drives Mass storage devices that read and write digital information magnetically on discs that spin under moving heads. Hard disk drives are precisely aligned and cannot normally be removed. Hard disk drives are an inexpensive way to store gigabytes of computer data permanently. Hard disk drives also store the installed software of a computer. See *Mass Storage Device*.

Hardware Abstraction Layer (HAL) A Windows NT service that provides basic input/output services such as timers, interrupts, and multiprocessor management for computer hardware. The HAL is a device driver for the motherboard circuitry that allows different families of computers to be treated the same by the Windows NT operating system. See *Driver, Interrupt Request, Service*.

Hardware Compatibility List (HCL) The listing of all hardware devices supported by Windows NT. Hardware on the HCL has been tested and verified as being compatible with NT. You can view the current HCL at http://microsoft.com/ntserver/hcl.

Hardware Profiles Used to manage portable computers that have different configurations based on their location.

HCL   See *Hardware Compatibility List.*

High Performance File System (HPFS)   The file system native to OS/2 that performs many of the same functions of NTFS when run under OS/2. See *File System, New Technology File System.*

Home Directory   The root directory of a Web server or virtual server that contains the default document or home page. See *Default Document, World Wide Web.*

Home Page   The default page returned by an HTTP server when a URL containing no specific document is requested. *See Hypertext Transfer Protocol, Uniform Resource Locator.*

Host   An Internet Server. Hosts are constantly connected to the Internet. See *Internet.*

HotJava   A Web browser written entirely in the Java programming language designed to show the capability of the language. HotJava was the first browser to support Java applications.

HPFS   See *High Performance File System.*

HTML   See *Hypertext Markup Language.*

HTTP   See *Hypertext Transfer Protocol.*

Hyperlink   A link embedded in text or graphics that has a Web address embedded within them. By clicking the link, you jump to another Web address. You can identify a hyperlink because it is a different color from the rest of the Web page. See *World Wide Web.*

Hypertext Markup Language (HTML)   A textual data format that identifies sections of a document as headers, lists, hypertext links, etc. HTML is the data format used on the World Wide Web for the publication of Web pages. See *Hypertext Transfer Protocol, World Wide Web.*

Hypertext Transfer Protocol (HTTP)   Hypertext transfer protocol is an Internet protocol that transfers HTML documents over the Internet and responds to context changes that happen when a user clicks a hypertext link. See *Hypertext Markup Language, World Wide Web.*

I

Icon   A graphical representation of a resource in a graphical user interface that usually takes the form of a small (32 x 32) bitmap. See *Graphical User Interface*.

IDE   See *Integrated Device Electronics*.

IIS   See *Internet Information Server*.

Index Server   A search engine ISAPI extension to IIS that indexes all the documents stored on a Web site. Users can then query the indexes to return Web pages that match the query. See *Internet Information Server, Search Engine*.

Industry Standard Architecture (ISA)   The design standard for 16-bit Intel compatible motherboards and peripheral buses. The 32/64-bit PCI bus standard is replacing the ISA standard. Adapters and interface cards must conform to the bus standard(s) used by the motherboard in order to be used with a computer.

Integrated Device Electronics (IDE)   A simple mass storage device interconnection bus that operates at 5Mbps and can handle no more than two attached devices. IDE devices are similar to but less expensive than SCSI devices. See *Mass Storage Device, Small Computer Systems Interface*.

Integrated Services Digital Network (ISDN)   A direct, digital dial-up PSTN data link layer connection that operates at 64KB per channel over regular twisted pair cable between a subscriber site and a PSTN central office. ISDN provides twice the data rate of the fastest modems per channel. Up to 24 channels can be multiplexed over two twisted pairs. See *Data Link Layer, Modem, Public Switched Telephone Network*.

Intel Architecture   A family of microprocessors descended directly from the Intel 8086, itself descended from the first microprocessor, the Intel 4004. The Intel architecture is the dominant microprocessor family. It was used in the original IBM PC microcomputer adopted by the business market and later adapted for home use.

Interactive User   A user who physically logs on to the computer where the user account resides is considered interactive, as opposed to a user who logs on over the network. See *Network User*.

Internet   A voluntarily interconnected global network of computers based upon the TCP/IP protocol suite. TCP/IP was originally developed by the U.S. Department of Defense's Advanced Research Projects Agency to facilitate the interconnection of military networks and was provided free to universities. The obvious utility of worldwide digital network connectivity and the availability of free complex networking software developed at universities doing military research attracted other universities, research institutions, private organizations, businesses, and finally the individual home user. The Internet is now available to all current commercial computing platforms. See *FTP, TCP/IP, Telnet, World Wide Web.*

Internet Database Connector   An extension to IIS that returns a database table formatted as an HTML document based on a query from the Web client. See *Database, IIS.*

Internet Explorer   A World Wide Web browser produced by Microsoft and included free with Windows 95 and Windows NT 4.0. See *Internet, World Wide Web.*

Internet Information Server (IIS)   Serves Internet higher-level protocols like HTTP and FTP to clients using Web browsers. See *File Transfer Protocol, Hypertext Transfer Protocol, World Wide Web.*

Internet Protocol (IP)   The network layer protocol upon which the Internet is based. IP provides a simple connectionless packet exchange. Other protocols such as UDP or TCP use IP to perform their connection-oriented or guaranteed delivery services. See *Internet, TCP/IP.*

Internet Relay Chat (IRC)   An informal Internet protocol for multiuser simultaneous conversation via relayed text strings between an IRC server and multiple IRC clients.

Internet Server   A server computer connected to the Internet or an intranet that serves Internet protocols such as HTTP, FTP, and Gopher based on the TCP/IP protocol suite. See *FTP, Gopher, HTTP, Internet, TCP/IP.*

Internet Server Application Programming Interface (ISAPI)   A specification to which extensions to IIS are written in order to expand its functionality or the services it provides.

Internet Service Provider (ISP)   A company that provides dial-up connections to the Internet. See *Internet.*

Internetwork A network of networks, usually based on a packet-switching scheme.

Internetwork Packet eXchange (IPX) The network and transport layer protocol developed by Novell for its NetWare product. IPX is a routable, connection-oriented protocol similar to TCP/IP but much easier to manage and with lower communication overhead. See *IP, NetWare, NWLink*.

InterNIC The agency that is responsible for assigning IP addresses. *See Internet Protocol, IP Address*.

Interpreter A program that executes the commands read from a script. See *Script, Scripting Language*.

Interprocess Communications (IPC) A generic term describing any manner of client/server communication protocol, specifically those operating in the application layer. Interprocess communications mechanisms provide a method for the client and server to trade information. See *Local Procedure Call, Mailslots, Named Pipes, NetBIOS, NetDDE, Remote Procedure Call*.

Interrupt Request (IRQ) A hardware signal from a peripheral device to the microcomputer indicating that it has I/O traffic to send. If the microprocessor is not running a more important service, it will interrupt its current activity and handle the interrupt request. IBM PC's have 16 levels of interrupt request lines. Under Windows NT each device must have a unique interrupt request line. See *Driver, Microprocessor, Peripheral*.

Intranet A privately owned network based on the TCP/IP protocol suite. See *Transmission Control Protocol/Internet Protocol*.

IP See *Internet Protocol*.

IP Address A 4-byte number that uniquely identifies a computer on an IP internetwork. InterNIC assigns the first bytes of Internet IP addresses and administers them in hierarchies. Organizations not attached to the Internet are free to assign IP addresses as they please. See *Internet, InterNIC, IP*.

IPC See *Interprocess Communications*.

IPX See *Internetwork Packet eXchange*.

IRQ See *Interrupt Request*.

ISA See *Industry Standard Architecture*.

ISDN   See *Integrated Services Digital Network*.

ISP   See *Internet Service Provider*.

J

Java   A compiled object-oriented cross-platform language based on the syntax of C++. Java uses the interpreted Java virtual machine as its machine language. Since Java applications and applets can be run on any platform, it is a natural candidate for Web-based programs.

JavaScript   A scripting language based on the syntax of Java that can be embedded in HTML documents to provide simple client-side active content. See *Script, Scripting Language*.

Java Virtual Machine   A fictitious machine language to which all Java applications are compiled. Java run-time environments can either interpret or compile JVM code to execute it on any computer or inside an application like a Web browser.

K

Kernel   The core process of a preemptive operating system, consisting of a multitasking scheduler and the basic services that provide security. Depending upon the operating system, other services such as virtual memory drivers may be built into the Kernel. The Kernel is responsible for managing the scheduling of threads and processes. See *Drivers, Operating System*.

Keys   Paired codes used to encrypt data in communication streams. One part of the key is kept private on the server, while the other (public) part of the key is transmitted to Web browsers. Web browsers can then encrypt data using the public portion that must be decrypted using the private portion of the key. The process is called *public key encryption* and is used in the Secure Socket Layer mechanism. See *Encryption, Secure Socket Layer*.

L

LAN See *Local Area Network*.

LAN Manager The Microsoft brand of a network product jointly developed by IBM and Microsoft that provided an early client/server environment. LAN Manager/Server was eclipsed by NetWare, but was the genesis of many important protocols and IPC mechanisms used today, such as NetBIOS, named pipes, and NetBEUI. Portions of this product exist today in OS/2 Warp Server. See *Interprocess Communications, OS/2*.

LAN Server The IBM brand of a network product jointly developed by IBM and Microsoft. See *LAN Manager*.

Lightweight Directory Access Protocol An open standard for storing user and group information independent of the operating system that hosts the WWW service.

Log A database stored in text format of time-based security and service-related information.

Local Area Network (LAN) A network of computers operating on the same high-speed, shared media network data link layer. The size of a local area network is defined by the limitations of high speed shared media networks to generally less than 1 kilometer in overall span. Some LAN backbone data link protocols such as FDDI can create larger LANs called metropolitan or medium area networks (MANs). See *Data Link Layer, Wide Area Network*.

Local Group A group that exists in a NT computer's local accounts database. Local groups can reside on NT workstations or NT servers and can contain users or global groups. See *Global Group*.

Local Printer A local printer is a printer that uses a physical port and that has not been shared. If a printer is defined as local, the only users who can use the printer are the local users of the computer to which that printer is attached. See *Network Printer, Printer, Printing Device*.

Local Procedure Call (LPC) A mechanism that loops remote procedure calls without the presence of a network so that the client and server portion of an application can reside on the same machine. Local procedure calls look like remote procedure calls (RPCs) to the client and server sides of a distributed application. See *Remote Procedure Call*.

Local Security   Security that governs a local or interactive user. Local security can be set through NTFS partitions. See *Interactive User, Network Security, New Technology File System, Security.*

Logging   The process of recording information about activities and errors in the operating system.

Logoff   The process of closing an open session with a server.

Logon   The process of opening a network session by providing a valid authentication consisting of a user account name and a password to a domain controller. After logon, network resources are available to the user according to the user's assigned permissions. See *Domain Controller.*

Logon Script   Command files that automate the logon process by performing utility functions such as attaching to additional server resources or automatically running different programs based upon the user account that established the logon. See *Logon.*

Long Filename (LFN)   A filename longer than the eight characters plus three-character extension allowed by MS-DOS. In Windows NT and Windows 95, long filenames may be up to 255 characters.

LPC   See *Local Procedure Call.*

M

Macintosh   A brand of computer manufactured by Apple. Macintosh is the only successful line of computers neither based upon the original IBM PC nor running the UNIX operating system. Windows NT Server supports Apple computers despite their use of proprietary network protocols.

MacOS   The operating system that runs on an Apple Macintosh computer. See *Macintosh.*

Mailslots   A connectionless messaging IPC mechanism that Windows NT uses for browse request and logon authentication. See *Interprocess Communications.*

Mass Storage Device   Any device capable of storing many megabytes of information permanently, but especially those capable of random access to any portion of the information, such as hard disk drives and CD-ROM drives. See *CD-ROM Drive, Hard Disk Drive, IDE, SCSI.*

Memory   Any device capable of storing information. This term is usually used to indicate volatile random access semiconductor memory (RAM) capable of high-speed access to any portion of the memory space, but incapable of storing information without power. See *Mass Storage Device, Random Access Memory.*

Merge   The process of joining temporary indexes (shadow merge) or of combining a temporary index into a master index (master merge) for the purpose of speeding queries to an index service. See *Index Server.*

Microprocessor   An integrated semiconductor circuit designed to automatically perform lists of logical and arithmetic operations. Modern microprocessors independently manage memory pools and support multiple instruction lists called threads. Microprocessors are also capable of responding to interrupt requests from peripherals and include onboard support for complex floating point arithmetic. Microprocessors must have instructions when they are first powered on. These instructions are contained in nonvolatile firmware called a BIOS. See *BIOS, Operating System.*

Microsoft Disk Operating System (MS-DOS)   A 16-bit operating system designed for the 8086 chip that was used in the original IBM PC. MS-DOS is a simple program loader and file system that turns over complete control of the computer to the running program and provides very little service beyond file system support and that provided by the BIOS.

Modem   Modulator/demodulator. A data link layer device used to create an analog signal suitable for transmission over telephone lines from a digital data stream. Modern modems also include a command set for negotiating connections and data rates with remote modems and for setting their default behavior. The fastest modems run at about 33Kbps. See *Data Link Layer.*

Module   A software component of a modular operating system that provides a certain defined service. Modules can be installed or removed depending upon the service requirements of the software running on the computer. Modules allow operating systems and applications to be customized to fit the needs of the user.

MPR   See *MultiProtocol Router.*

MS-DOS   See *Microsoft Disk Operating System.*

Multilink   A capability of RAS to combine multiple data streams into one network connection for the purpose of using more than one modem or ISDN channel in a single connection. This feature is new to Windows NT 4.0. See *Remote Access Service.*

Multiprocessing   Using two or more processors simultaneously to perform a computing task. Depending upon the operating system, processing may be done asymmetrically, wherein certain processors are assigned certain threads independent of the load they create, or symmetrically, wherein threads are dynamically assigned to processors according to an equitable scheduling scheme. The term usually describes a multiprocessing capacity built into the computer at a hardware level in that the computer itself supports more than one processor. However, *multiprocessing* can also be applied to network computing applications achieved through interprocess communication mechanisms. Client/server applications are, in fact, examples of multiprocessing. See *Asymmetrical Multiprocessing, Interprocess Communications, Symmetrical Multiprocessing.*

MultiProtocol Router (MPR)   Services included with NT Server that allow you to route traffic between IPX and TCP/IP subnets. MPR also allows you to facilitate DHCP requests and forward BOOTP relay agents. See *Bootstrap Protocol, Dynamic Host Configuration Protocol, Internetwork Packet Exchange, Transmission Control Protocol/Internet Protocol.*

Multimedia Internet Mail Extensions (MIME)   A specification for the content types of files transmitted over the Internet. Web servers identify the type of file being sent to Web browsers using MIME types.

Multitasking   The capacity of an operating system to rapidly switch among threads of execution. Multitasking allows processor time to be divided among threads as if each thread ran on its own slower processor. Multitasking operating systems allow two or more applications to run at the same time and can provide a greater degree of service to applications than single-tasking operating systems like MS-DOS. See *Multiprocessing.*

N

Named Pipes An interprocess communication mechanism that is implemented as a file system service, allowing programs to be modified to run on it without using a proprietary application programming interface. Named pipes were developed to support more robust client/server communications than those allowed by the simpler NetBIOS. See *File Systems, Interprocess Communications, OS/2.*

NDIS See *Network Driver Interface Specification.*

NetBEUI See *NetBIOS Extended User Interface.*

NetBIOS See *Network Basic Input/Output System.*

NetBIOS Extended User Interface (NetBEUI) A simple network layer transport developed to support NetBIOS installations. NetBEUI is not routable, and so it is not appropriate for larger networks. NetBEUI is the fastest transport protocol available for Windows NT.

NetBIOS Gateway A service provided by RAS that allows NetBIOS requests to be forwarded independent of transport protocol. For example, NetBIOS requests from a remote computer connected via NetBEUI can be sent over the network via NWLink. See *NetBEUI, NetBIOS over TCP/IP, Network Basic Input/Output System, NWLink.*

NetBIOS over TCP/IP (NetBT) A network service that implements the NetBIOS IPC over the TCP/IP protocol stack. See *Interprocess Communications, NetBIOS, TCP/IP.*

NetWare A popular network operating system developed by Novell in the early 1980s. NetWare is a cooperative, multitasking, highly optimized, dedicated-server network operating system that has client support for most major operating systems. Recent versions of NetWare include graphical client tools for management from client stations. At one time, NetWare accounted for more than 70 percent of the network operating system market. See *Client Services for NetWare, Gateway Services for NetWare, NWLink, Windows NT.*

Network A group of computers connected via some digital medium for the purpose of exchanging information. Networks can be based upon many types of media, such as twisted pair telephone-style cable, optical fiber, coaxial cable, radio, or infrared light. Certain computers are usually configured as service providers called *servers*. Computers that perform user tasks directly and that utilize the services of servers are called *clients*. See *Client/Server, Network Operating System, Server*.

Network Basic Input/Output System (NetBIOS)   A client/server interprocess communication service developed by IBM in the early 1980s. NetBIOS presents a relatively primitive mechanism for communication in client/server applications, but widespread acceptance and availability across most operating systems make NetBIOS a logical choice for simple network applications. Many of the network IPC mechanisms in Windows NT are implemented over NetBIOS. See *Client/Server, Interprocess Communication*.

Network Client Administrator   A utility within the Administrative Tools group that can be used to make installation startup disks, make installation disk sets, copy client-based administration tools, and view remote boot information.

Network Driver Interface Specification (NDIS)   A Microsoft specification to which network adapter drivers must conform in order to work with Microsoft network operating systems. NDIS provides a many-to-many binding between network adapter drivers and transport protocols. See *Transport Protocol*.

Network Interface Card (NIC)   A physical layer adapter device that allows a computer to connect to and communicate over a local area network. See *Adapter, Ethernet, Token Ring*.

Network Layer   The layer of the OSI model that creates a communication path between two computers via routed packets. Transport protocols implement both the network layer and the transport layer of the OSI stack. IP is a network layer service. See *Internet Protocol, Open Systems Interconnect Model, Transport Protocol*.

Network Monitor   A utility used to capture and display network traffic.

Network News Transfer Protocol (NNTP)   A protocol for the transmission of a database of topical message threads between news servers and newsreader clients.

Network Operating System A computer operating system specifically designed to optimize a computer's ability to respond to service requests. Servers run network operating systems. Windows NT Server and NetWare are both network operating systems. See *NetWare, Server, Windows NT*.

Network Security Security that governs a network. Network security can be set using share permissions. See *Local Security, Network User, Security*.

Network User A user who logs on to the network using the SAM from a remote domain controller. See *Interactive User*.

Newsgroups Internet-wide threads of topical discussion implemented using the NNTP protocol. See *Newsreader, NNTP, UseNet*.

New Technology File System (NTFS) A secure, transaction-oriented file system developed for Windows NT that incorporates the Windows NT security model for assigning permissions and shares. NTFS is optimized for hard drives larger than 500MB and requires too much overhead to be used on hard disk drives smaller than 50MB.

NNTP See *Network News Transfer Protocol*.

NT Directory Services The synchronized SAM database that exists between the PDC and the BDCs within a domain. Directory Services also controls the trust relationships that exist between domains. See *Backup Domain Controller, Primary Domain Controller, Security Accounts Manager, Trust Relationship*.

NTFS See *New Technology File System*.

O

Object A software service provider that encapsulates both the algorithm and the data structures necessary to provide a service. Usually, objects can inherit data and functionality from their parent objects, thus allowing complex services to be constructed from simpler objects. The term *object oriented* implies a tight relationship between algorithms and data structures. See *Module*.

Object Counters Containers built into each service object in Windows NT that store a count of the number of times an object performs its service or to what degree. You can use performance monitors to access object counters and measure how the different objects in Windows NT are operating. See *Object*.

Open Database Connectivity (ODBC) A standard for connecting database clients to database servers regardless of the vendors or systems involved.

Open Systems Interconnect Model (OSI Model) A model for network component interoperability developed by the International Standards Organization to promote cross-vendor compatibility of hardware and software network systems. The OSI model splits the process of networking into seven distinct services. Each layer uses the services of the layer below to provide its service to the layer above. See *Application Layer, Data Link Layer, Network Layer, Physical Layer, Presentation Layer, Session Layer, Transport Layer.*

Operating System A collection of services that form a foundation upon which applications run. Operating systems may be simple I/O service providers with a command shell, such as MS-DOS, or they may be sophisticated, preemptive, multitasking, multiprocessing applications platforms like Windows NT. See *Kernel, Network Operating System, Preemptive Multitasking.*

Operating System 2 (OS/2) A 16-bit (and later, 32-bit) operating system developed jointly by Microsoft and IBM as a successor to MS-DOS. Microsoft bowed out of the 32-bit development effort and produced its own product, Windows NT, as a competitor to OS/2. OS/2 is now a preemptive, multitasking 32-bit operating system with strong support for networking and the ability to run MS-DOS and Win16 applications, but IBM has been unable to entice a large number of developers to produce software that runs native under OS/2. See *Operating System, Preemptive Multitasking.*

Optimization Any effort to reduce the workload on a hardware component by eliminating, obviating, or reducing the amount of work required of the hardware component through any means. For instance, file caching is an optimization that reduces the workload of a hard disk drive.

OS/2 See *Operating System 2.*

OSI Model See *Open Systems Interconnect Model.*

Owner For NTFS files and directories, the user account that controls access and grants permissions to other users. By default, the owner is the creator of the file or directory. See *New Technology File System.*

P

Page File   See *Swap File*.

Partition   A section of a hard disk that can contain an independent file system volume. Partitions can be used to keep multiple operating systems and file systems on the same hard disk. See *Hard Disk Drive, Volume*.

Password   A secret code used to validate the identity of a user of a secure system. Passwords are used in tandem with account names to log on to most computer systems.

PC   See *Personal Computer*.

PCI   See *Peripheral Connection Interface*.

PDC   See *Primary Domain Controller*.

Peer   A networked computer that both shares resources with other computers and accesses the shared resources of other computers. A nondedicated server. See *Client, Server*.

Performance Monitor   NT utility that provides graphical statistics for measuring performance of your computer.

Peripheral   An input/output device attached to a computer. Peripherals can be printers, hard disk drives, monitors, and so on.

Peripheral Connection Interface (PCI)   A high speed 32/64-bit bus interface developed by Intel and widely accepted as the successor to the 16-bit ISA interface. PCI devices support I/O throughput about 40 times faster than the ISA bus.

Perl   A scripting language commonly used in CGI scripts to parse user input from Web pages and dynamically create HTML documents. See *Scripting Languages*.

Permissions   Assignments of levels of access to a resource made to groups or users. Security constructs used to regulate access to resources by user name or group affiliation. Permissions can be assigned by administrators to allow any level of access, such as read only, read/write, delete, etc., by controlling the ability of users to initiate object services. Security is implemented by checking the user's security identifier against each object's access control list. See *Access Control List, Security Identifier.*

Personal Computer (PC) A microcomputer used by one person at a time (i.e., not a multiuser computer). PCs are generally clients or peers in a networked environment. High-speed PCs are called *workstations.* Networks of PCs are called *LANs.* The term *PC* often refers to computers compatible with the IBM PC.

Physical Layer The cables, connectors, and connection ports of a network. The passive physical components required to create a network. See *OSI Model.*

Physical Port Printers can be connected directly to a computer through a serial (COM) or parallel (LPT) port. If a printer is connected in this manner, it is using a physical port. See *Print Device, Printer.*

Ping A protocol used to check the connected route between two systems on an IP network. Also the name of the utility used to generate Ping traffic. See *IP.*

Plug-ins Compiled components that extend the functionality of Web browsers, usually by interpreting specific types of data such as sound or video. See *Web Browser.*

Point-to-Point Protocol (PPP) A network layer transport that performs over point-to-point network connections such as serial or modem lines. PPP can negotiate any transport protocol used by both systems involved in the link and can automatically assign IP, DNS, and gateway addresses when used with TCP/IP. See *Domain Name Service, Gateway, Internet Protocol.*

Point-to-Point Tunneling Protocol (PPTP) Protocol used to connect to corporate networks through the Internet or an ISP. See *Internet, Internet Service Provider.*

Policies General controls that enhance the security of an operating environment. In Windows NT, policies affect restrictions on password use and rights assignment and determine which events will be recorded in the Security log.

POP, POP3 See *Post Office Protocol.*

Post Office Protocol A protocol used for off-line mail readers to manage the contents of their inbox on a mail server.

PowerPC   A microprocessor family developed by IBM to compete with the Intel family of microprocessors. The PowerPC is a RISC-architecture micro-processor with many advanced features that emulate other microprocessors. PowerPCs are currently used in a line of IBM computers and in the Apple Power Macintosh. Windows NT is available for the PowerPC, but is no longer actively supported.

PPP   See *Point-to-Point Protocol*.

PPTP   See *Point-to-Point Tunneling Protocol*.

Preemptive Multitasking   A multitasking implementation in which an inter-rupt routine in the Kernel manages the scheduling of processor time among run-ning threads. The threads themselves do not need to support multitasking in any way because the microprocessor will preempt the thread with an interrupt, save its state, update all thread priorities according to its scheduling algorithm, and pass control to the highest priority thread awaiting execution. Because of the preemptive nature, a thread that crashes will not affect the operation of other executing threads. See *Kernel, Operating System, Process, Thread*.

Preferences   Characteristics of user accounts, such as password, profile location, home directory and logon script.

Presentation Layer   That layer of the OSI model that converts and trans-lates (if necessary) information between the session and application layers. See *OSI Model*.

Primary Domain Controller (PDC)   The domain server that contains the master copy of the security, computer, and user accounts databases and that can authenticate workstations. The PDC can replicate its databases to one or more backup domain controllers. The PDC is usually also the Master Browser for the domain. See *Backup Domain Controller, Domain, Master Browser*.

Priority   A level of execution importance assigned to a thread. In combination with other factors, the priority level determines how often that thread will get computer time according to a scheduling algorithm. See *Preemptive Multitasking*.

Process   A running program containing one or more threads. A process encapsulates the protected memory and environment for its threads.

Processor   A circuit designed to automatically perform lists of logical and arithmetic operations. Unlike microprocessors, processors may be designed from discrete components rather than be a monolithic integrated circuit. See *Microprocessor*.

Program   A list of processor instructions designed to perform a certain function. A running program is called a process. A package of one or more programs and attendant data designed to meet a certain application is called software. See *Applications, Microprocessor, Process, Software*.

Programming Interfaces   Interprocess communications mechanisms that provide certain high-level services to running processes. Programming interfaces may provide network communication, graphical presentation, or any other type of software service. See *Interprocess Communication*.

Protocol   An established communication method that the parties involved understand. Protocols provide a context in which to interpret communicated information. Computer protocols are rules used by communicating devices and software services to format data in a way that all participants understand. See *Transport Protocol*.

Proxy Server   A server dedicated to the function of receiving Internet Web requests for clients, retrieving the requested pages, and forwarding them to client. Proxy servers cache retrieved Web pages to improve performance and reduce bandwidth; they also serve the security function of protecting the identity of internal clients.

Public Switched Telephone Network (PSTN)   A global network of interconnected digital and analog communication links originally designed to support voice communication between any two points in the world, but quickly adapted to handle digital data traffic when the computer revolution occurred. In addition to its traditional voice support role, the PSTN now functions as the physical layer of the Internet by providing dial-up and leased lines for the interconnections. See *Internet, Modem, Physical Layer*.

Q

Query   A request to an index or database server for a specific set of information. See *Database, Index Server, SQL*.

R

RAID   See *Redundant Array of Inexpensive Disks.*

Random Access Memory (RAM)   Integrated circuits that store digital bits in massive arrays of logical gates or capacitors. RAM is the primary memory store for modern computers, storing all running software processes and contextual data. See *Microprocessor.*

RARP   See *Reverse Address Resolution Protocol.*

RAS   See *Remote Access Service.*

Redirector   A software service that redirects user file I/O requests over the network. Novell implements the Workstation service and Client services for NetWare as redirectors. Redirectors allow servers to be used as mass storage devices that appear local to the user. See *Client Services for NetWare, File System.*

Reduced Instruction Set Computer (RISC)   A microprocessor technology that implements fewer and more primitive instructions than typical microprocessors and can therefore be implemented quickly with the most modern semiconductor technology and speeds. Programs written for RISC microprocessors require more instructions (longer programs) to perform the same task as a normal microprocessor but are capable of a greater degree of optimization and therefore usually run faster. See *Microprocessor.*

Redundant Array of Inexpensive Disks (RAID)   A collection of hard disk drives, coordinated by a special controller, that appears as one physical disk to a computer but stores its data across all the disks to take advantage of the speed and/or fault tolerance afforded by using more than one disk. RAID disk storage has several levels, including 0 (striping), 1 (mirroring), and 5 (striping with parity). RAID systems are typically used for very large storage volumes or to provide fault-tolerance features such as hot swapping of failed disks or automatically backing up data onto replacement disks.

Registry   A database of settings required and maintained by Windows NT and its components. The registry contains all of the configuration information used by the computer. It is stored as a hierarchical structure and is made up of keys, hives, and value entries. You can use the Registry Editor (REGEDT32 command) to change these settings.

Remote Access Service (RAS) A service that allows network connections to be established over PSTN lines with modems. The computer initiating the connection is called the RAS client; the answering computer is called the RAS host. See *Modem, Public Switched Telephone Network.*

Remote Procedure Calls (RPC) A network interprocess communication mechanism that allows an application to be distributed among many computers on the same network. See *Interprocess Communications, Local Procedure Call.*

Remoteboot The remoteboot service is used to start diskless workstations over the network.

Requests for Comments (RFCs) The set of standards defining the Internet protocols as determined by the Internet Engineering Task Force and available in the public domain on the Internet. RFCs define the functions and services provided by each of the many Internet protocols. Compliance with the RFCs guarantees cross-vendor compatibility. See *Internet.*

Resource Any useful service, such as a shared network directory or a printer. See *Share.*

Reverse Address Resolution Protocol (RARP) The TCP/IP protocol that allows a computer that has a physical layer address (such as an Ethernet address), but does not have an IP address, to request a numeric IP address from another computer on the network. See *TCP/IP.*

RFC See *Requests for Comments.*

RIP See *Routing Information Protocol.*

RISC See *Reduced Instruction Set Computer.*

Router A network layer device that moves packets between networks. Routers provide internetwork connectivity. See *Network Layer.*

Routing Information Protocol (RIP) A protocol within the TCP/IP protocol suite that allows routers to exchange routing information with other routers. See *Transmission Control Protocol/Internet Protocol.*

RPC See *Remote Procedure Calls.*

S

SAM See *Security Accounts Manager*.

Scheduling The process of determining which threads should be executed according to their priority and other factors. See *Preemptive Multitasking*.

Script A list of commands to be executed by an interpreter. Web browsers can be interpreters for scripts embedded in HTML documents. See *Interpreter, Scripting Language, Web Browser*.

Scripting Language A specific syntax and structure for commands in scripts. See *Interpreter, Script*.

SCSI See *Small Computer Systems Interface*.

Search Engine Web sites dedicated to responding to requests for specific information, searching massive locally stored databases of Web pages, and responding with the URLs of pages that fit the search phrase. See *Index Server, Universal Resource Locator, World Wide Web*.

Secure Socket Layer An encrypted transmission protocol that uses TCP/IP to implement a secure public key encrypted data channel between a client and a server. See *Encryption, TCP/IP*.

Security Measures taken to secure a system against accidental or intentional loss, usually in the form of accountability procedures and use restriction. See *Security Accounts Manager, Security Identifiers*.

Security Accounts Manager (SAM) The module of the Windows NT executive that authenticates a username and password against a database of accounts, generating an access token that includes the user's permissions. See *Access Token, Security, Security Identifier*.

Security Identifiers (SID) Unique codes that identify a specific user or group to the Windows NT security system. Security identifiers contain a complete set of permissions for that user or group.

Serial A method of communication that transfers data across a medium one bit at a time, usually adding stop, start and check bits to ensure quality transfer. See *COM Port, Modem*.

Serial Line Internet Protocol (SLIP)   An implementation of the IP protocol over serial lines. SLIP has been obviated by PPP. See *Internet Protocol, Point-to-Point Protocol*.

Server   A computer dedicated to servicing requests for resources from other computers on a network. Servers typically run network operating systems such as Windows NT Server or NetWare. See *Client/Server, NetWare, Windows NT*.

Server Manager   Utility in the Administrative Tools group used to manage domains and computers.

Server-Side Include (SSI)   A generic term for Web services that use embedded HTML tags to dynamically create HTML documents based on the contents of many different HTML documents.

Service   A process dedicated to implementing a specific function for other process. Most Windows NT components are services used by user-level applications.

Servlet   A server-side application written in Java. See *Java*.

Session layer   The layer of the OSI model dedicated to maintaining a bidirectional communication connection between two computers. The session layer uses the services of the transport layer to provide this service. See *OSI Model, Transport Layer*.

Share   A resource (e.g., directory, printer) shared by a server or a peer on a network. See *Peer, Resource, Server*.

SID   See *Security Identifier*.

Simple Mail Transfer Protocol (SMTP)   An Internet protocol for transferring mail between Internet hosts. SMTP is often used to upload mail directly from the client to an intermediate host, but only computers constantly connected to the Internet can use SMTP to receive mail. See *Internet*.

Simple Network Management Protocol (SNMP)   An Internet protocol that manages network hardware such as routers, switches, servers, and clients from a single client on the network. See *Internet Protocol*.

Site   A related collection of HTML documents at the same Internet address, usually oriented toward some specific information or purpose. See *Hypertext Markup Language, Internet*.

SLIP   See *Serial Line Internet Protocol.*

Small Computer Systems Interface (SCSI)   A high-speed, parallel-bus interface that connects hard disk drives, CD-ROM drives, tape drives, and many other peripherals to a computer. SCSI is the mass storage connection standard among all computers except IBM compatibles, which use SCSI or IDE.

SMTP   See *Simple Mail Transfer Protocol.*

Sniffer   Software or hardware troubleshooting device used for the low-level analysis of network protocols.

SNMP   See *Simple Network Management Protocol.*

Software   A suite of programs sold as a unit and dedicated to a specific application. See *Application, Process, Program.*

SQL   See *Structured Query Language.*

SQL Server   Microsoft's relational database server based on SQL syntax. See *Database, SQL.*

SSL   See *Secure Socket Layer.*

Stripe Set   A single volume created across multiple hard disk drives and accessed in parallel for the purpose of optimizing disk access time. NTFS can create stripe sets. See *File System, NTFS, Volume.*

Structured Query Language   An open syntax for the transmission of queries between clients and servers. Database servers interpret SQL to return the data described by the query.

Subdirectory   A directory contained in another directory. See *Directory.*

Subnet   A single network defined by the fact that any two computers in the subnet can communicate without any special routing. A subnet may consist of more than one subnetwork bridged together.

Subnet Mask   A number mathematically applied to Internet protocol addresses to determine which IP addresses are a part of the same subnetwork as the computer applying the subnet mask.

Subnetwork   A shared media network wherein all computers can communicate directly without intermediate routers or bridges.

Surf   To browse the Web randomly looking for interesting information. See *World Wide Web*.

Swap File   The virtual memory file on a hard disk containing the memory pages that have been moved out to disk to increase available RAM. See *Virtual Memory*.

Symmetrical Multiprocessing   A multiprocessing methodology wherein processes are assigned to processors on a fair share basis. This balances the processing load among processors and ensures that no processor will become a bottleneck. Symmetrical multiprocessing is more difficult to implement than asymmetrical multiprocessing as certain hardware functions such as interrupt handling must be shared between processors. See *Asymmetrical Multiprocessing, Multiprocessing*.

T

Task Manager   An application that manually views and closes running processes. Task Manager can also be used to view CPU and memory statistics. Press Ctrl+Alt+Del to launch the Task Manager.

TCP   See *Transmission Control Protocol*.

TCP/IP   See *Transmission Control Protocol/Internet Protocol*.

TDI   See *Transport Driver Interface*.

Telnet   A terminal application that allows a user to log into a multiuser UNIX computer from any computer connected to the Internet. See *Internet*.

TFTP   See *Trivial File Transfer Protocol*.

Thread   A list of instructions running in a computer to perform a certain task. Each thread runs in the context of a process, which embodies the protected memory space and the environment of the threads. Multithreaded processes can perform more than one task at the same time. See *Preemptive Multitasking, Process, Program*.

Throughput   The measure of information flow through a system in a specific time frame, usually one second. For instance, 28.8Kbps is the throughput of a modem: 28.8 kilobits per second can be transmitted.

Token Ring   The second most-popular data link layer standard for local area networking. Token ring implements the token passing method of arbitrating multiple-computer access to the same network. Token ring operates at either 4 or 16Mbps. FDDI is similar to token ring and operates at 100Mbps. See *Data Link Layer*.

Transmission Control Protocol (TCP)   A transport layer protocol that implements guaranteed packet delivery using the Internet Protocol (IP). See *Internet Protocol, TCP/IP*.

Transmission Control Protocol/Internet Protocol (TCP/IP)   A suite of Internet protocols upon which the global Internet is based. TCP/IP is a general term that can refer either to the TCP and IP protocols used together or to the complete set of Internet protocols. TCP/IP is the default protocol for Windows NT.

Transport Driver Interface (TDI)   A specification to which all Window NT transport protocols must be written in order to be used by higher level services such as programming interfaces, file systems, and interprocess communications mechanisms. See *Transport Protocol*.

Transport Layer   The OSI model layer responsible for the guaranteed serial delivery of packets between two computers over an internetwork. TCP is the transport layer protocol for the TCP/IP transport protocol.

Transport Protocol   A service that delivers discrete packets of information between any two computers in a network. Higher level connection-oriented services are built upon transport protocols. See *Internet, IP, NetBEUI, NWLink, TCP, TCP/IP, Transport Layer*.

Trivial File Transport Protocol   A simple file transport protocol often used during the booting of diskless workstations. FTP is more robust and therefore more common than TFTP. See *FTP*.

Trust Relationship   Administrative link that joins two or more domains. A trust relationship enables users to access resources in another domain if they have rights, even if they do not have a user account in the resource domain.

U

UDP   See *User Datagram Protocol.*

UNC   See *Universal Naming Convention.*

Uniform Resource Locator (URL)   An Internet standard naming convention for identifying resources available via various TCP/IP application protocols. For example, `http://www.microsoft.com` is the URL for Microsoft's World Wide Web server site, while `ftp://gateway.dec.com` is a popular FTP site. A URL allows easy hypertext references to a particular resource from within a document or mail message. See *HTTP, World Wide Web.*

Universal Naming Convention (UNC)   A multivendor, multiplatform convention for identifying shared resources on a network. See *MUP.*

UNIX   A multitasking, kernel-based operating system developed at AT&T in the early 1970s and provided (originally) free to universities as a research operating system. Because of its availability and ability to scale down to microprocessor-based computers, UNIX became the standard operating system of the Internet and its attendant network protocols and is the closest approximation to a universal operating system that exists. Most computers can run some variant of the UNIX operating system. See *Internet, Multitasking.*

UseNet News   A distributed news database implemented on NNTP, divided into topical discussion threads called newsgroups that are distributed among news servers. Clients using newsreaders can subscribe to specific newsgroups and have them automatically downloaded when they open their newsreader.

User Datagram Protocol (UDP)   A non-guaranteed network packet protocol implemented on IP that is far faster than TCP because of its lack of flow-control overhead. UDP can be implemented as a reliable transport when some higher level protocol (such as NetBIOS) exists to make sure that required data will eventually be retransmitted in local area environments. At the transport layer of the OSI model, UDP is connectionless service and TCP is connection-oriented service. See *Transmission Control Protocol.*

User Manager for Domains   A Windows NT application that administers user accounts, groups, and security policies at the domain level.

User Right Policies   Used to determine what rights users and groups have when trying to accomplish network tasks. User Rights Policies are set through User Manager for Domains. See *User Manager for Domains*.

Username   A user's account name in a logon-authenticated system. See *Security*.

V

VBScript   A variant of Visual Basic used as a scripting language in Internet Explorer and Active Server Pages. See *Scripting Language*.

VDM   See *Virtual DOS Machine*.

Virtual Directory   A directory accessible to IIS that has a registered alias so that it appears to be a subdirectory of a service root directory.

Virtual DOS Machine (VDM)   The DOS environment created by Windows NT for the execution of DOS and Win16 applications. See *MS-DOS, Win16*.

Virtual Machine   A fictitious machine language that can be interpreted on a number of actual machines. Programs compiled to the virtual machine specification can run on any computer that can interpret that virtual machine specification.

Virtual Memory   A kernel service that stores memory pages not currently in use on a mass storage device to free up the memory occupied for other uses. Virtual memory hides the memory swapping process from applications and higher-level services. See *Kernel, Swap File*.

Virtual Reality Modeling Language   A syntax that describes the position of three-dimensional objects in a space, which can be transmitted from a server to a client and rendered on the client.

Virtual Server   A set of directories that simulate the functionality of a wwwroot directory in that they appear to be a Web server unto themselves. IP addresses are unique to each virtual server and serve as the selection factor between them on the same machine. One actual server can embody many virtual servers.

Volume   A collection of data indexed by directories containing files and referred to by a drive letter. Volumes are normally contained in a single partition, but volume sets and stripe sets extend a single volume across multiple partitions.

WAN   See *Wide Area Network.*

Web Browser   An application that makes HTTP requests and formats the resultant HTML documents for the users. The preeminent Internet client, most Web browsers understand all standard Internet protocols and scripting languages. See *Hypertext Markup Language, Hypertext Transfer Protocol, Internet.*

Web Page   Any HTML document on an HTTP server. See *Hypertext Markup Language, Hypertext Transfer Protocol, Internet*

Webmaster   The administrator of a Web site.

Well-Known Port   The commonly accepted or defined TCP socket for a specific service.

Wide Area Information Service   An Internet-based distributed database connection protocol that allows the simultaneous query of multiple separate databases.

Wide Area Network (WAN)   A geographically dispersed network of networks, connected by routers and communication links. The Internet is the largest WAN. See *Internet, Local Area Network.*

Win16   The set of application services provided by the 16-bit versions of Microsoft Windows: Windows 3.1 and Windows for Workgroups 3.11, as well as OS/2.

Win32   The set of application services provided by the 32-bit versions of Microsoft Windows: Windows 95 and Windows NT.

WinCGI   The Windows adaptation of the CGI specification for UNIX computers.

Windows 3.11 for Workgroups   The current 16-bit version of Windows for less-powerful, Intel-based personal computers; this system includes peer networking services.

Windows 95   The current 32-bit version of Microsoft Windows for medium-range, Intel-based personal computers; this system includes peer networking services, Internet support, and strong support for older DOS applications and peripherals.

Windows Internet Name Service (WINS)   A network service for Microsoft networks that provides Windows computers with Internet numbers for specified NetBIOS names, facilitating browsing and intercommunication over TCP/IP networks.

Windows NT   The current 32-bit version of Microsoft Windows for powerful Intel, Alpha, PowerPC, or MIPS-based computers; the system includes peer networking services, server networking services, Internet client and server services, and a broad range of utilities.

Windows Sockets   An interprocess communications protocol that delivers connection-oriented data streams used by Internet software and software ported from UNIX environments. See *Interprocess Communications*.

WINS   See *Windows Internet Name Service*.

Workgroup   In Microsoft networks, a collection of related computers, such as a department, that don't require the uniform security and coordination of a domain. Workgroups are characterized by decentralized management as opposed to the centralized management that domains use. See *Domain*.

Workstation   A powerful personal computer, usually running a preemptive, multitasking operating system like UNIX or Windows NT.

World Wide Web (WWW)   A collection of Internet servers providing hypertext formatted documents for Internet clients running Web browsers. The World Wide Web provided the first easy-to-use graphical interface for the Internet and is largely responsible for the Internet's explosive growth.

X.25   Standard that defines packet-switching networks.

Index

Note to the Reader:

Page numbers in *italics* refer to figures or tables; page numbers in **bold** refer to significant discussions of the topic.

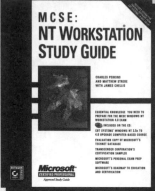

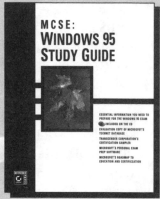

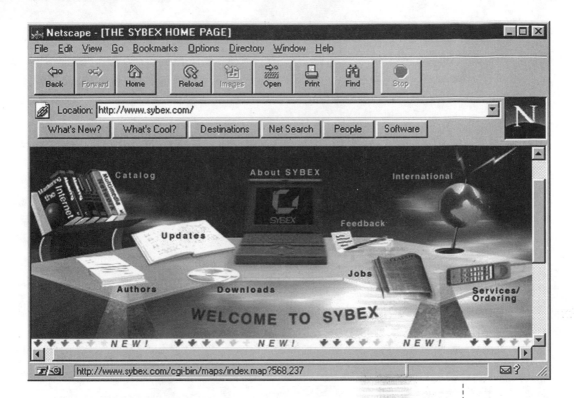